Reimagining the Gran Chaco

REIMAGINING THE GRAN CHACO

Identities, Politics, and the Environment
in South America

EDITED BY

Silvia Hirsch, Paola Canova,
and Mercedes Biocca

University of Florida Press
Gainesville

26 25 24 23 22 21   6 5 4 3 2 1

Library of Congress Cataloging-in-Publication Data
Names: Hirsch, Silvia María, editor. | Canova, Paola, editor. | Biocca,
   Mercedes, editor.
Title: Reimagining the Gran Chaco : identities, politics, and the
   environment in South America / edited by Silvia Hirsch, Paola Canova,
   Mercedes Biocca.
Description: Gainesville, FL : University of Florida Press, [2021] |
   Includes bibliographical references and index. | Summary: "This volume
   traces the socioeconomic and environmental changes taking place in the
   Gran Chaco, a vast and richly biodiverse ecoregion in South America,
   illuminating how the region's many indigenous groups are negotiating
   these transformations in their own terms"— Provided by publisher.
Identifiers: LCCN 2021007599 (print) | LCCN 2021007600 (ebook) | ISBN
   9781683402114 (cloth) | ISBN 9781683402862 (pbk) | ISBN 9781683402459 (pdf)
   | ISBN 9781683403357 (epub)
Subjects: LCSH: Indians of South America—Gran Chaco—Ethnic identity. |
   Indians of South America—Gran Chaco—Politics and government. | Indians
   of South America—Gran Chaco—Social conditions. | Gran
   Chaco—Environmental conditions. | Gran Chaco—History.
Classification: LCC F2230.1.E84 R45 2021 (print) | LCC F2230.1.E84
   (ebook) | DDC 982/.3—dc23
LC record available at https://lccn.loc.gov/2021007599
LC ebook record available at https://lccn.loc.gov/2021007600

University of Florida Press
2046 NE Waldo Road
Suite 2100
Gainesville, FL 32609
http://upress.ufl.edu

UF PRESS

UNIVERSITY
OF FLORIDA

A la juventud chaqueña
que lucha por sus territorios para forjar un futuro mejor

Contents

List of Illustrations   ix

Introduction: The Gran Chaco of South America in Transnational and Multidisciplinary Perspectives   1

Silvia Hirsch, Paola Canova, and Mercedes Biocca

1. The Rise and Fall of an Indigenous Homeland: The Itiyuro River Basin in Argentina   28

   Federico Bossert

2. Were the Chiriguano a Colonial Fabrication? Linguistic Arguments for Rethinking Guaraní and Chané Histories in the Chaco   53

   Bret Gustafson

3. Cosmology of Development: Humanitarian Narratives and Missionary Work in the Argentine Gran Chaco   73

   César Ceriani Cernadas

4. "They Only Know the Public Roads": Enlhet Territoriality during the Colonization of Their Lands   93

   Hannes Kalisch

5. Death Ritual as Ethnopoeisis: A Farewell to an Angaité Shaman   118

   Rodrigo Villagra Carron

6. Between Resistance and Acquiescence: Experiences of Agrarian Transformation in Two Indigenous Communities in Chaco Province, Argentina   141

   Mercedes Biocca

7. Infrastructures of Settler Colonialism: Geographies of Violence, Indigenous Labor, and Marginal Resistance in Paraguay's Chaco   166

   Joel E. Correia

8. Tense Territories: Negotiating Natural Gas in Weenhayek Society 186

   Denise Humphreys Bebbington and Guido Cortez

9. The Guaraní People's Struggle for Indigenous Autonomy in Bolivia 214

   Nancy Postero

10. Ayoreo Women and Access to Health Care: Negotiating the Multicultural Reform of the State in Paraguay 236

    Paola Canova

11. Multiterritoriality and the Tapiete Trinational Experience in the Chaco 256

    Silvia Hirsch

    Afterword: The Contested Terrain of the Gran Chaco 277

    Gastón Gordillo

    Works Cited 283

    List of Contributors 317

    Index 321

Illustrations

Figures

4.1. Maangvayaam'ay', January 2020   97

5.1. Gregorio Navarro, Wilfredo Navarro, and the shaman Laureano Ayala   126

7.1. Yakye Axa, 2016, seen from Ruta 5   170

8.1. Timeline of natural gas development and territorial recognition in Weenhayek lands   197

10.1. Indigenous people outside the INDI office in Asunción, 2019   239

10.2. Amistad Health Clinic in Filadelfia, Paraguay, 2020   245

11.1. Entrance to Guaraní Ñandeva community, near Filadelfia, Paraguay   267

11.2. Young women in an evangelical campaign, Tartagal, Argentina, 2019   270

11.3. Trinational Tapiete meeting, 2004, Tartagal, Argentina   272

Maps

0.1. The Gran Chaco region   4

0.2. Current areas of indigenous groups studied in this book   25

1.1. The first known cartographic reference to the Itiyuro indigenous village, circa 1800   31

1.2. Ranches in Chané territory, around mid-nineteenth century   45

4.1. Sites in Enlhet territory in Paraguay   94

7.1. Sawhoyamaxa and Yakye Axa study sites   168

8.1. Weenhayek TCO and surrounding hydrocarbon operations   188

Table

8.1. Hydrocarbon companies and projects affecting Weenhayek territory, 1960–2010   195

Introduction

The Gran Chaco of South America in Transnational and Multidisciplinary Perspectives

SILVIA HIRSCH, PAOLA CANOVA, AND MERCEDES BIOCCA

The Chaco is a vast ecoregion that stretches for more than a million square kilometers across four countries: Argentina, Bolivia, Brazil, and Paraguay. With enormous biodiversity, it is considered the second-largest biome in South America, after the Amazon basin (Krebs and Braunstein 2011). The region is inhabited by more than twenty-five indigenous groups, criollo settlers,[1] colonists of diverse nationalities, Mennonites, and Brazilian immigrants, among others. Its diverse social dynamic superimposed onto the intersection of four nation-states, each with a unique history of involvement in the region, has made the Chaco into a landscape marked by histories of unequal encounters and complex negotiations.

The region was also the site of a war between Bolivia and Paraguay at the beginning of the twentieth century over land and oil, and since then it has undergone massive transformations. In recent decades, this ecoregion has experienced fast-paced environmental, social, and economic changes as a result of an intensification of extractive industries such as agribusiness, ranching, logging, and the exploitation of hydrocarbons. In a few decades, the area has become a complex arena of political, cultural, and economic contestation between actors that include the state, environmental and developmental nongovernmental organizations (NGOs), and private businesses whose projects and agendas collide with the ways of life of local residents. This edited volume tracks these unequal encounters and the frictions the changes produce, revealing the ways local actors are experimenting and negotiating socioeconomic and environmental transformations in their own terms.

Specifically, the chapters in this book illuminate how local actors are contesting, accommodating, or redefining their subjectivities while reconfiguring their political agency as a response to these processes. Importantly also, this book traces the historical and contemporary trajectories that might unexpectedly link but also separate groups of people and the ecological landscapes in which their lives are embedded and beyond the territorial borders of each nation-state. In so doing, this volume ultimately brings greater visibility to the Gran Chaco as a site with a long history of ethnographic research that despite being underrepresented offers insightful outcomes, paradoxes, and peculiar parallels to similar processes under way elsewhere in Latin America and other locations such as the Southwest or the Plains regions in the United States (Combès, Villar, and Lowrey 2009). Taking a multidisciplinary approach, the authors of the chapters draw on fields such as anthropology, sociology, geography, and linguistics to convey the complex configuration of environmental, political, ethnic, cultural, and linguistic processes that have shaped and intervened in the region.

In this introduction we take a comparative approach to analyze the most outstanding historical, political, and social processes that constitute the Gran Chaco. We do not intend to provide an overview of the academic scholarship on the region, as several works have addressed this thoroughly.[2] We take a trinational perspective to examine five major processes that have shaped and continue to influence the socioeconomic, political, and cultural dynamics in the area: missionization, millenarian movements, the Chaco War, industrial enclaves, political mobilization, and the struggle for rights; we note the peculiarities of how these processes have developed and played out in each country and delineate present and future challenges that hinge upon the sustainability, both environmental and human, of this enormous and complex region.

The Chaco: A Peripheric Geography

In comparison to other geographical regions of Latin America, notably the Andes, Amazon, and Mesoamerica, the Chaco has been at the periphery of academic concerns and visibility in the media. It has been conceived as a last frontier to be domesticated and dominated (Wright 2008). The Gran Chaco is a subtropical ecoregion with low forests and two main rivers, the Pilcomayo and the Bermejo, that flow southeastward, flooding at times while disappearing during the dry season. The region is divided into the northern Chaco, known as the Chaco boreal, from the *llanos* (plains) of

Chiquitos in Bolivia to the Pilcomayo River; the central Chaco, between the Pilcomayo and Bermejo Rivers; and the southern Chaco, the Chaco *austral*, south of the Bermejo River. The northern Chaco includes eastern Bolivia, western Paraguay, and southwestern Brazil; it is a vast plain, slightly mountainous and with several large wetlands formed during the rainy season. Toward the east is a denser and more humid plain with more open savanna vegetation, and toward the center and west, drier and thornier forest vegetation prevails. The central Chaco encompasses the Argentine province of Formosa, with wetlands such as Bañado la Estrella, and eastern Salta Province, as well as southern Bolivia, with extensive dense forests. The southern Chaco covers Argentinian territory irrigated by several small streams, making for very rich vegetation that at the southernmost point blends with the Pampas.

The extraordinary diversity of flora and fauna and the vastness of the Chaco territory attracted industrial enterprises for the extraction of wood, production of cotton, and cattle ranching beginning in the mid-1800s. Since then, it has been extensively logged; trees such as quebracho (Schinopsis) were used for the production of tannin, wooden railway beams, and stakes for fencing, which had a brutal impact on the access of indigenous peoples to their territories. Even fruit trees such as algarrobo (carob) were used for the manufacturing of furniture; they were among innumerable plants and animals well known by the native population to be exploited by newcomers. The low cost of state lands, cheap labor force, and lack of environmental controls favored the extraction of resources. These enterprises have transformed the ecoregion, by depleting forests and wild animals, relocating the labor force, and overusing scarce water resources. More recently the environmental landscape is being dramatically changed once again by agribusiness and cattle-ranching activities that are driving the highest rates of deforestation in lowland South America (Guyra Paraguay 2018).

Since colonial times chroniclers and explorers have referred to the hostile, wild, and indomitable character of the region. Those who have conducted research in the Chaco and have traversed its immense spaces and ventured into its varied terrains know how unsettling the conditions can be, when temperatures reach 50 degrees Celsius and time passes without a drop of water or with endless rains and floods. Territorial control over the Gran Chaco has been a source of dispute since the independence of Argentina, Bolivia, and Paraguay from Spain, and the disputes led to several geographic and scientific explorations (Santamaría and Lagos 1992). By the late eighteenth century, Franciscan missions were established in the Bolivian

Map 0.1. The Gran Chaco region. Map by Ana Dell'Arciprete.

and Argentine Chaco; Jesuits also established missions in these places, although theirs were short-lived due to the expulsion of the order in 1767 by Spain. Similar to the greater Southwest region of the United States and Mexico (Guy and Sheridan 1998), the rugged ecological landscape, weather conditions, and perceived hostility of indigenous groups of the Gran Chaco frustrated the advance of Spaniards for centuries, impeding military efforts, missionary campaigns, and the formation of nonindigenous settlements.

Incursions into the region became more frequent by the nineteenth century, when European explorers provided rich accounts of the environment and the inhabitants. The travels of Alcide D'Orbigny in 1835–1847 were perhaps the most famous, but there were many more. In 1875 the Foster-Seelstrang expedition to the eastern Argentine Chaco had the objective of exploring its potential development. The report on the findings provides information on flora and fauna and the living conditions of indigenous and criollo inhabitants; it mentions the presence of fifteen timber mills that employed native people and describes the harsh working conditions they endured. The report also refers to the indiscriminate logging of forests that were sold by indigenous chiefs who did not anticipate the consequences (Seelstrang 1977 [1878]).

Other expeditions produced a large number of documents and maps on the region. One was conducted by Alfred Thouar starting in 1884 to the Bolivian Chaco in search of the French doctor and explorer Jules Crévaux, who was killed by indigenous peoples. Franciscan and Jesuit priests also provided numerous accounts of the Gran Chaco peoples who were under the custody of the missions.[3] While in Paraguay, the Italian ethnographer, photographer, and painter Guido Boggiani traveled in 1889 and in several other trips to the Chaco and produced rich descriptions and photographs of Chamacoco and Guaycurú groups that were published in 1900. In the twentieth century, other important ethnographers laid the groundwork for understanding the complex ethnohistory of the region; among these works are Nordenskiöld 2002 [1912], Métraux 1946, and Susnik 1978 and 1980.[4]

Braunstein and Miller argue that after independence the indigenous population "was of interest on two very different and mutually contradictory accounts. On the one hand, it was seen as a territorial obstruction requiring elimination; on the other, as an unskilled labor force" (1999, 9). The former of these two points of view gave rise to the notion of the "desert" in nineteenth-century Argentina, an ethnocentric metaphor for a space that had not been brought under the control of the rule of "law" and "progress" (Wright 2008). While Bolivia and Argentina lay claim to the Chaco, the distance of their capitals, La Paz and Buenos Aires, in addition to their social and cultural remoteness favored Paraguay with a *significant* part of the territory in relation to the new nation-state's size. Thus, Argentina holds 59 percent, Paraguay 23 percent, Bolivia 13 percent, and Brazil 5 percent of the Chaco territory (Metz and Wessling 2006).

The geopolitical borders between the four countries were established only after the War of the Triple Alliance (1864–1870). In 1876 Paraguay and Argentina signed a treaty over their geographical limits that assigned the area between the Verde River and the town of Bahía Negra to Paraguay; the area between the Pilcomayo and Bermejo Rivers would stay under Argentine sovereignty, and the area between the Verde and Pilcomayo Rivers would be submitted to arbitrage. In 1878, US President Rutherford B. Hayes decided in favor of Paraguay. The town of Yacuiba on the southern Bolivian border with Argentina was declared the capital of the Gran Chaco Province of Bolivia; although the border was on the Argentine side, a treaty signed in 1893 established the town as being part of Bolivia.

After 1870, a great proportion of state territory in the Paraguayan Chaco was sold to land speculators and mainly British, United States, and Argentine companies to raise livestock and build timber mills on the banks of the Paraguay River. Indigenous peoples had inhabited the region since precolonial times, and the presence of Europeans and other nonindigenous peoples was almost nonexistent. With investments in industrial enclaves, which were being built on several parts of the Paraguay and the Bermejo Rivers, a process of indigenous labor incorporation and exploitation was also initiated. Argentina developed its political and economic domain not only through the establishment of industrial companies but also through the development of fluvial transportation. During the same period, livestock ranches were established in the departments of Tarija and Santa Cruz on the banks of the Pilcomayo in Bolivia and in northern Argentina in the town of Tartagal (Figallo 2003). Bolivia began its colonization of the Chaco at the beginning of the twentieth century by establishing forts on the Pilcomayo and starting to build roads after 1920. At the turn of the twentieth century, the governments of Argentina, Bolivia, and Paraguay favored the presence of religious missions, and militarization of the borders was a priority. The Paraguayan government invited a group of Mennonites of Russian descent to settle the region as a geopolitical strategy of occupation.

The establishment of railways into the Chaco region became a turning point in the development of industrial enclaves, as they facilitated migrations from Bolivia to Argentina and led to the foundation of settler towns and the indigenous communities newly established by missionaries. The Spanish-Argentine company Carlos Casado established tannin factories by the end of the nineteenth century on the banks of the Paraguay River; it constructed a railway of 240 kilometers inland to a site known as Punta Riel, where raw material for the factory would be extracted. The company railway would later transport Mennonite settlers and military personnel during the Chaco War. Internal migration increased exponentially in the early twentieth century as the native population moved to work at sugarcane plantations, farms, and timber mills. By the 1930s several train stations were built on the western border of the Argentine Chaco in the provinces of Salta and Jujuy to reach Guaraní communities. By 1944 railroad tracks reached the border town of Pocitos in northern Argentina, thus establishing a connection to Bolivia. On the eastern part of the Argentine Chaco, a railroad was established in 1931 from Las Lomitas in Formosa Province to Embarcación in Salta Province, connecting a huge area of agricultural, wood, and livestock production. Finally, in 1938 the Argentine-Bolivian Railway Commission inaugurated the train from Santa Cruz de la Sierra, more than 500 kilometers from the town of Yacuiba on the southern border of Bolivia (Costello 2003).

The gradual improvement and development of infrastructure was instrumental in the founding of indigenous and nonindigenous settlements by the Paraguayan River and the mass migrations of indigenous peoples of the Bolivian Chaco to Argentina in search for work from the 1920s to the 1960s. These migrations led to their permanent settlement in Argentina, and the rapid transformation of the socioeconomic and environmental landscapes of the Chaco. A new social geography emerged, with fast-growing towns inhabited by a diversity of indigenous groups, criollos, European, and Syrian and Lebanese immigrants reconfiguring social, economic, and political relations.

Most Chaco native peoples were organized in seminomadic bands and practiced cyclical nomadism, fishing, hunting, collecting of edible plants, and moving about a *vast* territory. The groups circulated in and out of different nation-states; thus, their subsistence strategies and kinship networks extended beyond national geographic boundaries. With an increasing state presence in the Gran Chaco by the early twentieth century, the control of borders by agencies such as the military police (*gendarmería*) meant that indigenous peoples were now subject to new forms of control, reduction of their movements, and shift in access to their livelihoods. Numerous violent incidents took place in border areas starting in the 1940s in which indigenous peoples in groups were arrested, killed, or forbidden from crossing borders to engage in commerce, hunting, fishing, or simply visiting their relatives (Figallo 2003). Sometimes crossing the borders was easier, when the governments would issue various forms of documentation that allowed movement between countries for work in industrial enclaves. Now, transborder commerce and crossings to visit relatives and engage in evangelical campaigns or political transnational organizations are part of everyday practices of indigenous groups separated by nation-states (Hirsch 2014).

Missionization as a Complex Civilizing Project

Protestant and Catholic religious missions into the Chaco were spiritual endeavors intended to Christianize so-called heathen natives by introducing them to the Bible. Missions were also major civilizing projects that persist today, intertwined with the industrial and agricultural enclaves that have sought indigenous peoples as a labor force. Missions generated tensions and ambiguities. On the one hand, they provided safety from military incursions and introduced schooling and health services; on the other hand, missions imposed new belief systems and hygienic practices, appropriated indigenous land, and forbade native religious systems and forms of social organization (Ceriani Cernadas in this volume; Teruel 2005). Since the 1970s there has been a growing scholarship on the presence of missions among Chaco groups. Although the Catholic Church has had a longer presence in the region, the majority of indigenous peoples now belong to Protestant denominations such as Assembly of God, Baptists, Mennonites, and Mormons.

The Franciscan order settled in Bolivia during the late eighteenth century and developed a widespread network of missions throughout the Argentine and Bolivian Chaco, particularly among the Guaraní and Chané people (Langer 2009).[5] These missions established new settlements that became secularized in 1939, when the order withdrew from the region while continuing to maintain its influence. Protestant missionary work in the Gran Chaco can be traced back to the establishment of the British South American Missionary Society (SAMS) in 1886. The SAMS was founded in the Paraguayan Chaco among the Enlhet people and led by the missionary Barbrooke Grubb (Grubb 1993 [1911]). By 1911 the SAMS (South American Missionary Society) work would be expanded to the Argentine Chaco first among the Wichí and then among Qom by the 1930s. In Bolivia their work began in 1925 but was abandoned in 1932 due to the Chaco War. The SAMS missionaries had a lasting impact in Paraguay, especially among the Angaité (Villagra Carron this volume) as well as the Enxet people (Correia this volume). Anglicans established missions throughout the Argentinian Chaco among Wichí, Qom, Chorote, and Pilagá people, and in so doing they created schools and health dispensaries, trained pastors, and bought land for the settlement of dispersed groups.

Dutch and German-descended Mennonites, migrating from Russia via Canada, first reached the Paraguayan Chaco in 1926 and formed Menno Colony in 1927. Other groups of Mennonites would follow directly from Russia and form Fernheim Colony in 1930–1932 and lastly, Neu-Halbstadt Colony in 1947. Despite their initial geographic and social isolation, the main urban centers of these settlements, Loma Plata, Filadelfia, and Neu-land, respectively, would become some of the most economically dynamic hubs in the Paraguayan Chaco by the 2000s (Canova 2015; Vázquez Recalde 2013). Upon their arrival Mennonites sought to Christianize the Enlhet people (Kalisch this volume; Peter Klassen 2002), as well as the Ayoreo, Nivaclé, and other neighboring groups.

The US-based New Tribes Mission (since renamed Ethnos 360), a Christian missionary society, established a presence in the Bolivian Chaco in 1946 among the Ayoreo.[6] Some members of this missionary group moved to the Paraguayan Chaco in the 1960s and formed missions among the Ayoreo, Angaité, and Manjui; they became controversial for their mission-izing strategies of seeking uncontacted Ayoreo that resulted in fatal encounters (Escobar 1988, Perasso 1987). Scandinavian missionaries, Norwegian and Swedish, reached Argentina in 1940 and Bolivia in 1950 to preach the gospel and founded missions that have had long-lasting influence (Ceriani Cernadas 2011b). All these missionary endeavors would leave an indelible mark on the lives of Chaco groups, as new religious leadership emerged, churches were built, and everyday activities and religious practices were reconfigured. The emergence of millenarian movements spread among a population of underprivileged, deterritorialized, and exploited indigenous peoples.

Millenarian Movements and the Reconfiguration of Indigenous Settlements

From colonial times into the twentieth century, indigenous rebellions and millenarian movements swept through the Gran Chaco and generated fear and uncertainty among the criollo population. The policies of forced settlement, labor exploitation, mistreatment, and implementation of regulations preventing migration drew strong resistance from indigenous populations. In the nineteenth century, one of the most prominent movements took place in Bolivia among the Guaraní group known as the Chiriguano. Under the leadership of the prophet Apiaguaki Tumpa, in 1892 a massive upheaval evolved against the oppressive living and working conditions on the haciendas as well as their loss of lands and white domination. Hundreds of Chiriguano gathered and launched attacks but were defeated by the Bolivian army near the town of Kuruyuki.[7] Their defeat meant the death and persecution of hundreds of Chiriguano, but the final battle was reappropriated a century later by the Guaraní organization Asamblea del Pueblo Guaraní as a symbol of the organization and the strength of Guaraní warriors in their struggle for autonomy and independence (Albó 2012).

In Argentina, millenarian uprisings in the Formosa and Chaco Provinces were led by shamans and involved attacks on criollo colonies, theft of livestock, and refusal to work in criollos' agricultural fields. The shamans, who were believed by their followers to possess supernatural powers, organized rebellions and sometimes conflated biblical elements with mythological narratives, showing the growing influence of the religious missions (Cordeu and Siffredi 1971; Gordillo 2003; Miller 1979). One of the most important millenarian movements was the Napalpí rebellion. Napalpí was the name of a reservation founded by the national state in 1911 where approximately seven hundred Qom, Moqoit, and Vilela people were forced to settle.[8] Until 1915 the activities of the reservation were focused on lumber, but later it became a cotton-producing enclave. At Napalpí the administration provided indigenous peoples with temporary titles to the land and obliged them to hand over 15 percent of their production to the administration to pay for their working tools and the maintenance of roads inside the reservation. In 1923 the administration decided to reduce the wages and retain 10 percent from the price paid for a ton of cotton to cover transportation costs (Chico and Fernández 2011). Indigenous peoples began to gather and listen to leaders who claimed the ability to communicate with dead shamans. These voices enticed the native workers to stop working and announced a time of plenty when the dead would rise again (Gordillo 2006; Miller 1979). By May 1924, guided by these voices, the leaders began to organize attacks and robberies in the surrounding white settlements. The leader-shamans convinced their followers that the moment had come for confrontation with white people, that bullets wouldn't hurt them, and that they had nothing to fear. The attacks and the murder of two colonists resulted in an increased police presence and culminated on July 24, 1924, with the massacre of more than two hundred indigenous peoples in what came to be known as the Napalpí massacre.

In the following years, two more uprisings with similar characteristics occurred. The first of these took place in 1933 in the area of Pampa del Indio, where the Qom leader Tapanaik claimed that he foresaw the arrival of airplanes filled with goods. Their arrival would not only put an end to the scarcity of goods but also mark the beginning of an era of abundance. Meanwhile, to prepare for this new era, his followers were to avoid the consumption of agricultural crops. The second uprising took place from 1935 to 1937 in the village Zapallar the province of Chaco. Led by the shaman Natochí, Qom and Moqoit groups participated in the Zapallar movement. The uprising championed the resurgence of ancient practices, urging people to leave their work on the farms and cease any contact with the criollo population (Tamagno 2008). Both the Zapallar and Napalpí uprisings gathered large numbers of people attracted by the leaders, aggravating the lack of food in the settlements, which in turn led to attacks on nearby farms. These events created fear and anger among criollos, who subsequently campaigned for an intensification of security efforts by the state. The Pampa del Indio movement quickly ended after the imprisonment and murder of its leader, Tapanaik; the Zapallar uprising ended when Natochí, the leader, fled (Cordeu and Siffredi 1971; Miller 1979).

At the turn of the twentieth century, among the Enxet in the Paraguayan Chaco a religious movement called the *egyapam* cult took place. Stephen William Kidd (1992, 91) has found that it was "related to the measles epidemic of 1901 and the smallpox epidemic of 1903 which, according to missionaries, produced a 'spiritual awakening.'" Unlike those in Bolivia and Argentina, the *egyapam* movement was not related to labor exploitation; rather, it developed as a mixed discourse that critiqued missionaries and their teachings of the Ten Commandments and the related punishments. The millenarian movements in the Gran Chaco precipitated indigenous people's resistance to the demands and conditions imposed upon them by the capitalist system, which obliged them to abandon their nomadic life and reduced them to semislavery at work sites, colonies, and refineries (Tamagno 2008). But the millennial movements also entailed resistance to imposed culture change, loss of territory, and missionization. Today, that resistance still is evidenced in the ways the numerous churches of diverse denominations that operate in the region have been appropriated, transformed, and resignified by locals. Ceriani Cernadas (2017b) indicates that from the point of view of the native population, the arrival of the missionaries was a turning point that inaugurated an era marked by the end of interethnic wars and the introduction of writing, agriculture, and new ways of dressing and customs. The majority of the indigenous population has become evangelical, leading their own services and churches. Meanwhile, the criollo population, although still predominantly Catholic, has been increasingly shifting to evangelical churches as well.

The Chaco War: Displacements, Hardships, and Heterogeneous Interactions

Indigenous peoples of the Chaco were profoundly affected by the war between Bolivia and Paraguay that took place from 1932 to 1935 in which entire populations were displaced and villages devastated. Despite the profound transformations caused by the war, regional ethnography has largely omitted its legacy on indigenous groups, and few studies have addressed its impact on the inhabitants. Exceptions are the scholarship by Luc Capdevila and colleagues in both 2008 and 2010 and by Nicolás Richard, as editor, and contributors in *Mala guerra* (Richard 2008c). Their work has made a substantial analytical and ethnographic contribution toward understanding the relevance and impact of the Chaco War. Bolivia and Paraguay were concerned about oil exploration, territorial expansion, and national presence in what was considered a remote and practically uninhabited region. Indigenous peoples became an important resource for the Bolivian army because of their knowledge and adaptation to the environment, mostly unknown to highlanders who were drafted as soldiers and had enormous difficulties adjusting to the dire conditions of the Chaco. Though many Chaco indigenous peoples became guides and road construction workers for the army, they were represented and treated in diverse ways: as part of the natural environment, as helpers and guides of the enemy, as oppressed populations, or as savages and untamed inhabitants of an unknown territory (Capdevila et al. 2010).

Military documents as well as oral histories describe the positive and empathic attitudes of Paraguayan military toward the Guaraní groups of the Bolivian Chaco. The similarities in language and culture fostered a welcoming reception by Paraguayan soldiers. At the time, indigenous peoples living in the Bolivian Chaco did not have a nationalist sense of identity toward their country of residence. This in turn had an adverse impact on the Bolivian Guaraní, as many were taken prisoners or migrated to Paraguay and were considered traitors after the war ended and they returned to Bolivian territory. As indicated in Capdevila, Combès, and Richard (2008, 14), the ethnic cartography in place before the war brutally disintegrated in the war's violence.

The Chaco War had enormous consequences; huge populations were taken as prisoners to Paraguay, hundreds perished, infectious diseases and epidemics spread widely, and territorial loss and displacement destroyed communities. The war also signaled the consolidation of the presence of both Bolivia and Paraguay in the region. It differentially affected indigenous groups; some of them were living in the hinterland, and others were in the middle of the conflict in areas both armies traversed and where they confronted each other. Oral histories of the Enxet in Paraguay reveal how they had to remove and bury the bodies of soldiers or hide to protect themselves from bombings (Villagra Carron 2008, 88). The Wichí-Guisnay who inhabited the northern area along the Pilcomayo River left their territory in Paraguay permanently and migrated to Argentina. The Pilagá who lived mostly in Argentina were not as affected since they were considered Argentine citizens, while the Nivaclé and Maká were considered Paraguayan Indians (Córdoba and Braunstein 2008). Hence, cultural and spatial dynamics changed as a consequence of the Chaco War. In Paraguay, the Guaraní language was introduced, and as a result, several indigenous groups found their own native languages receding. Furthermore, they experienced a profound loss of autonomy and abandonment of their ancestral territories. For groups such as the Tapiete, Guaraní, and Nivaclé, Argentina became their permanent homeland.

Industrial Enclaves' Role in Labor Force and Capitalist Expansion

From the last decades of the nineteenth century to the mid-twentieth century, a cycle of capitalist expansion drastically altered the nature of indigenous territories in the Gran Chaco, much of which had previously been peripheral to colonial projects. The process of state control and expansion during the twentieth century became inseparable from the establishment of industrial, agricultural, and mining outposts. In this way, tanning companies, cotton production, sugarcane factories, and lumber mills systematically transformed the lives of Chaco indigenous groups by generating new interethnic relations, displacing entire villages, and creating a labor force that was key in the development of the region but underpaid and marginalized.

In Paraguay after the War of the Triple Alliance, the national government embarked on a massive campaign in 1885–1887 to sell state lands as a strategy to pay off debts incurred during the war. In just two years, the government sold off 98 percent of its national territory, most of it to large companies mainly owned by US, British, and Argentine capital (Villagra Carron and Bonifacio 2015, 234). By the mid-1920s, it was estimated that fourteen companies owned more than 14 million hectares in the Paraguayan Chaco alone (Glauser 2009). Following the sale of state lands and using third party individuals to get around restrictive Paraguayan laws, the Casado tannin company acquired a total of more than 5.6 million hectares, making it the largest landowner in the northern Chaco (Dalla-Corte 2012). At first, indigenous peoples from different regions did temporary work for the company before returning to their home settlements, but little by little they began to settle on the land permanently. A town quickly sprang up around the factory that would subsequently be called Puerto Casado with a population of mestizo and varied indigenous groups. Revealing the pivotal "civilizing" role of missionaries in supporting economic endeavors, the Casado family also encouraged the establishment of Salesian missions and aided the establishment of the Mennonite colonies through the sale of parcels of its land (Villagra and Bonifacio 2015).

At the tannery, indigenous workers were considered legal minors because they lacked identity documents. This status was used as an excuse by the Casado company to pay them less than other workers, and wages were only partially paid in cash, with the rest accounted for by foodstuffs. In addition to being paid less, indigenous workers were assigned the hardest jobs, such as working on the top floor of the factory next to the ovens, carrying fifty-kilogram sacks of tannin to the boats, and cleaning the factory and the streets outside. Company records reveal that the distinction made between indigenous and nonindigenous workers was only eliminated in 1977 (Bonifacio 2017:204). Besides exploitation in the workplace, indigenous peoples also suffered from other forms of discrimination such as the prohibition of community ceremonies, the use of physical violence as discipline, and the confiscation of their animals by the company. First the global financial and economic crisis of 1929 and soon after it the Chaco War dramatically debilitated the industrial enclaves on the Paraguay River. As a result, in the following decades nonindigenous workers would pressure the government for the redistribution of land, which eventually led in 1940 to the establishment of the first *estatuto agrario* (agricultural statute) (Glauser 2009). The *estatuto*, in turn, promoted the state's establishment of the first formal nonindigenous Paraguayan settlements known as *colonias*, composed mostly by factory and ranch employees. Until that time, the nonindigenous population in the region lived in work camps, temporary settlements by factories, or nearby military posts (Fritz 2011; Peter Klassen 2004). These informal settlements would also expand to become some of today's main urban centers in the Paraguayan Chaco. By the 1970s, new *colonias* were established with the support of the Catholic Church as well. Later attempts at colonization, in the 1990s, were furthered by the Paraguayan state (Vázquez Recalde 2011).

In Argentina once the military campaigns against the indigenous population were over, the newly created National Territory of Chaco, established before the provinces of Chaco and Formosa were created, was split into sections on which large enterprises were set up with foreign and mixed capital to produce lumber, mainly from quebracho, and cultivate sugarcane. These establishments included La Forestal Land, Timber, and Railways Company and the sugar refinery Las Palmas del Chaco Austral. The former was a company set up with French, German, and British capital established in the region in 1906. La Forestal grew to occupy 2.3 million hectares between the north of Santa Fe Province and Chaco Province. It also possessed 300 kilometers of railways and four ports on the Paraná River (Stunnenberg and Kleinpenning 1993). Las Palmas refinery was founded in 1909 by the Irish brothers Charles and Richard Hardy. At the time, the Hardys requested the concession of 100,000 hectares to grow sugarcane. A few years later, the company expanded to include livestock and tannin production. Most of the tannin production at this kind of establishment was exported to Europe until, after World War I, the United States became the main destination for these exports (Fuscaldo 1982).

Las Palmas refinery and La Forestal recruited indigenous peoples as woodcutters and harvesters. Usually the work was piecemeal and paid with merchandise; rarely was a cash wage offered. The small amount paid could only be used to purchase merchandise provided by the company, which increased its earnings even more. These conditions of semislavery were endorsed by national authorities, given the great influence large companies had over political and military power in the region (Cordeu and Siffredi 1971). Thus, although the report "The State of the Working Classes in Argentina," written by Bialet Masse (1986 [1904]) at the request of the national government in 1904, describes the role and power of these establishments as a "small despotic, monarchic state that exists within a democratic republic," their functioning was unaffected.

The 1920s saw the decline of the production of tannin caused in part by the reduction in global demand for it and the growing use of other substances to treat leather hides. In Argentina the efforts of the national government to encourage cotton cultivation were sustained by the rise in the international price of cotton in 1923 due to a fall in production in the United States. During this period, some of the larger establishments such as Las Palmas switched to cotton production while others such as La Forestal started selling parcels of land to contractors and administrators, giving rise to new private enterprises.

The growing number of agricultural colonies soon created a larger demand for a workforce. In 1924 a group of colonists requested that the government forbid the migration of indigenous peoples in order to guarantee a local workforce (Trinchero 2007). In response to their petitions, authorities issued a decree that prohibited hiring nonlocal indigenous labor. As the regulations were intended to ensure that they would carry out agricultural work, indigenous people were not only obliged to remain within the same province but also were prevented from selling unmarked animal hides. Thereafter, in accordance with the rural code, indigenous people began to be persecuted for cattle rustling. Harvesting and cotton picking became the only alternative jobs available in the region for indigenous people.

Perhaps no other enterprise encapsulates better the impact of industrial capitalism on the lives of indigenous and nonindigenous people than the sugarcane plantations and mills, whether as sites of fetishization of evil (Taussig 1980) or as forms of industrial production in the expansion of capitalism (Mintz 1985). At the edges of the Chaco, in the Argentine provinces of Salta and Jujuy, sugarcane plantations were established in the mid-nineteenth century. These were sites where thousands of Chaco indigenous peoples from Bolivia and Argentina and highlanders from the two countries formed a massive workforce. The plantations established a labor hierarchy whereby the indigenous groups who inhabited the lowest rungs of the ladder, such as the Qom, Wichí, Chorote, Tapiete, received the lowest wages and the harshest work and living conditions (Bialet Masse 1986 [1904]; Gordillo 2004; Lagos and Teruel 1991). Early ethnographers such as Erland Nordenskiöld (2002 [1912]) describe the life of Chaco groups on the plantations, emphasizing the harsh living conditions and cultural transformations imposed on them at these sites. Like other industrial enclaves, sugarcane plantations generated tensions and ambiguities. Inhabitants received new material goods and had different experiences and interactions that left lasting impressions and led to the formation of interethnic marriages, religious conversion, and sometimes access to schooling and health services. But the enclaves also were sites of exploitation, fear, and even death (Gordillo 2004). Several in-depth studies (Bossert 2013; Ceriani Cernadas 2015; Dasso and Franceschi 2015; Montani 2015) explore how new material goods, eating habits, forms of labor, religious conversion, and religious festivities were imposed and incorporated as new and indelible forms of life. Gordillo (2004, 154) asserts that although the sugarcane plantations produced a new class experience, they constituted sites of profound tensions and ambiguities, introducing forms of lives, resistance, negotiations, and adaptations, and they also generated profound forms of labor exploitation. Notably, the geography of the region has been transformed by decades of deforestation, extensive and intensive planting of sugarcane, use of water sources, and chemical contaminants. The presence of sugarcane plantations and other agricultural enterprises along an extended area known as the Ramal Salto-Jujeño has meant the emergence of towns and settlements inhabited by hundreds of descendants of sugarcane and agricultural workers. In these spaces, renewed indigenous identities are emerging, making new claims for recognition (Gordillo 2011).

Neo-Extractivism and New Territorial Dynamics in Ranching, Soybean Production, Hydrocarbons Exploration, and Infrastructure Projects

The Gran Chaco region is experiencing one of the fastest rates of deforestation in lowland South America, according to the NGO Guyra Paraguay (2018), which is monitoring the rates of deforestation in the region. In Paraguay, deforestation for cattle ranching has positioned the country as one of the top ten world exporters of cattle beef, alongside Argentina (Meador and Balbi 2019). In the Argentine Chaco, soybean production has similarly depleted enormous tracts of land, and indigenous peoples are finding themselves fighting for the territories against the economic interests of transnational corporations such as Cargill and Bunge. On the other side of the border, in the Paraguayan Chaco, soybean production dates back only to the 1990s, when trial production with transgenic varieties began. According to the Cámara Paraguaya de Exportadores y Comercializadores de Cereales y Oleaginosas (Paraguayan Chamber of Exporters of Cereals),

17,000 hectares had been planted by ranchers and agribusinesses by 2017. In 2018 that amount increased to 25,000 hectares (*Última Hora* 2018). This effervescence of soybean production in the region could have devastating effects on the fragile soils of the region.

Hydrocarbons exploration has also shaped the Gran Chaco in new ways. Paraguay initiated its petroleum explorations starting as early as 1944 but with little success; hydrocarbon extraction began in the Bolivian Chaco in the 1920s, and that area has experienced a boost in hydrocarbon explorations since the turn of the twenty-first century (Bebbington and Cortez in this volume). Though the Evo Morales government (2006–2019) emphasized indigenous autonomy and territorial rights, it also emphasized that hydrocarbon extraction is a national project of progress, development, and inclusion. In this way, extraction has entered into conflict with indigenous peoples' access and control of their own territories; scholars have suggested that these conflicts over extractivism produce new forms of political authority and state formation (Anthias 2016b; Fabricant and Gustafson 2016; Postero 2017).

Alongside a renewed extractivist logic taking root in the Chaco, major infrastructure investments supported by international investment institutions are also shaping the region in new ways. In 2013, financed by the Interamerican Development Bank, the Paraguayan government constructed an aqueduct to take water from the Paraguay River to the Mennonite colonies in the central Chaco. The aqueduct delivered an important natural resource to supply the Mennonite industry and ranching enterprises, but the project disregarded the needs of indigenous peoples to access this resource (Canova 2018). Another important infrastructure project spanning the Chaco region is the bioceanic highway. Planning for the project began in the early 1990s to link the Atlantic with the Pacific Ocean by building a system of roads across the Gran Chaco region (Vázquez Recalde 2013). In Paraguay, the project began to be executed in 2018. Financed by the Interamerican Development Bank and the Development Bank of Latin America (CAF, formerly Corporación Andina de Fomento), the project will link the town of Carmelo Peralta by the Paraguay-Brazil border with Pozo Hondo, where Paraguay, Argentina, and Bolivia meet. An international bridge is being built between the Paraguayan town of Carmelo Peralta and the Brazilian town of Porto Murtinho.

Taking advantage of this infrastructure boom, in 2018 the Bolivian government discussed with Paraguay the possibility of establishing a railway of 500 kilometers to link the town of Roboré in Bolivia with Carmelo Peralta in Paraguay. The Bolivian Ministry of Public Works promotes the project to "develop and promote culture, tourism, businesses, export and import in our countries" (EFE 2018). It goes unsaid, however, that these "mechanisms of integration" ultimately seek to facilitate the flow of commodities resultant from the extractive economic activities in the region. The ongoing infrastructure initiatives are rapidly changing the social and economic landscape of the region, with impacts mostly on marginalized communities. Simultaneously, the development of infrastructure is stimulating renewed economic interest in the region. By 2000, the Casado company, after depleting the quebracho forests, had sold 600,000 hectares to the Korean Holy Spirit Association for the Unification of World Christianity (now the Family Federation for World Peace and Unification), commonly known as the Moonies. The town of Puerto Casado, which was under private ownership of the Casado company, also was sold to the Moon sect, with total disregard of residents' opinions (Morínigo 2006). Alongside establishing their church in the Paraguayan Chaco, the Moonies planned to invest more than eighty million dollars in ranching and agriculture. Uruguayan real estate investors also have purchased large tracts of state land by the border between Paraguay and Bolivia since the mid-2000s and resold them to Uruguayan ranchers. These purchases have been conducted with the active support of the Paraguayan government Instituto Nacional del Desarrollo Rural y de la Tierra (National Institute for Land and Rural Development), despite national laws prohibiting foreigners to participate in the nation's agrarian reform programs (Pastore 2008).

Indigenous groups in voluntary isolation also experience impacts of rapid environmental changes taking place. The Chaco has been home to the last group of uncontacted Ayoreo. Although their numbers are hard to estimate, in 2009 a few small groups were known to be moving between the borders of Paraguay and Bolivia (IWGIA 2009). In 2004 a group of seventeen Ayoreo including children were contacted and introduced to sedentary life in the department of Alto Paraguay. NGOs have played an important role in assuring that the legal mechanisms for their protection are respected, but deforestation has continued to threaten the last patches of forests where they live and move. The dramatic pace of deforestation in the region has exacerbated the process of indigenous urbanization in which indigenous peoples have come to inhabit marginal spaces in urban towns and cities, forcing them to become dependent for survival on intermittent wage-labor activities. In these spaces, indigenous women are mostly marginalized and excluded (Canova this volume), although they are engaged in a growing process of activism and organizations (Castelnuovo Biraben 2019; Gómez and Sciortino 2015). Scholars of the Gran Chaco have identified multiple ways indigenous peoples such as the Guaraní, Qom, Ayoreo, and Tapiete are remaking their identities, engaging in new religious and political practices, and creating cultural practices in urban spaces as a result of growing urban migration (Canova 2019; Glauser and Patzi 2014; Hirsch 2006a; Tamagno 2001). Nonindigenous populations have been equally affected by these broader changes, but they have resorted to political mobilizations to denounce their living situations and have achieved some goals in unexpected ways. For example, in the fight against the Moon sect, in an unexpected move, the Paraguayan Congress sanctioned the expropriation of 52 million hectares in favor of the local population of Puerto Casado (Glauser 2009).

Political Mobilization, Ethnic Reemergence, and the Struggle for Rights

During the 1980s the end of military dictatorships, the ensuing process of democratization, and the increasing indigenous political mobilizations paved the way for the enactment of constitutional reforms. These reforms responded to indigenous demands and included the recognition of the pluricultural nature of the society, the existence of indigenous peoples, and the promotion of the use of native languages and cultural practices. Reforms have taken place at the international level as well, among them the ratification of the International Labor Organization Convention on Indigenous and Tribal Peoples (ILO 169), guaranteeing the rights of indigenous peoples, and the Declaration on the Rights of Indigenous Peoples, ratified in 2007 by the UN General Assembly, which includes the right of indigenous peoples to self-determination. Such advances constitute frameworks that support the demands of indigenous groups at the local and regional level.

In Argentina, the Ley de Protección y Apoyo a las Comunidades Indígenas (Law for the Protection and Support of Indigenous Communities), Law 23.302, implemented in 1989, includes granting of land titles, legal recognition (*personería jurídica*), and the creation of a National Institute of Indigenous Affairs (Instituto Nacional de Asuntos Indígenas) to oversee indigenous demands (Gordillo and Hirsch 2011). Importantly, in 1994, there was a constitutional reform and Article 75 was amended, in which the state recognizes the preexistence of indigenous peoples, their access to their lands, and their participation in management of natural resources and other aspects that might affect them. The reform of this article was the result of active lobbying by indigenous leaders, indigenist NGOs, and activists who for decades had struggled for cultural and language rights and collective possession of the land. By the mid-1990s, as indigenous activism increased, so did the visibility of their claims, and they achieved gradual improvements in the establishment of bilingual intercultural programs (Hirsch and Serrudo 2010), access to health services (Hirsch and Lorenzetti 2016), and limited access to land titling. The major challenge has been the dramatic expansion of extractivism (mineral, agroindustrial, hydrocarbon) in indigenous territories, and the activist resistance against it continues.

In Paraguay, indigenous rights were recognized in 1981 in Law 904/81, the Estatuto de las Comunidades Indígenas (Statute of Indigenous Communities), which also established the Instituto Nacional del Indígena (INDI), the governmental agency in charge of indigenous affairs, as an autonomous entity. Up to that point it had functioned as part of the Ministry of Defense since 1958. The law recognized indigenous peoples' territories and their right to self-determination for the first time. Moreover, after the fall of Alfredo Stroessner's dictatorship (1954–1989), indigenous peoples participated, with voice but no vote, in the Asamblea Constituyente (Constitutional Assembly), which resulted in the promulgation of the recognition of their rights at the national level, in Chapter 5 of the Constitution of 1992 (Susnik and Chase Sardi 1995). Since then, their rights have been recognized through several other legal mechanisms at the national level, such as the promulgation of Decree 1039/2018 for the establishment of a national protocol for the process of free prior and informed consent in activities pertaining to indigenous peoples. This has been a major achievement of indigenous social movements in Paraguay. Despite these efforts, however, the application of these legal mechanisms for the support and advancement of indigenous autonomous processes and protection of their territories continue to be actively contested by state and private interests (CODEHUPY 2017).

In the Paraguayan Chaco, the sale of land at the lowest prices in the market for cattle ranching and more recently soybean production is having an adverse impact on indigenous territories. As a result, NGOs and indigenous social movements are taking a prominent role in advancing demands for the protection of indigenous territories. Through their support, members of the Enxet people (Correia this volume) have taken their plight to the Inter-American Court of Human Rights and in an unprecedented move, won their case in 2005 against the Paraguayan state, forcing it to restore their traditional territories. Meanwhile in Bolivia, the Constitution of 2009, written by a Constituent Assembly with 55.8 percent of its representatives from indigenous groups defined the country as a plurinational state and granted collective rights and self-government. The constitution reinforced the indigenous autonomous territories called Tierras Comunitarias de Origen (TCOs) and guaranteed their rights to natural resources found in their lands.

The reformation of the constitution in granting of land titles led to the increase of revenues from hydrocarbon production that in turn were invested in state welfare programs, retirement accounts, social subsidies, national literacy programs, and other initiatives (Postero 2013). In 2009, the law of Indigenous Peasant Autonomy was established in the Bolivian constitution; it established two autonomous municipalities, one of them Charagua Iyambae in the Chaco region (Postero this volume). Previous to the Morales government, the Tapiete (Hirsch this volume) had obtained 21,840 hectares as Tierra Comunitaria de Origen (TCO). Despite pressure from neighboring settlers and expansion of the agricultural frontier, these legislative and political gains constitute major accomplishments in the struggle for territory and political self-determination of indigenous peoples. The experience of the indigenous population in the plurinational period was characterized by a clear and increasing contradiction between the legal-political framework that provided specific rights and guarantees to these groups and the consolidation of the extractivist model that undermined them (Postero 2017).

Overall, the neoliberal policies of the 1980s and 1990s had a profound impact on indigenous populations, reducing access to public health and education, supporting agricultural development, and leading to privatizations that affected people's livelihoods, environments, and access to resources. As a response to the political changes, indigenous political activism has increased since the 2000s, when protests took place in Argentina and Bolivia against privatizations, neoliberal policies, and the dire economic situation. In Argentina, increased stability, economic reactivation, and implementation of social programs has improved the situation of indigenous peoples, favoring their access to health, education, and economic development programs. However, land titling, a major demand throughout the country, did not improve, and extractivism and industrial agricultural production increased, affecting indigenous communities in the Chaco and other regions of the country (Biocca 2016).

Uncertain Futures in a Rapidly Changing Regional Landscape

The chapters in this volume delve into how aspects of the five broader processes explored in this introduction play out at the local level through specific case studies. The chapters present current ethnographic data to show the complex ways indigenous peoples have responded to the colonial process, to relations with the diverse social actors and institutions, and to global economic contingencies. Some of the starkest differences that the chapters illuminate relate to the role of the state in regard to the local populations in each country. In the case of the Argentine state, César Ceriani Cernadas explores how the humanitarian and development narratives and practices of religious organizations impinged upon indigenous groups. The author shows how religious missions initially occupied a role in education and health that later was assumed by the state, and in its so doing, humanitarianism and hygienic practices configured a cosmology of development. In the Paraguayan case, Paola Canova explores how the recent multicultural reform of the state is articulated as a contemporary form of governance. She focuses on how the reforms of the health system are experienced by young Ayoreo women, revealing radical disparities in the exercise of multicultural citizenship for indigenous women proclaimed by the state.

The loss of territories to contemporary extractive industries is another major theme that runs through several of the chapters. Federico Bossert takes a historical perspective to show how historical land claims and the struggle against hydrocarbon extraction among the Chané people were based on historical possession of land titles and knowledge of political bureaucracies. Mercedes Biocca focuses on the multiple perceptions and positions that members of Qom and Moqoit indigenous communities have adopted in relation to the model of agribusiness linked to the expansion of soybean production. She shows how in so doing they have reshaped the process of rural transformation wrought by neoliberal reform.

The chapters also underscore how colonial relations continue to be reproduced in the contemporary context and how indigenous peoples are navigating and furthering their own life projects in such contexts. In the Paraguayan case study among the Enxet people presented by Joel Correia, historical processes of missionization helped shape contemporary structures of settler colonialism, mainly through the expansion of cattle ranching, indigenous dispossession, and labor exploitation. He demonstrates that the role of ranching and its relation to settler colonialism in Paraguay are crucial to understanding the historical material and discursive processes that shape the present and future politics of Enxet struggles. Focusing on the Enlhet, Hannes Kalisch examines how interethnic relations construct notions of territory and territorial possession in the context of Mennonite settlers to the region. Drawing on the narrative of an Enlhet elder, he observes that the arrival of Mennonite settlers implied not only a process of dispossession but also a shift in Enlhet ontologies. In contexts such as this, marked by inequalities and discrimination, what does decolonization imply and look like? Nancy Postero examines this in the Bolivian Chaco by focusing on the building of Guaraní autonomy. Drawing on the case of the newly autonomous Charagua Iyambae government, she shows how decolonization is put into practice amid new structures of political power in a context of struggle to access resources.

Indigenous subjectivities are being constructed and resignified in a changing social landscape, as seen in the chapters. The work of Rodrigo Villagra Carron shows how the muddling of ethnonyms, origins, and displacement impinge on a death ritual. In the Bolivian Chaco, Bret Gustafson delves into a critical examination of the emergence of the Guaraní, historically known as the Chiriguano, in a historically and linguistically nuanced account of the complexity of ethnogenesis and influence of colonial discourse on the making of indigenous history. Silvia Hirsch takes a transnational perspective in focusing on the Tapiete of Argentina while also looking at how the Tapiete of Paraguay and Bolivia construct and experience a multiterritorial dynamic in which geopolitical borders are challenged and identities strengthened through contacts and evangelical membership. In a nearby region, where natural gas is being extracted in Weenhayek territory, Denise Bebbington and Guido Cortez explore the process of consultation and how complex relations between indigenous groups, leaders, and organizations, state officials, and a gas company are rife with tensions and contradictions that ultimately impinge on the livelihood of the Weenhayek people. Bringing into conversation theoretical and ethnographic approaches to understand processes of missionization, environmental pressures and degradation, struggles for indigenous autonomy, interactions between nonindigenous settlers and indigenous groups, land disputes, the intermittent presence of the state and its deployment of social and economic development programs, the chapters in this volume present the different struggles between members of civil society that emerge from the larger contested sociopolitical and economic dynamics rapidly transforming the Gran Chaco region.

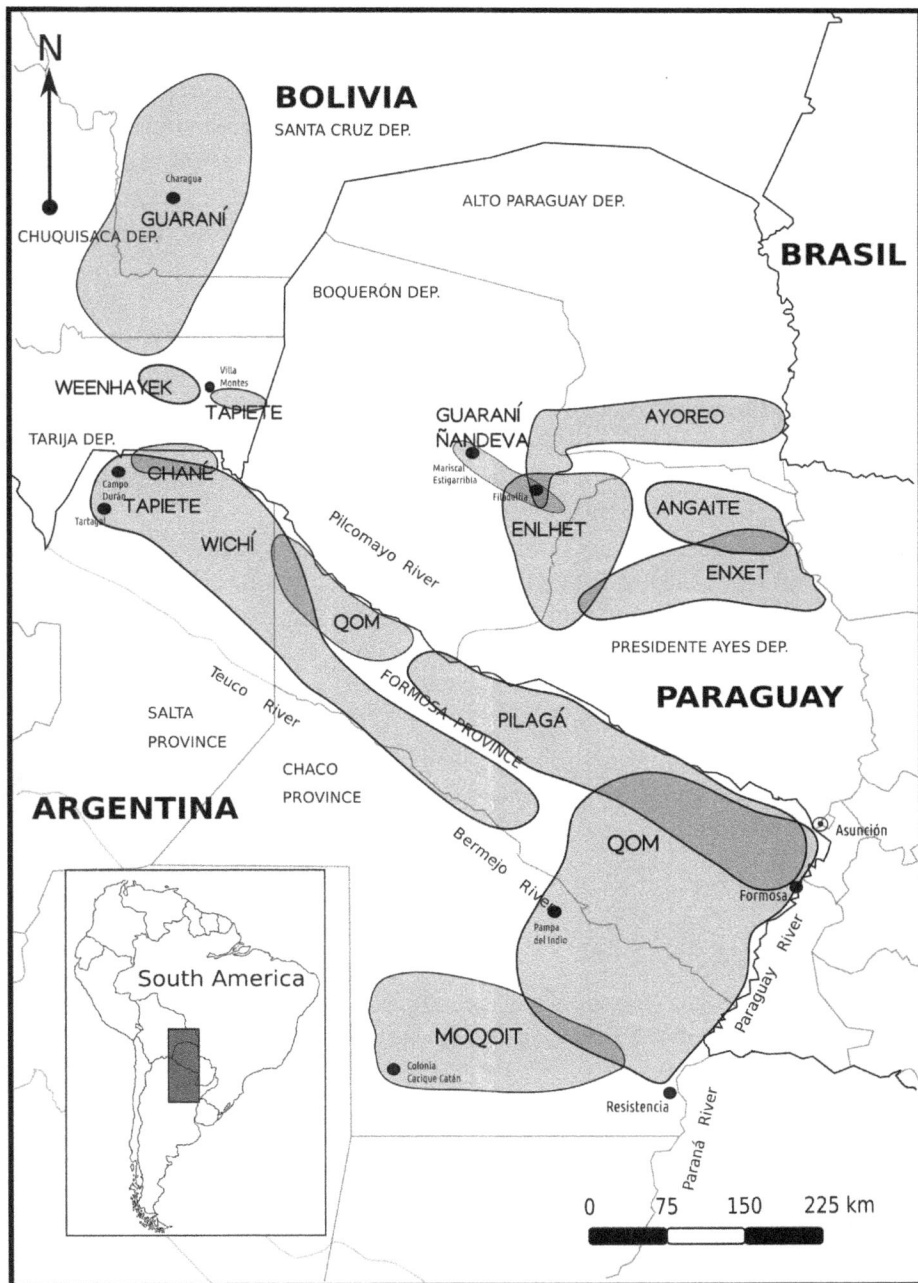

Map 0.2. Current areas of indigenous groups studied in this book. Map by Ana Dell'Arciprete.

Acknowledgments

The idea of this book was bolstered by our interest in granting visibility to the Chaco region and its peoples to English-speaking researchers and scholars and in thinking in transdisciplinary ways on the historical, social, economic, and political contingencies that have impacts on its people and geography. Foremost, we thank the contributors to this book for sharing not only insightful theoretical perspectives but also their diverse fieldwork experiences. We appreciate the time and efforts of all the authors to bring this collaborative project to completion; we are particularly thankful to Gastón Gordillo, who graciously accepted to write the afterword.

Other colleagues who have supported the making of this book include José Braunstein and Nancy Postero for their careful reading of the introduction, John Palmer for the translation of a chapter, and Ana Dell'Arciprete for crafting the maps in the introduction.

We thank the University of Florida Press, especially our editor Stephanye Hunter for believing in this project and insightfully guiding us through the process. We also appreciate the comments and suggestions of the anonymous reviewers who took an interest in our proposal and gave us the possibility to publish and stimulate future collaborations among the contributors to this volume.

Above all, we are profoundly grateful to all the people we have encountered in the field and in the libraries, archives, and museums who have opened their lives to us and provided access to sources and to their knowledge of the Gran Chaco.

Notes

1. The term "criollo" refers either to people of mixed race (indigenous and European) or only of European descent. It is a term usually used by indigenous peoples in reference to nonindigenous individuals.

2. Most publications that present state-of-the-art Chaco scholarship are in Spanish and predominantly on the Argentine Chaco. Since the first decades of the twentieth century, several Argentine universities and research centers have produced scholars who have conducted fieldwork in the Chaco and trained numerous students. In English, Braunstein and Miller 1999; Combès, Villar, and Lowrey 2009; and Krebs and Braunstein 2011 provide major contributions to the field. The Combès, Villar, and Lowrey article particularly also presents a comparative approach to Chaco studies. Gordillo (2006) presents a theoretically nuanced and critical account of Chaco studies in Argentina. Barúa and Rodríguez Mir 2009, the introduction to a dossier on the Chaco, presents

some of the current challenges in the region such as environmental deterioration, defor-estation, and hydrocarbon exploitation as well as the dire health conditions, particularly for the native population. Tola 2013, the introduction to the volume she coedited on ontology in the Chaco, provides an in-depth account of studies of political ecology, kin-ship, affectivity, and ontology that predominantly focus on the Argentine Chaco. Finally, Ceriani Cernadas 2015 updates scholarship on development, gender, power, and politics. These works largely refer to ethnographic studies conducted by anthropologists.

3. On the history and ethnography produced by Franciscans see Combès 2015, Langer 2009.

4. For more on the ethnohistory of the Chaco see Braunstein and Miller 1999; Santa-maría and Lagos 1992; Susnik 1978, 1981.

5. For a scholarly and thorough historical analysis of the Franciscan missions in nine-teenth century Bolivia see Langer 2009.

6. For a history of the New Tribes Mission in Bolivia see Johnson 1988.

7. For a thorough account of the Chiriguano rebellion see Combès 2014b.

8. Napalpí was officially called Reducción Aborigen Napalpí; it was created after a military campaign as a reservation to concentrate indigenous peoples and transform them into sedentary workers who would assist in developing productive agricultural projects.

1

The Rise and Fall of an Indigenous Homeland

The Itiyuro River Basin in Argentina

FEDERICO BOSSERT

ENGLISH TRANSLATION BY JOHN H. PALMER

One morning at dawn, in September 2016, the Chané of Campo Durán heard a thudding sound coming from the state road that separates their community from the adjacent forest. On inspection, they found a group of men unloading a truck replete with wooden posts, which they were then planting in the ground in order to build a fence on the opposite side of the road. The news spread quickly through the village, and a group led by the *mburuvicha* (headman) approached to inquire what the men were doing. Stepping forward, one of the intruders announced that he was the new landowner and that he was fencing off his property. To which the Chané replied that it was part of their territory: "We were born here, and no one can push his way in." Pulling out a bundle of papers, the man waved them in the air. "But you have none of these papers," he admonished the group. The Chané blocked the path of the fence, and the incident culminated in the arrival of the police and the departure of the supposed landowner, who left, threatening to return the following day to complete his task. He did not return, and the posts were left lying by the side of the road. The Chané took them back to their village and used them as firewood because, they said, the wood came from trees that had been logged on their land.

A few days later, the *mburuvicha* gave me his insight into the altercation. He said a neighboring settler, on hearing that the Chané were making headway with their land claim by securing "good papers" that would ensure the demarcation of their territory, had hastened to sell his holdings for a pittance to another local settler who chose to try his luck.[1]

Not unlike Brumaire's farce, the episode is a repeat of similar events that punctuate the history of Chané lands in the Itiyuro River basin. The following pages give an account of that history, from its nebulous beginnings at the end of the eighteenth century, when the Itiyuro River was barely a mark on one or two maps, to the Chané's territorial dispossession at the beginning of the twentieth century. By highlighting the contrast between oral ethnohistory and documentary sources, the Chané's memory of their traditional territory may be elucidated, along with their understanding of the causes behind their loss of that territory and their perception of the means they envisage for its recuperation.

The Unknown Itiyuro Basin

The Chané are an indigenous group in northwestern Argentina, with a population of scarcely two thousand distributed mainly in two communities: Campo Durán, a small cluster of households overshadowed by an imposing oil refinery on the banks of the Itiyuro River; and the former Franciscan mission of Tuyunti. A few other settlements are scattered across the river basin and at the foot of the Aguaragüe mountain range. Situated on the western edge of the Chaco, the region once formed part of the Bolivian provinces of Salinas and Gran Chaco, subsequently coming under the jurisdiction of the Department of Orán and since 1948, that of San Martín, both in the Argentine province of Salta. At an altitude between 300 and 600 meters above sea level, the Itiyuro basin ecosystem is characterized as a foothill forest, an ecological transition zone between the Andean Yungas and the Chaco Plain.

The Chané's presence along the course of the Itiyuro is attested to since at least the beginning of the nineteenth century. Until the end of that century, however, the area remained almost terra incognita, an ill-explored hinterland between the Bermejo and Pilcomayo Rivers that marked the limits of colonial and early republican exploration of the western Chaco. During the colonial period, incursions into this northern frontier zone had been few, as commerce and communication between Buenos Aires and the viceroyalty of Upper Peru followed either the highland Humahuaca route or the valleys of the Andean foothills. No known route traversed the low-lying Itiyuro basin, and indeed the river does not appear on most maps until well into the nineteenth century. So it was that in 1921 the engineer in charge of plotting the course of the railway line that was to skirt the foothills lamented the "defects of the existing maps" (Montagne 1941, 137).

In large measure, the Itiyuro and its inhabitants first appear indirectly, in documents referring to neighboring areas. The Chané's inconspicuousness was to a great extent the result of their not integrating into the townships founded between the end of the eighteenth century and the beginning of the nineteenth. Added to that, they succeeded in resisting missionary influence until well into the twentieth century. Thus, in documents of the 1790s relating to the upper Itiyuro's Itau and Caraparí districts, the Chané were mentioned only as a vague threat issuing from the obscure Chaco periphery, as bitter enemies of the local Chiriguano people and frequent allies of the Pilcomayo River Toba.[2]

Franciscan and military chronicles concur in the story they tell with regard, respectively, to the Itau and Salinas missions and the Caraparí fortress. In those regions, the enemy Chiriguano had become "Indian allies" open to being reduced to mission residence and evangelization, while the Chané were adversaries as "wild" and "uncivilized" as the peoples of the Chaco.[3] Their resistance was no longer the mere urge for freedom that thwarted all attempts at installing missions among them in the central mountain range; they had resorted to taking up arms. And their objective appeared to be that of bringing to an end the established pattern of interethnic relations. To this aim, they availed themselves of the Toba incursions into the upper reaches of the Pilcomayo that in the last years of the eighteenth century forced the retreat of Chiriguano villages in the Caiza region.[4]

Documents of the period record the names of at least two Chané villages—Caipependi and Sanandita—on opposite banks of the upper Pilcomayo. But it is well known that other Chané settlements existed to the south of the Pilcomayo, in the little-known Caiza Plain.[5] In 1795 a friar of the Itau mission reported that "the enemy Chané and Toba heathens who are advancing towards Itau have their villages to the east and to the south of the Reduction, and when they disperse they head in that direction."[6] Some years later, Father Comajuncosa (1971 [1800], 142) confirmed the friar's (imprecise) indications, stating that to the south of Caraparí were "the Chané and Mataguayo nations." Given that the said two villages of Sanandita and Caipependi were located to the northeast of Itau and Caraparí, who were those "enemy Chané" living to the south?

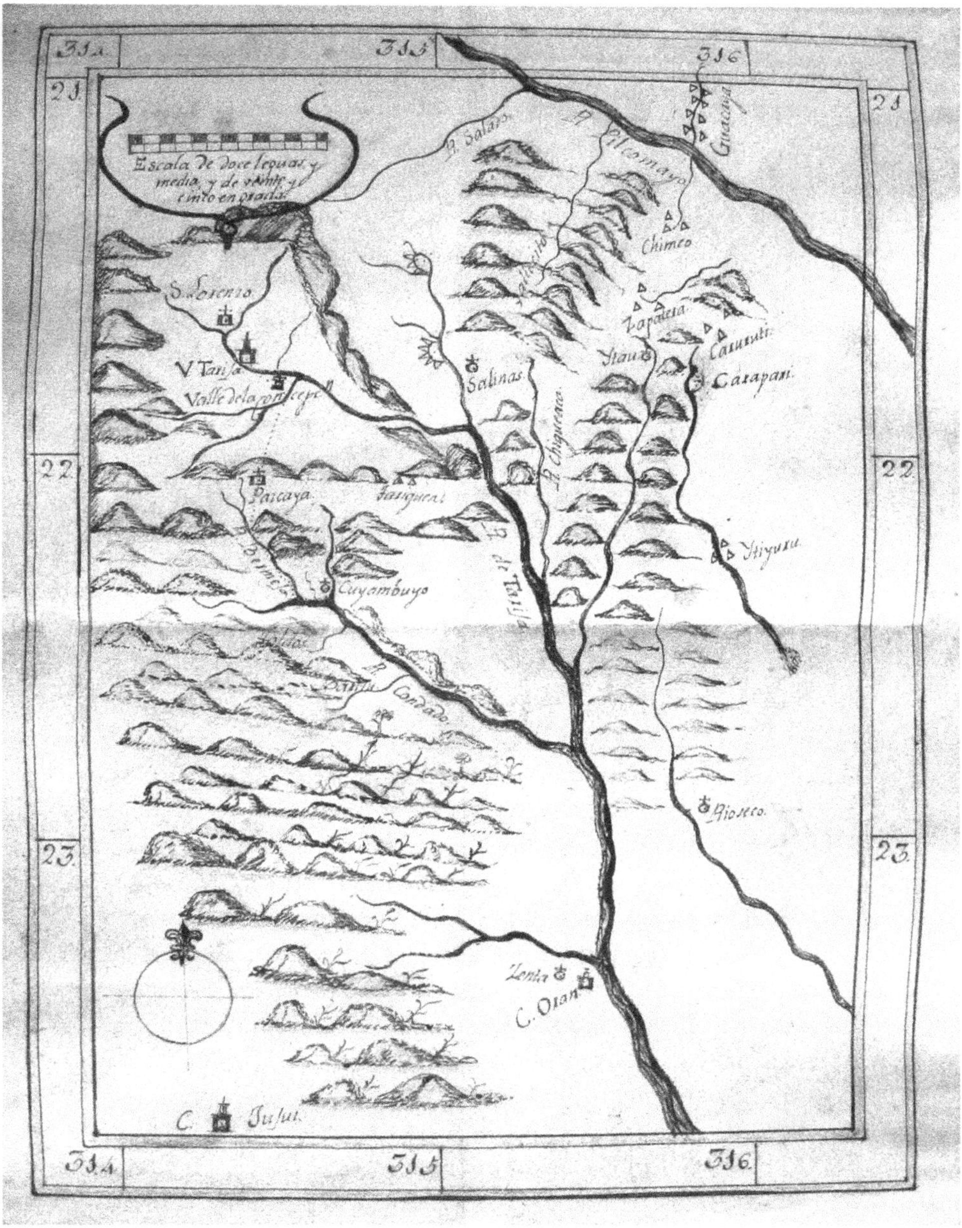

Map 1.1. The first known cartographic reference to the Itiyuro indigenous village, circa 1800. Fray Fernando Cano, interior, legajo 56, expediente 9, Archivo General Nacional.

Not by chance, that same friar was the author of one of the first maps featuring a previously unreported river and indigenous village: Itiyuro. And some years later Father Comajuncosa was to make what appears to have been the first precise reference to "the barbarous Chané Indians of the Itiyuro" some "sixteen leagues" from the Seco River mission (1884 [1810], 180).

One hundred years later, in a short note published after his 1908–1909 Chaco expedition, Erland Nordenskiöld wrote, "on the banks of the Itiyuro I found part of an isolated tribe that calls itself Chané" (1910a, 97). While such villages undoubtedly had formed part of the Chané network to the south of the Pilcomayo (Combès 2007), it is safe to say that their territory extended beyond the traditional limits of Chiriguanía in the lowlands, abutting lands inhabited by the Wichí (Palmer 2005, 50–51). Their singular distribution reflects two features of Chané history in the region: their distance (or enmity) with regard to the Chiriguano and their proximity (or alliance) vis-à-vis their Chaco neighbors. At the same time, their isolation protected them against the progressive installation of military and missionary outposts and, above all, against the expansion of cattle ranches on the Caiza Plain during the nineteenth century (Langer 1987, 308).

The late eighteenth-century perception of the Chané as "barbarous Indians," wild enemies like their Chaco allies, was to change in the first half of the nineteenth century. In 1843–1844 President José Ballivián (1841–1847) sent expeditions commanded by Generals Magariños and Van Nivel to make the Chaco stretch of the Pilcomayo frontier secure. Magariños explored the Caiza Plain, following a southerly route skirting the foothills, and allocated lands for colonization (Lista 1881, 30). On the banks of the Itiyuro he encountered the Chané captain Paragua, "principal cacique of all those peoples," who requested of him legal title to the lands inhabited by his people. Magariños consented, and in 1846 President Ballivián himself endorsed the land transfer with his signature in the course of an inspection of the region's fortresses. From the documentary evidence consulted, the transfer comprised an area of some 20,000 hectares in the Itiyuro basin, from west to east, from the "Itaki Outlet" to the "Itiyuro Narrows"; from north to south, from the river to the "Jakatimbae gorge."[7] According to Father Corrado (1884, 463), cacique Paragua proved from then on to be a "loyal friend to the Christians." The following pages trace the subsequent history of the territory with which he was endowed.

The Ethnohistorical Record

One of the most pessimistic tenets of Chiriguano and Chané ethnology is that for various reasons, the oral histories of both ethnic groups have, like their scant mythologies, ceased to be narrated. Alfred Métraux, one of their most influential ethnographers, was an active exponent of that pessimism. In nearly all his writings on the two groups, he predicted that their cultural traditions would not be long in dying out (Bossert and Villar 2007). Andrés Campanella, his secretary at the Tucumán Ethnological Institute, furnished a revealing account of an incident that can only have added fuel to that somber forecast. In a Chiriguano village in which Métraux asked to be introduced to the person most knowledgeable in their cultural traditions, the headman replied, "Don't delude yourself, my friend. There are no Indians here, only such as mix with their masters—the *karai*, as he put it—and forget the most elementary episodes in their history" (Campanella 1935, 260). The commentary replicates, in secular key, the complaint lodged by Chiriguano elders before the missionary Giannecchini, a half century earlier. They lamented that while their ancestors had educated their offspring in Chiriguano warriorhood, "the present generation, having established relations both with missionaries and with mestizos, no longer sets store by its *immiani* (oral traditions). On the contrary, it despises and derides those traditions" (Giannecchini 1996 [1898], 358). So it was that historical amnesia in all its variant forms, the result of military incursion and colonization, was to become a recurrent topic in many texts dedicated to the ethnic groups in question (Bernard 1973; Saignes 1984, 35; 1990, 200).

Nonetheless, the Itiyuro Chané maintain a discrete set of historical narratives that are transmitted from generation to generation and unlike personal and family memories, are widely known. Their central theme is precisely the defense of Chané territory by captains of the distant past. Two of the most representative of such accounts are of Cochou's repulsion of a Chiriguano invasion and Mocapoi's journey in pursuit of land titles.[8]

Both events can be placed in time. In 1908 Nordenskiöld collected genealogical evidence relating to the line of captains from which the then headman of the Itiyuro Chané descended. On the basis of that evidence and of scattered genealogical data supplied by other sources, it can be surmised that although there is no record of Paragua as the great captain or corporate headman who had secured title to his people's lands, he was none other than the Hinu Parava who heads the chiefly lineage recorded by the Swede. Chané historical reconstruction dates back to the next generation and the warfare feats of Cochou, one of Hinu Parava's sons who was corporate headman at a time when Chané possessions in the Itiyuro basin were still undisputed.[9]

Cochou's Combat

As in a good number of Chané historical narratives, the story opens with a reference to their original territory: "In those days the Chané had total freedom. There were no townships, and Chané dominion was unrestricted. Cochou lived in Tëtaiguate, at the top of one of the foothills. Ava [Chiriguano] land began beyond the third village to the north."[10] The narrative describes how Cochou and a small party of men defended their village, with the support of settlers, by launching a counterattack against Chiriguano enemies who, under the pretense of traveling to the sugar plantations, had taken it upon themselves to massacre and cannibalize the Chané. Forewarned of the attack by allies from the Isoso region and with the protection of shamanic conjuration, Cochou and his men rode down Mount Tëtaiguate and clubbed all the assailants to death. They then headed north, to the fourth village, to interrogate the Ava *mburuvicha*, who, in fear of his life, claimed to know nothing of the attack, since the culprits had said that they were going to work on the sugarcane harvest south of the Itiyuro River. Nevertheless, he offered to compensate the Chané with articles of clothing, personal adornments, and money.

In all probability, Cochou's captaincy can be situated in the 1880s. The estimate follows from the consistency of the territory evoked in the oral text with the nineteenth-century territory as one that was relatively marginal in relation to the colonist front and markedly distanced from Chiriguano areas of occupation, which "began beyond the third village to the north." The oral narrative also indicates ethnic relations that radically diverge from those now seen; the antagonism toward and warfare with the Chiriguano, not to mention the anthropophagy suffered at their hands, contrast with the current situation, in which even the oldest Chané villages have for several decades been profoundly multiethnic. The Chiriguano migrated massively to the region during the Chaco War (1932–1935), established themselves in communities along the road beside the foothills, and frequently entered into affinal relations with neighboring Chané villages. As a result, Chané genealogies are today very different from the proud lineage recorded by Nordenskiöld. With few exceptions, they comprise complex intertwinings of the two peoples.

The Chané territory defined in the narrative was not only situated at a safe remove from Chiriguanía; it was also strategically placed on the access route between the Caiza Plain and *mbaporenda*, the area of sugar plantations to which, from the mid-nineteenth century, large numbers of Chiriguano traveled each year. At the time, there were two paths of communication between the Orán and Tarija regions; Chané elders maintain that the Chiriguano chose the mountain route, although longer and more tortuous, to avoid Chané lookout posts in the route skirting the foothills, a choice that corroborates the story of Cochou.

The historian Branislava Susnik (1968, 123–124) has pointed out, additionally, that around 1840 colonist pressure in the Tarija region drove the large Chiriguano nuclei of Chimeo, Itau, and Caraparí to fragment and disperse toward the Pilcomayo and that their dispersion was obstructed by the control exerted by the Chané over the Itiyuro River: "the banks of the river Caraparí [another name for the Itiyuro] were always predominantly Chané. Chiriguano mobility to the south of the river was obstructed, in the 19th century, by their former 'tapíis' [slaves]" (230). Her analysis would appear to find confirmation in the narrative of Cochou's combat in which, mythological elaboration notwithstanding, real historical events of the 1870s and 1880s can be discerned. The conclusion is that in keeping with Chané ethnohistory, interethnic relations underwent an inversion such that it was now the Chiriguano masters who were paying tribute to their former Chané slaves.

Mocapoi's Journey

The second narrative is an account of events that took place a couple of decades later, with the defense of their territory at the forefront of Chané concerns. When Nordenskiöld visited the Itiyuro in 1908, the corporate great captain Mocapoi told him that settlers were usurping his land rather than renting it as tenants. Together they surveyed and drew up a map of the territory, and the Swede advised Mocapoi to address his grievances to the country's president. A few years later, back in Sweden, Nordenskiöld harked back on the matter: "regrettably, I do not know whether Vocapoy ever made the long journey to the great white chief's village" (2002 [1912], 140). He probably considered it unlikely, but what follows is the account of that journey narrated in 2007 by Mandasai, a woman elder of Campo Durán.

Long, long ago, Mocapoi went on a journey. Others went with him, both Chané and Toba. The guide was a Toba, because the Chané couldn't go alone. They, the Tobas, spoke our language well. Some came from a place called Irua, in Villa Montes, and the rest were from the Chaco. The Chané were from Ñatiurenda. As a young girl, I understood nothing; I didn't understand why they were having those meetings. It was only later that I knew that they were going to Buenos Aires. Every night they gathered to hold meetings. Kapura, Tumbakiki, and Taikoriki were headmen. Taikoriki was a squint-eyed Toba, fluent in the Chané language.[11] They were going to accompany our fathers—and others from here, such as Kaamiri—to Buenos Aires. People of Campo Durán also went. I don't know how many traveled with Mocapoi, but they were many. There was Kapi and Pipa, who were called "little captains." They had all joined together to make their voice heard far away. Before starting the journey, they made themselves cowhide sandals, because there were no shoes. For food, they prepared *atikui* and *aitipí*, and they took water in gourds, carrying it all on their shoulders. As far as I know, they traveled first through Bolivia and then across Paraguay. . . .

I vaguely remember their departure. It made me very sad. They went in groups of four, and their numbers swelled on the way through Bolivia and Paraguay. They went through the forest, not via Salta. Not until they reached Buenos Aires did they break the news in Salta. They were gone for a long time. They passed through Salta on their return and finally arrived safe and well, with a military escort.

They suffered greatly. My grandfather's brother, who made the journey, recounted that one of the leaders instructed them to observe the path carefully: "If you find cattle tracks, we must follow them to the house of the owner." They came across goat tracks and decided to follow them. After walking until late afternoon, they heard a cock crowing: *cocoreóooo*. "The house can't be far away," they said; "we'll spend the night there." They reached the house and went to ask to sleep there: "We're on our way to Buenos Aires and we're stopping here." The settler stood looking at them: "You can camp over there," he said; "fetch some firewood." . . .

Who, I ask, would travel in that fashion? But that is how they made the journey, on foot. How many days would it have taken them to walk through the forest, with stopovers at different ranches? During one such stopover, the settler's son was bitten by a snake while rounding up his father's cattle. "Who knows how to heal?" the settler asked the group of wayfarers. "My son's been bitten by a snake." My grandmother's brother was a healer, and he sent the settler to bring him uapere bark [bark of the tusca tree (*Acacia aroma*)]. The settler returned with a long strip of the prescribed plant medicine, which my great-uncle wrapped firmly round the victim's ankle. After various repeats of the treatment, the victim's pain subsided. He slept and recovered, cured of the snakebite. The settler invited the group to stay, and he slaughtered and barbecued a calf to share with them.

By my grandfather's account, they continued walking till they reached Buenos Aires. They encountered many Toba groups who obstructed their transit and wanted to kill them, but Kapura spoke with them and ensured the group's safe passage. And so they proceeded until Kapura at one point announced, "We now have only two groups to pass, and then we're there." Those two remaining groups were bad Toba, disguised like carnival dancers. (That is why I am always reminded of Mocapoi's ordeal at Carnival time!) They brandished weapons and jumped to the rhythm of the drumbeat, spears in hand. Our grandfathers had set out with nothing but a knife and they kept it out of sight. Thanks, though, to the Toba "captains" who accompanied them, they arrived unharmed. They also returned safely. Such is the story.

The Toba "captains" married Chané women . . . and everyone lived well because the land adjudicated to us was extensive. But settlers have taken our land. All was well after the delegation's return because they came with papers which, it seems, were the land title. What else can they have been? The limit was Yakatimbae, where, long ago, there used to be a boundary marker. The boundary descended via Chilkara, along the Itiyuro, past Ikua, to Yerba Buena. My grandfather, my mother's father, took me on horseback to see it. Over there in Pocitos, we saw a *timbo-i* tree [pacará (*Enterolobium sp.*)] with large letters inscribed on it by the *karai* [members of the settler population].

Drafted by the government, the map included the foothills near here. It was drawn on a very large sheet of paper and stated that we could sell the land and timber. That's what it said. My father gave me the paper, and I wrapped it up and took good care of it. Then it got into the hands of the Centeno family [which exercises the headmanship of Tuyunti community]. Where can they have put it? The papers given to the delegation in Paraguay and Bolivia were smaller, but all this land was ours, and the large map said that we could sell stone and gravel. Now anyone can come and take the stone and the wood, and we are left in poverty.

For the Chané, the story of Mocapoi, with its multifarious variants, is a historical point of reference and a principal proof of their legitimate right to their ancestral territory. The most immediately relevant aspect of the narrative consists in its geographical and toponymic references, which, in the absence of the missing maps, constitute an oral cartography of the ancestral homeland. Such references are a fundamental part of Chané discourse, to the extent that narrators always locate their subject matters in space with every available detail. Mandasai will state, for example, "My father was from Algarrobal, from a place known as Irua. Beyond that lay Iopeité and, beyond that, ran the track to Itika." The conservation of the memory of their homeland's coordinates is a prime value of Chané ethnohistory.

References to the ancestral homeland typically contrast the former territorial splendor with the current situation, regarded as banefully antithetical to an agriculturalist mode of subsistence. The differences between the two are self-evident. In the narrative of Cochou, the Chané still had "total freedom" and their "dominion was unrestricted" in that terra incognita deplored by late nineteenth-century explorers. A few years later, in the narrative of Mocapoi, the colonization of the Itiyuro had begun and was marked from its inception by the distinguishing feature of servile labor. Chané autonomy on lands of their own contrasts with the regime of working for colonists in exchange for food.

Ethnic relations had also shifted. In the earlier of the two stories, settlers were allies of the Chané, and the invaders were the long-standing Chiriguano adversaries; in the second narrative the invaders were neighboring settlers, and it was long-standing Toba allies who provided the Chané with support. Invariably, Mocapoi's journey was the result of abuses such as those that he related to Nordenskiöld. For example, in 2005 Koronsai recalled that a colonist, Juan Moreno, forced the Chané to work for him under conditions that led to a situation in which "the men hid in the forest and only the terrified women remained in the community. No one could plant crops." Koronsai's aged mother, Jerusai, recalled, "My grandfather went to Buenos Aires on account of that Chaco settler, who never left us in peace and made it impossible for us to do our own work. He used to come into our houses as though he owned them."[12] The ethnohistorical record assumes proportions that are both timeless and ubiquitous: past troubles, be they those that triggered Mocapoi's journey or those ensuing from the loss of the land title papers, are interspersed with allusions to similar events lived by the storytellers. Mandasai incorporated the following personal reminiscence in her narration:

> My vegetable garden was not wired off. It had only a stick fence. In those days, the colonists' livestock intruded unhindered, even into my front yard. There I had a large clay water-pitcher, which was shattered by their cattle. I had to wake up before dawn to keep watch. I berated the settlers, telling them that it was very pleasant before, not like it is now, with nobody giving us the slightest consideration. They cut the wire fence and sent in their cows, their horses, all their animals.

The story of Mocapoi thus serves as testimony not only to the traditional territory but also to the abuses suffered in connection with the colonization of that territory. The structure of the narrative, comprising the advance of the colonist front, the protection afforded by the authorities, and the eventual loss of the land title, adapts itself to any historical or biographical episode in the bitter record of territorial degradation experienced by the Chané.

The Documentary Record

Many Chané take a keen interest in all written materials related to their history, including the pages devoted to the subject by Nordenskiöld. That interest is evident in the complaint that a Chiriguano headman lucidly articulated to Father Giannecchini that the missionized members of his society had forgotten their own historiographic tradition, but its best exponents were the missionaries because they wrote all they heard on their strips of *tüpa-pire* (skin of god, sacred skin), one of the Guaraní terms for paper. Having probed indigenous historical memory, a review of the literary version of history is due.

Lawsuits

While missionary and military texts were until the mid-nineteenth century the principal documentary sources regarding the Chané's homeland, from then on a labyrinth of judicial case files constitutes a record of the land disputes that impinged on their territory. The switch in the documentary record reflects the change to which the colonization process was subject as it moved from the exploratory stage to that of de facto occupation and exploitation.

Father Corrado bore witness to the land transfer that the Bolivian government conceded to the Chané captain Paragua. Mocapoi's journey fifty years later came in response to the damages inflicted on that property in the intervening half century but also since the outset of colonist encroachment on the region. Fortresses and ranches had been established to the north, in the upper Pilcomayo and Caiza area, and the commercial route skirting the foothills between the Orán zone to the south and southern Bolivia had been in operation since the last decades of the nineteenth century. The Chané, in other words, were already familiar with the impact of cattle-raising colonization on the fringes of their territory. At the turn of the twentieth century, however, that impact made itself felt within their territory with the establishment of the small settlement of Campo Durán on the banks of the Itiyuro.

Corrado himself acknowledged that Paragua, despite remaining an ally after the transfer of lands to his people, consistently rejected the advances of Franciscan missionaries from Aguairenda. A few years later, however, colonists' harassment forced him to seek protection, and he approached the mission with a request for assistance although for unknown reasons a mission was never founded on the Itiyuro.

Traces of the tensions arising between Paragua and neighboring settlers, of the sort attested to by Corrado, are to be found in lawsuits pertaining to landownership in the region. In 1846, the very year of the Chané's land entitlement, the province of Salinas, the jurisdiction to which the Itiyuro belonged until the creation of the Gran Chaco Province, awarded land to a soldier who had participated in General Magariños's colonization campaign. Known as the Itiyuro Narrows, the terrain lay to the east of the Chané's concession. The deeds of possession indicate that at the point where the river narrows, a boundary marker was placed in the ground "adjacent to the lands of the Chané Indians."[13] Some five years later, the soldier lodged a complaint with the authorities about a superimposition of titles. His holding had been turned over to another colonist by a successor to the governor of Salinas Province. The complaint states, "Since this person has not been able to deprive the allied Chané Indians of their land, he has acted to the detriment of third parties, in violation of my own property rights and those of others." The governor replied that it was a matter of two different holdings, adding that the land adjudicated to the colonist was "compensation for the area allocated to the Chané allies in order to curtail their dissension."[14]

Similar conflicts and dissension resurface, in greater detail, in lawsuits concerning lands on the western limit of Chané territory, namely, the lands of the Itaki Outlet, an area covering the piedmont fringe between the Itiyuro and the Capiazuti rivulet. Also awarded in 1846 to a soldier who had served on the Chaco frontier, the beneficiary quickly sold his endowment to a settler resident in the region. The buyer, for his part, soon discovered that his acquisition belonged to the Chané of the Itiyuro by virtue of the land conceded to them by President Ballivián. His protestations, presented in 1849, give a tendentious account of the origins of the Chané's land claim but attest to the fact that certain of their villages were already then in existence:

> No Chané Indians have at any point been present therein, nor have they ever had settlements, livestock, or plantations there. Nor even a single house. They live in [such places as] Itiyuro, Capiazuti, Iquira, [and] Piquirenda and occupy a very great many immense tracts of land. In keeping with current practice, however, several neighbors and cattle owners induced the Chané to put to Ballivián a claim to Itaque ranch, as a means of availing themselves of my estate.[15]

In 1852 the state prosecutor for the district validated the settler's possession with the proviso that it be free of Chané domestic constructions and livestock since the land in question had been "previously kept for the Indians by General Magariños, sole official with authority to establish a military colony and distribute the Caiza wastelands." But the dispute was to continue, and in 1869 the provincial prefect ordered that the contested land be returned to the "Chané Indian Paragua" and that "all Christian title holders be dispossessed."[16]

After the death of Paragua, other Itiyuro Chané headmen faced similar threats to Chané land rights, to which they consistently responded with the strategy of appealing to the highest authorities. One such headman was the captain Guarumbaque, representative of the Itiyuro Chané in various legal proceedings in the 1890s. He engaged in lawsuits against two colonists who attempted to secure ownership of the land that they were renting from the Chané. Around 1890 a certain Nicanor Galarza sought to register Chané lands in his own name. The case led to the intervention of the Bolivian minister of colonies, who resolved in the Chané's favor:

> Captain Guarumbaque, who belongs to the native alliance of the Itiy-uro foothills and gives to understand that the citizen Nicanor Galarza seeks to dispossess him of his lawfully endowed lands, pleas for the endorsement of his proprietary rights. . . . It being convenient that the native allies of that part of the frontier be persuaded of the justice and protection dispensed by the established authorities, I recommend, Mr. President of the Republic, that you undertake to issue binding decrees to safeguard the property rights of the said Captain, in accordance with his land titles.[17]

In the second lawsuit, around 1898 another of the Chané's tenants also sought to gain possession of the land he was renting, the domain known as Itiyuro Outlet or Pampa Blanca. Under the circumstances, Guarumbaque traveled to La Paz, where, according to the case file, he won the support of none other than the Bolivian President Pando and thereby "secured title to the land in question." With the title before his eyes, the prefect of Yacuiba confirmed the indigenous land rights:

> In view of the appearance of ally captain Guarumbaque of Itiyuro in the offices of this Prefecture and General Headquarters, and in the light of his demonstration of the right to possession of certain land that was legally conferred on his ancestors by the late General Magariños—which right, he declares, is threatened by attempts to dispossess him of certain of his properties—I hereby prevail upon you in your capacity as Sub-Prefect to safeguard his possessions and protect his interests, in keeping with the ownership deeds and other documents which the said captain will present to you.[18]

Various conclusions can be drawn from the foregoing cases. First, the colonization of the Itiyuro region, mainly by small-scale livestock ranchers, had already begun by the 1850s despite its not having been recorded on maps of the period. Second, the Chané allowed colonists onto their territory provided that they accepted the Chané as the legitimate owners of the land by entering into lease agreements. Although such agreements may well have proven to be more symbolic than effectual, witness statements by members of the regional workforce indicate that the Chané's territorial dominion was acknowledged by their tenants. According to one such witness statement, headman Guarumbaque "has on his property a fair number of colonists and tenants who, since the distant past, have always paid him rent and grazing dues."[19] Father Corrado, for his part, provides a telling illustration of the strictures of Chané diplomacy with regard to nonindigenous occupants. Around 1846, he recounts (1884, 463), an Anglican missionary tried to win over the indigenous people of the Itiyuro. He was received hospitably at the outset, but a few days later, after having expressed his desire to buy a parcel of land and install himself among them, "Paragua, without further ado, enjoined him to remove himself from their midst, on pain of death."

Third and foremost, the lawsuits in question demonstrate that Paragua and his successors had successfully learned to defend their lands against the threat of usurpation by appealing to Bolivian authorities. Bolivia's land grant to the Chané was not a symbolic act but part and parcel of a well-defined strategy aimed at the colonization of indigenous frontiers. The strategy was sustained over time; for more than fifty years, governments and regional authorities honored the land entitlement conferred on the Chané by Magariños and in cases of conflict endorsed Chané property rights.[20] In Chané historical memory, it translates into an unshakeable faith in authority, be it military or administrative. A compelling example is Mandasai's gloss on the military escort that accompanied Mocapoi's return from Buenos Aires, officially proclaimed as a measure aimed at restoring order: "In those days, the border guard took care of us round the clock. Nowadays, no one takes care of us."[21]

Loss of the Homeland

As Mocapoi explained to Nordenskiöld, Chané control over their territory, as in the days when "all the land was free for us," was in crisis at the beginning of the nineteenth century. The crisis was largely a consequence of the protracted border negotiations between Bolivia and Argentina that resulted in the Itiyuro zone being unexpectedly transferred into Argentine hands by a treaty of 1889 whereby, on the basis of the imperfect existing cartography, the frontier was set along the longitude 22° south parallel. Negotiations continued, with certain modifications being made during the 1890s, until the jurisdictional handover, already in place by about 1904, was definitively signed in 1925.[22]

In addition to such cadastral uncertainties and no doubt exacerbated by them, the Chané captaincy was in thrall to internal political instability, of which colonist intruders were quick to take advantage. Nordenskiöld was witness in 1908 to a stable captaincy and a unified indigenous territory. Mocapoi, he was informed, was the great captain of the whole region, and the names both of his predecessors and of his future successor to the office were given with precision. In the same period, however, two other captains appeared, claiming to hold the same office and engaging in judicial and commercial proceedings in relation to the same lands.

The first of the said captains is Guarumbaque of the Campo Durán residential group, who acted as political representative of the Itiyuro Chané at the same time as Mocapoi. In 1904 Guarumbaque conferred power of attorney on a certain Justo Alba, a tradesman from the distant town of Yacuiba, in order for him to intercede with Bolivian authorities for the procurement of the documentation necessary for the validation of Chané landownership. On that occasion, however, the Bolivian minister of colonies declined to issue any land title on the grounds that the land was now under Argentine jurisdiction, to whose authorities he advised the petitioner to address his claim. That same year, despite the course of action not having prospered, Guarumbaque signed a document ceding one half of Chané land to Alba as undivided joint owner and as payment for his services. As such, Alba would, in the event of an Argentine court of justice validating the property, acquire identical proprietary rights to those of the Chané as a whole.[23]

Two years later, in 1907, Guarumbaque sold certain tracts of land to another colonist, the Campo de Durán and Aguaray ranches, which largely coincide with what the Chané remember as their territory to the south of the Itiyuro. In his capacity as joint owner, Alba managed to annul the land sale, demonstrating that the Chané were now no longer sole owners of their own land, nor even could they lease it out without the consent of their new "associate." The legal dispute petered out in 1910 when, after the death of Guarumbaque, three of his sons traveled to Salta in the company of Alba to sell all their domains to a landed resident of the city.[24]

Simultaneously, about 1908, the Chané headman Chukuri presented himself as "Great Captain of the Chané tribes of Campo de Alcoba, Algarrobal, and Itiyuro," with a view to selling off a vast area of the ancestral territory to the east, downriver, of the possessions claimed by Guarumbaque. He based his right to that land on an inheritance from his father, the great captain Catia.[25] According to the genealogy recorded that same year by Nordenskiöld, Catia was a son of Basavi, brother of Paragua. The Chané identified him simply as a village chief within Mocapoi's overarching captaincy. In 1911, the Algarrobal section became the object of a judicial dispute when a colonist claimed it as his property and sought to have it demarcated. Thereupon, a certain Delgado formulated his opposition, presenting himself in representation of the rights of Captain Chucuri, the original titleholder to the contested terrain "by virtue of the land-endowment awarded to his father, Captain Catia, by the Bolivian Government."[26] The

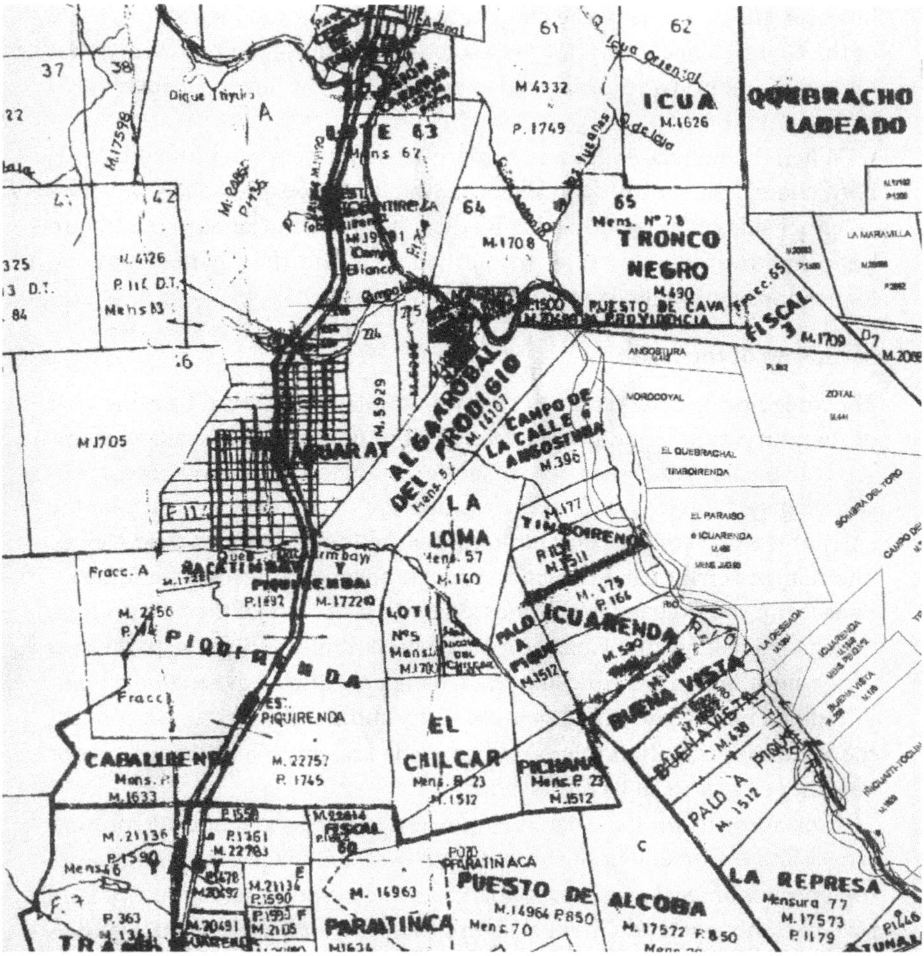

Map 1.2. Ranches in Chané territory, around mid-nineteenth century. Land register map, Dirección General de Inmuebles, Provincia de Salta, Argentina.

legal proceedings followed the now familiar course. Witnesses confirmed that the colonist had been a tenant of Chukuri, that he had performed some kind of representation on the latter's behalf, and that he had abused that responsibility by attempting to claim the property in his own name. They also confirmed that the Chané headman "has always had material possession of the properties described, . . . exploiting them with productive activities based on livestock-management and crop-cultivation." Despite such representations, the courts found in favor of the colonist, to whom therefore accrued a huge landholding on the eastern edge of Chané territory. By then, however, the outcome of the court case was of no consequence to the fate of the Chané, since it was not their interests that Delgado represented but his own; Chukuri had already sold to him, in 1910, the "approximately 5,000 hectares" in dispute.

When the Bolivia-Argentina border was definitively established in 1925, both countries committed to honoring the land titles previously obtained on either side of the new frontier. By then, however, the lands of the Itiyuro basin had been divided into private holdings, and the Chané's name no longer appeared in the land titles.[27]

Memories of the Loss

The foregoing episodes share in common the same historical baseline, that of the usurpation of indigenous territory by colonists who, availing themselves of the legal uncertainty born of the protracted border settlement process, engaged in ploys such as the assumption of power of attorney on the basis of leonine contracts or, directly, the staking of spurious land claims. The change of national jurisdiction brought to an end the long-standing alliance with the Bolivian authorities and with it the loss of their protection, which for a half century Chané captains had skillfully cultivated. In the eyes of the new Argentine judiciary, the Chané captaincy was an amorphous, ill-defined entity that lacked political unity and stability. In such a context, the disturbing situation that Mocapoi made known to his Swedish visitor becomes clearer in all its dimensions.

Even allowing for the Chané's empowerment of unscrupulous representatives and endorsement of ruinous joint ownership agreements that were the product of legal confusion, how does one account for the sale of land by Guarumbaque and Chukuri? Were the sales straightforward swindles or signs of desperation and loss of principles? At a century's remove, the answer cannot be known with certainty, though everything suggests that the colonists and the proxies knew how to take advantage not only of the jurisdictional fluctuation but also of the inherent tensions within the indigenous system of political organization. There is no doubt that at the time, the Itiyuro captaincy was, to say the least, lacking in stability. Mocapoi was little more than a surrogate for his aged aunt, the true heir to the office, and it is very possible that there were other candidates for the position. The simultaneous emergence of three headmen with the title of "great captain," all acting in the name of the Chané people as a whole and invoking different lines of descent to legitimate their status, indicates that at the beginning of the twentieth century, either the Itiyuro captaincy was an unconsolidated amalgam of lesser political units between which no permanent hierarchical order existed, or the captaincy was subject to rivalry between opposed lineages.

The first hypothesis would appear to be upheld by the measures taken by Chukuri in respect of one sector of the territory independently of the rest. The second hypothesis is supported by the scarce references that we have recorded during fieldwork with respect to the two rival headmen, Chukuri and Guarumbaque. Chukuri was depicted in 2006 by Taparindu, then *mburuvicha* of Tuyunti, in a light that by and large coincides with the image conveyed by the historical case files: "Chukuri was kin to Mocapoi, but they fought over the papers that Mocapoi brought from Buenos Aires. Chukuri wanted to become cacique, so he killed Mocapoi by bewitchment. Then he made off with all the papers and land titles and handed them over—to whom, who knows?" Guarumbaque is portrayed in a similar light; posted by Mocapoi to a tip of the territory as a mere watch-keeper captain, his ambition to become overall chief led him to betray Mocapoi and steal the land titles.

Memories of land sales and betrayals, however, are few and far between. The standard explanation is that the territorial usurpation was a direct result of the loss of the multiple land titles. This is a recurrent theme in Chané ethnohistory, as in the conclusion to the account of Mocapoi's journey, of which the variants are innumerable. By some accounts the papers were destroyed by enemy settlers, as maintained in 2004 by Jerusai of Tuyunti, who accused a certain Molina of having burned the titles acquired by her grandfather, the headman Acharei: "Molina was a bad man. He disliked my grandfather, and he came and set fire to all the papers that he [Acharei] had brought with him from Buenos Aires." Usually, however, the disappearance of the documents is attributed in some way to the Chané's work on the sugar plantations. In the words of the elder Arasari of Campo Durán in 2007, "Cacique Uacapi [brother to Mocapoi] lost the land title during a trip to the sugar plantation. On his return, he stopped to rest in Tartagal, where the shoulder bag made of cactus-fiber string in which he was carrying the documents was stolen. Someone from Tartagal stole the land titles." Such accounts are corroborated by documentary evidence to the effect that the land titles secured by Guarumbaque during his trip to La Paz in 1899 went astray shortly thereafter, between 1900 and 1904, while he and his people were working on the Ledesma sugar plantation. Given the dire consequences that the loss entailed, it was to become a traumatic leitmotif of Chané ethnohistory.[28]

Historical memory condenses paradigms of collective thought such that the value, or efficacy, of the Chané recollections under study lies not in their factual accuracy but in their reaffirmation of certain principles of this group's identity and social organization. A precept of Chané geopolitical thought is that possession of the territory over which the captaincy has jurisdiction depends on political stability and continuity. Accordingly, the original Chané territory was, in ideal ethnohistorical terms, organized on the basis of politically stable relations between its regions. Chané elders explain that those to whom Nordenskiöld referred as "village captains" were like guardians of the territory, sent to distant outposts by the great captain. Such a politically organized system of land use gave rise to a unified territory that was greater than the sum of its parts, a far cry from the state of fragmentation into independent communities that now prevails. Chané ethnohistory thus attests to a far more extensive territory than the sparse parcels of land they possess today but also to a broader and more complex collective identity, one that amply surpassed the limits of the local residential unit.[29] As such, their loss of land also comes to be seen by the Chané as a consequence of the passing of the great leaders of Campo Durán: "When Mocapoi died, nothing remained; our lands were sold off," reflected Arasari. The written history that we have examined confirms that view: the demise of the territory coincides with the collapse of the great captaincy. Under that ideal model of the traditional captaincy, the loss of the homeland is viewed as a consequence of processes that are, in fact, the same; the loss of the land title coexists with and even stands for the political and territorial fragmentation.

Chané ethnohistory gives expression as well to another central feature of their projected identity, that of territorial preexistence. Guaraní communities of the region explicitly invoke the memory of their arrival in Argentina in the first decades of the twentieth century, while Chané communities declare themselves to be autochthonous. This status typically translates into their assumption of Argentine nationality to the point that the accounts of the heroic deeds of their captains become entwined with those of renowned national figures. They say Cochou's Chiriguano enemies were intent on overrunning Chané lands in the name of Bolivia and that the annexation was forestalled by the defense that he mounted, "Had they killed us all, this would have become part of Bolivia." And the aim of Mocapoi's journey was, by certain accounts, to instate Argentine jurisdiction over the land to which he laid claim. It is even held that the military escort that accompanied his return—commanded, supposedly, by none other than the hero of

Argentine independence, General José de San Martín—had as its objective that of demarcating the international border.

The evidently paradoxical nature of the Chané's assumed national identity goes beyond the mere adoption of a feature that distinguishes them from the immigrant Guaraní population. Throughout the second half of the nineteenth century, they successfully fostered the role of "allied Indians" in their diplomatic relations, engaging directly with state authorities to defend their territory against the encroachment of settlers and lessees. It would seem that the memory of that strategic alliance has permeated their reconstruction of the change of national jurisdiction, hiding from view the disastrous consequences of the latter on the Chané captaincy. That is to say, Chané ethnohistory sublimates the severely damaging role played by Argentine state agents in the loss of the indigenous homeland.

Epilogue

In the course of the following decades, colonization of the Itiyuro basin accelerated. In the locality known as Campo Durán, squarely situated in Chané territory, a small but important township was to appear that by 1917 had become the seat of a judicial office. In the years 1925–1930, a railway line traversed the region, leading to the emergence of a sizable town at the foot of the mountains and leading also, to be sure, to headman Acharei's journey to Buenos Aires in 1927. Since the late 1920s the colonization of this region of the Argentine foothills was led by the oil companies Standard Oil and Yacimientos Petrolíferos Fiscales (YPF), whose headquarters were installed some twenty-five miles south of the Itiyuro, and by loggers and cattle ranches. In 1950, Chané territory was directly disrupted when the discovery of an important oil deposit near the river led to the rapid installation of drilling and pumping operations, refineries, and pipelines. This incursion abruptly transformed the environment and forced them to abandon their age-old dispersed settlements and to relocate at Campo Durán, where they still live today. Many adult men of this village were employed as unskilled workers in the YPF plants, leading to a new and deep colonization of the group's historical imaginary.[30]

Despite many decades of prosaic bureaucratic procedures, the long-held perception still persists that territorial dispossession resulted from the loss, in the distant past, of *iwi papire*, the authentic "land papers," described as "big" and "good" documents, in contrast to others that are smaller and less authentic. The land claim upheld by the many *mburuvicha* is therefore understood as a search, in the literal sense of the term. As such, warlike defense of the land has been replaced by journeys to the far-off capital, and such journeys are of equal status in terms of the political legitimacy they confer.[31] As Mandasai explained, the previous headman of Campo Durán had rightfully held the post not because he was voted to it by the assembly but because his grandfather had participated in Mocapoi's journey.

At a symbolic level, history reproduces myth. The loss of the land titles is a historical equivalent of the mistaken choice of weapons made by the Chané's mythical forebears; both imply subjection to so-called white society. The two differ, however, inasmuch as the historical episode entertains the possibility of reverting the land loss. Knowing that copies of the original maps and titles are conserved in an archive in Buenos Aires, La Paz, or some other city, their discovery would be sufficient to ensure the recovery of the land. The dream of elderly headman Taparindu was to travel to Bolivia to find them. Clutching a bundle of papers, maps, and photocopies inherited from his father and grandfather, the treasure of his headmanship, he once mused, laconically, "We have certain papers, yes, but not all of them."

The profound implications of the incident with which this chapter opened are now perfectly clear: after almost a century of confinement to missions and communities, the Chané great captaincy has been dismantled and their territory dismembered. Whereas, in the past, residential groups were distributed in small *tenta* (villages) throughout the homeland, today they are mainly agglomerated in two large communities. Tuyunti mission is crowded into one hundred hectares secured for them by Franciscans, and Campo Durán community strives to finalize the official survey of the lands that it has occupied for at least two and a half centuries. The files go astray or are subject to bureaucratic delay on account of changes of authority in state organisms, financial hiatuses, and endless administrative meetings. But Chané historical memory imbues the procedures with an inviolate purpose. Likening his task to the legendary exploits of the great captains of the past, the young, computer-literate *mburuvicha* of Campo Durán, who was appointed to the position within the past few years, encodes his aspirations in terms of the canonical political agenda of his people. His goal is to be remembered as the *mburuvicha* who recovered Mocapoi's missing land titles.

Notes

1. The papers in question comprise the survey carried out by the National Institute for Indigenous Affairs in compliance with Emergency Law 26.061, which requires that the

Argentine government delimit the territories of the country's indigenous communities. Sanctioned in 2006, the law has to date been implemented in little over one third of the country's indigenous communities.

2. In early colonial chronicles, the Chané normally appear as being under the yoke of Chiriguano invaders, but by the eighteenth century a number of independent Chané groups were identified throughout Chiriguanía (Combès 2004a, 225).

3. On Chané attacks against the Itau and Salinas missions, see Comajuncosa 1884 [1810], 223–225, 1971 [1800], 142; Corrado 1884, 369; Mingo de la Concepción 1981 [1799], 368–369.

4. On the Toba of the Pilcomayo frontier, see Combès 2014a; Santamaría 1988, 182; 2001, 87. Susnik (1968, 225) considers that the Toba offensive was "fomented by the southern Chané [who], taking their first steps towards independence, sought to avenge themselves on their former 'masters.'"

5. Susnik 1968, 232. For a thorough study on the Caiza Plain's Chané villages and their historical relation to the Itiyuro basin, see Combès 2007.

6. Report by Fernando Cano, prior of the Franciscan College of Tarija, Justice, file 32, Case 932, IX-31-6-5, folio 18, Archivo General de la Nación, Buenos Aires.

7. Civil Justice, Case 325, 1910, folio 35, Archivo Histórico de Salta (hereafter AHS). The "ï" denotes a nasal phoneme in the Guaraní language.

8. The accounts here reproduced were narrated by Mandasai, a Chané female elder of Campo Durán. Their translation was done with the inestimable collaboration of Catalina Huenuán of Tuyunti. The accounts in the chapter come from interviews conducted by the author. For an analysis of the narrative genre in question, see Bossert and Villar 2005.

9. Nordenskiöld 2002 [1912], 212. According to Nordenskiöld's genealogy, the "principal chief" Hinu Parava had several children, including Cochou. His position was inherited by his daughter, Vuaruyi; but, given her advanced age, it passed (circa 1908) to her brother Cochou's son Mocapoi, protagonist of the second ethnohistorical episode.

10. In Chané oral texts, Mount Tëtaiguate was the seat of residence of the "great captain" of the Itiyuro basin.

11. The Chané term for the Chaco region in general is Itika, the name they also give to the Pilcomayo River. By "Toba" they refer to all the indigenous inhabitants of the Chaco, although the inclusion of the renowned Toba cacique Taokoriki in the company of allied headmen suggests that it was members of his ethnic group, precisely, who traveled with Mocapoi.

12. Juan Moreno was indeed a settler who took possession of land on the left bank of the Itiyuro in the first decade of the twentieth century.

13. Notarial Protocol, Enrique Klix, November 1910, deeds 456 and 457, AHS.

14. Notarial Protocol, Enrique Klix, November 1910, deeds 456 and 457, AHS.

15. Civil Justice, Case 325, 1910, folios 35–36, AHS.

16. Civil Justice, Case 325, 1910, folios 50–51, AHS.

17. Notarial Protocol, David Gudiño, October 1906, folio 469, AHS.

18. Notarial Protocol, David Gudiño, October 1906, folio 466; January 1905, folio 20, AHS.

19. Notarial Protocol, David Gudiño, October 1906, folio 450, AHS.

20. In 1854, when the government granted land to the south of Chané territory, it did so "with due regard for the rights of third parties, including the Indians of the Itiyuro" (Notarial Protocol, Enrique Klix, 1910, folios 1109–1149, AHS).

21. The incident is reminiscent of the legendary case of Enrique Iyambae of the Isoso region and his bureaucratic battle to secure land titles in the face of mistreatment by certain settlers. In that case, reportedly persons of power in the distant Bolivian capital lent their support to the indigenous leader by recognizing his authority and aligning themselves with the indigenous cause (Combès 2005; Schuchard 1986, 77–79).

22. For a synthesis of the matter, see Cobos 1926; Fifer 1976, 269–270, 295–299, 333–334; Sánchez 1926.

23. Notarial Protocol, David Gudiño, January 1905, folio 18, AHS. Undivided joint ownership entails not the physical division of the property but the approval of both owners with regard to any transaction affecting it.

24. Notarial Protocol, Ernesto Guibert, June 1910, deed 821, AHS.

25. Notarial Protocol, Enrique Klix, November 1910, deeds 410 and 411, AHS.

26. Civil Justice, Case 713, 1922, folio 14, AHS.

27. The settler intruders of bygone years had been replaced by new actors on the colonist front. By 1922, much of Chané territory was in the hands of the region's main landowning family, that of Patrón Costas (Civil Justice, Case 713, 1922, folio 133, AHS).

28. Witness statements were collected to verify Guarumbaque's account, and many Itiyuro settlers declared that they had seen the titles in his hands. One such declaration stated that "the loss of their titles is well known here in the Chaco" (Notarial Protocol, David Gudiño, October 1906, folio 455, AHS).

29. Villar and Bossert 2008. The territorial attributes of Chané leadership, institutionalized in the figure of the *mburuvicha*, the headman, are reflected in their agrarian customs. Various prerogatives in the past and the present give the *mburuvicha* something of the character of an owner of the land who is to authorize building a house or cultivating a new plot of land (Nordenskiöld 2002 [1912], 214).

30. As a result, Chané active resistance against oil firms is a fairly recent occurrence. Only over the course of recent decades they began to regard the companies as colonial invaders into their lands. Quite a few of them had endured indignities such as witnessing the unearthing of their ancestors' funerary vessels during the companies' excavations and seeing them taken by "engineers" to unknown destinations. This resistance mostly arose following the privatization of YPF in 1993–1999, which drastically decreased the demand for indigenous labor and was fueled some years later by the legal struggle of a nearby Guaraní village against the incursion of a gas pipeline through its territory.

31. The story of Mocapoi seems to synthesize details of journeys made by other Chané headmen in different times. The version reproduced here incorporates elements pertaining to earlier and later trips, such as those of Guarumbaque to La Paz in 1899 for which Bolivia is mentioned among the destinations and of Acharei to Buenos Aires in 1927. Conversely, narrations of Acharei's journey usually repeat details of the story of Mocapoi.

2

Were the Chiriguano a Colonial Fabrication?

Linguistic Arguments for Rethinking Guaraní and Chané Histories in the Chaco

BRET GUSTAFSON

In virtually all of the ethnological and historical literature on the Chaco, the historical origins of the Guaraní who live in what is now Bolivia are condensed into what, for this chapter, I will refer to as the Chiriguano thesis. In short, the Chiriguano thesis suggests that these westernmost Guaraní speakers are not, in fact, Guaraní. Rather, it is argued, they are Chiriguano, the result of ethnogenetic fusion between Guaraní peoples who invaded from the east and Arawak-speaking Chané peoples who were already living in the Andean foothills and valleys. Proponents of the Chiriguano thesis argue that the warlike, marauding Guaraní enslaved the peaceful, agriculturalist Chané. Some say this occurred before the Spanish invasion; others say it occurred during and after it. In some versions, Guaraní cannibalism is invoked, such that the Guaraní ate the Chané men and took the Arawak women. The Chané gave their women to the Guaraní, and the Guaraní gave their language to the Chané. Both disappeared into a new being, the Chiriguano (Combès and Saignes 1991). Following this argument, the Guarani (Chiriguano) have been said to be a "mestizo" people (Combès 1992; Saignes 1990). It has been further argued that while the Guarani language prevailed, Arawak culture persisted in certain social formations, leading to a new being, the "Chiriguano" (Combès and Lowrey 2006). The Chiriguano thesis—invasion, language displacement, ethnogenesis—has been replicated, rather uncritically, by historians, linguists, and anthropologists writing about cultural and linguistic histories of the Chaco (e.g., Jensen 1999; Schwartz and Salomon 1999; Weber 2005). Given the linguistic evidence, I find the Chiriguano thesis at best deeply problematic. In many of its expressions it is apocryphal, having emerged from colonial narratives. I point out the limitations of the thesis in its crude form and offer observations on the need for rethinking histories of contact and exchange in the western Chaco.

The argument put forth here is not a claim to Guaraní purity or a denial of the existence of peoples who self-identify as Chané in the past and present. The word is still used by contemporary peoples, although they all speak Guaraní, who refer to themselves as Chané or claim some link to Chané ancestry (Bossert, Combès, and Villar 2008, 208n1). The presence of such communities does not in itself validate the Chiriguano thesis or even the existence of a distinct pre-Hispanic ethnolinguistic Chané population in the past. The geographic specificity of these self-ascriptions today in the lower parts of Isoso and in Itiyuro, Argentina, in relation to the wider Guaraní-speaking region supports my wider point. The only robust linguistic evidence for the existence of a pre-Hispanic Arawak-speaking people referred to as Chané is that of the peoples now known as Terena and closely related peoples living along the Paraguay River in what is now Mato Grosso state in western Brazil.

I offer a revised historical thesis as follows: Guaraní-speaking peoples lived in the Andean foothills prior to the Spanish invasion. We simply do not know precisely when they might have arrived or exactly from where they came, whether from the north or the east, or who may have lived there prior to the Guaraní. In subsequent years, perhaps centuries, other Guaraní most certainly came to the region from the east, either on their own or with Spanish *entradas*, the organized incursions into the region from Paraguay. So too came peoples called "Chané" from the Paraguay River region. Mixing, violence, and enslavement, a product of Spanish demand for slaves, were doubtless part of this process. In addition to being plagued by its deeply politicized usage, the notion of the Chiriguano as Guaraní-Chané fusion is empirically flawed. There is no convincing historical evidence for the invasion-cannibalism-exchange thesis as a preconquest historical process, despite its frequent repetition. Our current understandings are considerably distorted by the continuing reproduction of what is largely a colonial narrative. Space does not allow for a full historical revision. I offer some observations on the linguistic evidence, the absence thereof, and the contradictions therein, for the Chiriguano thesis. My goal is to open up space for reexamination of what has come to be held as doctrine on the Chaco and the Guaraní.[1]

The Chiriguano Thesis as Colonial Narrative

While scholars, as cited above, have intellectualized the Chiriguano thesis as a plausible story of frontier ethnogenesis, colonial writers created the Chiriguano thesis as a tale shaped by racist and imperialist categorizations of native peoples. Based on the earliest colonial accounts, the peoples of the Andean *cordillera*, despite being Guaraní speakers, were referred to by the Spanish as "Chiriguanos" or "Chiriguanaes." Encapsulating a range of meanings, the word "Chiriguano" eventually sedimented as an ethnonym to distinguish these Guaraní from the mission Guaraní of Paraguay. Even so, the terms "Guaraní" and "Carío," also applied to Paraguayan Guaraní, were sometimes used to refer as well to these Chiriguano. The colonial, and now national, border-making usage of indigenous ethnonyms continues to the present. The colonial origins of the word "Chiriguano," as much political instrument as a descriptor of any particular ethnolinguistic group, is the first of many problems associated with the Chiriguano thesis.

Over time the meanings of "Chiriguano" condensed around a colonial narrative about the origins of these other Guaraní in the Andean foothills. "Chiriguano" was an ethnochronotope. Like "Chichimeca," which marked the unconquered frontier of northern Mexico, or "Caribe" to describe unconquered peoples around the Caribbean, "Chiriguano" delineated a place, a people, and a history in relation to the political situation of the Spanish colonial frontier. These Chiriguano (Guaraní) were said to be outsiders on the Andean frontier, warrior invaders from the Río de la Plata who had attacked, cannibalized, and enslaved the more peaceful indigenous subjects (*naturales*) of the Andean front, called Chané. An attentive reader will note here a second significant problem of the ethnonym and the narrative: they replicate the colonial binary between *indios mansos* (calm or tame Indians) and *indios salvajes* (savage Indians), a politically productive binary that allowed for distinguishing bodies subject to legitimate violence from those available for labor. As a corollary, "Chiriguano" as a word and as an imagined subject worked as a "colonial mirror of production" (Taussig 1993, 66), through which the very characteristics of the colonizer—invasion, enslavement, rape, and *mestizaje*—were imputed to the Chiriguano as the supposed oppressors of the Chané. The only distinction, that these Chiriguano were cannibals, was deployed as a legal means of justifying enslavement and land seizure without adhering to the more cumbersome colonial laws.

Despite the risks inherent in taking up colonial narratives as historical explanation, Chiriguano thesis proponents collapse complex geographic, demographic, and historical encounters into a singular process of transformation: Guaraní migrants confronted the native Chané, gradually overcame them, and created Chiriguano society. Though it is sometimes suggested that there were many native peoples involved with (or subjugated by) the Guaraní, the Chiriguano thesis argues that the *mestizaje* was either wholly (Combès 2005; Combès and Saignes 1991) or primarily (Pifarré 1988) a Guaraní-Chané affair. In its colonial context, Spanish colonizers deployed the Chiriguano thesis because these Guaraní were an obstacle. In the academic context, the Chiriguano thesis similarly offered an explanation for what some saw as a linguistic anomaly: the presence of Guaraní-speaking people in a supposedly Andean geographic and cultural area.[2] Yet it is unclear how the Guaraní can be at once labeled "mestizo migrants" and "mestizo-ized invaders." Were they the former, the fusion would have occurred elsewhere, undermining the idea that the Chané were well established in the Andean foothills. If the latter, the process suggests a rapid transformation from Guaraní to Chiriguano that contradicts conventional understandings of more complex migratory and ethnogenetic processes.[3]

Other proponents of the Chiriguano thesis now argue for a process that lasted over generations, as Guaraní gradually absorbed and erased the Chané (Combès and Villar 2007). Yet this is also inconsistent. The terms "Chiriguano" and "Chané" are maintained and distinguished right up to the present, suggesting not absorption but coexistence. A more elaborate set of hypotheses, largely speculative, is offered by Bossert (2008), who argues that the "guaranization" of the Chané would have been largely completed by the end of the sixteenth century. Yet were the process to have lasted over generations, we would have more reason to expect to find Arawak language traces, whether in contemporary language use or in colonial documentation. Save Erland Nordenskiöld's enigmatic data, about which more below, there are none.

What or Who Was Chané?

In considering whether an Arawak Chané people might have once lived along the Andean front, it is useful to situate the Guaraní in relation to the most proximate historical and contemporary Arawak populations in the circum-Chaco region. These are the Guana Chané (also Tsané, Xaané, Xâne), who today live in Mato Grosso, Brazil, and the Moxeño (Ignaciano, Trinitario, Moxeño) of the Bolivian Amazon. Part of the southern Arawak subgroup, these are the southernmost expressions of the Arawak diaspora that had its origins, perhaps around 3000 before present, in the northwestern Amazon (Aikhenvald 1999; Heckenberger 2002, 106). In the past there may have been more subgroups of Guana Chané. Yet today there are four: Tereno, Kinikinau, Echoaladi, and Layana. In all of these languages, the word *xaane* or *tsaane* (*chané*) means person or companion and *indio*, Indian, as distinguished from whites (Martins Ladeira 2001; De Souza 2008). Confirming an argument that I made in Gustafson 2014, Fernando Carvalho has argued that "Terena, Chané, Guaná, and Kinikinau are one and the same language" (2016).

Farther north, speakers of Moxeño, today known as Trinitario and Ignaciano, may also have been referred to as Chané. In their language, *nuchané* means person or people, literally "we people." Historically, the Moxeño also interacted with Chiquitano and the Chiriguano (Guaraní) and Itatines (Guarayu) in what was then the province of Santa Cruz. These were often violent relations mediated by the Spaniards' frenzied pursuit of El Dorado and slaves as they faced chronic labor shortages and pressures from soldiers for grants of land (*encomiendas*) (Radding 2005). The early distinction of Moxos, as a people and a province, from the Chiriguano, also a people and a province, has meant that both were subjected to war, evangelization, and reduction as juridical, territorial, and linguistic entities. The term "Chané" may have made reference to Moxeño peoples, though they lived north of the Andean front. It is fairly well established that around the time of European contact, the Arawak Guana Chané peoples along the Paraguay River lived both to the east and west of the river in what is now part of the Paraguayan Chaco. It is unclear how far these peoples ranged westward across the Chaco.[4]

From the early colonial period, observers argued that the Guana Chané along the upper Paraguay River lived as slaves of the Mbaya-Guaykuru, or Kadiweu people. Early texts reported this relationship as one between masters (the Mbaya) and slaves (the Guana). In Schmidl's early account (1881 [1567]), the Chané were like "Bavarian serfs." This well-studied history created a paradigm of hierarchical interindigenous social relations in South American ethnology and has also shaped questions of language imposition and exchange as such relations continue in an attenuated form today (De Souza 2008). Yet contemporary researchers see the relation more as a kind of symbiosis than as slavery since the Guana Chané moved freely in and out of Kadiweu communities (De Souza 2008; Oberg 1949, 1–2). Early observers like Mason (1946, cited in De Souza 2008) also suggested that cultural docility of the Chané led them to easily give up their languages in the face of more warlike Indian masters. Yet the Jesuit José Sánchez Labrador, the closest observer of the Guana Chané, though perhaps trying to embellish his own reputation, described these Chané in the mid-1700s as a "feared" and "bellicose" people (1910 [1770], 39–41). As observed by the contemporary linguist Ilda de Souza (personal communication, 2012), the early assumption that the Kadiweu imposed their language on the Chané who served them and forced its disappearance was mistaken. Arawak language shift in Mato Grosso was a result of later nation-building pressures and evangelization, not servitude to the Kadiweu. Since the supposed cultural docility of the Chané is often cited in support of the Chiriguano thesis, I make these points simply as a counter to formulaic arguments. In the Kadiweu-Chané case, the relationship did not generate cultural fusion, ethnogenesis, or linguistic assimilation.

Were there other Chané peoples beyond the Paraguay River area? The term "Chané" was used often in colonial and historical documents to refer to servant Indians, friendly Indians, companions, socios, and guides regardless of their linguistic identity. "Chané" as such appear in accounts ranging from Asunción to Lima. Much of this echoes writings like that of Reginaldo Lizárraga (1987 [ca. 1600]), who wrote from Lima of "indios de servicio Chanéses" without reference to their ethnic or linguistic specificity but of their social relations to Spaniards or other Indians whom they accompanied. Chanena also means, in extant Chané Guaná languages, "my companion." Other colonial documents place Chané or Chaneses in the circum-Chaco area, though none along the Andean front. Schmidl's early account from the Irala expedition (1881 [1567], 252) speaks of Chané (serving Mbaya) only along the upper Paraguay River. However, Schmidl also writes of numerous other groups who may have been Arawak speakers that the Spaniards encountered (and attacked) in their wanderings north and east across the Chaco (not along the Andean front) as they made their way to Santa Cruz. This is one area of unsettled debate.[5] Indians called Chanés(es) were encountered by Domingo Martínez de Irala (1555) and Cabeza de Vaca in the Pantanal region near an island that still maintains the name Isla Chané, today the Bolivia-Brazil border area.

Paradoxically, these Chané were reported to speak a Guaraní similar to that of Asunción. It is plausible that many Guaraní of Paraguay who were indeed accompanying the Spaniards on their *entradas* were also called Chané. A mythical-historical account also places a Chané war chief, Grigotá, in the province of Santa Cruz. The story has become folklorized and politicized as a marker of the region's identity. Yet Grigotá, as a name, is a Guaraní form, with the suffix *tá* indicating masculine warrior status. Chané references also survive in toponyms to the north of Santa Cruz, sites where enslaved Indian of various origins were put to work. Jolis (1789, 397) described Chané communities north of Santa Cruz but referred to them as amalgams, people from various nations who had escaped slavery. These were likely Spanish resettlements, as were putative Chané communities, though Guaraní-speaking, at Porongo and Acero in the Guaraní area. They may have been Guaraní or Guaraní speakers of various origins who had accompanied Spaniards to the region or aided them in war and were later resettled. Chané were also said to be living in the Llanos de Manso, an area that was at the northern and eastern edge of the Guaraní Andean front. Similarly, Ñuflo de Chávez, in a recording of lands and native bodies to be distributed to *encomenderos* (Spanish landlords) reported the existence of a "Province of the Chanés," which he did not in fact visit (Julien 2006). In my reading it appears to be east of Santa Cruz, though others suggest it refers again to the Llanos de Manso, a disputed area between Santa Cruz and the Parapetí River. This is at best the only somewhat convincing reference we have to Chané peoples outside of the upper Paraguay River. However, these references were deeply politicized by the dispute between the conquistadors of Peru and Paraguay. This contest centered for a time on the lands of the Llanos de Manso, which Ñuflo de Chávez sought to claim for himself by establishing a claim over the putative Chané, then a generic marker for any "Indian of the plains" (*indio de los llanos*).

Historically speaking, then, the only solid evidence for the historical existence of Moxeño and Guana Chané Arawak peoples at the time of the European invasion places them to the north and east of the Andean front. Whether another population of Arawak Chané, said to have numbered up to 100,000 people, lived in the lowlands and valleys along the southern Andean front on the western edge of the Chaco is at best doubtful. In efforts to make this claim and thus defend the Chiriguano thesis, there is much ambiguity, contradiction, and political manipulation. This becomes further apparent in past and present disputes over the meaning of the terms "Chiriguano" and "Chané."

Etymological Debates: Chiriguano and Chané

Proponents of the Chiriguano thesis argue unequivocally that the word "Chiriguano" itself provides indisputable evidence of Arawak-Guaraní "mestizaje" because it means "mestizo" (Combès and Saignes 1991; Combès and Villar 2007). There is no linguistic argument made for this claim. Rather, the etymology relies primarily on an early report of the governor of Santa Cruz, Lorenzo Suares de Figueroa (1965 [ca. 1568], 404, my translation):

> The proper name of this generation [*generación*, seen as a "nation" or "ethnic group"] is Cario, from which is derived the name that they have, Caribes, which means eaters of human flesh. They call themselves as well Guaranis and Guarayus, which means people of war. They are also called Chiriguanaes, a corrupted word that derives from "Chiriones," which means mestizos, their sons with Indian women (*yndias*) of other nations. Their origin and beginning it is said is the coast of Brazil, and they have extended themselves across many parts and provinces, populating where there are many people, to execute their natural cruelty against the human species.

The text is ambiguous, suggesting that these people are Guaraní or Darío, and the term "Chiriguanae" is an ascribed name rather than a self-ascription. Suares makes no reference to the term "Chané." The word "Chiriguano" and its synonyms are all positioned in a series of legally binding tropes, since each ethnonym is part of a triad—cannibalism, migration, warfare—that negates these peoples' rights to certain protections in the lands they now inhabit. Yet Combès and Saignes (1991) rely heavily on this singular reference to "mestizos" to suggest that "Chiriguano" means "one who has taken a Chané wife." I can find no linguistic justification for this interpretation.[6] Furthermore, the Suares reference to the Chiriguano as mestizos is itself ambiguous. A few paragraphs later, in the same report (1965 [1568], 465), Suares distinguishes the supposed mestizos from the Chiriguanos, writing that of the four thousand Indians of war (*indios de guerra*) in the Chiriguano *cordillera*, "not even half of the *naturales* are Chiriguanaes, but mestizos, their sons with women of other nations, who are as bad as or worse than the legitimate and natural [Indians]" ("e que no son la mitad de los naturales Chiriguanaes, sino mestizos, hijos dellos y de mujeres de otras naciones, los cuales son tan malos y peores que los legítimos y naturales"). In Suares's account and a later version of Suares's text (in Cepeda 1914 [1584]), the term "Chiriguano" is also applied both to Guaraní and Guarayu, much farther north in Itatines. The latter group is not considered in the Chiriguano thesis or referred to as mestizo, but both are referred to as "Chiriguanaes" because they were Guaraní speakers in open rebellion against Spaniards at the time. In the Lic. Cepeda version (1914 [1584], 255), they are thus defined not in opposition to Chané but as rebellious Indians distinct from another category of generic "domestic Indians" (*indios domésticos*). Spaniards hailing from Upper Peru and seeking land and power in the Santa Cruz area claimed purity of blood by deploying the term "mestizo" disparagingly against Spaniards arriving from Paraguay, who were said to have been sons (as Suares implies of the Chiriguanae) of Spaniards and *indias*. This equivocal and shifting use of politicized terms does not offer a strong case for accepting "mestizo" as the meaning of "Chiriguano."

Work by scholars of colonial narrative suggests that political and legal concerns and categories aimed at justifying war were determining factors in almost all written representations of native languages and territories during the colonial period, more so in contested frontier regions like the Andean-Chaco borderlands (Adorno 2007; Giudicelli 2005). Yet proponents of the Chiriguano thesis do not critically interrogate the political context in which the term "Chiriguano" takes meaning and these accounts were produced. A 1574 letter to the king from the famed colonial jurist Juan Polo de Ondegardo, crucial in the viceroy of Lima's attempt to justify a war of enslavement against the Guaraní, is revealing of the flexibility of the meaning of "Chiriguanaes" (1914 [1574], 87, emphasis added):

And these Chiriguano Indians are a large and well-known nation although those err who are not aware that *by this name are called all of the Indians who live from war, and which are many nations*, that even if they are similar in their traits and order of life are very different and opponents and enemies ["son muy diferentes y contrarios y enemigos"]. This is better understood in the Rio de la Plata than in this land [Lima, Upper Peru] because the Spaniards that have settled in those *comarcas*, and even in Brazil, because there are Chiriguanos of different names, some Guatataes, Aguazes, Guaycuros, and Topis [Tupi] and Carivez [Caribe] and many others who do not have different names, being one and all without cult or idol as I have said that in their *comarcas* they engage each other in warfare and eat and enslave and ransom [sell] each other, and among them the heads [skulls] that they have taken in war are kept in their houses and are cherished cups from which they drink, and they all have different customs among themselves but all share in this—living at war and eating one another and their role is to conquer and fight.

"Chiriguanae" or "Chiriguano" was thus a term that indexed various political characteristics (warlike, cannibalistic, slaver), a usage more frequent than the singular association between the term and "mestizo." Lizárraga himself expressed both confidence and insecurity in his use of the term, placing "Chiriguanaes" all over the place and writing at one point of "a horrible people who did damages to Charruas in Buenos Aires, a nation [whose name] I cannot remember so I will call them Chiriguanas" (Lizárraga 1987 [ca. 1600], 427).

Despite this ambiguity, the Chiriguano thesis depends ultimately on an empirically unsustainable foundation, the argument that the word "Chiriguano" was from the early colonial era to the present a continuous reference to the same people and place and unequivocally meant "mestizo" (Combès and Saignes 1991, 9n1).[7] Conversely, the word "Chané" accrued geographic, racial, and cultural meanings associated with assumed docility and servitude. These supposed traits were later projected back in time as Arawak cultural norms when this category entered into ethnology and linguistics, yet they were likely derivative of the colonial association between "Chané" and *indio de servicio*. The figure of the domestic Chané living in submission to the savage Chiriguano was quite useful, as it placed Spaniards in the position of reestablishing a natural and legal order in the world by liberating the Chané and enslaving the Chiriguano. It is not clear that such traits were actually accurate representations of Arawak culture.

Columbus initiated such misreading of local ethnic and linguistic boundaries by grouping Indians into "tractable (guatiao, arauaca) and . . . savage (caribe, caniba)" peoples (Whitehead 2002, 52). The Chiriguano thesis of Guaraní invaders (Columbus's "caribe") and Chané victims (Columbus's tractable "arauaca") is formulaic in the same way. It echoes the foundational imperialist binary between enemy and friend that helped to constitute a frontier space as one of barbarism, as with Chichimeca, Auca, and Caribe, posed against the Spaniards' own sense of noble heroism and legitimation in pursuing wars of enslavement (Giudicelli 2005). Combined with the inconsistencies in colonial accounts, this formulaic quality itself should also raise questions about the empirical validity of the Chiriguano thesis.

Colonial Language Documentation

There is no linguistic documentation, past or present, of a Chané language community outside of the Paraguay River area, despite a handful of references to its possible existence. According to Diego Martínez (1944 [1601]), a Jesuit priest in the Mission of Santa Cruz, his colleague Dionisio Velásquez learned the Chané language and wrote a grammar and catechizing materials in it. This material has not been recovered, but the statement itself is questionable. Chiriguano thesis proponents rely heavily on two of Martinez's statements, that the "principal languages of the [Santa Cruz] province are Guaraní, Chané, and Gorgotoqui [Chiquitano]" and that "Chiriguano and Chané" are the principal languages of Cordillera Province, on the Andean front (Combès 2005, 70; Combès and Saignes 1991). Yet in the first case, Martínez was speaking of Santa Cruz, then situated at Chiquitos, north and east of its current location. There may indeed have been Chané there from nearby Mato Grosso or from the Moxos area. In reference to the Guaraní *cordillera* to the south ("la Provincia de los Chiriguanos"), Martínez spoke of Chané but had never been there. These invocations of linguistic territoriality and knowledge were linked to Jesuit appeals for grants from the crown of evangelizing permission in new areas. In the letter, Martínez added that in addition to his Chiquitano work, he himself was also partially fluent in Chané. The missive had no other details about language use and concluded with the lament that with the decimation of the population there were no longer areas to missionize in Santa Cruz. Save references to Chané from what is now the Mato Grosso region, yet with no documentation of actual lexical items, I have found no colonial linguistic references to confirm Chané speech or Chané-Guaraní bilingualism in the *cordillera* region of the Andean front.

The Nordenskiöld Data

Missionary and explorer accounts during the 1800s and 1900s, as during the colonial period, identified communities distinguished as Chané and Chiriguano along the Andean front, though all spoke Guaraní (e.g., Combès and Saignes 1991; Nino 1912). The only linguistic data are from the Swedish explorer-ethnologist Erland Nordenskiöld (1910b), on which all other later attestations of Chané rely. On his third Bolivian expedition, Nordenskiöld visited the Guaraní region in 1908 and 1909. There, nestled within the wider Guaraní territory he identified three key areas of Chané: lower Isoso, Itiyuro in northern Argentina (then Bolivia), and Kaipependi. The eastern distribution that this sketches suggests a history distinct from that of the Chiriguano invasion thesis. Nordenskiöld wrote that Chiriguano and Chané were indistinguishable in cultural and linguistic terms, but he pointed out that there was a west-to-east layering of Chiriguano (Guaraní), Chané, and other indigenous peoples along the Parapetí River (1910b, 142): "Along the Parapetí River, in the heights live Quechua Indians, then come the Chiriguano, then near the river the Tapiete, sometimes called Yanaygua, then come the Chané, and then in the unknown wildlands, the Tsirakua Indians."

In his 1908 visit Nordenskiöld went to the Isoso region on the lower Parapetí and reported encountering the "first Chané or Tapuy" at Isiporenda. Here there is slippage between "Chané" and "Tapuy" (Guaraní: servant, slave), a term that referred to a social inferior, not an ethnic other. He recorded no Chané data on this first visit. On his 1909 return, Nordenskiöld went back to Isoso to see an old friend, Batirayu. Batirayu spoke Guaraní as well as "excellent Spanish" but called himself Chané (Nordenskiöld 1910b, 142–143). Nordenskiöld and Batirayu visited Guirapembi, said to be the community where the "Indians best knew how to speak Chané," which he described as a secret "ritual" language (1910b, 145). One elderly woman reputed to speak "an excellent Chané" told Nordenskiöld she would teach it to him once they were in the "land of the dead." This place, Nordenskiöld wrote wryly, was likely closed to white men and ethnographers. Though "it was not easy to get their secrets out of them," some young men reportedly provided Nordenskiöld a few words and phrases.

Nordenskiöld recorded six words: maize, *sopóro*; water, *úné*; fire, *yucu*; dog, *tamúco*; chicha, *liqui*; and rat, *cóvo* (1910b, table 1). He collected three phrases: the lines of a song "siparakinánoye, siparakinánoye, siparakinánoye tonéya, tonéya, tonéya" (no translation); *karitimisoyti* (son of a whore), and *pocóne* (the invitation to coitus) (1910b, 145–146). Four of the words (corn, water, fire, dog) are indeed Arawak. They are practically the same words in Terena and Kinikinau, Arawak languages of Mato Grosso. Water, fire, and dog are also Moxeño. Corn is a close cognate in all of these Arawak languages. Cognates of *tamuku*, dog, are also present in non-Arawak Chiquitano to the north (*tamokorr*), and Ayoreo in the eastern Chaco (*tamokoi*), but not in Bolivian Guaraní. I have not found *kovo* attested as an Arawak form. Nordenskiöld glosses Moxeño rat as *cozo* (after Marban

1894 [1701]). These fragments are all we have. It would be a stretch indeed to suggest that this validates the Chiriguano thesis.

There are also problems with Nordenskiöld's data. *Liqui* (chicha), *pocóne* (the invitation to coitus), and the song phrases are enigmatic.[8] Nordenskiöld translated *karitimisoyti* in his Swedish original text as "*son af en h_a*" (*hynda* or *hora*, son of a bitch, whore, *hijo de puta*). Common in Spanish, the phrase does not translate easily to Guaraní. He included a Guaraní gloss presumably offered by his hosts, *barágue* (*mbarague*), child without a father. I have found no confirmation of *karitimisoyti* from an Arawak language, though in Terena and Kinikinau, *-ti* is a common verbal suffix that can indicate states of being (De Souza 2008, Ekdahl and Grimes 1964). Eternal jokesters, probably annoyed with Nordenskiöld, it is highly plausible that the young men in Guirapembi were pulling his leg or insulting him to his face with their own inventions.

According to what Nordenskiöld was told, Chané was spoken mostly during drinking events. This would fit the use of marginal languages, as Guaraní who claim to have lost their language (now seen unfavorably by Spanish speakers) often speak it fluently while drinking. Yet the tenor of the words shared also suggests a domain of interethnic (Indian-Indian or Indian-white) relations in the Chaco that were shaped by labor exchanges, generally in male-dominant and competitive settings, and often involving drinking and violence. The nineteenth-century rubber boom in the north and seasonal migration to cane plantations in Argentina brought together Indians and whites, including many Guaraní, of various origins in such contexts. The seasonal migrations might explain the semantic field Nordenskiöld gathered: insults (son of a whore), songs (usually associated with drinking events), a word for fermented corn beer, and a crude invitation to sex. Nordenskiöld offers bits of contextual data that seem to both confirm and undermine the Chiriguano thesis (1910b, 156):

When one speaks with the Indians, of their own history, their tradition does not go far back in time. Chané on the Parapetí River told me that they first lived on the upper Parapetí, from where they were driven out by a great chief. Some stopped where they now live, others went across the Chaco to the Paraguay River, a river, as mentioned, that is not unknown to them. On the Paraguay River, Arawak are also found. The Chiriguano lived first on the lower Parapetí, from where they were expelled by Chané. This is the [Chané] official story, for, if anything, it was the Chiriguano who drove out the Chané from the fertile valleys of the upper Parapetí. Batirayu told me what he knew of the Chané-Indians' history on the Parapetí. The last big chief was his father's brother, Aringui. He took many Indians of his tribe to work in Argentina.

In combination with the words and strange phrases, the Chané data are at best curious. If authentic, they attest to some connection between these Guaraní speakers and the Arawak of the Paraguay River and may also explain the presence of claimants on Chané identity in northern Argentina. Yet it is not clear that the data, if authentic, survived from the precolonial era or derived from more recent trans-Chaco or Amazonian connections between these Guaraní communities and Moxeño or Guana Chané.

Bernardino de Nino (1912, 69), a Franciscan priest and contemporary of Nordenskiöld, also argued that Guaraní traveled frequently to Argentina, a well-established fact. Adding to the enigma, he also suggested that Guaraní oral tradition spoke of visits between Guaraní and Corumbá (Brazil, home to the Terena and Kinikinau) as well as back and forth visits to the Paraguay River, where "Chiriguano" relatives were found. Were these Chané Arawak connections, it would suggest again that these links derived from more recent origins rather than from residues of ethnogenesis on the Andean front.

For his part, Nino, as a Franciscan priest, faced a peculiar historical and political dilemma. He was then writing in defense of beleaguered missions for a Bolivian military state then making claims on the Chaco lands all the way to the Paraguay River and Corumbá. He may have fabricated oral traditions as a means to bolster Bolivian claims and garner state favoritism. Immediately following the statements on Guaraní travels to the Paraguay River, Nino writes two paragraphs that address the question of language and Paraguay's claims on the Chaco (1912, 69):

Neither the Chiriguano language, nor the invasion of this race give rights to Paraguay, because all of the authors and explorers agree in affirming that this race did not exist here before the thirteenth century. . . . [T]he Bolivian nation has exercised authority here since before and after the War of Independence and the Missions progressed and prospered under the shadow of the Bolivian flag that has always waved in these distant lands.

Nordenskiöld was equivocal. When he later wrote of the Guaraní "invasion" of the Inca Empire, he cited his Chané discovery to conclude that the Portuguese confronted the Inca before the Spaniards. But he concluded that "in large tracts of Bolivia now inhabited by Guaraní Indians, the Arawaks *presumably* constituted the original population" (1917, 121, emphasis added). Yet he also expressed reservations, writing that the "Chiriguano were a conquering people, who *probably* subjugated the Chané" ("Chiriguano har varit ett eröfrande folk, som troligen underkufvat chané") (1910b, 215, emphasis added). Though I hesitate to question Nordenskiöld's Chané data, he was a guest explorer whose work unfolded under the aegis of the Bolivian state. He may have faced political pressures similar to those Nino encountered, to offer data in support of the Chiriguano thesis.[9] That is to say, by drawing a sharp distinction between the Guaraní (of Paraguay) and the Chiriguano (of Bolivia) and referring to the latter as invaders, Paraguay could not use the Guaraní language or presence to justify its own claims on the Bolivian Chaco. During this same period, Ricardo Mujía (1914) was compiling colonial documents in the archive of Seville to make Bolivia's case against Paraguay, many of which revolved around the relations of the Chiriguano to Bolivia's claim on the Chaco.

Contemporary Chané?

Contemporary scholars have struggled to replicate Nordenskiöld's findings in Isoso, claiming but never demonstrating the ongoing survival of Chané in these areas. Juergen Riester and Barbara Schuchard accept the Chiriguano thesis and claim to have found three people with (reported) rudimentary knowledge of it in the late twentieth century. They do not offer lexical examples (Schuchard 1979, vi). Riester, Schuchard, and Brigitte Simon (1979) suggest that a ritual song, the "Ajarise" (*ayarise*) remembered by some elder Isoseños, is derived from Chané, though no evidence is given. The word *ayarise* is Guaraní. Many Isoso Guaraní still claim that somebody, usually someone's grandmother, still knows Chané. However, the secret nature of such knowledge—and the clear understanding that outsiders are interested in paying for such things, as Nordenskiöld did—makes it difficult to ascertain what these claims might mean in fact. Despite the extensive pursuit by the linguist Wolf Dietrich, perhaps the world's foremost expert on Bolivian Guaraní, there is no evidence of Arawak influence in contemporary Bolivian Guaraní (Dietrich 1986, 197–198; Dietrich, personal communication,

2008; Gustafson 1995). Although Isoseño Guaraní does show slightly more unexplained lexical roots than other Guaraní variants, these forms are numerically limited, to around twenty roots, and Dietrich was unable to trace them to Arawak (Dietrich 1986, 197–198; Dietrich, personal communication, 2008).

Though it undermines their own version of the Chiriguano thesis, Combès and Villar (2004, 47) also describe three nuclei of Chané said to have fled from their Guaraní masters. These included a group that moved down the Parapetí in the sixteenth century, the so-called Isoso group; a group from Saipurú on the eastern fringe of the foothills that moved west to Acero in the eighteenth century; and a third Kaipependi group of uncertain origins. This argument suggests a significant inconsistency in the Chiriguano thesis since all these purported Chané had their origins on the eastern borders of the region, not across the totality of the Andean front. It also highlights the maintenance of clear social identities, not Chiriguanization. But whether these were Arawak speakers is unclear, as we have no evidence other than the ascription to them of the generic term "Chané," which may well have meant something else entirely. These doubts persist because Combès and Villar misrepresent the colonial-era document in their quotation of a supposed Chané leader.[10] They cite a captain named Chindika of the supposed Acero Chané who told the Franciscans "I am happy being Chané" ("eu satisfeito por ser Chané" in the published Portuguese version, Combès and Villar 2007, 46). The statement seems to confirm an unambiguous Chané identity. However, the primary document (Mingo de la Concepción 1996 [1791], 133) actually reads, "You are content to be Christian, and I am content with being Chanés or Chiriguano" ("Tú contento con ser cristiano, pues yo contento con ser chanés o chiriguano"). Of course we can never know if Chindika said anything of the sort. What we do know is that the combination of Chané and Chiriguano was crucial to Mingo's account of who was who. In fact, the document also details how some of these Chanéses came from Porongo to the north, echoing Jolis's argument (1789) that these communities emerged from Spanish resettlement tactics of various enslaved or reduced peoples of different nations, even perhaps Guaraní, but they were not the last representatives of a singular ancient ethnicity.

In Isoso (Bolivia) and Itiyuro (northern Argentina) some Guaraní-speaking communities reportedly still use the term "Chané" to refer to themselves and to distinguish themselves from their Guaraní-speaking Chiriguano neighbors. In Isoso, where Nordenskiöld made his find,

Guaraní-speaking communities on the lower Parapetí River are said to be the ancestors of the most ancient and authentic of the real Chané, though they call themselves Isoseños or Guaraní (Combès 2005). In the Itiyuro area, Dietrich collected Guaraní (Chiriguano) language data from self-described Chané in the 1970s and 1980s. He used the label "Chané" to refer to one of the dialects of Guaraní in his Chiriguano grammar (Dietrich 1986). Another contemporary anthropologist (Villar 2006) also argues that the Itiyuro Chané in northern Argentina are the authentic descendants of the original Arawak peoples. Chiriguano thesis proponents now suggest that while other Chané were absorbed completely into the Chiriguano ethnicity, the subregion of Isoso, especially the lower reaches of the Parapetí, and Itiyuro, now in Argentina, maintained a marked and distinct essence as Chané. In this account, all Chiriguano are Arawak-Guaraní mestizos, but some have remained more Arawak than others (Combès and Lowrey 2006; Combès and Villar 2007).

To sustain these arguments, minor phonetic distinctions in the Isoso and Itiyuro variants of Guaraní are taken as signs of Arawak influence. Yet again, no linguistic analysis is offered. If true, Isoso and Itiyuro Guaraní should be similar. In fact, the variants spoken by Isoseños, the supposed Bolivian Chané, are distinct from the variants spoken by those of Itiyuro, the supposed Argentine Chané. Dietrich describes in detail how those calling themselves Chané in Itiyuro differentiated themselves and spoke differently from Guaraní who spoke the Isoso variant. Dietrich's reported Chané spoke the Simba variant (Dietrich 1986, personal communication 2008). Leading to further doubts about these claims, Villar (2006, 207) has sought to authenticate the Itiyuro Guaraní of Argentina as Arawak Chané by writing that Nordenskiöld had collected his word list from Itiyuro. Nordenskiöld's data were in fact from Isoso, several hundred kilometers to the north.[11] Though outside the space of this chapter, I have also sought Chané connections in various loan words used around the Chaco. The evidence suggests a complex history of multidirectional exchanges rather than any validation of the Chiriguano thesis.

It is simply unclear what Nordenskiöld's data and the ongoing survival of the term "Chané" actually mean. Geographically limited, temporally ambiguous, linguistically enigmatic, and politically manipulated in colonial and contemporary writings, these Chané invocations are insufficient to sustain the Chiriguano thesis. In the end Nordenskiöld offered four of the most common words in regional languages, of which he already had intimate knowledge from his work in Bolivia and which many peoples of the circum-Chaco perhaps also knew. He also added two vulgar insults that have little meaning other than their probable expression of native rejection of white attempts to label them.

The Chané Enigma

Cases of ethnogenesis before and after the European invasion, intra-indigenous violence and slavery, and cultural and linguistic erasure of one indigenous people by another are well attested in South American history (Aikhenvald 2002; Hornborg 2005; Whitehead 1992, 2002). The entire region between the Andean front, the Chaco, and the Paraguay-Paraná basin was a complex crossroads of migration, conflict, and exchange, generating a mosaic of languages and peoples. This dynamic space was further complicated by Spanish and Portuguese colonial incursions, which led to population movements, an intensification of slave raiding, trading, and movement of people. There were clearly exchanges of various kinds between Arawak and Guaraní peoples in southern South America, and indeed, there are Arawak peoples known as Guana Chané who lived and remain along the upper Paraguay River. It is not my purpose to argue that contemporary Guaraní language use reflects unified cultural origins or seamless historical continuity.

Yet the entanglement of contradiction, coloniality, and contemporary sleight of hand involved in the making and remaking of the story of Chiriguano and Chané suggest that historical processes were radically different and more complex than the Chiriguano thesis offers. There are also multiple political agendas at work, frequently tied to the division of linguistic communities, the denial of certain Indigenous rights in certain places, and the reinforcement of national and academic boundaries. There is no single convincing explanatory narrative about Guaraní origins or the Chané enigma in the Andean front. I have argued here that the evidence for the Chiriguano thesis is empirically weak and analytically inconsistent. The colonial origin of the word "Chiriguano" clearly suggests that much of the thesis lies not in empirical evidence but in colonial narrative and thus merits a radical rethinking.

Notes

1. I first developed these arguments in Gustafson 2014. For exchanges that contributed to this article, I thank Isabelle Combès, Fernando O. de Carvalho, Wolf Dietrich, Harriet Klein, Christer Lindberg, Kathleen Lowrey, Carl Masthay, Dercir Pedro de Oliveira,

Giovani José da Silva, Frank Siefert, and Phil Young. A special thanks to Alexandra Aikhenvald and Ilda de Souza for their generosity in sharing knowledge and references on Arawak and Guana Chané. Nancy Twilley, Nicole Solawetz, and Marly Cardona provided research assistance. Thanks to Guaraní scholars Ceferino Manuel, Sabino Manuel, Marcia Mandepora, Guido Chumiray, and many others for their long-term collaboration and debate. My claims are based on an ongoing rereading of colonial materials, and I welcome critical engagement. I do not purport to represent others' views, Guaraní or otherwise, on this contentious issue, and any errors of fact or interpretation are my own.

2. Saignes (1990) describes the Guaraní of the Andean foothills as an anomaly, the explanation of which should be the task of all who study their history. Métraux (1946) evidenced similar discomfort with the apparent disjuncture between geographic zones and language and culture areas in the Chaco, speaking of the "Chiriguano" in relation to where linguistic and cultural borders and peoples *should* have been, based on assumptions about the relations between environment and culture. Similar to the colonial Spaniards though with different purposes, these views presuppose the existence of atemporal founding moments of indigenous authenticity, naturalizing ties between certain kinds of peoples, languages, and places. There is, of course, a political arbitrariness in how and when one seeks to "fix" these notions of identity, territory, and origin.

3. Saignes seems to view indigenous peoples as bearing identities and territories rooted in nature (and without history), while identities rooted in "historical constructions" are necessarily hybrid, mestizo, or inauthentic. This outmoded concept of indigeneity persists in contemporary reframings of the Chiriguano thesis.

4. Today the Guana Chané live in Brazil, north and east of their location at the time of conquest. Sometime in the eighteenth century the Guana Chané who lived west of the Paraguay River moved or were forced east in the context of geopolitical shifts between competing colonial powers. They were later pushed northward when Brazil confronted Paraguay in the War of the Triple Alliance in the late 1800s (Martins Ladeira 2001; see also Carvalho 2016 and Taunay 1868, 1875).

5. Schmidl's account (1881 [1567]) of Irala's bloody campaign across the Chaco details encounters with a number of peoples whose ethnonyms end in *no*, possibly a sign of Arawak ethnonymics. Yet it is hard to decipher the location of these peoples or the precise route of Irala, which extended northwesterly from the middle of Paraguay toward Santa Cruz and never entered the Guaraní area of the Andean front. Their route came nearest Guaraní country, possibly at the Salinas salt flats of southern Santa Cruz, the closest point to the far reaches of Isoso. All of this is intriguing but does not shed light on the Andean front.

6. Other etymologies of "Chiriguano" derive the word from Quechua roots (*chiri* = cold; guano = feces) as a label said to have been used to refer to Guaraní war prisoners held by Inca forces in the highlands (Pifarré 1989). The etymology is equally speculative.

7. Restrictions of space prevent full accounting of the colonial historiography of "Chiriguano." But consider, as a sample, these diverse usages: "Chiriguanos" was used to refer to *indios* "levantados en Asunción" (Matienzo 1566); to "Caríos de la sierra" (Martínez de Irala 1555); to "caríos" or "chiriguanas" in Asunción as well as those of Itatines, as distinct from Portuguese "Topi" ("Comisión al gobernador de Santa Cruz . . . ," in Mujía 1914,

supplement 2, pp. 40–44); as "caríos and carives [but not mestizos]" in Cepeda (1914 [1584]); as "chiriguanas caribes" and as "no caribes" of Paraguay and the Río de la Plata (Lizárraga 1987 [ca. 1600], 424, 426, 427).

8. Neither Ilda de Souza, who works with the Kinikinau of Mato Grosso (personal communication, 2007), nor the Arawak specialist Alexandra Aikhenvald (personal communication, 2007) saw obvious Arawak origins in these phrases.

9. On the paradigms and pressures that sometimes led Nordenskiöld to construct accounts that veered away from the empirical evidence, see Howe's work (2009) with the Guna (Kuna) of Panama.

10. I reserve judgement on whether this erroneous citation was intentional.

11. Whether Villar's erroneous citation was intentional or not, Loukotka (1968, 143), citing Nordenskiöld, commits the same error, attributing his Isoso "Chané" data to Itiyuro. In point of fact, Nordenskiöld provides little data on the Itiyuro Chané. He states that "he could tell some histories of the Chané of Itiyuro, but does not want to tire the reader with too many names" (1910b, 157). Villar (2006) and Combès and Lowrey (2006) argue that other Arawak traces, including hierarchical leadership and certain kinship patterns but particularly weaving, are further evidence of authentic Chané roots among the Isoso Guaraní. Though weaving is important in Isoso, what little Nordenskiöld does note of Itityuro (Villar's so-called authentic Chané) includes the observation, "I saw no looms among the Chané in the Itiyuro Valley and indigenous textiles were scarce" (1910b, 228; see also Hald 1962).

3

Cosmology of Development

Humanitarian Narratives and Missionary Work in the Argentine Gran Chaco

CÉSAR CERIANI CERNADAS

Among indigenous peoples of the Argentine Chaco, the adoption of Christianity involved a complex process of cultural change and sociopolitical rearrangement that spanned much of the twentieth century. The impact of Protestant and Catholic missionary experiences on the creation of new communities, such as the subsequent formation of an independent indigenous evangelical movement, are revealed as central elements of this long historical process. Anthropological studies dating back to the 1930s constitute an area of pioneering research on indigenous Christianity in South America (Ceriani Cernadas and Citro 2005; Cordeu and Siffredi 1971; Métraux 1933; Miller 1979; Reyburn 1954; Wright 1983, 2002a). In previous works I have sought to understand the social, symbolic, and political forms involved in the indigenous appropriation of Protestant Christianity, focusing on the cultural creativity of the Qom and Wichí peoples in their relations with missionary agencies and within the independent evangelical churches. I also have studied the changes in leadership structure and the multiple meanings and experiences that indigenous people attribute to evangelism (Ceriani Cernadas 2005, 2011a, 2014). In the present study I examine another dimension: the intersection between humanitarian and development narratives of outside religious organizations that have worked on the social and moral transformation of indigenous peoples.

In particular, my research centers on humanitarianism as a moral narrative of modernity and how Christian missions and faith-based nongovernmental organizations (NGOs) build a cosmology of development among indigenous societies in the Gran Chaco. This cosmology entangles definitions of culture, person, social rights, and gender in cultural imaginaries about modernity, development, and social change sustained in Christian values. The notion of a "cosmology of development" is a heuristic device, an intuitive theoretical tool that allows me to develop a comprehensive interpretation of Argentine Gran Chaco missionary and development processes.

Therefore, this analysis is also situated in the context of anthropological and historical studies on the discursive construction of the Chaco as a conceptual and visual geography of alterity. In this field, two main studies sustain my approach: Pablo Wright's (1998) conceptualization of the Chaco as a "desert narrative," a symbolic, moral, and ideological device that motivated a territorial intervention conducted by explorers, missionaries, military, and colonizers; and Mariana Giordano's (2004) study of the visual and discursive imaginary of Chaco indigenous peoples historically constructed by missionaries and state and social agents since the mid-nineteenth century and synthesized in three schemes: civilizational, integrationist, and reparational.

The sociohistorical dimension of this analysis is the long process of conquest, colonization, Christian missionization, and socioeconomic subordination of the Qom, Wichí, Mocoví, and Pilagá peoples during the 19th and 20th centuries (Gordillo 2004; Miller 1979; Trinchero 2000). Likewise, I consider four additional social processes. First is the creation of an independent evangelical movement among the eastern Qom during the 1940s and 1950s and its institutionalization between 1958 and 1961, when twenty-nine native congregations joined to create the United Evangelical Church (Iglesia Evangélica Unida) (Buckwalter 2009, 197). Second are the development policies in the Chaco territory during the 1970s and 1980s carried out by national and provincial governments, international cooperation agencies, and humanitarian aid organizations (Hermitte 1995). Third, the restoration of the Argentine democratic government in 1983 enabled the emergence of a new ethnopolitical configuration that led to constitutional reform, the enactment of indigenous laws, and the recognition of "ancestral land ownership" in 1994. The fourth social process I examine is the discontinuous territorial regulation and social, health, and educational inclusion policies established since the mid-2000s under a human rights paradigm. In this social process, indigenous religious and political associations, political parties, and NGOs became intertwined in the struggles for the political claims of indigenous rights to territory, education, labor, and health care.

In a critical inquiry on missionization and sociocultural change in the Argentine Gran Chaco, I resort to an anthropological review of "modernity" and "development" as social categories and ideological constructions of Western societies. I examine the link between hygienism and humanitarianism in the moral configuration of the Chaco cosmology of development, focusing on the health interventions of the missionaries in terms of their representations and praxis as well as on indigenous memories. Following a chronological pattern, I focus on ways faith-based NGOs among the Qom and Wichí communities worked for cultural revitalization and socioeconomic improvement of indigenous people.

Chaco Modernity, Missionization, and Development Narratives

Research on missionization processes among the Qom and Wichí in the twentieth century shows how missionary styles and contact adapted in different ways to the diverse contexts but were oriented toward a civilizing ethos, humanitarianism, and social engineering (Ceriani Cernadas and López 2017). The first involves the general ideological framework in which Christian missionary enterprises developed beyond the borders of Euro-Western civilization, that is, Christianity as synonymous with a disciplined social order in which moral and bodily reform, as well as literacy, were key projects (Comaroff and Comaroff 1992; Wright 2003). The second involves thinking about humanitarianism as a moral narrative of the civilizing ethos, which emerged during the nineteenth and twentieth centuries of Western colonial expansion and was based on feelings of empathy for the suffering of ostensibly neglected human groups and the management of palliative actions (Ballantyne 2011; Fassin 2012; Laqueur 1987). The third characteristic is based on the rationalized social restructuring of each missionary project, where the symbolic, economic, legal, territorial, and political order of the communities was fundamental for their survival (Miller 1979; Torres Fernández 2007).

Within this framework, moral discourses and practices, medical and hygienist actions, literacy projects and economic organization were oriented toward aiding, encouraging religious conversion, and incorporating indigenous peoples into the national society. The emphasis is on these three terms, aid, religion, and social integration, in order to define the cosmology of development as a religious-secular theodicy of modern Christian missions. "Theodicy" here refers to the ethical composition of the world as a space of inequality and suffering where the developed, developing, and underdeveloped members of states live in unequal conditions and where it is necessary to engage (Das 1997). "Religious-secular" refers to a framework whereby Christian morality, economic rationality, naturalistic worldview, and scientific knowledge are intertwined (Miller 1970).

The historical relations between Christian missionary agencies, imaginaries, and community development policies in the Argentine Chaco designed since the 1960s are linked to this worldview. I refer to a universe of projects directed to indigenous groups and deployed in a network of relations between state agencies, international cooperation agencies, mission teams, and faith-based NGOs. Several contemporary studies in the area allow deepening the knowledge about the cultural mediation structures that are carried out by faith-based organizations in their relations with the indigenous communities of the Gran Chaco territory. A key issue is the impact that discourses carried out by *indigenista* Catholic organizations had on the reconstructions of social categories such as "indigenous peoples" and "indigenous communities."[1] The works of Laura Zapata (2013), Miguel Leone (2016), and Leone and Cristian Vázquez (2016) analyze the meaning, circulation, and use of these categories in the sociopolitical interventions of several Catholic-based groups in the provinces of Formosa and Chaco between 1960 and 1984. These studies illustrate the links between religious and political ideals, development narratives, academic knowledge appropriations, and state policies in the construction of social and ethnic categories. Another important issue involves the rhetorical and political strategies on women's rights, cooperative work, and gender roles defined by religious faith-based organizations, such as the Institute of Popular Culture (INCUPO),[2] the Foundation for Development in Justice and Peace (FUNDAPAZ),[3] and among others, the National Aboriginal Pastoral Team (ENDEPA).[4] The ethnographic studies of Laurie Occhipinti (2003, 2005, 2011), Mariana Gómez (2016), and Natalia Castelnuovo Biraben (2019) have contributed to broadening this area of research by analyzing the progressive protagonism of women in activist organizations, in correlation with a global multicultural emphasis aimed at enhancing the role of indigenous women.

Recent research also locates the political, economic, and transnational dimensions involved in social development projects. Sergio Braticevic's (2009) study of faith-based NGOs in western Formosa centers on a "reconversion" of the evangelizing model as a result of the closure of traditional missions, a crisis of legitimacy of indigenous churches, and new evangelization strategies. Castelnuovo Biraben's inquiries (2010, 2015, 2017), on the other hand, shed light on the political culture of development agencies in the western Chaco from an ethnographic perspective and focusing on "brokers of development," alliance relations, and tensions between faith-based NGOs and indigenous populations.

Therefore, I review some key aspects of the development narrative by exploring the ways in which these ideas and technical knowledge were anticipated and spread by missionary practices. As is well known in the academic literature, the notion of "social development" and its policies were influenced by European evolutionist and colonial ideologies, by a geopolitical redefinition after World War II, and by the impact of decolonization processes in Africa and Asia. The development episteme was forged in the 1950s, when the notion of the "Third World" was invented (Escobar 1996). The international cooperation networks together with the NGOs of global influence emerged in northern European countries, mostly in Germany, Sweden, and Norway. In the Gran Chaco, decisive funds were provided by the organization Misereor, which is self-defined as "the episcopal work of the German Catholic Church for development cooperation."[5] This organization was created in 1958 under the promotion of community development and the fight against global poverty, excluding all proselytizing and missionary religious activity (Castelnuovo Biraben 2017).

In addition to this, we must consider the relation between the development narrative and the encompassing narrative of modernity, understood as a set of unilineal, objective traits, in which literacy, democracy, industrialization, economic well-being, access to health care, and individual freedom prevail (Foster 2002). The anthropological perspective has allowed a critical reflection on the sociohistorical construction of this Eurocentric narrative of modernity and its influence on the ideologies and practices of development programs (Asad 2003; Ferguson 1994; Knauft 2002). Along with this construction, following Webb Keane's argument (2007), these programs are sustained by a moral narrative. The core of the narrative is that the strength of the idea of progress lies not only in technological improvements or quality of life but also in the possibilities of "human emancipation and self-mastery" (Keane 2007, 7). In this moral narrative, especially embodied in the Protestant habitus and in tune with the modern, secular, and enlightened ethos, the problem of human agency becomes central. Here, the modern notion of person and its ideological emphasis on individual responsibility and cooperative action will be central to the various Christian-developmentalist conceptions carried out by missions or NGOs, as can be observed regarding the Argentine Gran Chaco.

Institutions and groups such as religious orders, missions, foundations, lay pastoral teams, volunteers, and others have a long history of involvement in social problems. Furthermore, these groups have focused on poverty alleviation, social inequality, literacy, and health and have been pioneers in the implementation of "social development projects" and "human promotion" (Leone 2016). Charity, piety, and social assistance have had diverse interpretations according to the religious institutions and the sociopolitical and economic contexts where they were situated. Hence, some religious groups emphasized charity in their work with impoverished or excluded populations without making explicit in their discourses critical visions about the social structures in which poverty or exclusion developed. The concern for justice, social equity, and human dignity would be resignified by Catholic religious movements and emerging Protestants between the 1960s and 1970s; the relations between sociopolitical change and religion had a marked impact in Latin America after the Second Vatican Council (1962–1965) and the Medellin Bishops Conference (1968). The Second Vatican Council promoted the role of lay practitioners as protagonists of social and moral change in their respective societies. This context enabled a space for the emergence of critical positions toward social inequality, embodied in the "option for the poor" of the so-called Liberation Theology and in Argentina, the movement Priests for the Third World.

The Catholic Church and Argentine Catholicism experienced significant changes from the 1920s to the 1950s, a time considered to be marked by a strong discourse against modernity, understood as a secular, materialistic tendency, and ultimately a source of perversion of the constitutive moral values of society. During the 1950s and 1960s, the emergence of an "antibourgeois sensibility," in the words of Miranda Lida (2012), characterized the developmental enthusiasm of young Catholics after the military coup that ended the Peronist government in 1955. In this context, summer camps of engaged young people in remote villages of the country, labor cooperatives, and new indigenous and criollo imaginary were cultural signs of the renewed Latin American "Catholic culture" (Ludueña 2009).[6]

From Max Weber onward, the characterization of Protestantism as possessing a special link with the modern imaginary and "the spirit of capitalism" has had a powerful influence. The sociologist and theologian Ernst Troeltsch has argued that Protestantism embodies the "last characteristic of the modern spirit, its optimism full of trust and faith in progress" (1951, 23). Beyond the range of direct influence between Protestant ethics and economic development, I emphasize the self-perceptions of these churches and missions in the context of the Latin American experience during the twentieth century. The cultural imaginary of the Protestant missions shaped meanings articulated in a semantic chain: modernity = freedom = democracy = educational, economic, technical progress.

In this way, the Christian missions were inserted into the same process of social and ideological change that took place throughout the twentieth century. That is, the missions moved from the philanthropic policies of the first decades, followed by the sociopolitical transformation projects of the 1960s and 1970s, to the "new planetary consciousness" of the last twenty years of the century, marked by multicultural, ecological, and gender policies (Mölle 2008).

Missionary Humanitarianism

Around April 2010, during my fieldwork in Embarcación, Salta Province, I spoke with Marcos, a pastor there, about the impact of missionary evangelization. Embarcación has one of the oldest indigenous missions, founded in 1920 by Scandinavians. Marcos, a criollo, became senior pastor of the Evangelical Mission Assembly of God in 2000. He is a descendant of one of the leading indigenous evangelists who worked with Norwegian and Swedish missionaries between 1930 and 1950. In one of our many conversations on the subject, he did not hesitate to affirm, "The missions were the first to defend indigenous rights, although they have been criticized for killing aboriginal culture and many other things, but the missionaries helped a lot." For his part, Diego, a musician and religious leader of the same mission, made another interesting statement: "The Protestant missions were pioneers in social work throughout this area, because until these gringos arrived there was no one to take charge of the health and education of the Indians, and that lasted a long time." Diego mentioned another significant factor in the history and memory of the Chaco missionization process, a story that crosses different parts of the territory: the missionary role in social and bureaucratic mediation in order for natives to obtain citizenship.

A decade earlier, between 2000 and 2006, I did fieldwork among the Qom of Colonia La Primavera and Naineck in Formosa Province. Miguel, then in his sixties, was not only the head of the family that hosted me but one of the most reputable evangelical preachers in the area and an active member of the United Evangelical Church. Likewise, his political family was one of the main lineages linked to the origin of both settlements. "All the Qom are *evangelio*. We are not Catholics; that is the religion of the whites, who smoke, are drunk, homosexual, and do nothing for the indigenous people," Miguel said in one of our first conversations. He told me his relatives settled in that place due to the action of the English missionary John Church, known as Juan Chur, after a retinue of Qom leaders from the area requested his help. It was 1937, and the Emmanuel Mission, to which Chur belonged, had set up a mission station in the town of Espinillo in Chaco Province and a school for indigenous children in Formosa city. The cacique Sanabria entourage arrived in Formosa and met with Chur, an event that led to the installation of a new mission in Laguna Blanca.[7] These indigenous mobility practices in search of a Protestant missionary to install a mission, in a critical context based on military control, territorial dispossession, and the progressive colonization of the territory, have been common throughout Argentine Chaco territory since 1910 (Gordillo 2004). As we note in a previous work, these strategies account for how the indigenous agency of the Qom, Wichí, and Pilagá was involved from the beginning in the missionization processes (Ceriani Cernadas and Lavazza 2013).

Miguel also recalled that Chur "told us about the power of God and taught us how to write and how to eat, how to be clean." Together with Church's wife, who was a nurse, and trained Qom assistants, they took care of people's health "because there was so much disease." It is important to note that both statements refer to two intertwined themes of indigenous Chaco evangelism. Miguel places that identification as radically opposed to that of the Catholic, marked as a religion by whites who forcibly entered the territory (Wright 2002b, 2003). The second refers to the ambiguity of the past in indigenous evangelical reconstructions of memory, in which the lack of material culture and writing contrasts with the wisdom, learning capacity, and physical and spiritual strength of the bodies of the ancients (Ceriani Cernadas 2014; Citro 2009; Tola 2009).[8]

In the Chaco territory, the action of religious institutions has had an active and heterogeneous presence since the beginning of the twentieth century in social projects with indigenous and peasant populations marginalized by regional and national power structures. In northwestern Argentina, specifically in the provinces of Salta, Jujuy, and Tucumán, the process was more linked to and controlled by Catholic institutions. At the beginning of the twentieth century, the Franciscan missions were supported by the state for the purpose of civilizing, Christianizing, and nationalizing the natives of the border areas of the National Territories of Chaco and Formosa (Dalla-Corte and Vázquez Recalde 2011; Teruel 2005).[9] The arrival of Anglicans in 1910 and the progressive installation of several Protestant missions in nodal points of the territory, mediated by indigenous agency, gave impulse to a dynamic of cultural (re)production (Sahlins 1985) under the creation of new social configurations. The most complete expression of this process was the formation of the Qom independent evangelical churches in the 1950s and their progressive expansion in the following decades among the Wichí, Pilagá, and Mocoví peoples. Here it is not possible to review this complex process, documented in influential works mentioned above. What is important for the core argument in this chapter is to highlight the ideological and practical articulations between Christian missions and development undertakings, observing the representations, moral sensibilities, and methodologies involved.

The Protestant missionary expansion among those who were called "wild" peoples constituted a transnational cultural enterprise that disseminated modern ideologies of progress, scientific perspectives especially in medicine and ethnography, aesthetic languages, and material culture (Nielssen, Okkenhaug, and Skeie 2011). In the case of the Gran Chaco, I emphasize the importance of the hygienist and educational projects of the missions as well as the strategies to integrate indigenous peoples into the labor market and assist in accessing citizenship by obtaining ID cards. As noted in the previous testimonies, a large majority of indigenous people have viewed the installation of Protestant missions as a beneficial historical milestone, inaugurating an era of defense against the abuses of the army, the end of interethnic wars, the cure of certain diseases, the acquisition of literacy, and the transformation of attire (Ceriani Cernadas 2007). English, Scandinavian, and North American missionaries of different denominations built a fluid missionary field in the region toward the middle of the twentieth century, crossed by alliances and territorial cooperation (López 2017). Beyond their differences, these groups shared the central idea that the conversion to Christianity and the experience of civilized life in the missions would lead them to progressive social and economic development.

The three shared characteristics of the missions and their cosmology of development (civilizing ethos, humanitarianism, and social engineering) implicitly defined them as social and symbolic centers for the production of civilized life. Hence, the spatial ordering of missionary settlements in the Gran Chaco hinterland was organized under the model of the agricultural village, with the religious temple, the medical dispensary, the school, a grocery store (ruled by a monetized economy), and the homes of missionaries and natives, built in the manner of the criollo settlers of the region (Miller 1979).

In this context, the history of access to health services and Christian missions in the territory is central to understanding the role of a humanitarian narrative in the moral configuration of this particular cosmology of development (Hirsch and Lorenzetti 2016). In other words, it is important to inquire into the imaginaries of the missionary doctors and nurses about the health of the indigenous people, their forms of healing, and their own interactions and reciprocal perceptions with the Qom, Pilagá, Wichí, or Guaraní, among other populations. As happened in many other regions of the Americas, the arrival of contagious diseases such as smallpox, tuberculosis, and influenza were related to the process of conquest, colonization, and plundering of indigenous territories. The plague (*la peste*), for example, is remembered by the elderly Qom of Formosa as something that came from the west, from the sugar mills and cane fields in the provinces of Salta and Jujuy (Gordillo 2004, Tola and Suárez 2016). For the Qom and Wichí groups that inhabited the evangelical mission founded by Norwegian preacher Bergen Johnsen in Embarcación, the smallpox epidemic of 1960 unleashed a health panic that led to the relocation of the settlement under the accusation of contamination, as pointed out by social elites (Ceriani Cernadas y Lavazza 2013).

Examples like these resurface in the memories of elderly *paisanos* (indigenous people) in the vast territory of the Gran Chaco. I want to emphasize here that the web of social and discursive connections between biomedicine and Christianity, especially in the experiences of missionization in the supposed frontiers of civilization, exposes the ways the humanitarian narrative of modernity also sought to reconcile the development of scientific knowledge and religious praxis. John and Jean Comaroff in their seminal study on Christianity in colonial South Africa point out the ambiguity between hygienist medical discourse, racialized in metaphors of past contamination and civilizing redemption, and the sensitive practice of medical missionaries. The authors state that "healing remained, in large measure, a tactile process, one in which the physical separations of the civilizing mission were most often ruptured-and where feelings of recognition, even compassion, flowed across the cleavages of a racially divided society" (Comaroff and Comaroff 1997, 324). Throughout the twentieth century, British and American doctors and nurses were part of a movement, as Pamela Klassen points out, "in which biomedical care was a public good open to all; and as believers in the spirit they insisted that the science behind biomedicine was itself a gift of divine wisdom" (2011, xi).

In the Argentine Gran Chaco, access to biomedicine was inextricably linked to indigenous Protestant missions. Doctors, nurses, missionaries, and indigenous people articulated social relations and biopolitical agendas in specific historical-regional junctures. In the Anglican missions of Salta and Formosa between 1914 and 1940, physicians and nurses were in charge of vaccinating people and reducing the incidence of infant mortality. "This method is achieved by saving countless lives, while the new generations breed stronger," wrote the anthropologist Alfred Métraux in his famous humanistic apologetic text about Anglican missions (Métraux 1933, 206).

Toward 1935 in the mission led by Johnsen in Embarcación, the public health of the settlement and the sanitary control of its disciplined inhabitants were priorities (Ceriani Cernadas 2011b). Disinfection campaigns, vaccination, weekly household cleaning, and prohibition of drinking mate with sorbet because of the danger of catching tuberculosis were some of the measures implemented by Johnsen (Palavecino 1959/1960). The last elders who lived during the foundational period still remembered that the first thing they did when they met Berger and his wife, Hedvig Berg, a Swedish missionary, was to give them white soap and new clothes, which symbolized a new status and social contract for the Indians. "Missionary Berger was very strict about cleaning the house and clothes. Every day that he made inspection rounds in the mission houses, he first went up to the roof of the temple to survey the cleanliness of the streets from there," recalled Indalecio, a Wichí raised in the mission during the 1940s.

In the 1950s the Norwegian mission took a more extensive evangelizing turn under the leadership of Per Pedersen. The doctor in charge of the Municipal Hospital of Embarcación, Virgilio Coutada, treated indigenous people of the mission without their having ID cards, something unprecedented at that time. In November 2016, during the centennial commemoration of the Evangelical Mission Assembly of God, I spoke with Cyril Pedersen, one of the renowned missionaries who retired in 1995, about the mission's great dedication to health issues. Cyril recalled the importance of missionary nurses in caring for the health of indigenous mothers and children, and he highlighted the valuable help provided by Dr. Coutada: "This person was a great man, an idealist, a humanist. He was not religious, but he did a great good to the indigenous people of the mission."

Paradigmatic in this coincidence between medicine, humanitarianism, and Christian missions in the Gran Chaco was the experience of Dr. Enrique Cicchetti, whose conversion to Methodism in the city of Rosario, Santa Fe Province, led him to settle in the city of Castelli in the heart of Chaco Province in 1964 and focus on the indigenous people's health and the spread of the Christian message. This would become the basis of the United Missions Board (Junta Unida de Misiones), an active ecumenical

Protestant organization since 1964 formed by the Evangelical Methodist Church of Argentina, the Evangelical Church of the Río de la Plata, the Disciples of Christ, and the Waldensian Church of the Río de la Plata (Barroso 2015).

This missionary field boomed from the 1930s into the 1970s in a political and economic geography in which the Argentine state was still an actor of scarce presence; the state presence went through changes during the Peronist governments of 1946–1955 and then with the impulse of the development policies in the following decades (Lenton 2005; Zapata 2013). The religious policies of the Peronist government were ambivalent and changing. During the first government (1946–1952), a strategic alliance with the Catholic Church implied, among other issues, an eagerness to regulate the non-Catholic religious field and especially to impose strict control over Protestant confessions. Members of the political elite who identified with Catholic nationalism saw the growth of evangelical churches as an affront to the national identity and encouraged restrictive policies. Among the regulations, those with the greatest impact were the creation of the National Register of Non-Catholic Religious Associations in 1946 and the prohibition of Protestant proselytizing and land purchases in the National Territories of Chaco and Formosa (Bianchi 2001; Caimari 1995; Canclini 1970; López 2017). However, from 1952 to 1955, the relations of the Peronist government with the Catholic hierarchy deteriorated, while the pressures and regulations toward the Protestant churches diminished. Christian missions in the Gran Chaco followed this pattern. Thus, during 1946–1952, the Protestant missions litigated with the government and the Catholic Church for the freedom to evangelize the indigenous populations, but after 1952 the pressures decreased. Control over education, work, health care, and territory, that is, the institutionalized instances of social production, were the key points in the power play between Christian missions, the Peronist government, and indigenous peoples (Ceriani Cernadas 2017; Dalla-Corte 2014). But it is also important to point out the political pragmatism of indigenous agency, since it was precisely in 1947 that the independent Qom evangelical movement began to grow after the leader Pedro Martínez went to Buenos Aires to make a claim for land to President Juan Perón (Miller 1979, 139–140; Reyburn 1954, 36). The trip brought Martínez into contact with Pentecostal pastors from the Church of God who agreed to let him lead the creation of Qom churches in the Chaco hinterland. Among the Qom, the confluence of having a Peronist political affiliation through someone of evangelical religious affiliation would be constitutive, Silvia

Citro has explained (2009, 133–168), of new forms of social and cultural identification.

Along with this encompassing social process, changes in missiology paradigms had an impact on the agenda of Protestant evangelization policies and their development imaginary. The transnational dimension of these socioreligious enterprises was, and still is, an important factor in their symbolic and political economies. The best-known case is that of the Mennonites missionaries who organized the Nam Cum Mission in the then National Territory of the Chaco from 1943 to 1954, when they dismantled it. According to these missionaries, it was the 1954 anthropological and linguistic report by William Reyburn, linked to the United Bible Societies, that persuaded them of the need to radically change the mission's philosophy and praxis. Their realization gave rise to Mennonite Fraternal Workers (Obreros Fraternales Menonitas), a group that encouraged a new type of missionary practice. It was led for forty-three years by the couple Albert and Loida Buckwalter, based in the town of Roque Sáenz Peña, Chaco Province, and accompanied by other American missionary couples and later by Europeans and Argentines (Altman 2017; Buckwalter 2009; Miller 2002). To support the Qom in their choice of Pentecostal Christianity, Mennonite Fraternal Workers dedicated themselves to assisting them in the bureaucratic legal procedures of the churches for enrollment in the National Register of Non-Catholic Religious Organizations. Coupled with this assistance, the missionaries engaged in linguistic work on Qom language (*qom'lactaq*), Bible translations, and regular visits to indigenous congregations in rural communities. Horst, one of the main Fraternal Mennonites, has pointed out, "In the late 1950s, Mennonite missionaries and some leading Toba/Qom believers agreed on the idea of organizing a totally Indigenous church" (2001, 171). The project to curb internal mergers and rivalries as well as conflicts with nonindigenous religious agencies led the Qom's religious leaders to create the United Evangelical Church.

Faithful representatives of the Protestant written culture, the Mennonite missionaries from Indiana, USA, in 1958 began publishing *Qad'aq-taxanaxanec* (*Our Messenger*), the first publication on the Qom evangelical movement; later it would cover pan-indigenous issues. Published in the Qom and Spanish languages, this news bulletin about the indigenous churches, with biblical commentaries, over time became involved in indigenous rights, land, identity, language, health, and education. Contents in Pilagá, Mocoví, and Wichí languages and some news from their evangelical churches were added to the bulletins during the 1980s and 1990s.

"As Fraternal Workers we try to collaborate with indigenous organizations that seek ways to demand from the State the fulfillment of their rights," declared the German missionaries Ute Mueller-Eckhardt and Frank Paul (2009, 162).

Despite their commitment to the secular cause of indigenous rights to land, language, and culture, Mennonite missionaries in the Argentine Chaco have not been involved in development projects. Unlike other missions in the region, Mennonite Fraternal Workers refrained from distributing goods under the ideal of avoiding economic dependence by the Qom and the reproduction of the patronage system (Miller 1995, 62). In this sense, there is a tension between Mennonite perceptions and practices and the humanitarian and development narrative of other missions such as Anglicans, Scandinavian Pentecostals, and Catholics. Knowing how difficult it is to avoid a relationship of material dependence with indigenous people, Fraternal Workers seemed to be disenchanted with the Gran Chaco's cosmology of development. However, from the Qom point of view, the missionary, leader, collaborator, and politician must control and dispose of material goods (Ceriani Cernadas 2013). The elder Salustiano López, a historical Qom religious leader and the brother of Aurelio López, one of the most influential and remembered Qom evangelists, said, "We are grateful for the arrival of the Mennonite brothers although they do not bring money. But they arrived." (Horst, Mueller-Eckhardt, and Paul 2009, 176).

During the 1970s the growth of indigenous evangelical churches paralleled a greater commitment to development policies and community work by old and new missionary agencies. Mennonites and some other missionary groups continued their religious and legal support for indigenous communities, while others exercised different approaches to alleviate economic and health problems as well as to support indigenous political and cultural activism. This process allowed new forms of engagement with the indigenous populations of the Chaco, a distinctive sign of a different scenario.

The Faith-Based NGO Turn

After the impact of the forced exile of British missionaries during the Malvinas/Falklands War in 1982, the shift in the missiology paradigm took place in two fundamental movements. One was a retraction of the missionaries' presence in the daily lives of the communities and at the same time a revitalization of biblical translation into the Wichí and Chorote languages and in the bilingual graphic production oriented to the interweaving of religious and cultural themes. The other was an emphasis on social, educational, developmental, and cooperative activities, institutionally channeled through the intersectional work carried out by ASOCIANA,[10] the Foundation of Social Accompaniment of the Anglican Church of Northern Argentina. This organization, formalized in 1994, had its pioneering action in the Christian Initiative social plan launched in 1972 (Lunt 2011). Aligned with the developmental spirit of the time, ASOCIANA established agricultural programs in irrigation, health, education, and carpentry in various missions. Its work prioritized territorial and agroforestry issues that included management with the communities to gain land titles and activism against deforestation of their territory. ASOCIANA committed to advancing the long territorial claim of the Association of Aboriginal Communities Lhaka Honhat including a resolution of conflict with the criollo populations, which has been described in detail by Morita Carrasco (2009, 175–186). Further research by Castelnuovo Biraben (2017) compares ASOCIANA and FUNDAPAZ, a lay Catholic NGO for rural development and land rights for the indigenous peoples, their culture, and their relations with the criollo populations. These and other works initiated a discussion of the politics that Christian missions and NGOs deployed in their interaction with the indigenous peoples of the Chaco, where relativistic approaches of ethnic safeguard, romantic imaginaries of the "poor and good Christian Indian," and anthropological knowledge left a lasting predicament (Miller and Wynarczyk 1988).

The experience of the United Missions Board among the Qom of Castelli and Villa Bermejito since 1964 has promoted a creative synthesis between social action and evangelical commitment in the heart of the Chaco territory. Originally the mission was a humanitarian medical assistance program in an area that had the highest rates of tuberculosis, chronic malnutrition, and maternal and infant mortality in the entire country. During the 1970s, social development and economic programs were incorporated and directed toward alleviating structural poverty through social and health assistance and the implementation of handicraft and carpentry programs. During the 1980s, the United Missions Board assumed the defense of the territorial and educational rights of the Qom settlements, integrating itself in the legal-political contest for the recovery of the 150,000 hectares of the Interfluvio Teuco-Bermejito. The board still directs its projects toward the religious, social, and educational self-management of the indigenous Chaco population. The rhetoric of human agency, the dominant symbol of the narrative of modernity, incorporated the issues of women's empowerment, educational support for indigenous youth, training in civil rights, and advice on territorial claims. Coupled with this model, the United Missions Board has maintained religious activities such as the theological training courses organized in the 1990s by the renowned Evangelical Superior Institute of Theological Studies (ISEDET)[11] and has more recently developed "intercultural ecumenical camps."

In the Catholic religious field, the Institute of Popular Culture stands out as an organization "of Christian inspiration" that focuses on community support for indigenous and peasant groups of the region. It emerged in 1968 under the guidance of bishops motivated in literacy tasks and community development in indigenous and peasant communities (Castelnuovo Biraben 2017; Zapata 2013). Since the 1980s, in parallel with the aforementioned Protestant organizations, its priorities have moved progressively toward the problems of access to land, agro-ecological production, the promotion of rights, food security, sustainable use of natural resources, and fair trade of agricultural products. However, the core of its social work has been in the field of communications and popular education including workshops, courses, seminars, and proposals of greater scope.

In 2002, with the foundational support of the United Missions Board, indigenous associations such as the Federación Pilagá of Formosa and Cacique Taigoyik of Chaco, and the Institute of Popular Culture led in the formation of the Indigenous Communication Network (Red de Comunicación Indígena, RCI). The network has its center of action in Resistencia, Chaco Province, as a space for training and articulation of organizations committed to indigenous rights. Under an intercultural perspective, the RCI set out to communicate the problems of the indigenous communities of northern Argentina from within and according to the perspectives of native agents themselves. This ideal of indigenous media sovereignty is the cornerstone of this collective enterprise that foster the practical training of native reporters in numerous communities throughout Argentina. The network focuses on a topic familiar to the peoples of the Gran Chaco: training of social communicators as a new form of transactional leadership, that is, as cultural mediators. This is the type of leadership conducted by traditional caciques who later become Christian religious leaders and political and cultural activists. One of its key promoters, Elisa del Carmen Zenteno, indicates the folds that articulate the religious-secular theodicy that characterizes the notion of a cosmology of development. As host of the RCI radio program *Voces originarias* (Aboriginal Voices) in Jujuy Province, Zenteno expressed the notion of "appropriation" to mean adapting nonindigenous knowledge and technologies to shape modern indigenous sensibilities. In an article on the role of local indigenous communicators in the RCI newsletter of July 2008, Zenteno asserts, "We only depend on ourselves, on our ability to appropriate ourselves and assume a real and true commitment." After defining the purpose of these reporters, she concludes the article with the prayer "that God, our Father, who is the way, truth, and life, guide us to carry out our mission as journalists and communicators to fight for justice, to defend human rights, and to work for peace."

Another Catholic organization with a strong commitment and presence in the region is the National Aboriginal Pastoral Team, created in 1984 after the first national meeting of pastoral workers in indigenous areas was held in Buenos Aires in 1980 and brought to light the dramatic situation of the peoples of the Gran Chaco. This organization, linked to the diocese of Formosa, promotes numerous activities and projects in social areas. It and other missions reinforce the notions of culture, community, family, and land that have had an important impact on legal reforms from the 1980s onward (Lenton 2005; Leone 2016; Zapata 2013).

These religious organizations established new meanings and practices in their work, marked by humanitarianism and the development expectations of the Chaco communities. They also catalyzed the political sensibilities of the time that implied the self-criticism of traditional missiological approaches and new agendas in defense of indigenous rights, the empowerment of native languages and cultural identities, and the inclusion of gender issues.

Religious Modernities, Back and Forth

Relations between missionization, humanitarianism, and community work in the Argentine Gran Chaco have reflected the notions of cosmology and development. Semantic and moral articulations are evident between religion, modernity and development that missionaries and NGOs built in historical and social contexts of the Argentine Gran Chaco.

Maria Barroso (2009) demonstrates in her ethnographic study of the relations between Norwegian international cooperation agencies and Brazilian indigenous peoples that one of the main reasons for the persistence of development agencies is the interference of religious actors. In a later work (Barroso 2015, 190), she points out that the presence of missionary discourses in "the definition of the rights of the 'poor,' 'vulnerable,' and of other categories that were traditional objects of the philanthropic actions of the Christian world" established the deployment of the cooperation apparatus "as a space for debates not only technical but also moral."

Humanitarian narratives and their relations with modernity and development can be illuminated by focusing on the sociocultural dynamics of religious organizations among the indigenous populations of the Argentine Chaco in the fields of education, health care, agriculture, cultural revitalization, and land rights. The historical journey that goes from the "poor and neglected Indians," as the Norwegian missionary Johnsen wrote in 1915, to the claims of cultural sovereignty and indigenous rights directed by missionary, postmissionary, and faith-based groups reveals some of the changes in the interfaces between religious undertakings and development agendas in the experience of the indigenous peoples of the Argentine Chaco. From there emerge three ideological and practical axes of the Protestant missionary processes—a civilizing ethos, humanitarianism, and social engineering—that would influence the future configuration of a cosmology of development, understood as a secular-religious theodicy of contemporary Christian missions and faith-based NGOs.

In the context of social change that permeated many religious and political projects in the 1960s and 1970s, religious missionary organizations that pioneered development projects in the civilizational style turned the object of philanthropic work that they carried out toward integrating the principles of social emancipation and cultural autonomy. Since the 1990s, new guidelines and critical redefinitions have been incorporated into the global discourse of faith-based NGOs and religious organizations. In this new context, five main themes are observed: cultural diversity, human rights, ecology, integral human development,[12] and gender issues.

Examining a cosmology of development of the Argentine Gran Chaco built by the missionization process and the faith-based NGOs community work does not detract from the active role of indigenous women and men involved in these interdependent relations. Research on Protestant and Catholic missions has advanced the problematizing of the reciprocal effects of missionary and indigenous agencies and the creative adaptations of worldviews, leadership, and religious practices (Ceriani Cernadas y López 2017). Future research will require expanding the ethnographic scope to understand the social construction of religious languages of development to understand how community projects sponsored by religious institutions are incorporated into local indigenous contexts. Here it is necessary to be aware of the national and transnational sociopolitical articulations in the current definitions of "society," "culture," "human rights," "poverty," "environment," and "gender" as categories that have been decisive in the shift in religious development policies from the 1980s to the present. Anthropological research must address two symmetrical and inverse questions: How has the notion of development been represented and practiced by institutions and religion? How do actors of faith-based development projects interact with "beneficiary" populations? These issues cannot be raised in the abstract but should be explored in the context of concrete social, cultural, and economic processes.

Notes

1. The term *indigenista* refers to the conception that emerged in Latin American intellectual and political circles during the first decades of the twentieth century that indigenous populations constitute an object of protection subject to integration policies in the national economic and social process.

2. INCUPO, the Instituto de Cultura Popular, is a civil society organization founded in 1968 in the city of Reconquista, Santa Fe Province, under the auspices of the diocese of the northeast region. Since then, it has spread in Chaco, Corrientes, Santiago del Estero, Formosa, and north of Santa Fe, focusing on community development, agroecology, indigenous rights, and environmental activism.

3. FUNDAPAZ, the Fundación para el Desarrollo en Justicia y Paz, is a civil organization created in 1973 in Santa Fe Province for the purpose of accompanying and strengthening the sustainable rural work of peasant and indigenous communities of the Gran Chaco. As was INCUPO in 1968, the creation of FUNDAPAZ was sponsored by Bishop Juan José Iriarte of the Northeast diocese.

4. ENDEPA, the Equipo Nacional de Pastoral Aborigen, was founded in 1984 by the Argentine Episcopal Conference. This Catholic institution promoted from its beginnings a form of social work in indigenous communities from a non-proselytizing and ecumenical vision. Composed of priests, nuns and laity, it is organized into three regions, northwest, northeast, and south, under a National Coordination and an itinerant Headquarters.

5. "About Us," Misereor, https://www.misereor.org/about-us/.

6. The term "criollo" refers to the local population of the Argentine provinces. In addition, from the point of view of the indigenous peoples of the Gran Chaco, the category designates the "white" Argentine population as opposed to foreigners, who are generally known as "gringos."

7. On the historical vicissitudes and the Toba memoirs about the Emmanuel Mission between 1937 and 1951, see Ceriani Cernadas 2007, 2009, 2017; Citro 2009; Wright 2008.

8. "Ancients" refers to the forefathers, their ancestors.

9. National territories, unlike provinces, were areas that depended directly on central government power. In the 1950s the federalization process began, as with the provinces of Chaco in 1951 and of Formosa in 1955.

10. ASOCIANA, Fundación de Acompañamiento Social de la Iglesia Anglicana del Norte Argentino.

11. ISEDET, Instituto Superior Evangélico de Estudios Teológicos.

12. "Integral human development" was a paradigm proposed by the Catholic Church in 1967 that focused on the holistic dimension of human experience, in which the spiritual, the affective, the ethical, and the material engaged in the production of a renewed notion of a universal human family.

4

"They Only Know the Public Roads"

Enlhet Territoriality during the Colonization of Their Lands

HANNES KALISCH

> The Enlhet had many places in the Chaco . . . ; a large circle describes the Land of the Enlhet. Today we live within a very small circle in Campo Largo. Nevertheless, we maintain the memory of the places of our ancestors, because it is very important that the young be able to compare both circles, so that we don't think it is impossible to have more space than we have today. We want the youth to learn more of the Land of the Enlhet, so in that way they have a vision for the future; to . . . broaden . . . the possibilities that they have today.
>
> Simeón Negro, former leader of the Enlhet community of Campo Largo, 2012, in Kalisch 2018c, 186

With around 8,200 members, the Enlhet people are the largest group in the Enlhet-Enenlhet language family (Fabre 2005), which also includes the Enxet, Angaité, Sanapaná, Guaná and Toba-Enenlhet. Their traditional territory coincides approximately with the Mennonite colonies that began settling in the central Paraguayan Chaco in 1927.[1] The arrival of Mennonite immigrants and the Chaco War between Bolivia and Paraguay (1932–1935) signaled the abrupt onset of the colonial process in that part of the region. Within a few years, the living conditions and the ways in which the Enlhet related with their territory changed radically (Kalisch and Unruh 2014, 2018).

The Enlhet people have lost their lands almost completely, and their traditional territory now exists solely as a memory-image, albeit one that could translate into a struggle to reclaim the land. The idea of a territory of one's own may indeed survive the complete loss of the lands that constitute the territory, because a territory is more than land: it is a "space of relation"

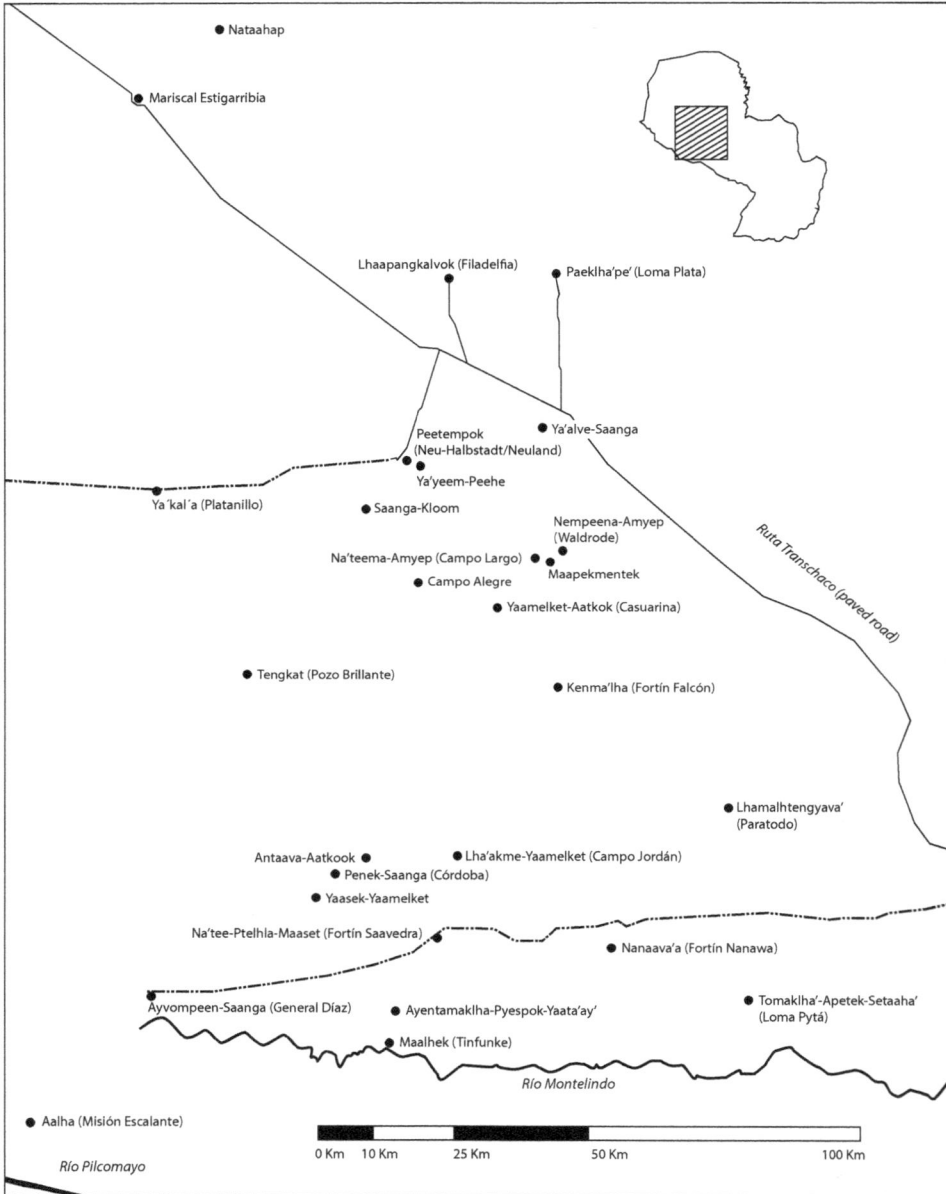

Map 4.1. Sites in Enlhet territory in Paraguay. Map by Hannes Kalisch, 2020.

with the world (García Hierro and Surrallés 2004, 22). Thus, Enlhet territory goes beyond its measurable, physical dimensions. It involves ideas and practices through which the indigenous society constructs relations with and within that space. Since Enlhet notions of territory are completely unknown outside their society,[2] it is almost inevitable that outsiders, when speaking of Enlhet territory, inadvertently impose external concepts and categories, thus interfering in communication between the Enlhet and actors from the surrounding society (Tytelman 2016, Viveiros de Castro 2004).

The Enlhet use the term *nengaoklha'* to refer to the geographic space with which they relate. In addition, elders use the term *nengeleyvomaklha'* ("the space in which we move"), which expresses the linguistic concept of a distributed movement and points in this way to a space of multiple movements. Though the two indigenous concepts can be understood as equivalents of the notion of territory, they do not imply a geographic, social, cultural, or political totality (Briones and Cairo 2015, 33). To reflect the difference between Enlhet concepts and the notion of territory, I additionally use the term "space" or "own space." Understood as a "web of relations and practices that conforms it" (Tytelman 2016, 17), I should point out that this notion of space should not be thought of as an abstract concept that can be separated from concrete places and regions.

Land, in the form of concrete places, is constitutive of the notion of "own space" in the Enlhet sense of "territory." *Mutatis mutandis*, certain "ways of seeing and inhabiting landscapes" (Anthias 2014, 9) repeat themselves in different spatial configurations (Pierce et al. 2011, 60). Henceforth, I use the term "territoriality" to refer to the *ideas* surrounding "own space" and to the social *practices* that underpin the construct of "own space"; that is, I understand "territory" as describing multiple, historically established articulations between the physical world, humans, and nonhuman beings (Barabas 2001, 16). This relational approach places the concept of territoriality in close proximity to processes of identification (Barabas 2004, 115; Spíndola Zago 2016, 48). At the same time, the approach allows us to address the notion of *perception of space* (Surrallés 2004). The notion of "perception" differs from that of "perspective" in that it highlights the idea of articulation, implying both the subject that observes and the substance of what is seen; one looks at something, and simultaneously one perceives it in such and such a way. We are thus reminded that ideas about space respond to a reality that is not the same for all (Ingold 2010).

Sousa Santos (2010) has noted that metropolitan societies take a similar perception of the environment as their baseline conviction that there exists only one world, or as Blaser (2009, 17) puts it, that "the environment is one reality 'out there.'" At the same time, such societies maintain that they are the ones that have the most adequate access to that reality (Kalisch 2018b, 204–208), while the perspectives of indigenous societies are classed as mere beliefs, "perhaps worthy of preservation as long as they did not claim their right to define reality" (Cadena 2010, 346). If, however, there is more than one world, then the idiosyncrasies of an indigenous society cannot be reduced to cultural metaphors about a unique world (Ingold 2010, 30), and different ways of accessing reality are not simply the product of epistemological differences (Blaser 2013, 21). Such idiosyncrasies point, rather, to the existence of realities that are "differently composed" (Kalisch 2018b, 210); they touch on the ontological axis.

If different cultures—above all, radically different cultures—inhabit different worlds, and if they refer with their specific categories to different realities, this raises the question of mutual commensurability and ultimately, the possibility of mutual communication (Blaser 2009, 15; Kalisch 2018b, 211). To talk about one culture in the ontological terms of another is at the very least problematic (Kalisch 2018b, 211–214), making the inclusion of Enlhet descriptions and reasoning a theoretical necessity for the understanding of their perspective. Such inclusion requires recognizing indigenous thinkers as subjects of a particular perspective, as protagonists of a particular tradition of perceiving the world. Furthermore, if we wish to talk of their world without from the very outset imposing our own categories, we need to recognize them as agents within our epistemic process in a way that allows us to be in dialogue with their ideas. This in turn implies recognizing them as authors and not simply as sources of information, even though their discourse is constructed differently from one's own. The Enlhet express themselves not with abstractions or formulas but with descriptions of concrete experiences that they put into circulation within their society (Kalisch 2018b, 219).

Here I reproduce the observations and reflections of one Enlhet thinker, Maangvayaam'ay', drawing on more than fifty hours' recordings of oral discourse spoken by him in Enlhet to his people from 2001 to 2018.[3] Maangvayaam'ay' was born around 1935 on the southwestern edge of Enlhet territory, in the area of the present-day town of Ávalos Sánchez. My choice of an elder as narrator responds to the focus of the present text on examining the changes in Enlhet territoriality caused by colonization; in it I do not examine in detail the younger generations' perceptions of their

Figure 4.1. Maangvayaam'ay', January 2020. Photo by Hannes Kalisch.

territory. Maangvayaam'ay' is chosen specifically because he treats the topic of Enlhet territoriality and its recent changes with particular clarity.[4] At the same time, his observations are representative of similar observations made by his contemporaries. It is for that reason that I occasionally complement his voice with that of other narrators who, like him, were settled in 1963 at the Campo Largo mission, named in Enlhet Na'teema-Amyep.[5]

*　*　*

In his narrative Maangvayaam'ay' highlights varied relational contexts, emphasizing articulation with other actors. In the first section, he describes the Enlhet practice of constructing their territory in a shared way with the Nivaclé through a cross-identification that makes Enlhet territoriality highly dynamic and renders the creation of interconnected territories possible.

From the Enlhet ontological perspective, the relational dimension is not limited to the human sphere but also includes nonhuman actors (Blaser 2009; Cadena 2010; Descola 2004; Viveiros de Castro 1998). In this regard, in the second section Maangvayaam'ay' looks at territoriality from the standpoint of the interaction between humans and invisible beings. In the third and final section, he describes the encounter with Mennonite colonists that culminated in his group's settlement at the mission in 1963. He makes clear how interference in the interaction between humans and invisible beings paved the way for Mennonite actions aimed at subordinating the Enlhet to colonist interests. As a result of that subjugation, Enlhet space was substantially and definitively reconfigured in geographic, environmental, economic, social, and relational terms. In the process, the basic traits of present-day Enlhet territoriality crystallized, as a territoriality characterized by a reduction not only in geographic terms but also in terms of the possibilities for articulation both among humans and between humans and nonhumans.

Mother Was Nivaclé, but She Married an Enlhet

Maangvayaam'ay' sketches the relations between Enlhet and Nivaclé in his region of origin, delimited by Tinfunke, Campo Jordán, and Córdoba. He describes dynamics that are no longer present, in a region that has been abandoned but which in his youth was the southwestern edge of the geographic space inhabited by the Enlhet. I speak of edge because there were no borders. Such a perspective from the edges is only one among many, but it offers a general comprehension of certain aspects of traditional Enlhet territoriality. Besides, dominant perspectives are put to the test on the margins and are, for that reason, particularly visible.

*　　*　　*

The father of Maangvayaam'ay', an Enlhet, was from Kenma'lha, where in December 1927 Paraguayans founded Fort Falcón (Joy 1992, 135). In his youth, he spent some time at the Nanaava'a (Nanawa) mission that Anglicans had founded in 1916 about fifty kilometers to the south; there the missionaries brought Enlhet, Maká, and Nivaclé from the region (Hunt 1932, 301). After marrying her, he joined the group of his Nivaclé wife, and Maangvayaam'ay' was born there.

> My mother was Nivaclé, but she married an Enlhet; she had two languages, Enlhet and Nivaclé. Her mother, my grandmother, was pure Nivaclé. I think she belonged to the people of Tengkat [Pozo Brillante]; she was a *kooyo'oklhelhma' sevhen* [Nivaclé of the open

savanna]. I too am *kooyoʼoklhelhmaʼ sevhen*. My grandmother didn't speak Enlhet. She understood it but spoke to me in Nivaclé. Hence, when I reached the age at which children start pronouncing words, I spoke in Nivaclé. There was a real possibility that I might never learn Enlhet.

Mother was Nivaclé, but Father was pure Enlhet. I learned both languages at once. My father knew Nivaclé; he didn't speak it well, but he understood perfectly when they spoke to him in Nivaclé. He spoke in Enlhet. Mother understood him and answered in Nivaclé. Sometimes she used Enlhet, which she also spoke. I learned two languages at once.

Maangvayaamʼayʼ describes an intense coexistence between Enlhet and Nivaclé that was typical of the entire western edge of Enlhet space, going from Nataahap in the region of Mariscal Estigarribia, through Yaʼkalʼa (Platanillo) and Tengkat, all the way to Maalhek (Tinfunke) and Tomaklhaʼ-Apetek-Setaahaʼ (Loma Pytá). Many present-day families in both groups still remember the kinship links between them.

When the water level dropped in Ayentamaklha-Pyespok-Yaataʼayʼ, we used to go to Maalhek to get fish, living there with Nivaclé. Maalhek was in Nivaclé space and was part of the region in which my mother moved. The Nivaclé also inhabited Penek-Saanga, a place named Córdoba by a Paraguayan, Lieutenant Mora, who had his ranch there. My mother used to live there with the Nivaclé. There were no Enlhet there, only Nivaclé; it was a Nivaclé settlement. The Enlhet lived to the east, in Antaava-Aatkook.

Maangvayaamʼayʼ identifies Antaava-Aatkook, an Enlhet settlement, as his place of origin. He thus defines himself as Enlhet, even though he had earlier stated that he is *koo* yoʼoklhelhma sevhen. This double identification operates simultaneously rather than describing a sequence in time. He says, for example, that only Nivaclé lived in Penek-Saanga, insinuating that when he lived there, he did so as a Nivaclé. This means he does not identify himself as Enlhet or Nivaclé because he speaks a certain language or because of his personal history or because he thinks he is one or the other. His place of residence allows him to identify in one way or another; the same person can be Enlhet in one place and Nivaclé in another. The possibility of having recourse to different modes of identification creates manners of belonging that can be activated or deactivated according to circumstances. At certain times, it is important to present oneself as an equal; at other times, it is important to differentiate oneself.

> The Nivaclé stayed in Maalhek, next to the river. They call the place Tenjoke', a name that Enlhet who understood Nivaclé must have translated into their language as Maalhek. We ate fish, *kamaata'* [Prochilodus lineatus], until we were full and then returned to Yaasek-Yaamelket, which the Nivaclé called Nukkachi and which is southwest of Penek-Saanga, known to the Nivaclé as Makok'jey. As to Antaava-Aatkook, I never heard a Nivaclé name for the place or for Lha'akme-Yaamelket, in the region of Campo Jordán. I think that they didn't have Nivaclé names. Nor did Na'tee-Ptelhla-Maaset [Fort Saavedra]. Ayentamaklha-Pyespok-Yaata'ay' was Enlhet as well, though some Nivaclé used to live there; we were together. I haven't heard a Nivaclé name for that place either.

Maangvayaam'ay' makes a clear distinction between Enlhet places and Nivaclé places. Such a distinction appears to contradict the practice of sharing the same space in a framework of intense and intimate coexistence. In reality, however, the distinction makes possible, through a practice of identification that finds support in local identities, an interaction that integrates such undeniable differences as are language and culture without producing any lines of separation. The description shared by Maangvayaam'ay' thus expresses a territoriality that is markedly different from that of colonial societies, which, on the basis of the assumption that a territory is a discrete unit counterposed to other territories, impose and affirm borders in order to exercise dominion (Bartolomé 2010, 17).

The absence of a clearly delimited ethnic boundary is compatible with the absence of centralized political units or, indeed, of a totalizing conception of the Enlhet people as a whole such as would support a view of Enlhet territory as a discrete, consolidated space. Instead, the Enlhet thought of their geographic space in terms of concrete social and linguistic experience. The region they shared with the Nivaclé constituted a geographic space belonging to a complex society comprising distinct social, cultural, and linguistic dynamics incompatible with the concept of superimposed territories. In keeping with the internal diversity of the society, its members activated or intensified different identity mechanisms, thereby creating varied possibilities for relations beyond the geographic and social space of the shared region. It is, then, a society interconnected with others. The potential for varied associations is reflected in the way relatives of Maangvayaam'ay' did not gather into a single homogeneous Nivaclé or Enlhet group during the changes after the Chaco War. Rather, for a variety of reasons, some adopted Nivaclé existence and others Enlhet existence, with the result that some died in a Nivaclé mission while others died in an Enlhet mission.

> Many people lived in Antaava-Aatkook. My Nivaclé grandmother was the elder sister of Kaymaap-Tes's father, who died here in Campo Largo as an Enlhet. Uncles of mine also lived in Antaava-Aatkook. One of them was So'khalheem, a Nivaclé who died in Campo Alegre as a Nivaclé. It was the Enlhet who called him So'khalheem; the Nivaclé called him Chu'qlayich. My uncles used to live in Antaava-Aatkook, but they also spent time in Penek-Saanga. They were part of our group in my childhood.

The idea of a territory as a discrete unit did not exist, and *nengeleyvomaklha'*, the space in which beings move, was not exclusive. These are among the reasons the Enlhet have not defended their space as a physical possession. On the contrary, at the time of their first contact with white people they acted according to a logic of sharing, even helping military explorers to find their way in the region (Kalisch 2018a, 149–150).

To this day, the Enlhet do not perceive their space and their society in terms of a totality such as would allow for an assembly of the people as a whole or support land claims. By the same token, since the concepts of territory and people are not familiar to the Enlhet, they do not come up in their internal discussions and reflections. Admittedly, leaders have had to appropriate those terms in order to articulate with the dominant society, and they use them in their struggle to secure more physical space. Their usage, however, entails two risks. First, insofar as the people do not use them in their internal discussions, the terms do not convince or move them to action. For that reason, the discourse of the leaders toward the outside world, their demand-discourse, finds little echo in the communicative processes of the people. Second, the usage of the terms restructures the reflective process, promoting a reconfiguration of indigenous territoriality along the lines of a colonial logic that, in addition to being reductionist, tends toward internal homogenization. It thus becomes another step toward subordinating indigenous concepts to hegemonic categories.

In the face of such dangers, it is essential that local practices such as those that have to do with forms of constituting oneself in and with space be understood in their own terms and not in terms of the dominant system (Cadena 2010; Viveiros de Castro 2004). In accompanying indigenous articulation with the white world, one needs to understand the indigenous perspective in depth, on the basis of its own categories. Only in that way is it possible to position oneself critically vis-à-vis competing perspectives.

*   *   *

After the Chaco War, the space in which Maangvayaam'ay' moved was slowly populated by criollos of Paraguayan or Argentine origin and scattered Mennonite colonists who settled around the strategic arid water sites of the Chaco, thereby interfering with traditional Enlhet movement within the region.[6] At the same time, the Mennonites were establishing colonies in the north and had a growing need for indigenous labor.

> The Mennonites didn't reach our region. However, when the news of their arrival spread, the Enlhet started visiting Paeklha'pe' [Loma Plata], Lhaapangkalvok [Filadelfia], and other settlements of theirs. We ourselves used to go only to the Loma Plata region. The Mennonites planted cotton, a lot of it, and the Enlhet worked the harvest. We liked working for them, as it enabled us to get cloth, pants, shirts, and blankets. We took those clothes to our region, and we used to dress up when we were with the Nivaclé, during a festivity, for instance. They would ask us for pieces of our clothing, which we shared with them. We went about as affluent people, and the Nivaclé would give us a knife in exchange for cloth.

Until approximately 1947, Maangvayaam'ay' and his parents traveled on foot along the military roads to the Loma Plata region, a distance of about 140 kilometers. There they would work for the Mennonites, visit the Enlhet of the area, and then return south.

> After the harvest, we used to return to my region and to where my mother stored the algarrobo [carob] meal. There we found a great variety of foods, including fish, *kamaata'* [*Prochilodus lineatus*]. We never experienced hunger in my area.

As the Loma Plata and Filadelfia colonies developed, Maangvayaam'ay' and his parents took longer to return home because the colonists, needing their labor, held them back. At a certain point in time, they decided that they would not be returning to Antaava-Aatkook, so the relator's father butchered all his goats. Thereafter, when they returned from the colonies, they stayed at Yaamelket-Aatkok (Casuarina), a place on their route to the south where an Argentine lived with his Enlhet wife in the company of an Enlhet group that had gathered around them. Over the course of several minor adjustments, the family began to reorient itself in relation to the external settlers, be they criollos or Mennonites.

The Enlhet continued to make decisions in a relatively free way, but they moved in a context of disquiet and anxiety. The wounds caused by the Chaco War and a smallpox epidemic (1932–1933) that together cost the lives of more than half the population were far from healing (Kalisch and Unruh 2018). Also, the rise in the number of external settlers was increasingly felt, generating centrifugal forces of expulsion in some areas and gravitational forces of attraction in others. Traditional Enlhet settlements dispersed, and new social units emerged in new physical spaces. Certain families from the Antaava-Aatkook region resettled in the area of Lhamal-htengyava', the future Paratodo colony, sixty kilometers to the east. Others, like Maangvayaam'ay' and his family, settled on the southern edge of the future Neuland colony seventy kilometers to the north. Those families would later live in Enlhet missions, while people and families of the same origin who followed Nivaclé dynamics would settle in a future Nivaclé mission.

There are no general patterns that explain the course of this reorientation. The multiplicity of dynamics that characterized the period, such as the contradictory processes of expulsion and attraction, meant that families of the same group underwent different sets of circumstances and resettled in a variety of separate contexts. One clear consequence is that the social space shared by the Enlhet and the Nivaclé has disappeared. Although kinship ties between families are still remembered and reaffirmed in the later generations, the loss of frequent interaction and with it, the loss of the daily construction of a shared social space has led to the two peoples becoming distanced, as is clearly reflected in the disappearance of the generalized bilingualism reported by Maangvayaam'ay'. It should be mentioned that the distancing of Enlhet and Nivaclé societies has not given rise to the Enlhet perceiving themselves as a social, political, and territorial totality.

The reconfiguration of physical and social space constitutes a basic premise of Enlhet life after the Chaco War.

Take Care of Them! Articulation with Nonhumans

Maangvayaam'ay' refers next to a second relational context, in which he focuses on observes human societies that share the world with societies of nonhuman beings (Blaser 2013; Cadena 2010). Like human societies, nonhuman societies inhabit particular geographic spaces. Some relate to specific sites, especially the people of the water sites, who live underground. Others occupy extensive regions, as did the Enlhet themselves, living in small settlements and moving constantly throughout the region.

As among human societies, there are a variety of invisible, nonhuman societies such as the *koonamyepaek* (those of the savanna), the *koonalhma'* (those of the bush), the *koonaasangaek* (those of the water sites), and the *yaavey*.[7] Their members enter into contact with humans and act on them in ways that are perceptible to all. However, only those with power, called *kelyoholhma'* (wise men) or *kelvaanyam'* (elders), can interact with the invisible people and mediate between them and human beings.

> I met the *koonamyepaek*. My *sekvanmongkama* [the soul of a living being] was among them.[8] I arrived at a large settlement of theirs in the west. They are people like ourselves, the Enlhet. . . . They live as the Enlhet [did], traveling not with the aim of reaching a certain location, but in order just to move within their region. . . .
>
> Another large western *koonamyepaek* settlement is that of short and stocky people with rounded bodies like the *yavayke'* [black widow spider], which is itself a person like ourselves. After once swallowing a *yavayke'*, I was taken by one of them to their place. . . .
>
> "*Lheep nak!* [It's you!]," they greeted me.
>
> "*Eehe, ko'o!* [Yes, it's me!]," I replied.
>
> "He's *engmook* [a relative, an ally]," explained my companion. "Take care of him."

Each of the invisible societies is characterized by a specific way of acting on the *nengvanmongkama*. Thus, when a member of a certain society takes a person's *akvanmongkama* to its place, its actions produce interferences that are visible in the person's body.

> The [angel-like] *yaame'enlhet-neeten* have numerous settlements. I have just returned from a *yaame'enlhet-neeten* village in the "Region of the Crying Women," located to the southwest, in *yo'oklhelhma'* [open savanna covered with algarrobo]. The resident *koonamyepaek*—

persons like ourselves, the Enlhet—abduct the souls of women. The abducted souls gather together at dusk and weep, hunched over their knees. At such times, a woman, in her real body, weeps miserably, overcome with deep sorrow.

The possibility that invisible beings impinge on human existence demands of the Enlhet that they constantly remember that they share the same space with those beings. It is dangerous to move without keeping the invisible inhabitants as *engmook* [relatives, allies]; conversely, it is beneficial to be in harmony with them. Real and potential encounters with invisible beings thus define the way the Enlhet situate themselves in geographic space. Another elder, Sekhay'-Pva', described the ways they related to humans. His narrative below is from excerpts of more than thirty hours of recordings of oral histories he shared in Enlhet with his people between 2006 and 2016.

A few years ago, in 2010, a small group of us visited the place that I am from. We moved calmly, and none of the *apkaoklha'* [those who are from there] caused us any harm, neither those of the bush nor those of the savanna, the *koonalhma'* and the *koonamyepaek*. They took care of us, and my companions killed *pomaap* [peccaries], and I myself killed a *popyet* [deer]. When other Enlhet went to the same area, however, they didn't kill anything. Those who are from there did not give them any prey, which is how, the Enlhet formerly used to say, they act with those whom they don't know. They discriminate between visitors whom they know, whom they treat well and to whom they make prey available, and those whom they don't know, whom they reject and may even harm. So, one has to talk to them:

"I have returned!" one has to say.

That's how it was when I returned after many years to Saanga-Kloom:

"Grandmother, I'm back!"

Later, when I went looking for *yelhem* [eel] in the lagoon, I found several large ones.

The invisible beings react to human activities and attitudes. At the same time, they relate to the physical space inhabited by the Enlhet. This combination of attributes is not without consequences, as the elder Kam'aatkok-Ketsek relates in one of her accounts from the more than seventy hours of recorded oral histories she shared in Enlhet with her people between 2002 and 2015:

> The great illness appeared, known to those who are no longer with us as *nengelyeetapaykam'* [smallpox, literally "We break apart"]. In their lifetime, our elders used to say that the Enlhet were numerous people in the past but that they were destroyed by an illness that appeared after the war on account of the soldiers. We Enlhet live beneath the *enlhet-neeten* [people above, angels], who were displeased that the criollos shot one another on our land. They abhorred such killing. So, as the blood of the soldiers rose, they demanded compensation from the owners of the land, who paid for it with smallpox. . . . The *Enlhet-neeten* brought the illness, incited by the killings among the criollos to act against those with whom they shared the region, the Enlhet. Since the Enlhet couldn't preempt the killings, another death befell them. (Kam'aatkok-Ketsek 2018)

From being potential *engmook* (relatives, allies), the invisible beings had turned against the Enlhet. From then on, every step the people took became dangerous, and their movements in their own space, in their *apkeleyvomaklha'* (the spaces in which they move), were increasingly problematic.[9] In the wake of the immense disturbances that befell them in the years after the Chaco War, the Enlhet's fatal rupture with their *apkeleyvomaklha'* could not be adequately healed. On the contrary, the Enlhet themselves felt that as their daily relations with specific places and their invisible inhabitants were curtailed, the latter's displeasure with them grew, and it became ever more dangerous for them to traverse the region. Thus reinforced, the rupture crystallized in the form of an inverted territoriality in which the familiar, friendly connotations of their own space gave way to a sense of diffuse but constant danger.

The disruption of the relations between Enlhet society, the invisible societies, and the geographic space that they shared constitutes a second premise of Enlhet life after the Chaco War.

They Decided to Tame Us

Here, Maangvayaam'ay' describes the massive changes that shaped the perception of space that is now dominant among the Enlhet people. The abandonment of Antaava-Aatkook in the south and the reorientation toward Yaamelket-Aatkok were already in progress in 1947 when colonists from Neuland founded villages in the Yaamelket-Aatkok area. Given that the immigrants were now directly populating the group's spaces, their *apkeleyvomaklha',* contact with the settlers acquired a different quality from that which it had been during visits to Menno Colony; relations with the colonists ceased being an option and became inevitable. The change combined with other impacts on the people's daily lives, the recent traumas of war and the smallpox epidemic, the rupture with invisible societies, the gradual colonization of Enlhet space by criollo settlers, the immigrants' increasing incorporation of the Enlhet as a labor force albeit as yet outside the latter's *apkeleyvomaklha',* the group's progressive abandonment of their own space, and the process of social reconfiguration. The underlying pressures, uncertainties, and fears that accompanied those experiences for the Enlhet, in addition to the purposeful actions of the Mennonite immigrants aimed at channeling "the indigenous question" in their favor, explain how the settlers managed, in only fifteen years, to reduce the Enlhet groups in the region (Kalisch 2018c).[10] In 1963 Mennonite immigrants founded the Campo Largo mission, where they settled all the Enlhet living within their colony. Maangvayaam'ay' recounts the interactions:

At that time we lived according to our own mores. If someone fell sick, another would heal him with his song, and he would be truly healed. The elders took care of us; the wise men saved us from ailment. . . . The elders also acted on Mennonites who mistreated our people. For that reason, the colonists decided to tame us; they feared that the elders would finish them off. At first, we weren't Christians. We were like wild people although in reality, we were not wild; we are and always have been Enlhet. It was under those circumstances that the missionary appeared. . . . On Sundays, we used to visit the houses of the Mennonites. We would get a bit of dry bread or some sorghum flour. . . . When the woman of the household brought it out, she opened the door very slightly and stretched out her arm to give it to us. We disgusted her. That must have been another reason why the Mennonites, tired of our visits, decided to tame us, in order that we stop asking them for food.

We lived near the Mennonite houses in Nempeena-Amyep, on the edge of the small swath of forest at the far end of their field. They had fenced off their field, but the rest of the land remained open and their cows moved freely on it. We lived on the other side of the fence until we were approached by Haako'-Pya'yeem, a Mennonite from Nempeena-Amyep:

"Do you want to hear the word of God?"

From then on we lived in Haako'-Pya'yeem's yard; no longer did we stay on the other side of the fence. We received *vaetka'hak* [paper, written documents], and he set up a hospital, in which his wife worked as a nurse. His teaching was designed to domesticate us; his actions made us tame. Yes, that's it, he rendered us harmless. From then on, the Enlhet would not react fiercely when a Mennonite berated them. They had become friends of the colonists or, as we say, their *engmook*. . . . Today, the Enlhet are passive and don't offer resistance. They are Christians; they have been tamed. We are Christian like the Mennonites.

The colonists faced a dilemma; their rejection of the Enlhet clashed with their dire need for labor (Kalisch and Unruh 2014, 536–537). The dilemma was reflected in a discussion within the Mennonite community in the early 1960s about whether it was more convenient to settle the indigenous people far from the colonies or to keep them nearby (Kalisch and Unruh 2014, 551–554). In the end, the indigenous settlements were set up on the edges of the colonies, as Maangvayaam'ay' describes:

The Mennonites proceeded to tame the Enlhet. They also decided to look for ways for us to acquire our own possessions. To that end, they settled us on a plot of our own, at Maapekmentek.

"You will no longer work for the Mennonites," they said. "Plant cotton and you will have your own money."

The Mennonites disliked the Enlhet's mobility because they needed us as a labor force. They planted cotton, sweet potatoes, corn, sorghum, peanuts, and they needed us to weed their plots. They decided to look for ways to have us stay in one place, with our own possessions. That is why they settled us on the plot, because in that way it would be easier for them to find people to work for them. It would be part of their taming us.

Maangvayaam'ay' had staked out certain milestones in the process of "taming" the Enlhet. With their acceptance of the Mennonites' attempts at proselytism, the Enlhet imagined themselves to be part of the same social fabric as the colonists, sharing a project of coexistence; no longer on the other side of the fence, they lived in the missionary's yard, received medical attention, and gained access to *vaetka'hak*, books and documents. By being "Christian like the Mennonites," they assumed that the latter became their friends, their allies, their relatives, even. But Maangvayaam'ay' was aware that such apparent inclusion was based on a lie; the colonists argued that once settled, it wouldn't be necessary for the Enlhet to work for them. In reality, however, they were settled in order to provide the Mennonites with a workforce. Their taming, therefore, had clear benefits for the Mennonites; the Enlhet ceased to be feared and even became manageable and controllable. They could be included as functional to the immigrants' system, not as equals, but subordinated to the latter's economic aspirations. Furthermore, by limiting the Enlhet's freedom of movement, colonist interventions imposed a reconfiguration of Enlhet territoriality that mainly obeys alien principles and interests.

*   *   *

Maangvayaam'ay' presents a clear analysis: the Mennonites' taming of the Enlhet was motivated by the colonists' fear of them, by the discomfort and disgust that they felt in the Enlhet's presence, and by the need for labor. The procedure consisted of missionary teaching, in the feigned inclusion of the Enlhet and their sedentarization and in the attempt to destroy their practice of sharing. The Mennonite solution to their dilemma of needing and at the same time rejecting the Enlhet was to reduce them by taming and isolating them. By such means, it was the Enlhet's possibilities of agency in relation to the colonists that were reduced, as the colonists increasingly decided for them. Maangvayaam'ay' was well aware that the supposed inclusion of the Enlhet, part of the strategy to tame them, had to be complemented by their subsequent isolation.

> After a few years at Maapekmentek, a message arrived from Peetem-pok [Neu-Halbstadt, the center of Neuland Colony]:
> "The people of Ya'yeem-Peehe [on the outskirts of Neu-Halbstadt] are going to join you."
> The Mennonites disliked there being Enlhet living in Ya'yeem-Peehe, a place close to their own houses. Such must have been their reasoning. . . . It wasn't the Enlhet of Ya'yeem-Peehe who were looking for somewhere to live. In reality, they didn't want to leave where they were; they wanted to stay in the region they were from. However, the words of the Mennonite leader indicated otherwise.

Known as a "mission" on the outskirts of Neu-Halbstadt, Ya'yeem-Peehe was a place where the colonists initially settled the Enlhet from the surrounding area. Maapekmentek, approximately thirty kilometers from Ya'yeem-Peehe, was likewise a "mission." Therefore, the residents' unwillingness to leave Ya'yeem-Peehe, which went unheeded, was not motivated by a rejection of being geographically reduced to a mission; rather, it was based on a reluctance to abandon the Neu-Halbstadt region. Indeed, their reduction, or confinement, was not immediately apparent to the Enlhet. In those days, they could still move in a relatively free way outside the missions. They could visit their places of origin, and they had access to their traditional resources. At the same time, they received material support from the Mennonites, which strengthened their illusion of having entered upon a shared project of life with them. They soon realized, however, that geographic reduction went together with the suppression of their own practices and symbols:

> Haako'-Pya'yeem disliked it when the wise men cured with their songs. He forbade it. . . . Nor did he like it when elders smoked tobacco. He took away their pipe and threw it on the fire. The elders offered no resistance; they said nothing.

The repression Maangvayaam'ay' mentions in reference to the wise men goes beyond the domain of practices and symbols. It implies the negation and suppression of the Enlhet ontological system, in which nonhumans, the invisibles, were gradually made to disappear. In contrast to their geographic reduction, the violence of that repression and suppression was clearly visible to the Enlhet. They saw the colonization of the spaces in which they moved, their *apkeleyvomaklha'*, as primarily a struggle in the domain of practices, symbols, and words. For that reason, their acceptance of the aggressions of the missionary without resistance, that is, without defending themselves or withdrawing from the mission because they were now Christians, a tame people, indicates that they had accepted that life there had its own rules, that it was a life in a world belonging to others. Equally, the acceptance of the missionary as the authority who directs the conversion process and shows the path of life evinces a subjection to the society that sent him. The mission thus embodies a space of defeat that Maangvayaam'ay' acknowledges:

> The elders stopped working, and the wise men's activities went into abeyance. My father used to comment that when he converted, he lost his power. His powers dispersed, and he could no longer heal and protect his people. He was aware that that would happen, but he converted nevertheless. The missionary insisted greatly on him doing so.

"I have lost my power; I no longer have light," the elders used to say when they converted.

"I have nothing left," said my father. "No longer can I save my people from their suffering."

Concomitantly, the parallel phenomenon of mass baptisms that occurred in the late 1950s symbolized surrender from the Enlhet's perspective (Kalisch 2018a; Kalisch and Unruh 2014).

*   *   *

Sekhay'-Pva' recalls these changes with regard to his people's current situation:

We used to relocate frequently. . . . In order to satisfy our constant desire for bush meat, our occupation was to find it. Later, however, our space was cut up by Mennonite fences. We couldn't cross the fences because we already used horse-drawn buggies, and we only had the sides of the roads on which to spend the night. In due course, as the number of vehicles rose, the Mennonites pointed out to us that we were not to stay by the side of the road.

We stopped looking toward our *nengeleyvomaklha'* [the spaces in which we move], as our names were registered in the mission. We could still today return, but no, we can't. Everything is fenced off, and we have forgotten our places. The young don't know about them.

We used to move at ease and we lived well, with nothing to fear. The Enlhet walked the savanna and the bush, and when they met another person, they knew who it was. Today it is different. Today we move with fear; we fear encountering dangerous people, Paraguayans or Mennonites, who might kill us. Our families frequently warn us against going out alone; they exhort us not to go far, though, in reality, the Enlhet no longer have much space in which to move. All that is left for us are the public roads. Access to the rest is forbidden.

The young no longer know the bush. They only know the roads. For that reason, when they wake up they think of the things they see on the road. They think of motorcycles. They think of alcohol, of money, of many things. That makes them anxious and deprives them of tranquility. . . . They no longer accept our own bush food; they have grown accustomed to the food of the Paraguayans.

The world before subjugation had its dangers and conflicts, but it allowed for agency and for articulation with other social actors. Nevertheless, along with the loss of *apkeleyvomaklha'* came the violence that is characteristic of dispossession, subjugation, and exclusion. With the violence, the world around the *comunidad* (community), the term that has substituted "mission," is not only dangerous but also full of aggressions. It has become a hostile world. The Enlhet have lost the possibility of constructing amicable relations with the invisible cohabitants of their territory. At the same time, they fear the human owners of the land, be they Mennonite or Paraguayan, who discriminate against them and even abuse them (Kalisch 2018a, 154–155). The possibility of learning on the basis of their own agency has been replaced by an anxiety that spells dependence on external agency (Kalisch 2018b). Subjugation has led to the Enlhet's becoming outsiders in their own land. With such an imbalance, the conditions for *el buen convivir* (peaceful coexistence) are denied them, and tranquility is put beyond their reach (Kalisch 2011). Maangvayaam'ay' put it in these words:

> Insofar as the present is concerned, it's true that there is food in the garden plot. But the sweet potatoes take a long time to ripen, as do the watermelons and the squash. In order to get food, therefore, we need to work for the Mennonites. In the face of such difficulties, the Enlhet were happy when they received a *vaetka'hak* [document] called *tetolo* [community land title, from the Spanish *título*]. We recovered our tranquility when we received that document. We live without worrisome news. God gave us a piece of land because we trusted the Mennonite leaders when they proposed that we accept the word of God. There's no doubt that with the word of God, one avoids problems. However, today's youth confront many problems, and I cannot help thinking that they won't live well.

Maangvayaam'ay' expresses the hope, common in present-day Enlhet society, that the tensions and contradictions that they experience will be eliminated by their embracing the central emblems of the white world: the word of God as a symbol of their relations with Mennonite society and the community land title as a symbol of their relations with the Paraguayan state and society. With the land title, says Maangvayaam'ay', "we recovered our tranquility"; with the word of God, "we avoid problems" in a world dominated by its exponents. Nevertheless, he worries that in reality, the young "won't live well." The tranquility of which he speaks, then, doesn't refer to the *sas nengleyvaam* (*buen vivir*, good life) associated with an autonomous existence in which it was unnecessary to sell one's labor in order to obtain food. It refers rather to a new perception of space, in which the *comunidad*—a social, political, and economic construct with which the colonists undertake to reduce the Enlhet—presents itself as a safe haven in a world that exudes a sense of diffuse but constant danger, a place to which the people are exiled in the midst of their own territory (Kalisch and Unruh 2014, 262).

*　*　*

The image of the safe haven is ambivalent in that it combines the notions of reduction and protection. It is simultaneously a space of subjection and one in which the Enlhet actively shape their lives. It stands for manifest exclusion and at the same time represents the space from which the Enlhet forge links with the outside world, a world they are obliged to relate to but they also wish to relate to. It is the embodiment of the systemic imbalance that was imposed and consolidated in the lifetime of Maangvayaam'ay' by nontraditional actors and by means of an incremental process of dispossession and exclusion. The Enlhet, then, have had and still have to situate and redefine themselves in the face of realities imposed, commanded, and manipulated by new actors. The space occupied by those new actors and the control they exercise make their opportunities for agency much ampler than those of the Enlhet. The two circles to which the Enlhet leader Simeón Negro refers in the epigraph pertain not only to the geographic dimension but also to the opportunity for agency. Maangvayaam'ay' describes the process that took them from the large circle to the small one. The shrunken circle circumscribes a situation in which the Enlhet struggle to maintain a life and lifestyle of their own. It is a complex struggle that continues despite all its ambivalences. Simeón Negro stresses that the words of the elders are essential to the furtherance of that struggle.

*　*　*

Besides being geographically restricted, the *comunidad*'s safe haven presupposes compact coexistence and loss of opportunities for agency. Additionally, it conceals the ontological predicates relating to a reality that, as the Enlhet know well, impinges on their being. All know that they are surrounded by invisible beings, but the younger generations have lost many of the tools with which to relate to those beings. With the drastic reduction of potential experiences and of the communicative processes through which society constantly reconstituted itself in all of its aspects, the possibilities for interacting with their own reality have diminished, as the knowledge required to read that reality has been hidden. As a result, people observe phenomena that they are unable to interpret; they fail to see things that they should be able to discern, and they think they see phenomena that are not really there. In short, the phenomenological world itself ceases to be coherent, and the Enlhet are overwhelmed by it.

The feeling of being exposed to a world that can neither be read nor controlled raises a fear that echoes throughout Enlhet existence. Correlatively, the perception of the *comunidad* as a safe haven is constantly reaffirmed. Today, people are not in favor of the young marrying into other Enlhet *comunidades*, whereas formerly one's partner could speak a different language. Trips into the bush are avoided for fear of animals and invisible beings, whereas formerly the people coexisted with the bush and with the invisible beings. There is even fear of moving alone on public roads. New ideas have arisen about space and about the Enlhet's position within it, where territoriality has been reworked on the basis of reduction and marginality. It is a territoriality of exclusion, a territoriality without territory. At best, the territory has become a network of isolated *comunidades*.

The reworking of Enlhet territoriality—the inversion of their territoriality—has an impact on the collective imagination, and emotional ties with a space of their own relate only to the marginal refuges that remain. Such ties go hand-in-hand with new loyalties that are functional to the interests of those who profit from the situation and convert the fact of "reduction" into a tacitly accepted solution.

Closures and Openings

I have shown an Enlhet perspective on their *apkeleyvomaklha'*—the spaces in which they moved—that predates the extensive colonization of the region. Those *apkeleyvomaklha'* do not comprise a discrete totality, but consist rather of interconnected spaces that are created through complex practices of cross-identification. They may even be inhabited by members of different ethnic groups, without there being any grounds for interpreting the ethnic diversity in terms of superimposed territories. Despite the enormous changes that have taken place over the past few decades, the Enlhet's nontotalizing perspective with regard to their own space has persevered, with the limitations and potentialities that go with it. That perspective makes the struggle for land rights difficult as a people, but it facilitates the organic inclusion of other indigenous societies in a new social fabric present within traditional Enlhet territory.

Enlhet society also shares its territory with invisible societies whose abodes form part of Enlhet oral cartography. Any infringement of the balance between humans, or of that between humans and nonhumans, angers the invisible beings and jeopardizes the physical, psychological, and social integrity of human society. It was therefore inevitable that the invisible beings should have reacted against the Chaco War. Their reaction came in the form of a smallpox epidemic that in addition to decimating the Enlhet population instilled in the people a fear of circulating on their traditional lands. Such a rupture between the Enlhet and their *apkeleyvomaklha'* facilitated the occupation of the region by colonist immigrants and the reduction of the Enlhet, without great resistance, into missionary settlements. Geographical reduction was concomitant with the denial and suppression of Enlhet ontology. With few exceptions, the people have lost access not only to their physical territory but also to the places peopled by nonhumans; the mission therefore defines a territoriality that is, in a double sense, without a territory. What is more, the Enlhet, dispossessed of the opportunities for agency that are essential to the construction of their own space, reinterpret such reduction as the solution to the pressures to which they are subjected.

*   *   *

The use of space has always to be negotiated and renegotiated; territoriality itself is linked with an identity process in continuous flux. Enlhet perception of space today reflects the personal and ethnic histories that have been developing in the context of three or four generations of reduction, the perpetuation of which is, like its inception, the product of intense pressure. They have redefined their territoriality, or, better said, they have had to redefine their territoriality in the face of a colonial logic that is angled toward the acceptance and reproduction of systemic imbalance and exclusion. The resulting inversion of a territoriality that was inclusive and interconnected with other societies is highly functional to the colonists' purpose of occupying Enlhet land and keeping it under their dominion. Their inverted sense of territoriality led to the Enlhet's abandoning of their territory; it also silences potential land claims.

As long as the Enlhet continue to understand reduction as a solution—their means of overcoming the pressures they suffer—it will be difficult for them to rethink themselves in a way that includes their own traditional categories, still tacitly upheld in their daily life. The continued relevance of those categories makes it essential for the Enlhet to embrace them when they negotiate the future, even if only, ultimately, to put them aside. Under such a constellation of circumstances, the importance of the memory of which the Enlhet leader Simeón Negro speaks is clear with regard, for instance, to the narratives of the elders. Both male and female elders speak of a world that is radically different from the present-day world, one that is, moreover, historically approved. Their narratives invoke many categories connected with present-day daily life, which is full of reminiscences from the past. As such, they have an invaluable potential as tools with which to rebuild life on the basis of an agency that reverts the condition of being reduced without promoting the glorification of the past.

As Maangvayaam'ay' makes clear, Mennonite immigrants suppressed Enlhet elders possessed of the power to relate with invisible beings. He describes their actions not in terms of a religious or symbolic conflict but as a political act; the colonists eliminated their opponents because they feared them. In so doing, the Mennonite immigrants assailed the Enlhet practice of keeping the balance among humans through complex interactions with invisible beings, a practice that in itself is of political significance. The inclusion of invisible beings as actors goes beyond the limits of what is normally thought of as the domain of politics. Nevertheless, rather than a negotiation of power, politics comes to be understood in the Enlhet perspective as a relationship that articulates conflicts between worlds (Cadena 2010, 360; Kalisch 2018b, 180–182). Acceptance of such a framework for political negotiation would be a step on the part of external actors toward conferring opportunities for agency on Enlhet society, allowing it to work with and build on its own disempowered but ever-present potential.

Acknowledgments

I thank Paola Canova, Mercedes Biocca, Silvia Hirsch, and Rodrigo Villagra Carron for their comments on an earlier version of this chapter. I further wish to thank Andrés Pablo Salanova for translating the chapter from Spanish into English. I have carried out the compilation and editing of accounts by Enlhet elders in their language over the past two decades in close collaboration with Ernesto Unruh, an Enlhet in Ya'alve-Saanga.

Notes

1. Three different groups of Mennonite immigrants arrived from Canada and Russia, speaking a language that belongs to the German linguistic family. Between 1927 and 1947, they founded three colonies: Menno, Fernheim, and Neuland, with their main urban centers being Loma Plata, Filadelfia, and Neu-Halbstadt, respectively. They soon undertook to convert the Enlhet to their religion and assign them a place within their colonist project. In addition to the Mennonites, the Enlhet had contact with criollos of Paraguayan or Argentine origin who gradually populated their territory in small family groups after the Chaco War. As the Mennonite colonies expanded, the criollo settlers had to abandon the spaces they had recently occupied. The Nivaclé, an indigenous people belonging to the Mataco-Mataguayo language family, shared with the Enlhet a large swath of land on the western edge of the latter's territory.

2. The literature on the Enlhet is extremely scarce (Fabre 2005), which partly explains the widespread lack of knowledge of their society. Important publications exist about other peoples of the Enlhet-Enenlhet family; these include Kidd 1999 b about the Enxet, and Glauser 2019, Leake 1998, and Villagra Carron 2010 about the Angaité.

3. The quotations in this chapter are extracts from the unpublished transcription of those recordings. The oral narratives by Maangvayaam'ay' are partly published in the Biblioteca de la Memoria Hablada, available at https://enlhet.org/audio.html.

4. Given limitations of space, the focus on a single voice allows for a much more detailed account of historical processes than would have been possible through an exhaustive presentation of the various sources that we have recorded over two decades.

5. Campo Largo is one of the Mennonite missions installed to settle and evangelize the Enlhet (Kalisch and Unruh 2014). A note is required here on Enlhet toponyms. Many of these lack an equivalent on criollo and Mennonite maps and cannot be translated. However, in the cases where such equivalents exist for colonist societies, they are cited within brackets in the text. Map 4.1 indicates the relative positions of all locations mentioned in this chapter.

6. The term "criollo" is used here to refer to a person from the western part of Paraguay who speaks Guaraní and Spanish or a person from Formosa in Argentina who speaks Spanish.

7. *Yaavey* is the name of a particular category of invisible being and as such, cannot be translated.

8. The term *nengvanmongkama* is qualified by a possessive prefix that varies according to the grammatical person of the possessor; thus it appears in different forms throughout the chapter.

9. The term *nengeleyvomaklha'* is another variant term as explained in note 8.

10. At the time, the Paraguayan state was entirely absent from the central Paraguayan Chaco. Only after the end of the Stroessner dictatorship in 1989 did state institutions begin to be established in the area of the Mennonite colonies.

5

Death Ritual as Ethnopoeisis

A Farewell to an Angaité Shaman

RODRIGO VILLAGRA CARRON

On a hot December day in 2015, Agapito Navarro, an Angaité shaman and friend of mine, passed away in a public hospital in Asunción. A couple of months after his death, following his burial, a sort of improvised ritual was organized in his community. The ritual constituted ethnopoeisis, a phenomenon related to the ever-changing nature of ethnonyms; the ethnonyms visibilize characteristic social, linguistic, and ethnic reconfigurations of indigenous peoples of the Gran Chaco.

I understand ethnopoeisis as the somehow conscious process of self-ascription of a given ethnic group, influenced by historical phenomena such as migrations, contact, and colonization that have impinged upon the group's sociopolitical reconfiguration. Among the indigenous peoples of Chaco, such reconfiguration occurs through defined although variable elements of transformations such as charismatic leadership; linguistic permeability; diacritical cultural, mythical, and ritual traits; and kinship alliances. Thus, ethnopoeisis contrasts the way ethnonyms and rituals have been externally ascribed in the Chaco, as indexes of ethnic and cultural identities that are categorically reproduced throughout time as separated and bounded units. In today's Paraguay, to be a distinct indigenous group requires possession of an equally distinct set of cultural traits such as a specific language that distinguishes one group from another, myths, material culture, and so on. The Angaité have attempted to conform to such external and categorically applied criteria while retaining some of their own aspects and creating and incorporating external elements and transforming them. In this way, Angaité rituals are the result of their complex ethnogenesis and a constant and concrete interaction with diverse indigenous and nonindigenous groups in a specific moment in time.

The Angaité are part of the Enlhet-Enenlhet linguistic family also formed by five other indigenous groups with distinct but closely related languages: Enxet, Enlhet, Sanapaná, Enenlhet, and Guaná (Kalisch and Unruh 2003). A seventh group could eventually be added, the Maskoy of Riacho Mosquito, but they represent a particular case of ethnogenesis. The Enlhet-Enenlhet inhabited the Central Chaco and the northern and mid regions of the lower Paraguayan Chaco at the time of colonization by the nation-state, about 1880, when the Angaité had recently emerged as a distinctive ethnic group.

I base this analysis on both ethnographic and ethnohistorical materials I collected intensively from 2004 to 2007 and afterward in specific events and encounters as well as on further research until 2019. I refer to the colonization of the Paraguayan Chaco and the events that have impinged adversely upon Angaité's lives such as the impact of capitalism and globalization and the territorial dispossession and subsequent environmental and social impoverishment (Bello M. and Aylwin O. 2008). The death ritual of Agapito offers an ethnographic case with apparently incongruent elements that illustrates nonetheless my argument. In an analysis of the ethnohistorical record, the ethnographic cartographies of the Chaco reveal dialectical transformations subjacent to the rebellious variation of ethnonyms and languages throughout the history of the Chaco. And by resorting to classic and new anthropological perspectives on death, ritual, and shamanism, Agapito's death is seen as a manifestation of the Angaité's ethnopoeisis.

A Bit More Than One Hundred Years of Solitude

The Spanish colonized the eastern territory between the Paraguay and Paraná Rivers that were inhabited mostly by Guaraní peoples during the first half of the sixteenth century. However, for various reasons, the indigenous peoples of the Paraguayan Chaco remained politically autonomous in their territories until the late nineteenth century. Nevertheless, the newly independent Paraguayan state assumed de jure proprietorship of the Chaco by means of a decree issued by the dictator Rodríguez de Francia in 1825 (Miranda, cited in Kidd 1992, 57). After the War of the Triple Alliance (1865–1870) and in order to pay off its debts, in 1885–1887 Paraguay sold off most of its nominally public lands in the Chaco and the eastern region (Casaccia and Vázquez 1986). Most of the territory occupied by the Angaité was bought by the Argentinean company Rosarina. At that time, the encompassing ethnonym was solely known and used along the Paraguay River, and the Angaité precolonial groups distinguished themselves from each other by certain labels such as the Kovalhok, "those who come from the marshes" (sometimes written Koalhvok); the Konhongnava, "those who come from the quebracho blanco tree (*Aspidoperma quebracho blanco*) area"; the Koeteves, "those who come from the black algarrobo tree (*Prosopis nigra*) area" (Villagra Carron 2010, 43, 182). Such labels could be or not be recognized as self-ascribed and could designate people who shared a geographical space but who had different, however related, ethnic and linguistic backgrounds. Thus, some names could refer to the multifarious inhabitants of a common geographic area, such the Koonaava'atsam, "those from the Paraguay River," and Koonalhma or Chanalhma (the prefix *ko/koo/cha/chaa* varies according to the Enlhet-Enenlhet language), "those from the forest" (Kalisch and Unruh 2003, 15), or Chanameshma in Branislava Susnik's writing (1978, 110).

In 1907 the Rosarina company founded the town of Puerto Pinasco on the west bank of the River Paraguay. A few years later, about 1918, the International Product Corporation (IPC), a US quebracho colorado (*Schinopsis balansae*) tannin and lumber extracting company, bought this territory of nearly one million hectares from the river to the west. The IPC established two lines of railways, lumber camps, and cattle ranches, reaching and encroaching on indigenous villages along the way. The indigenous peoples of the area were forced to limit their foraging and hunting activities as well as social and cyclical mobility within their territory; subsequently they were obliged to increasingly depend on wage labor for IPC. The Chaco War between Paraguay and Bolivia (1932–1935) caused further migration of the western Angaité villages toward the Paraguay River. Some indigenous people acted as guides and troops for the Paraguayan army (Villagra Carron 2008), which even carried out massacres on entire villages as punishment for allegedly stealing cattle from IPC (J. Sanderson 1941). All these factors disciplined, concentrated, and reduced the Angaité population (Delporte 1998; Villagra Carron 2010, 224–231).

Alongside the IPC and the military, Anglican missionaries also had an impact on the Angaité. They founded three main missions and an outpost on Angaité territory: Yave Sage, 1914–1920 (Farrow 1914, 146); Laguna Rey, 1928–1929 (A. Sanderson 1929); Campo Flores or Maskoykaha, 1930–1946 (W. Sanderson 1930, 127); and the outpost Xakmok Kásek, 1939 to unknown year (Webb 1939, 87). The Anglican missions and outpost did not last as long as their counterparts among the Enxet. The proselytism of the missionaries declined over the years, and most of the missions were abandoned after World War II. However, the missionary work of the Anglican Church continued. In 1978 the Anglicans carried out a census that registered numerous Angaité, Enxet, and Sanapaná families and individuals who suffered labor exploitation and poverty on the *estancias* (ranches) in the lower Chaco region (Brunn, Chase Sardi, and Enciso 1990, 66). To alleviate their predicaments, Anglicans began the program La Herencia, which among other actions entailed purchasing private land and resettling families on those lands, where they were expected to become farmers. In 1983 the Anglican Church bought 22,520 hectares known as Colonia La Patria mostly for Angaité but also for Sanapaná and Enxet families who had been working and living on the IPC's or neighboring ranches. Nonetheless, the missionaries' expectations and productive endeavors did not turn out very successfully at La Patria for several reasons. From the 1990s onward and with the advent of democracy, after the demise in 1989 of Stroessner's dictatorship, the Angaité joined other Enxet and Sanapaná leaders and communities in a land restitution campaign requesting more than 160,000 hectares to the Paraguayan state (Kidd 1995). Initially the land claims received legal assistance from the Anglican Church and from 1994 to the present the political and legal support of Tierraviva, a nongovernmental organization (NGO). The Angaité now live on relatively small portions of land, titled to eight geographically disperse communities, totaling 50,185 hectares (Paraguay, DGEEC 2015, 204–252). These communities are subdivided into several villages each and organized legally and politically under the authority of elected leaders.

Most of the Angaité men from these communities work as wage laborers on neighboring or faraway cattle ranches (Bedoya Silva-Santiesteban and Bedoya Garland 2005; Delporte 1998). There, the laborers and their visiting relatives also continue to hunt, gather, and fish with the permission of the *patrones* in the remaining forests that have not been cleared for raising livestock (Glauser 2019, 91–130; Leake 1998). Sometimes, they do these subsistence activities clandestinely outside their lands at their own risk. Since the early 2000s, the Angaité have received more assistance from other NGOs and state programs such as for housing and drinking-water infrastructure, elementary school education, health care, small-scale agriculture, conditional cash transfers, and pensions.

Anglican involvement has been irregular among the Angaité since the closure of La Herencia program about 1993, and other Christian denominations, Mennonite and Pentecostal, have been disputing for followers among La Patria's villages for two decades. The expansion of Christian denominations creates internal differentiations, but more importantly it causes tensions between those who identify as *cultureros* (culture adherents) versus the *evangelios* (gospel adherents). The *cultureros* are reputed to follow shamanic practices and mainly the traditional dance called *choqueo* in Guaraní and Spanish and *weigke néten* in Enxet (Bonifacio 2009; Villagra Carron 2011, Kalisch 2012). The *evangelios* are those who attend Christian services and receive social assistance as acolytes (Glauser 2019, 185–187). The *choqueo* begins with a main drummer and singer who has some shamanic training. Standing in the center of an open area, he starts drumming and singing as an initial round of men holding each other by the waist dance around him echoing his chant, and old and young women may join the male round afterward, following innumerable rounds till the dance is over (Villagra Carron 2010, 325). One should bear in mind that Christianity and shamanism have been expressed in alternate but also intertwined ways throughout time in the Gran Chaco as complex, transformational, and relational processes, described by many authors (Kidd 1999a, Miller 1975, Tola 2012, Villagra Carron 2010, Wright 2008).

Angaité have been referred to as one of the most culturally assimilated indigenous peoples in Paraguay, as a result of their participation in wage labor exploitation and cultural subordination while working for the tannin companies and *estancias* (Brunn, Chase Sardi, and Enciso 1990, 66). In fact, the Paraguayan state considers language the principal marker for ethnic classification; the Ministry of Linguistic Policies (Secretaría de Políticas Lingüísticas) reports that, according to the 2012 national census, a shift from the Angaité language to Paraguayan Guaraní resulted in only 235 of 5,992 Angaité speaking their native language (Ávalos et al. 2018, 16). In order to reverse the loss, several NGOs and the ministry have supported cultural revitalization programs for language use and ritual practices in La Patria in recent decades. Their efforts have led to an increase in printed materials (Franco and Imaz 2006) and audiovisual productions (Elizeche 2007) in Angaité language, including a FM community radio station in the villages 6 de Marzo and Paraiso. Furthermore, the practice of *choqueo*, after years of abandonment, has been reestablished and performed since 2005 in La Patria's villages of Puente Kaigue, La Leona, and 6 de Marzo. The passing away of Agapito, as lived experience of present Angaité, connects with and exemplifies these long processes and larger socioeconomic circumstances.

Agapito's Death and Farewell

Agapito Navarro died at the hospital Juan Max Boettner on December 14, 2015. He had gone through a critical period when the symptoms of tuberculosis worsened and a further diagnosis of cirrhosis. In order to receive treatment for his illnesses Agapito spent time in the hospital and also tried some alternative therapies with an Enxet shaman from the community La Herencia and a nonindigenous medicine woman from the suburbs of Asunción. The weekend before he died, one of his sons suggested that Agapito be taken out of hospital—at his own risk, the physician in charge admonished him—to be treated by a more powerful shaman who lived in the Enxet community El Estribo. Accompanying him to the Chaco locality of Rio Verde were Agapito's daughter María; her two children, Mario and Lorena, who were raised as Agapito's own children and were twenty-two and seventeen years old, respectively; and Agapito's wife, Agustina Aguilera. There, they waited for the powerful shaman, who never arrived. As Agapito's health condition worsened he was sent back to the hospital in an ambulance, a scarce luxury in the Chaco, which was obtained with the help of an anthropologist colleague, but he did not make it. He died not quite twenty-four hours later. Lorena called to tell me the bad news, and her voice and crying were profoundly desperate. As neither Agapito's family nor I could afford the costs of a private burial in Asunción, a friend who worked for Indigenous Peoples Health Division of the Ministry of Health aided Agapito's relatives in obtaining the necessary assistance to treat Agapito's corpse, buy a coffin, and transport the body to bury in his village.

I did not accompany Agapito during the last phase of his disease and treatment, nor did I see him as much as I would have wanted. At that time, I was living 230 miles south from Asunción, my wife was pregnant, but more than anything, my father suffered terminal cancer, and his care demanded most of my time and emotional support. I visited Agapito once in the hospital, in November 2015; he could hardly recognize me and cried when he did so. He probably feared and foresaw what was coming. A couple of months later, after Agapito's death, I managed to visit Agapito's village, Karova Guazu, in La Patria with a colleague from Tierraviva, his son, and my nephew to give my condolences to Agapito's wife, Agustina, his children, and his grandchildren Remigio, Mario, and Lorena. Agapito's absence was still in the air, but as the Angaité's social etiquette requires, not much crying or open expression of sadness was displayed by anyone. Agustina greeted me with a hug, a rare gesture, and some tears; María did the same. After that, the typical round of *tereré* (cold infusion of yerba mate, *Ilex paraguayensis*) was offered to visitors and became a way of sharing the initial moments of sadness that later turned into a cheerful conversation. Sitting in the hammock I observed quietly that Agapito and Agustina's one-room hut was already dismantled, and she was living nearby with her grandson Remigio and his family. At some point I expressed that I wanted to know where Agapito was buried; agreeing to my request, most of the people and some neighbors and relatives accompanied and guided us to the place of the burial.

We walked for 500 meters to the south of the village and took a small path that meandered within the high plain forest unaffected by the seasonal floods of the nearby *riacho* (small stream). There was Agapito's tomb with a wooden cross that barely marked its location. As we silently surrounded it, I thought I had to say a few words to express my sorrow and love to the family and give Agapito a proper farewell. Clumsily in Angaité I said that he had been my teacher, that he taught me his language and many stories of his people, and that he was like my father. Some of the women shed a few tears and started to moan softly. It was my colleague's turn to speak, and in Guaraní he mentioned Agapito's presence in indigenous leaders' meetings in the past and spoke of him as a representative of his culture who would probably be in heaven by God's will, at which point people responded "Amen." Lastly, my nephew gave in Spanish his condolences and expressed his gratitude to Agapito's relatives for receiving him at their village. That was it. Or so I thought it to be the last farewell, for as far as I knew at the time, there would not be further public mourning manifestations and less so any traditional rituals to come. I thought the processes of Christianization and labor exploitation at the ranches would have diminished most known rituals, such as the boys' *vaingka* or girls' *yamana* initiations, and that they were abandoned because the missionaries prohibited them and the *patrones* also disliked them, except for the *choqueo* for reasons I have analyzed elsewhere (Villagra Carron 2011).

A few months later, Gregorio Navarro, Agapito's oldest son, proposed that we should do a tribute taking advantage of a traditional gathering that would take place at La Patria to celebrate the national official indigenous day, held every April 19. Gregorio, his younger brother Félix, and Agapito had been the leaders of their village. Before Agapito died, Félix had decided to leave Karova Guazu after a family conflict over the community's cattle. In 2007 he established a new village, 6 de Marzo, with a couple of families who followed him (Villagra Carron 2010, 273). Gregorio continued as the single leader in Karova Guazu, and later he summoned his other younger brother, Victor, to accompany him in leadership.

Close to the date of the tribute, sometime in March 2016, Gregorio called to inform me about his request for support from several external allies, including the NGO Tierraviva, the governor's office,[1] and the Anglican church. He was basically asking for food provisions to be cooked and shared with everyone who participated in the tribute. However, the planned homage would eventually collide with other intervillage events planned for the same date in La Patria. This, Gregorio told me, made everyone less interested or reluctant to support him, as the main event scheduled for the indigenous day was a leader's meeting of most villages to be held in La Leona village, a new center for congregation of the fluid internal political alliances within La Patria.

I told Gregorio I would leave from Asunción on April 18 in one of Tierraviva's vehicles. Gregorio had a word with Laureano Ayala, an Enxet shaman of the Palo Blanco village in the Enxet community Sombrero Piri. He and Gregorio were members of the Coordinadora de Líderes del Bajo Chaco, an organization of leaders of the Lower Chaco. I left Asunción accompanied by Serafín López, one of the leaders of the Sanapaná village of Xakmok Kásek, and by the photographer Pascual Glauser, and we picked up Laureano from his village on the way. As we reached the village of Xakmok Kásek, several families had gathered by the entrance gate to go to Asunción to protest before the Ministry of Finance to pressure the government to pay for the land they recovered from private owners. This was just another chapter of thirty years of struggle for their land.[2] It started in 1986 with the claim made by the former Sanapaná leader Ramón Oviedo for around two hundred hectares. By then Oviedo and his people lived in an area of less than four hectares within the Salazar ranch that belonged to the Eaton family of US origin although it and neighboring cattle ranches were established in their ancestral territory. In 1993 the Xakmok Kásek community presented a larger claim, of 10,000 hectares, before the Paraguayan Institute for Indigenous Affairs. In 2001 the community unsuccessfully claimed the land through an expropriation bill before the Paraguayan parliament. Finally, in 2010, the Inter-American Court of Human Rights ruled against the Paraguayan government and ordered it to grant 10,700 hectares to the community.

After exchanging greetings with the Xakmok Kásek families, Laureano said he wanted to give his shamanic blessing to them. He did so by briefly

Figure 5.1. Gregorio Navarro (*center*), Wilfredo Navarro (*left*), and the shaman Laureano Ayala (*right*) at Agapito's tribute. 2016. Photo by Pascual Glauser.

singing a chant, after which we continued our trip to La Patria. We arrived at night, but instead of going to the village Karova Guazu, to my surprise we went to María Navarro's new house in her brother Félix's village 6 de Marzo. Laureano introduced himself to Agustina and María as Agapito's nephew; called María "niece" as she and Agustina offered us a nice dinner. Agapito never told me that Laureano was his relative when I tried to register his full genealogy and figure out who his relatives were within and outside La Patria. Nonetheless, I learned long after, by asking Remigio, that Laureano and Agapito were probably related on Agustina's maternal side, Laureano being the son of one of her female cousins and hence of mixed Enxet-Angaité descent.

The next day, the tribute was set to begin in the morning, and the location chosen was María's courtyard shaded by a few algarrobo trees. People began to arrive, mainly from the same village but also from some other close ones such as Karova Guazu and Paraiso. However, as the meeting in La Leona was the central act that festive day, probably no more than forty people were present at the tribute, including authorities and representatives from La Patria and others. Gregorio acted as the host of the tribute for Félix, the village leader, went to La Leona's meeting. Although he did not organize a program, he previously asked some of the people invited to give speeches, and he let some others to speak spontaneously. I summarize below the presentations of the designated speakers.

Gregorio, with a visible excitement, began the event saying that it was to honor the memory of his father, Agapito Navarro, a leader and shaman "who had done a lot for his family and fellow community members." Then it was my turn to pronounce a few words, with the book I wrote entitled *Meike makha valayo* (Villagra Carron 2014) in my hands that included Agapito's photograph and short biography on the back flap. I explained both in Angaité and Guaraní that Agapito had taught me his language and told me many stories of his people that were transcribed in the book. I said that it was clear from these narratives that the Chaco was originally inhabited by Indians who lived by hunting and cultivating their gardens, but later the Paraguayans came and imposed their rules and *estancias*.

Then it was the turn of Ruben Fernández, leader of the village of San Fernandez and one of the most important leaders of La Patria at the time. He showed his authority, dressed for the occasion in the uniform of a Paraguayan policeman. Rubén said that *by looking* at the histories and teachings collected in the book and the things Agapito and other allies, anthropologists, and NGOs went through, "we could attain and defend our rights as indigenous people." Next, the director of the school, Eulogia Ruiz from Karova Guazu, took the floor. She said, seized with strong emotion, that she started teaching at Karova Guazu sixteen years earlier. "Agapito was like a father to me," she said. Next she read a short biography of him in Spanish and translated it into Guaraní.

Laureano then introduced himself as a member of the Lower Chaco leadership organization and as a shaman, and he asked everyone, particularly addressing Agapito's closest relatives, to step forward to receive his blessing, adding, "We come here to cry, not to party." He asked Gregorio and me to get his bag and to start a campfire from which he would smoke a *ñana* (remedy plant, in Guaraní) and then chant to show us *yavahalhma* (Angaité: outer place), where Agapito soul's would be taken. He told participants, "You will sleep peacefully and will not dream about him." Gregorio took out of Laureano's bag a long bead necklace, and Agustina and I lit the firewood and placed the unknown leaves on the fire to release a gray smoke and mild scent. Laureano started to sing loudly, shaking his maraca, and Gregorio began to dance, uttering broken sobs; he was joined mostly by his female relatives, who cried and covered their faces with their hands. The shamanic ritual did not last more than fifteen minutes, and when it finished, Laureano said that he safely took Agapito's soul to the west and last dwelling place. He told me later that Agapito's powers as auxiliary spirits could easily turn against his relatives. After that, the food was distributed among those present.

Later we went to the village of Puente Kaigue to participate in a *choqueo* dance. There, the circle of dancers surrounded and echoed the single drummer and singer at the center, and the circle grew larger each time a round started. Bright moonshine illuminated the evening, while small plastic bottles of *caña* (rum) generously circulated among the participants. Gregorio and Laureano also took turns drumming and singing. As the night advanced and we shared the steady rounds of *caña*, I believed, as the Angaité would have it, our *valhok*, the physical, cognitive, affective center of a person (Kidd 1999b, 47), "leaned over" (to indicate sadness). At a certain point Gregorio looked at me, mentioned Agapito, and started to cry, and so did I, and we hugged. My tears were also triggered by the thought of my father, who had just passed away. There I also met an old couple from Puente Kaigue who remembered Agapito and said that they missed the tribute; they shed a few tears to show their sorrow about his death. The next day, before leaving La Patria, I stopped to say goodbye to some acquaintances at the village of Urundey, on our way out of 6 de Marzo. There, another celebration was taking place, with the support of a Mennonite church and its *evangelio* followers, among whom were some of Agapito's grandchildren. The leader, Chico, and his wife also shared with me their sorrow for Agapito's death.

A few months after the farewell ritual I ran into Agustina and Gregorio at the Tierraviva office, and he mentioned that Agustina was recently diagnosed with kidney stones, but she did not need an operation, as he was treating her with medicinal plants in his role of shaman. This took me by surprise, as he had told me before that although he began his studies as a shaman by fasting and ingesting certain plants, he discontinued his training because he could not endure such trials (Villagra Carron 2010, 325). Agapito's granddaughter Lorena and Osvaldo González, a young man from the neighboring village Paraiso of La Patria, had a son, Josué Emanuel, their first baby, in August 2017. Some months later Lorena started to lose weight until she seemed quite ill. At that point she went with Agustina, María, Osvaldo, and the baby to Asunción. Lorena could hardly breastfeed and did not receive a clear diagnosis at the hospital, as apparently the doctors did not know what illness she had. The couple turned to a shamanic cure and found a suitable shaman in the Enxet village of Nueva Jerusalem, a man named Eligio González. After observing Lorena for a few days, the shaman told her that it was Agapito, or more precisely Agapito's ghost, who wanted to take her with him, as he was alone and she was the one who was present at the time of his death. Eligio chanted for Lorena's recovery, and he said that the shaman who officiated at Agapito's farewell ceremony had lied, for he was not able to usher Agapito's ghost to the abode of the dead. The term he used, *aphag'ak*, means the biggest *vangmagko* of the multiple "soul/dream" of a person that after death becomes a ghost (Kidd 1999b, 33–45). Thus the shaman Laureano had not prevented Agapito's *aphag'ak* from being a peril to his living relatives. Lorena was eventually diagnosed with tuberculosis and also received treatment at the hospital. Progressively, her health improved.

On July 13, 2018, Lorena married Osvaldo on the same occasion as Remigio Navarro and Carolina and other couples were married in 6 de Marzo with a Christian ceremony sponsored by the Anglican church and officiated by Pastor Agripino. Lorena and the other brides wore traditional white wedding dresses, and the grooms dressed in fine Paraguayan-style suits. They all received their marriage certificates, valuable documents that grant recognition as equals to nonindigenous people. Mario sent me the wedding photos, and I responded that Agapito would have been very happy to be there. He replied, "Maybe he will always be watching over us, taking care of us. Papá is still alive, and he never left us."

The Angaité's Trajectory from "Unknown" People to a Dubious Name

The Angaité were first mentioned in the ethnographic record more than a century ago. The nineteenth-century Spanish explorer Juan de Cominges was the first individual to mention the Angaité with this ethnonym in his book *Exploraciones* (Cominges 1892, 97).[3] He was commissioned by the Bravo Company on his expeditions into the Chaco and later by Carlos Casado's tannin company, which bought huge areas of land in the region, some of it in Angaité territory. We can presume that Angaité (ethno)history, like that of other Enlhet-Enenlhet peoples, goes back much deeper in time, but they became more visible when they reached the west bank of the Paraguay River by the mid-nineteenth century. By then, the predominance of the Mbayá peoples had ceased as they crossed the Paraguay River and settled on the other side in Brazil's Mato Grosso do Sul (Fabre 2005, 515; Susnik 1981). Before this time, just a handful of missionaries and explorers had noticed the Enlhet-Enenlhet, among them the Jesuit José Sanchéz Labrador in the late eighteenth century (1910 [1770], 1:40, 2:266). The priest's contemporary, the Spanish military captain Juan Francisco Aguirre (2017 [1948]), used the testimony of the *pardo* (brown-skinned) Asencio Flecha to draw a cartography and ethnic classification of the Chaco based on the point of view of the Mbayá and Payagua Indians as well as the mestizos from the riverine frontiers of the Chaco. A century later, the Anglican missionary Barbrooke Grubb ventured by himself into far-off lands of the Chaco. There he met Enxet and later fully described the encounters in a book titled "An unknown people in an unknown land: An account of the life and customs of the Lengua Indians of the Paraguayan Chaco, with adventures and experiences met with during twenty years' pioneering and exploration amongst them" (Grubb 1993 [1911]).

The result of the veil of uncertainty about the inhabitants of the Chaco interior brought about a picture of multiple ethnonyms and languages that varied endlessly; each explorer or missionary attempted a taxonomy of the Chaco's people and claimed the failure of the ones who preceded him. As the Argentine anthropologist José Braunstein brilliantly proposes, such paradigmatic shortcomings and discontinuities may look different if we observe a subjacent logic to such puzzle: "Like a kaleidoscope that rotates with a certain periodicity, its [the Chaco's] ethnography presents ever-changing images, although composed again and again by similar elements. That is to say, the Gran Chaco offers a variable ethnic panorama, but composed of a more or less stable amount of elements; and these, in turn, always present new combinations of components" (2016, 57, my translation). The kaleidoscope metaphor explains the apparently arbitrary sociocultural discontinuities that are exemplified in Agapitos's death ritual. In this ritual in particular, Angaité contemporary life is formed by a "stable amount of elements" that present "new combinations."

Based on the ethnography and cartography of Chaco Indians collected and written by the Jesuits Joaquín Camaño y Bazán (1931) and Guillermo Furlong (1936), Braunstein (2016) offers a critical review and typology and distinguishes the early sixteenth-century chroniclers such as Ulrico Schmidl; the seventeenth- and eighteenth-century Jesuit missionaries-ethnographers such as Camaño; the late eighteenth-century Spanish Bourbonic functionaries such as Aguirre and Félix Azara; early and mid-nineteenth century travelers and the Argentine military; the late nineteenth-century ethnographers such as Guido Boggiani and Erland Nordenskiöld; and the twentieth-century anthropologists Herbert Baldus, Alfred Métraux, Enrique Palavecino, and Branislava Susnik. From Camaño's cartography Braunstein identifies four distinct groups: the western Mataguayo, with subdivisions; the eastern Guaykuru (Toba, Mocoví, and Apipón); the northeastern Zamuco, Guaná, and Guaykurú (Mbaya-Caduveo) of Alto Paraguay; and the southwestern Lule, Vilela, and Malvala along the Salado River. These four groups can also transversally disaggregate into three categories distributed also geographically: the agricultural and pottery peoples who circumscribe the whole Chaco region at its borders, the hunters and gatherers of the interior or "peripheral bonfires" who become later Equestrian peoples, and the archaic hunters of the north (Braunstein 2016, 58–60, 70–71). In addition, Braunstein explains the characteristic social and ethnic plasticity of the Chaco peoples: "The existing sociopolitical units are descendants of others that consisted of groups of politically allied bands—usually exogamic and integrated by extended uxorilocal families—who lived in the region at the end of the nineteenth century" (83, my translation).

Both the bands and the allied groups merged or fissured according to variable conjunctures and internal or external causes such as "the prestige of charismatic chieftainships or access to resources, with the frequent occurrence of the decomposition of concurrent bands and tribal recomposition with allies who could be quite distant linguistically and culturally" (84–85). Furthermore, such constant socioethnic reconfiguration has been more feasible depending on the affinity that certain groups have in their type of leadership (Braunstein 2008). Braunstein finds that the *chaqueños centrales*, inhabitants of the basins of the Bermejo and Pilcomayo Rivers and belonging to the linguistic groups of Mataco-Mataguayo, Guaykuru, and Enlhet-Enenlhet (Maskoy), had similar sociopolitical institutions. These include seminomadic bands, bilateral kinship, uxorilocal residence, and a ritual framework of "ancient drinking ceremonies and war trophies . . . [as] symbolic attributes" of their mostly shamanic leaders, events Braunstein names as "charisma tournaments" (2008, 19–20).

Hence, the stable elements may be the result of four historical and geographic groups of peoples, three different geographical, material, and productive traditions, three reversible levels of social organization (band, tribe, and their respective alliances), and correlated social characteristics such as a ritually charismatic shamanic leadership in a specific area. All of these elements may help to imagine and visualize their endless combinations expressed in ethnonyms that vary and alter their meaning and use. How does this kaleidoscopic ethnicity pertain to the specific case of the Angaité? Or how can one trace such ethnic reconfiguration as a characteristic pattern that affects them? The ethnonym's genealogy and winding trajectory of the Enlhet-Enenlhet linguistic family in the Chaco's ethnic cartography will lead to the specificity of the Angaité.

In order to illustrate this complex configuration, I analyze the genealogy of four different ethnonyms that remain related to the Enlhet-Enenlhet family: Lengua, Machikúy, Maskoy, and Enimaga. All four ethnonyms or better said, exonyms designate a supposedly distinct ethnic group, at least from a particular ethnic point of view, and at some point were used to designate the whole group. Machikuy and Enimaga were used as names for the whole linguistic Enlhet-Enenlhet family up to the late nineteenth century; since then the term Maskoy was used instead. Later on, the terms Maskoy and Lengua were used to designate specific peoples within that family, such as the Lengua-Maskoy, Toba-Maskoy, and Maskoy.

With regard to the first ethnonym, Azara notes (1850, 225), "*Lenguas.* This nation gave itself the name *Yuiadgé* later written *Juidgé*; the Payaguás call them *Cadalu*: the Machicuys *Quiesmagpipo*; the Enimagas *Cochaboth*; the Tobas and other Indians *Cocoloth*; and the Spaniards name them Lenguas,[4] because of the particular shape of the lip plate they use." The "tongues" (*lenguas*) allusive to the lip plate they used was a colonial denomination extended to various peoples of the Chaco, but it referred, Azara notes, to a group that was already near extinction by the late eighteenth century (225); therefore he uses the name Machicui, Machicuys, or Machikúy to classify the whole linguistic group (227). This term, however, was used specifically by the Toba (linguistically Guaykurú) from the Pilcomayo River area to refer to their supposed linguistic relatives to the north (Braunstein 2016, 82). Boggiani (1900, 149) reused the name Machicui as a general category but included among its members the Kaskiha people, who no longer exist or ever existed, according to Kalisch (personal communication). Boggiani also included in that group the Sújen, Sujin, or Seugen (the modern Nivaclé, the Mataco-Mataguayo linguistic family group) and the Toothli (Grubb 1993 [1911], 244), the present-day Toba (Guaikurú linguistic family group), names the Enxet and other Enlhet-Enenlhet peoples gave respectively to their neighbors.

The term Maskoi or Maskoy replaced Machikúy in the twentieth century to refer to the whole current Enlhet-Enenlhet linguistic family. Such former name is of unknown origin but attributed to the modern Toba (Boggiani 1900, 149; Fabre 2005, 515). However, Azara already mentioned that the Lengua people named the Machikúy with this appellative but written as Markoy (1850, 227). Until quite recently, the compound name

Lengua-Maskoy was used in the indigenous peoples national taxonomy to designate indistinctly two specific peoples of the Enlhet-Enenlhet family, the Enxet (south) and Enlhet (north) peoples, who ethnically distinguished themselves from one another based on their albeit close linguistic and sociogeographical differences (Paraguay, DGEEC *2003*). The term Maskoy, in turn, has been used as a distinctive complementary noun of other groups of the same linguistic family, such as the Toba-Maskoy or Enenlhet. Finally, Maskoy as a noun alone has been used as self-denomination in a specific case. In 1983 an intricate mix of people whose common denominator was their involvement as workers with the Casado quebracho tannin and cattle company for about one hundred years agreed to call themselves Maskoy. In a simplified version of past denominations, accepted and retold by the protagonists themselves, Maskoy people are constituted by five different ethnic groups: Toba, Angaité, Sanapaná, Guaná, and Enxet (Bonifacio 2009, 30). The self-emergence of the Maskoy people is completely intertwined with their land claim as a sociopolitical and ethnic unit before the Paraguayan state (Bonifacio 2009, 28–71; Casaccia and Vázquez 1986).

The fourth term, Enimaga, was associated in the late eighteenth century with the Lengua. The former inhabited the areas between the Bermejo River to the west and the Pilcomayo River during the seventeenth century (Susnik and Chase Sardi 1995, 22), and both terms were indistinctly used to call two closely related social units (Braunstein 2016, 96). We can observe the ethnophonetic and written variations of terms such as Ñimaqa, as Toba and Pilagá of the Pilcomayo named the Maká (linguistic family group Mataco-Mataguayo) (89), and Ennimá, as the Yshir named their southern Enlhet-Enenlhet neighbors (Boggiani, cited in Fabre 2005, 511), Enimaga, Enimagos, or even Inimicá or Imaca (Braunstein 1981, 97). In fact, the Maká language shares 40 percent of its vocabulary with the Lengua and Enimaga registered by Amancio González in the eighteenth century (Tovar, cited in Braunstein 2016, 89).

This complex reconfiguration of groups reflects the variation fueled by several causes. Among the oldest were Indian rebellions against the Spanish *encomienda* system and the Calchaquies wars during the seventeenth century; the Spanish military campaigns from Tucumán to the west of the Chaco drove several peoples to take refuge in the Jesuit missions on the Salado River, to later disperse themselves into the northern and central Chaco after the expulsion of the Jesuit order in 1767. Thus, culturally transformed peoples from the borders, also characterized as farmers and potters, merged at different points and directions into the Chaco, with the hunters and gatherers cum equestrians of the interior of the Chaco (Braunstein 2016, 75–88).

One of the areas where migration exerted pressure on cohabitation and merging becomes evident for the Enlhet-Enenlhet linguistic family was at the geographical funnel of the Pilcomayo River, as mentioned by Susnik (cited in Braunstein 2016). There the ancestors of present-day Enxet and Enlhet, Maká, Nivaclé, and Toba peoples merged at the turn of the eighteenth century, as revealed by records of the Melodía mission of González. The Enimaga were located at the headwaters of the Aguaray Guazu River, a tributary of the Paraguay River, in a lagoon named "*Flagmagmegtempela*, or *Etacametguischi* or *Tahaaguí*" (Aguirre, cited in Braunstein, 1981, 108 (quote); Azara 1850, 229). The former term means "place of many chajá birds" (*Chauna torquata*) in both Enxet and Enlhet languages; the two latter denominations are unknown to me but could be Toba. Such multiethnic composition and numerous ethnonyms in the Pilcomayo River funnel proved to be resilient throughout time. In 1916 the Anglican missionaries who founded the Nanawa mission among the Nivaclé with the aid of Enxet acolytes mentioned that the whole area, not too distant from the Aguaray River's headwaters and the Montelindo River, was variously inhabited by Enxet, Maká, Toba Qom, and Nivaclé groups, named by the Enxet as A'ii, Towothli/Tootlhi and Sujin/Seugen, respectively. The missionaries even proposed that "these traditions point to a common origin . . . they all came from the upper reaches of the river Pilcomayo" (Hunt 1933, 66–67, 301). In May 2018, in a visit to the Toba Qom community of Cerrito, the elder shaman Tranquilino Flores, whose mother was Enxet and father was Toba Qom, told me that in the Lower Chaco not long before there was a "triangle" composed of the Maká in the west, the Enxet to the east, and the Toba Qom in the south at the tip of the Pilcomayo River.

These groups, as a distinct sociopolitical nucleus formed by kinship and political alliances favored by migration and cohabitation, centrifugally homogenized their cultural and linguistic characteristics and gradually expressed their differences (Braunstein 2016, 101). Boggiani noticed that among the Enlhet-Enenlhet there was a variation of cultural aspects displayed in an extended geographical region from north to south. The northern Guaná, Kaskiha, and Sanapaná had a more sophisticated type of pottery, variety of species cultivated, and use of cotton (Boggiani, cited by Braunstein 2016, 102–103). The southern Angaité and Enxet, as well as the Toba and Nivaclé whom Boggiani included in the same family, had less-developed pottery and agriculture but crafted wool textiles and were inclined toward hunting rather than cultivating (102–103).

A century after Boggiani's observations, Hannes Kalisch and Ernesto Unruh speak of a linguistic "nucleus" instead of discrete languages, claiming, similarly to Boggiani's register, that there is a variable continuum among the Enlhet-Enenlhet languages "following the line Enlhet, Enxet, Angaité, Sanapaná, Guaná, Toba, that correspond to the traditional territories" (2003, 5–8). In such a continuum, boundaries are flexible, showing both genetic and areal commonalities between the different linguistic nucleus and the former traditional groups that originally composed them. These ethnographers and linguists speak of cultural (Braunstein) and linguistic (Kalisch and Unruh) nucleus to stress the quality of openness rather than of enclosure, as permeable variations within a common family of peoples.

If ethnonyms represent a geographical, cultural, linguistic, and gradual variation, for the case of the Enlhet-Enenlhet, they can also express a relational quality, that is, relations between people or groups, and reveal a system or set of such relations as Isabelle Combès (2009) in her study of the ethnohistory of the ancient Zamucos and Nicolás Richard (2008a) in his study of the Yshir-Chamacoco have shown. Both authors, like Braunstein, drew inspiration from Susnik's proposition (1981) that there was a "socioperipheric dependence" of the peoples of the interior areas of the Chaco to the predominant Chiriguano, Mbayá, Chaná, and Chiquitos who were at its geographical limits and thus mediated various types of exchanges with colonial actors. Richard and Combès show that the many ethnonyms qualify sociopolitical relations between different peoples at specific historical and geographical contexts. The names establish a "chain of mediations" (Richard 2008a, 55). Thus, the Mbaya at the colonial frontier called the people they subjugated *niloyolas* (slaves) and specifically named *layanas* the Guaná-Chané they colonized and allied with through a "soft slavery" (Azara 1850, 206) by marrying their *capitanas* (female captains) (Susnik and Chase Sardi 1995, 121–122). The latter, in turn, called the far-off people who would be the last link in the chain *tamkok* (dogs) and eventually *chané-má* (companions, relatives, associates) (Susnik 1978, 114) and "crowd" (Susnik and Chase Sardi 1995, 176). *Chané-má* resembles the ethnotoponymal Enlhet-Enenlhet voice of Koonalhma, alternatively written as Kyoinithma by Grubb (1993 [1911], 319) and as Chanameshma by Susnik (1978, 110) to mean "those of the forest," bushmen. Susnik explicitly connects the ends of the chain with the Angaité by mentioning that they were sometimes called "Chanameshma" and "Koitïiwish / Chaatïwïsh" (algarrobo eaters), that is, as an Angaité precolonial group of the Chaco interior (110). In the Chané language they were called *nigati ciboe* and in Mbaya, *negueca temigi* (110).

Following the variation of ethnonyms in the Chaco and having paid particular attention to the Enlhet-Enenlhet family, one can see how half these people have adopted as their self-denomination the terms Enlhet, Enxet, and Enenlhet, a noun that translates as "person" or "people." The Angaité, unlike most ethnic cognates, have opted to keep their former ethnonym of dubious origin, which an old Angaité interpreted in mythological terms as the peculiar attribution of a Paraguayan military officer who asked an Angaité *vese* (shaman, leader) when the Chaco War (1932–1935) would end, to which the old man replied, "Ãngaite opata" (Guaraní: "It will finish in a short while"); thereafter his people were labeled the Angaité, literally the "short whiles" (Villagra Carron 2010, 19). The Maskoy of Puerto Casado and Riacho Mosquito do not have a common language, although they have claimed a common ethnicity unified under that term. Finally, the Sanapaná and the Guaná keep for themselves their former exonym, the latter one indistinguishable from the Chaná of the eighteenth and nineteenth centuries. Nonetheless, whether it is a self-denomination, a former (re)adopted exonym, and/or a dubious denomination such as the Angaité's, these terms reveal a certain relational quality with an underlying colonial or neocolonial form of ethnic identification.

At this point, I return to the interpretation of Agapito's death ritual as an index of Angaité's ethnopoeisis. The Angaité, and the rest of the Enlhet-Enenlhet peoples, are simultaneously the result and the producers of long-term processes of ethnogenesis in particular historical, geographical, and political contexts in which they instantiate and condense as social units. The wide variation of the ethnonyms related to the family, within and beyond their linguistic specificity, show the geographically interrelated diversity, gradual material and linguistic transition, open and malleable sociopolitical structure, and interethnic relational asymmetry as "chains of mediations" within colonial frontiers. Particularly, a flexible "fission-fusion" (Braunstein 2016, 83) society that could relatively recompose itself around a ritually charismatic shamanic leadership characteristic of the central *chaqueños* (Grant 2006, 26), proves to be the case for the Enlhet-Enenlhet's society and leadership. This may be facilitated by their more egalitarian political, socioeconomic, and moral ethos (Kidd 1999b, 1; Bonifacio 2009, 146–178; Kalisch 2010), which contrasts with the much more hierarchical ancient Mbayá and Guaná-Chané, whose nobles, cavaliers, *capitanas*, slaves, and relatives crowded into their villages on the west banks of the Paraguay River (Rodrígues de Prado 1839 [1795]; Sánchez Labrador 1910 [1770], 2:19–20; Susnik and Chase Sardi 1995, 176) or with the present-day Yshir and their ethnic, clan, gender, and age divisions (Richard 2008a, 337–338). In this sense, the rituals as charisma tournaments held and played by leaders-shamans (*wese/vese*) helped to reproduce such features and made their practices meaningful.

Why Then Does a Death Ritual Index Angaité's Ethnopoeisis?

In Robert Hertz's classic *Death and the Right Hand* (1960 [1909]) there are interpretive parallels to Agapito's death ritual. The most important is that "death has a specific meaning for the social consciousness; it is the object of a collective representation. This representation is neither simple nor unchangeable: it calls for an analysis of its elements as well as a search for its origin" (28). Without dwelling on what would be "social consciousness," it is clear that Agapito's death and tribute ritual was, to say the least, a common representation to all of us who were involved, although those events were neither simple nor unique for anyone nor unchangeable in any way. After Agapito's death, following Hertz's scheme, "a more or less prolonged period of mourning" (28) began. Neither the burial of his body in the forest, under circumstances that I did not witness or ask about, nor our own later visit in January 2016 to his tomb marked the end of such period. The burial and the speeches and prayers were still part of the mourning, which lasted with its effects for much longer. Regarding the temporary stay of the soul on earth Agapito's *apvangmagko* (soul) turned into *aphangak* (ghost) and thus did "not reach its final destination immediately after death" (28) as "it stay[ed] on earth in the proximity of the body, wandering in the forest or frequenting the places it inhabited while it was alive," his old hut was dismantled and Agustina moved to Remigio's house after Agapito's death. The mourning left Agapito's family quite "vulnerable" (37), and eventually some of the members were more affected than others "according to the degree of kinship" (39) or similarly in Angaité terms, those "emotionally attached." The mourning period was not over for Lorena, Agapito's granddaughter, until Agapito entered the land of the dead (39). Why did Agapito's farewell become a new death ritual? And was it symbolically effective?

The special mourning ceremony for Enlhet-Enenlhet peoples has been described by Jacob Loewen (1967, 21) as

The *Yocsac* [*sic*] or the "festival of the dead" [Yooksa'a or "end of the tears," according to the Enlhet (Kalisch 2012, 355)] was designed to help the surviving relatives over their fear and bereavement and to integrate them into the community circle once more. Since immediate relatives always were the most vulnerable to the soul of the deceased, the bereaved were partially isolated during the period of mourning, and . . . [the] festival was designed to decontaminate the bereaved and to rid them of the great fear . . . friends and neighbors helped the . . . relatives to wash off their black paint with which they had disguised themselves from the pursuing soul of the dead. The . . . relatives joined the rest of the community to spend the night in eating, drinking, and making merry. Meanwhile, everyone spoke words of encouragement assuring them that the soul of the departed was no longer in the vicinity . . . At last, under the influence of great quantities of liquor and heavy tobacco smoking, the people finally became drowsy (if not drunk) and fell asleep. When they awoke . . . the whole community including the bereaved, freed from fear, went about their ordinary way of life which . . . permitted the bereaved to again eat from the common pot which had been forbidden during the mourning period.

Similar to other rituals, Yooksa'a was supposed to disappear under colonial pressure, although, by chance, I witnessed one in the Karanday Puku community in 2008 (Villagra Carron 2010, 347). The conspicuous trait of ritual tradition at Agapito's tribute was Laureano's smoke decontamination of Agapito's close female relatives and the alleged sending of his soul to the dwelling of the dead. A similar practice was observed by Grubb in Enxet funerary rites: "In the case of dropsy, the body is shot at, and a bunch of herbs are held by the man conducting the burial. This is afterwards burnt, and each of the party swallows some of the smoke" (1993 [1911], 162).

Thus, the motives of the rituals in Yooksa'a and in Agapito's death ritual seemed to be somehow similar, to forget the fear and bereavement of the surviving relatives and to send away the dead person's haunted soul. The procedures for achieving these goals were dissimilar: a purifying washing, a night performance, partying, and dancing in contrast to a tribute ceremony with foreign guests and speakers where commensality was assured although partying and dancing were relegated. Nonetheless, the words of encouragement, the dance circle, the liquor and smoking, the postmourning sharing of food at the Yooksa'a, in comparison with the compassionate tears of more distant relatives and friends, the available *choqueo, caña*, and smoking and the communal food sharing at Agapito's tribute can be seen as transformed practices although not completely different ones (Kalisch 2012, 357).

Last but not least, does this improvised death ritual to appease the dead and establish alliances with foreigners constitute an index of ethnopoeisis? In order to answer this question, I must recall that the Angaité emerged in relatively recent times with an odd (exo)ethnonym out of a long process of ethnic, social, and linguistic miscegenation that involved the Enlhet-En-enlhet and other peoples in the Chaco. I also have to take into account the plasticity of their society, their egalitarian ethos, and the charismatic sha-manic leadership. For the Angaité as well as other indigenous peoples, the boundaries with the outside world have become blurred, and paradoxically, being indigenous is equated with being poor and discriminated against. To allow themselves certain control over their lives, they have to manipulate and control nonindigenous elements in their society. These may be not only material and productive aspects for subsistence such as land, cattle, money, and commodities but also the various ideological discourses and practices of development, anthropology, religion, ethnicity, and so forth that confine them to a more or less stereotypical position as beneficiaries, qualified or unqualified indigenous informants, faithful or rebellious acolytes, authen-tic with written mythologies and stories or acculturated Indians who have lost their language.

Then, "new" rituals such as Agapito's farewell tribute are a means to make sense of the present while proving that relationships and alliances that help constitute the moral, individual, and social self constantly chal-lenge and are affected by historical events and diverse external influences. To be "authentic" in both Angaité and nonindigenous terms, it is important to achieve a tranquil life, one that overcomes the perils of mourning the dead, a life in which good relatives, neighbors, and external benefactors make the most of it in the present day. Thus, ethnopoeisis is to make effec-tive and affective being and becoming a social identity that an ethnonym may represent despite its equivocal origin, as in the Angaité case. A new ritual that conflates both indigenous traditional and new nonindigenous elements, including a mythical and oral narrative told in their vanishing language and materialized in various books, helps to instantiate yet another episode of the ethnic variation of the Chaco, that of the Angaité-Koalhvok,[5] a compound name that is concomitantly affirming its usage (Ávalos et al. 2018; Elizeche 2007; Franco and Imaz 2006).

Finally, we cannot categorically determine which was the "final ceremony" (Hertz 1960 [1909], 53) that ended the mourning for Agapito. The tribute and other related events, somehow cathartic expressions of affliction by Gregorio and others including myself, seemed to work fine as a closure. Nonetheless, Laureano's attempt to dispatch Agapito's soul was notably unsuccessful in view of the malevolent disease Lorena suffered as Agapito's soul wanted to take her with him. Thus, the final ceremony seemed to be successful in terms of the "effectiveness of symbols" (Lévi-Strauss, 1963 [1958]), carried out by the shaman who discovered such an attack and was effective in curing Lorena. Again, it could be said that the multiple weddings officiated by an Anglican pastor were the end of "the mourning of the relatives of the deceased" that brought "these back into communion with society" (Hertz 1960 [1909], 61–62). All these rituals show the Angaité's agency and conscious manipulation of foreign elements. Agapito "will always be watching over us, taking care of us," his grandson Mario remarked. I hope so, for the sake and good of all of us who loved him.

Notes

1. This was the governor of the Department of Presidente Hayes. Departments are administrative jurisdictions in Paraguay.

2. See Villagra and Bonifacio 2015 for an account of some of the legal and shamanic efforts of the community of Xakmok Kásek toward the successful recovery of their land.

3. Rufino Enéas Gustavo Galvão, Brazil's minister of foreign relations and a member of the Brazil-Paraguay Demarcation Commission, while working in the Apa River area in 1872 noticed the "Ingaetés" (Galvão 1875, 229). I thank Pablo Antunha Barbosa for calling my attention to this reference.

4. *Lengua* means "tongue" in Spanish.

5. The Angaité Damacio Flores explains that this ethnomyn means "the real souls" (in Franco and Imaz 2006, 15).

6

Between Resistance and Acquiescence

Experiences of Agrarian Transformation in Two Indigenous Communities in Chaco Province, Argentina

MERCEDES BIOCCA

> Here in Chaco Province, thousands and thousands of hectares are plant-ed with soybeans. The landowners grow it, about twenty-nine families, a small but powerful group that owns half of Chaco. We don't have a good relationship with the soybean producers because they exploit the forest, buy more land and take it away from indigenous people. An indigenous family might own just a single hectare while the big landowners own prop-erties of 120,000, 140,000 hectares. Ever since the land was privatized, ev-erything has been fenced off. We have almost nothing left. They force us out of our homes so businesspeople can come to plant soybeans. So we had to organize to take our protest to the government.
>
> Mártires, 2010

Similar transformations to those described by Mártires, a Qom leader, dur-ing one of our first meetings have been analyzed in numerous studies across the globe as processes of "accumulation by dispossession." This concept, developed by David Harvey (2003, 2006, 2007), has been established in recent years as a key tool for explaining the changes that occurred in rural areas during the neoliberal era. The speed at which studies of accumulation by dispossession proliferated following the term's coinage provides compel-ling evidence of the descriptive effectiveness of the concept and its ability to expose the links between global and local processes (Bailey 2014; Hart 2006). However, it has also contributed to the establishment of a perspec-tive in which new dynamics are reduced to simple processes of appropria-tion of goods or the invariably successful imposition of the objectives of the dominant sectors. This has led to the presumption that as a counterpoint to these processes, whatever the type of dispossession or enclosure under discussion, resistance by subaltern groups will arise.

Paradoxically, however, in Argentina and many other countries across the world, the transformations generally associated with accumulation by dispossession do not always generate opposition or resistance. On the contrary, in many cases, subaltern groups demand to be included in industrial agriculture or seek to benefit from the creation of special economic areas, encouraging the commercialization of areas that had previously been outside the market to some degree (Borras and Franco 2013; Castellanos-Navarrete and Jansen 2015; Hall et al. 2015; Li 2014; Mamonova 2015).

In this context, emphasizing the subaltern's agency contributes to the debate on processes of accumulation by dispossession. Understanding accumulation by dispossession as a process perceived and experienced differently by diverse actors, taking into account not only the actions of the dominant groups but also the "local rationalities" of subaltern actors (Nilsen and Cox 2013), may help to replace the dichotomous conception of spaces of power and spaces of resistance usually presented, more or less explicitly, in works on neoliberal transformations (Nilsen 2010; Nilsen and Cox 2013). In other words, placing the memories, perceptions, and positions of indigenous communities in Chaco Province at center stage in the analysis and interpreting these local rationalities as integral parts of the processes is an essential step toward understanding "the way in which power is lived and inequality is normalized at the nexus of force, consent, and the production of desires for particular ways of living" (Li 2014, 17).

I first analyze the main features of the concept of accumulation by dispossession developed by David Harvey and examine the main criticisms it has received. The perspective of local rationalities helps explain the different positions subalterns adopt and the multiple paths these processes can take. The process of accumulation by dispossession is seen from the perspective of local rationalities in two indigenous communities in Chaco Province. Their dispossession involved deforestation, environmental pollution, and shifts in access to resources due to the cultivation of transgenic soybeans. In the Qom community of Pampa del Indio the expansion of transgenic crops brought resistance, while in the Moqoit community in Colonia Cacique Catán a similar process did not lead to collective action. Data presented are based on ethnographic fieldwork I conducted between 2010 and 2016 in Chaco Province.[1]

From Primitive Accumulation to Accumulation by Dispossession

The concept of accumulation by dispossession presented by David Harvey (2003, 2006, 2007) is a reformulation of the concept of primitive accumulation proposed by Karl Marx in *Das Kapital*. In general terms, primitive accumulation can be understood as a historical process by which the human being is deprived of a means of subsistence. This process, which transforms the social relations of production into capitalist ones, is achieved by different methods, such as "the spoliation of the Church's property, the fraudulent alienation of state domains, the theft of the commons lands, the usurpation of feudal and clan property and its transformation into modern private property under circumstances of ruthless terrorism, all these things were just so many idyllic methods of primitive accumulation" (Marx 1990 [1867], 895).

In *The New Imperialism* (2003, 156), Harvey argues that in the neoliberal era, to avoid crises of overaccumulation, capital sought out new territories and commercialized social sectors that had previously been partially or completely free of market influence. Accumulation by dispossession includes not only coopting existing structures but also confronting and violently suppressing them where they are inconsistent with the needs of capital (146). The final objective is the liberation of a series of goods at a very low cost so that capital can make use of them in highly profitable ways (149).

In addition to a significant transfer of assets to the dominant classes, Harvey argues (2003, 162–179), the current preeminence of this form of accumulation has created a new politics of resistance. In contrast to traditional forms of resistance against the expanded reproduction of capital, these new struggles are characterized by pursuing fragmentary and contingent objectives, function on different scales, and tend to remain in the form of social movements.

The versatility of the concept of accumulation by dispossession explains why it became so important to contemporary agricultural studies (Levien 2013). First, the main advantage of the concept is its multifaceted nature. In contrast to studies in which primitive accumulation is limited to the conversion of "the commons," Harvey's concept addresses the conversion—or reconversion—of different kinds of property into private property. This theory encompasses a wide range of contemporary dispossessions brought about through both extra-economic and economic mechanisms. Second, the concept is not limited just to the sphere of production but also includes other economic sectors, such as the financial and public spheres, making it possible to better analyze the role of national states in these processes. Third, it allows us to establish links between different kinds of struggle, such as organized rural resistance to the appropriation of land and urban resistance to the closure of factories and privatizations (Kasmir and Carbonella 2008). However, in Harvey's original formulation, the role of the subaltern is reduced to simple reaction, thus limiting the understanding of these processes and how they reproduce and last over time.

The main criticisms of the concept of accumulation by dispossession can be classified in two large groups: the structural, and the suprastructural or political. The former, which focus on structural issues, identify the limitations of the concept in the development of capitalism. Scholars such as Ellen Wood (2007) contend that the emphasis Harvey places on the crisis of overaccumulation as the driver of the process makes his theoretical approach of accumulation by dispossession more a liberal analysis than a Marxist one. Wood argues that primitive accumulation is characterized not by the concentration of wealth but by the transformation of social relations. From this perspective, the accumulation of the neoliberal era would be defined less by the hoarding of goods, a crisis of overaccumulation, or the use of coercion than by the subjection of an increasing number of spheres of human life to the imperatives of the market. Other structural critiques of the concept include Brenner 2007, Webber 2008, and Negi and Auerbach 2009. Although these criticisms are important, exploring them further would go beyond the scope of this text, so I will move on to the second group, analyses that note the lack of attention in Harvey's focus to the suprastructural, or political, dimension of the process. These critics call for a greater emphasis not on the functions of the process but on the means by which the dispossession is produced. Scholars such as Jim Glassman (2006, 2009) and Michael Levien (2011, 2013, 2015) assert that the use of extra-economic means is the definitive condition for accumulation by dispossession. Levien, who has developed this critique to the greatest extent, holds that by including processes of displacement caused by both economic and extra-economic means, "Harvey underemphasizes the most significant aspect of land dispossession: namely, that it is a deeply political process in which owners of the means of coercion transparently redistribute assets from one class to another" (2015, 149). Levien contends that if only processes generated by extra-economic means are considered, the role of the states and national capitalist sectors can be better understood, thus providing a more specific, less generic perspective.

Even when this criticism is applied, processes of accumulation by dispossession continue to be described and understood as top-down phenomena, as events that are imposed on subalterns mainly through the use of force. In my opinion, this is mainly because the processes continue to be explained solely from the point of view of the logic of capital and its dominant sectors. This aspect is similar to what Michael Lebowitz has described as "one-sided Marxism," in reference to those analyses that have a deterministic perspective in which everything that occurs is exhaustively explained by the needs of capital or the capitalist faction in power. Subaltern groups here are represented as being a necessary instrument of capital, and the fact that they are also subjects who act and struggle to satisfy their "own development needs" is ignored (Lebowitz 1982, 1997, 2003, 2007).

This "one-sided" perspective hinders the analysis of several processes of transformation that have occurred in the neoliberal era. It does not explain why some indigenous communities seek to get involved in soybean cultivation, albeit in a marginal fashion, in an attempt to alleviate the poverty suffered by their community while others resist and take their protests and demands to the state. Although I agree with some authors who have highlighted the importance of understanding accumulation by dispossession as a political process (Levien 2013, 2015), it is important to remember that politics cannot be limited to the realm of dominant social groups. Nor can politics be seen as simple coercion. On the contrary, accumulation by dispossession comprises interaction, cooperative actions, and resistance across different groups.

Understanding the Agrarian Transformations through the Local Rationalities

Given the relevance of the concept of accumulation by dispossession and the need to consider the different positions of subaltern groups, I now return to an approach focused on "local rationalities" (Nilsen 2010; Nilsen and Cox 2013). This concept can be defined as "those oppositional ways of doing, being, and thinking that people develop in their situated, everyday effort to cope with, negotiate, and resist such restraints and encroachments" (Nilsen 2010, 15). It is important to note that the local rationalities of subalterns are not constructed in a space located outside relations of dominance. On the contrary, they are shaped by and interwoven with relations of power. This concept of rationality seeks to avoid explanations based on the notion of a "false consciousness" as well as those that abstract subalterns from the power relations in which they are immersed (Cox 1999; Nilsen 2010; 2012).

To apply this approach to concrete cases of dispossession, it is necessary to draw on the concept of "local rationalities" developed by Nilsen and Cox (2013). To do so, I propose to focus on three dimensions: memories of past experiences, the actual experiences of dispossession to which Moqoit and Qom peoples have been exposed, and their positions of subalternity. Understanding the positions of subalterns in a neoliberal context requires consideration of how these actors' desires, objectives, and needs have transformed over the different phases of capitalist development (Lebowitz 2003). The analysis of collective and individual memories of prior periods can contribute to an understanding of when a process is perceived and experienced as dispossession or not as well as why resistance arises in some cases and not in others. This approach also acknowledges that rationalities are multiple and constantly evolving, and they cannot be separated from emotion; they are subconscious expressions of how one understands and interprets the world (Lapegna 2016).

The second aspect I analyze is what I call actual experiences of dispossession. I refer to specific ways in which the process of accumulation by dispossession took place in each of the indigenous communities studied. This includes both a consideration of the role played by the resource being appropriated, as has been proposed by Susan Spronk and Jeffery Webber (2007), and the change in the formal and informal regulations that govern access to these resources (Cáceres 2015; Ribot and Peluso 2003). In addition, within actual experiences of dispossession, it is necessary to consider the period during which each process occurred, whether it was a process that can be described as "piecemeal dispossession," as in the case of Moqoit, or a more abrupt dispossession, as occurred in the Qom case, and to reflect on how this temporal aspect affects the actions of the different groups involved (Li 2010).

Finally, "position of subalternity" refers to the complex matrices of power relations that exist within subaltern groups and between them and dominant sectors. The position of subalternity is thus linked to what Lapegna (2016) has described as "dual pressure" and "institutional recognition," concepts that shed light on the many different pressures created by the ties that exist between leaders, community members, their allies, and the state, which may facilitate or restrict the emergence of resistance. In other words, resistance or acquiescence is also the result of the presence or absence of traditional political movements, more confrontational social movements, clientelist practices, and the different historical ties with the state. In the following sections, the various ways in which the process of accumulation by dispossession materialized in Pampa del Indio and Colonia Cacique Catán can be observed through the lens of the local rationalities of indigenous communities.

Agribusiness and Resistance in Pampa del Indio

Pampa del Indio, in the far north of the department of General San Martín, Chaco Province, is one of the most populous indigenous enclaves in Argentina. Historically, the Qom communities that inhabit the area were organized in bilateral *bandas* of two or more extended families.[2] These units were nomadic hunter-gatherers within a defined territory on both margins of the Bermejo River (Miller 1979).

When the national army occupied the south shore of the Bermejo River in 1884, the Qom settled on the north shore and stayed there until the early decades of the twentieth century. At this time, rather than seeking their extermination, the Argentine state began its process of incorporating them into the labor force. A group of families led by the cacique Taigoyik moved south, where they provided most of the workforce at Las Palmas sugar mill (Fernández and Braunstein 2001). Given the importance of the sugar mill to the economy of the region,[3] President Hypólito Yrigoyen granted Taigoyik a temporary occupation permit for forty square leagues for his group (interviews with Qom inhabitants of Pampa del Indio, 2012).[4]

Decades later, due to successive economic crises suffered by Las Palmas and the modification of the law of colonization, some of the land that had been granted to the indigenous people was withdrawn and given to new settlers arriving in the region to promote cotton production. "When Taigoyik died, people came from all over, from I don't know where, strange people looking for land," recalled Mariana, a Qom woman whom I interviewed in 2010.

This dispossession of the Qom was partially reversed in the mid-1940s when the state introduced redistribution policies, with the land of large-scale criollo landowners being expropriated on this occasion.[5] With these and other measures that benefited small-scale producers and rural workers, the new government of President Juan D. Perón sought to challenge the power and legitimacy of the large landowners. In this context, several indigenous communities acquired rights of occupation or ownership of land and received different kinds of benefits from the government to encourage agricultural production. During these years, several Qom families received deeds to individual lots of twenty-five or fifty hectares. Oral histories report that the cacique Pedro Martínez negotiated with President Perón to obtain the land where the settlements of Campo Medina and Pampa Chica were founded.

The access to small parcels of land continued after the Peronist decade. By the late 1970s, the Misión Evangélica Bautista granted 704 hectares for the settlement named Campo Nuevo. During those years, most of the Qom families were contracted to perform clearance and harvest work in the fields of criollo farms.[6] Many of them also produced their own cotton, which was sold through the Cooperativa Pampa del Indio, founded in 1975.

By the late 1980s, when the cotton period was coming to an end, the rural population of Pampa del Indio was plunged into a profound crisis. The fall in the price of cotton prevented farmers from paying their debts, and many sold their land. This situation exacerbated the unemployment and contributed to increased migration to urban areas.

Neoliberal policies, mostly those implemented after 1990, together with the introduction of transgenic crop technologies and high international prices, encouraged the expansion of agribusiness in northern Argentina (Cáceres 2015; Lapegna 2016). Unitec Agro bought large tracts of land, some of it from the state and other sections from cotton producers in the region. Several Qom residents said these lands were part of the original area given to Taigoyik in 1922. Today they belong to Unitec Agro, which founded the Don Panos establishment that occupies a 120,000-hectare area in the provinces of Chaco and Formosa on both sides of the Bermejo River; 53,000 hectares are in Chaco Province and border the indigenous settlements of Campo Medina, Pampa Chica, and Campo Nuevo.

Initially, during a deep recession at the end of the 1990s and beginning of 2000, the inhabitants of Pampa del Indio were hopeful about the news that a large company had moved in. To the great majority of indigenous people living there, the company represented the prospect of employment. "It was good, we had work, and they were going to pay us every fifteen days," said Luis, who took part in the first clearance work, in 2010. Several members of the community were temporarily hired to carry out clearance work, a process not always done in accordance with the law.[7] Some were employed to build a landing strip, a hangar, and an aqueduct connecting the company's facilities with the Bermejo River.[8]

Once all the construction was finished, the far-reaching reconstruction of the territory and the new rural dynamics that came with it began to be felt. The arrival of Don Panos in Pampa del Indio led to a process of accumulation by dispossession linked to the loss of seasonal work, the inability to practice *marisca* (foraging activities), and increasing difficulties with producing food for consumption at home, raising animals, and growing cotton for sale. The loss of seasonal labor was due to the company's high degree of mechanization typical of transgenic agriculture (Cáceres 2015; Newell 2009; Reboratti 2010). Engaging in *marisca* ceased due to the loss of biodiversity caused by deforestation and increased pollution associated with the frequent agrochemical spraying. Also, a perimeter fence was built and security personnel were hired to prevent trespassing on the company's land. This enclosure represented a profound change in the rules that governed access to resources; criollo producers had traditionally allowed indigenous people to cross their lands to gather food or fish in the river. Finally, increasing difficulties with producing cotton, vegetables for consumption at home, and raising animals were linked to the intensive use of agrichemicals as well as a scarcity of water caused in part by the diversion of the Bermejo River and the perimeter fence, which limited the amount of grazing land available to the animals.

In June 2006, with the support of some state officials from the undersecretary of family agriculture and the National Institute of Indigenous Affairs, the Qom filed a complaint with the public attorney in General San Martín requesting that the agrochemical spraying be halted and that the Ministry of Social Development and Human Rights intervene to resolve the conflicts arising from the construction of the company's facilities. Despite gathered evidence, the complaint was rejected.

Two years later, in the context of "the countryside conflict,"[9] the problems with Eduardo Eurnekian, the main shareholder of Unitec Agro S.A. and Don Panos and one of the wealthiest and most powerful businessmen in Argentina, took on greater national prominence. The three main indigenous organizations of Pampa del Indio (Unión Campesina, Comisión Zonal de Tierras, and Asociación Cacique Taigoyik)[10] used this conflict as an example not just of the problems caused by the expansion of the agribusiness model but also of the history of dispossession and marginalization suffered by the indigenous population of the country.

After holding several marches and roadblocks, in 2008 the organizations signed an agreement with the governor that granted a large part of the organizations' demands. These included the delivery of seeds, fuel, and tools; repairs of pumps; and the delivery of titles to the land owned. However, a year later, the agreement had not yet been implemented. As a result, in July

2009 the three organizations held a march from Pampa del Indio to Resistencia, the provincial capital, where members set up a camp in front of the house of government.

Despite the continuous complaints and marches of the three organizations, the problems caused by the agrochemical spraying and the lack of water continued. Once more, the Qom decided to present their complaints, but this time to the national press. The visibility of their complaints in the national newspaper *Página 12* resulted in a temporary halt to the spraying along with promises of support from national authority.[11]

By 2011 the company resumed its agrochemical spraying, and the water scarcity grew more acute. At this time, one of the three organizations, the Unión Campesina (UC), reached an agreement with the provincial government. The indigenous organization would receive transgenic cotton seeds, which also required spraying and larger scales of production. The UC leaders viewed this agreement as an achievement, although it created new challenges for both the group and its relations with the other organizations. Some members of the Unión Campesina began to withdraw from lawsuits against Don Panos regarding pollution caused by agrochemicals.

Without the participation of the UC, in June 2012 the Qom signed an agreement with the company as part of the Alternative Program for Conflict Resolution run by the public attorney of Chaco Province and the national government. This agreement stated that the company was committed to leaving a 600-meter strip free of agrochemical spraying, while the Ministry of Planning and the Environment committed to a sustainable development plan to reestablish indigenous farms. The agreement also established a plan by which the Ministry of Planning and the Environment, the Water and Maintenance Provincial Company Service, and the Provincial Water Administration would resolve the water shortage. Paradoxically, the plan consisted of providing a national governmental loan to Unitec Agro as part of the Bicentennial Production Financing Program. The loan, whose objective was to triple the company's production by improving its irrigation system, was granted on the condition that the company build a water reservoir on its land and a new 30-kilometer aqueduct to provide a supply to the urban area of Pampa del Indio. Meanwhile, the rural areas would continue to depend on water distribution trucks. The conflicts over the agrochemical spraying stopped, but problems related to unemployment and the scarcity of water, hunting, and gathering practices continued.

Memories of Past Experiences

For the majority of the Qom whom I interviewed in Pampa del Indio, the beginning of the cotton period in the middle of the 1940s was described as a key moment in the community's history. In the words of Aristóbulo, that was a prosperous time: "There was a lot of *acompañamiento* [continued support, followup], and we saw the results. We produced cotton, sunflowers, sorghum, and vegetables. There were a lot. In those years, the production got a little more democratic, and more people could be served" (September 2012).

Acompañamiento refers to the training and supervision carried out by experts from state programs as well as the representatives of political parties and religious institutions. Similarly, Dario, a Qom language teacher, referred to that time:

> The cotton period was great. I was a harvester. It was great because it was a very important source of income when cotton was worth something. In my area, there were a lot of families attached to the agricultural cooperative, indigenous families; they had been guided and shepherded by the Evangelical Baptist Church at the time. Those who became members of the Pampa del Indio cooperative were mostly members of the Evangelical Baptist mission. There was a missionary who took charge of teaching the communities, and the mission helped with the planting, the subsidy, and everything that might help. With the help of the mission, we rented land and planted there. We organized ourselves with the evangelical mission, and it subsidized us. I don't know where the subsidies came from; I suppose that they also had a political link with the state, the government, maybe. At that time, my grandfather didn't have the deed; he only had the political word. He had fifty hectares, which were then divided up. (August 2012)

As expressed by both interviewees, this was a time when they received external support from different actors. These paternalistic relations contributed to shaping the way dispossession is perceived and addressed. Just as "progress" achieved since the 1940s was related to the amount of *acompañamiento*, the current problems are associated with a lack of it, and the solutions inevitably entail greater support.

In the words of Luis, "We have received a few things, and now we've presented projects for vegetable cultivation. Later, we'll see what other opportunities are available. We need projects, and experts to accompany us" (October 2012).

Actual Experiences of Dispossession and Their Perceptions

During my stay in Pampa del Indio, my conversations with the Qom about the problems they faced rarely started out with mentions of the conflict with Don Panos. The narratives mostly focused on the absence of the state and the lack of support for working in the fields. The lack of support was almost always synonymous with the absence of the state and other actors such as missions and churches that had been important during the cotton period as providers of goods and services.

On some occasions, the lack of support appeared to be associated with the role of being a small producer without differentiation from the situation of the poor criollos. However, in most cases, it was the Qom's status as indigenous people that explained the lack of support. The problem, ultimately, was that they continued to be victims of a priori perceptions of what it means to be indigenous, or as Tania Li has suggested (2000, 2010b), they were in the "indigenous slot." Sebastián explained it as follows:

> People are renting because they don't have the resources, because they don't have tools. Why don't they bring us a tractor? Indigenous people can drive too. But no, they don't give them a loan facility because they see you're an aborigine, and they get stingy. But if a gringo comes along, they give him everything. "Oh, yes! How much do you want? Take it; here's a loan for some machinery too," they say to the gringos. And us? They say no because you're indigenous; you don't get anything. (2010)

The focus on the lack of support in perceptions of dispossession does not mean that the Qom do not mention the arrival of Don Panos and the subsequent lack of water, increased pollution, and barriers to *marisca* as threats to their ability to remain in the countryside. Those who had direct contact with the company, indigenous health agents, and teachers in Campo Medina emphasized the responsibility of the company in preventing them from staying on their land, as Mariano described:

> A lot of things were grown here before the spraying. When my parents were still alive, we produced cotton. Every week, we gathered up to forty-five tons of cotton. We also delivered to the cooperative as partners. But with all the spraying, all those problems, we can't even

produce sweet potatoes or mandioca. And we're struggling with the animals now. We have difficulties because the cows and goats are having miscarriages or dying because of the spraying. (2012)

Ángel, another Qom whose land borders that of Don Panos, also stated on several occasions that the arrival of the company had altered practices in the community. He said the company not only ended his honey production but also that cultural practices were disappearing:

Here, we're 300 meters from his [Eurnekian's] farm. And when the plane sprays with a southerly wind . . . we don't have any hives any more. We're just left with the boxes. The beehive was important because it provided honey, and you can't go looking for it in the fields any more. And we can't make natural medicines. Some of them are inside that large company's [Don Panos's] land, and they've closed it all off. The plants don't grow here, in our area, maybe a little but not enough to make medicines. Before, when we had open land, there were a lot of plants and roots to make them. In the open fields, people knew where to go, and they made medicine. But not any more. (September 2012)

Overall, only the people who lived next to Don Panos along with the teachers and health care workers were able to locate the impact of the company on their lives. For the majority, however, the neoliberal restructuring and the new agricultural model in Pampa del Indio were associated with the lack of state help and recognition.

Position of Subalternity

Dispossession for one group is not a homogeneous or unchanging experience. In some cases the experience can be focused on the lack of support, in others on the impossibility of reproducing cultural practices or practicing agriculture. These distinctions are important insofar as the actions of subaltern groups depend on the way the dispossession is experienced and perceived. The experiences and perceptions also are intimated in relation to the position of subalternity, that is, the transformative power that each actor has according to the complexity of the relations in which he or she is immersed.

The Unión Campesina, the indigenous organization with more political weight in Pampa del Indio, chose a position from which to negotiate a more successful inclusion rather than rejecting the model. This position was reflected in the words of Nora, who temporarily assumed its leadership in 2012 after her husband, Mártires López, passed away. Remembering him, she told me,

> He said that we had to try to turn back the wind: first, that we should be reorganized as peasants. Although we are aborigines, we needed to be recognized as peasants. Because we always had the idea that a peasant is a gringo who works the land, but if you go into the interior, you'll find Qom who want to work the land, who don't want to leave the countryside. . . . We chose cotton because it is the only product that we can sell. That's what the government must understand, that there must be a price for cotton. That if we plant a lot of squash and watermelons, who's going to buy them? The government helps the soybean producers more than the cotton producers. (2012)

This position of the UC is also reflected in the willingness to use transgenic seeds. One of its members stated, "The weed killer is messed up because it messes with the farms, but we as a community are trained in using the transgenic seeds; that's why we have an expert, and we are always in contact with them, and they tell us how to plant" (Daniel, 2012).

In contrast to the perspective of the UC, many other Qom in Pampa del Indio have said their struggle should not be focused on ensuring access to the same technology that other producers in the region have. They do not agree that it would be beneficial to use transgenic seeds, for economic reasons and health concerns, as stated by Mariano: "Transgenic seeds aren't worth it, because they need a lot of treatment and are also bad for your health. We must cultivate organic, nontransgenic seeds because otherwise we'll be needing more and more chemicals to maintain production. How much do we have to spend? Instead of cultivating healthy crops like before, we're going to wipe out the town" (2012).

The differences in criteria between the Unión Campesina and other Qom regarding the type of agriculture that should be practiced presents a serious challenge, especially because of the political weight of the UC. Luis, a health care worker, said the decision of the UC to plant transgenic seeds has caused great damage to the community: "Now some brothers plant transgenic cotton, which sank us. Until the maize starts to flower, the transgenic screws us. When your seeds flower, you're still screwed because of the bugs that come one after another" (2012).

This assessment has led in great part to the Qom directing their efforts not just toward confronting Don Panos but also toward achieving a new agreement among the organizations. During my visit in 2012, Mariano was very worried by the situation, and in an interview he gave to the provincial radio program *A Buen Tiempo Nacional*, he expressed his discontent: "Now what I'm asking the organizations is for them to support us, who have always lived at a disadvantage." While for the UC the struggle is against adverse incorporation into the agroindustrial model and ceasing to be "the bottom, the poorest of the poor"(Mártires, 2010), for the Qom who live near Don Panos and whose organizations have less political weight, the adverse incorporation can be reversed only if another kind of agriculture is practiced.

Colonia Cacique Catán and the Dynamics of Resignation

The history of Colonia Cacique Catán, also known as Paraje Las Tolderías, began in 1911,[12] when a group of Moqoit people led by the cacique Pedro José Nolasco Mendoza was forced to migrate from the province of Santa Fe as a consequence of the advance of the state's line of forts. By 1922, they were divided into two bands, one settling in Colonia El Pastoril and the other in Pampa del Cielo (López 2009). The latter group was evicted in 1924 and had to settle in its present location inside the General Necochea Agricultural Colony, which was created by President Hipólito Yrigoyen. Their narratives reveal that families had no fixed place to live or lived as *agregados* (additions) on other people's land. As José described it, the Moqoit "had no communities like our brothers the Qom and the Wichí, who got large stretches of land; we were spread out across the colony in the places left unoccupied" (2012).

The region inhabited by the Moqoit was one of the main cotton-producing centers of Chaco. In contrast to the Qom, who were surrounded by large estates, the Moqoit lived next to small farms. The interethnic relations established in this context are exemplified by a family tale told by Antonio Mocoví:

My grandfather told me that when we came with the group of 1,500 Indians from Santa Fe to Chaco, we came as a group, and then the carts of the gringos came. A caravan of gringos came after the indigenous people accompanying the caravan. So they came to Chaco and settled in Pampa del Cielo, throughout the Charata area. If a war arose during that period, the gringos were there, behind the indigenous people, to fight against the army. It was the army that trapped people, that sought out indigenous people to kill them. (2012)[13]

Given that indigenous access to free land was reduced, work as day laborers and harvesters in the fields of the colonists became, until the mid-1970s, the main source of livelihood for Moqoit families. They complemented this activity with subsistence farming and the *marisca* on the colonists' land (interviews, 2010–2012).

The 1980s brought major changes for the Moqoit. Although the colony had been founded in the 1920s, only by 1984 did they receive provisional deeds to parcels of land, which varied between twenty and twenty-five hectares (interviews, 2012). Along with obtaining the titles to their land they received tools and funds for production. In Narciso's words, "Help came, because they now knew the people had fixed places, and so help began to flow. Everyone now had their own little parcel, so the next step was to help them. After a while, the house came too, because they knew that we were the owners" (2012).

The help referred to by Narciso was a rural development project run by the Inter-American Foundation.[14] For five years, the foundation granted the funds to clear land and increase existing crops (Bray 1989). For the funds to be transferred, the Moqoit had to create the Asociación Comunitaria Colonia Las Tolderías, which was one of the first indigenous organizations in Chaco Province with legal personhood. The association had to coordinate the use of machinery and jointly organize the sale of the produce. However, shortly after the project began, conflicts arose that eventually led to the division of the community and the formation of two neighborhoods, Santa Rosa and San Lorenzo.

By the mid-1990s, a group of business people from Córdoba Province began to rent and buy fields from criollo colonists, progressively replacing cotton crops with soybeans.[15] In contrast to the previous case study, which involved a large enterprise, Don Panos, here, soybean production is carried out by three mid-sized establishments. The new producers are barely known by the people in the area. The interviewees referred to them as the "rich men," "millionaires," or "capitalists," but their identities remained anonymous, unlike those of the previous small-scale farmers (interviews, 2012). The only contact between the Moqoit families and the soybean producers occurs through "managers," employees who occasionally come to spray, plant, and harvest the fields.

The departure of the criollo colonists and the introduction of soybeans, similar to events in Pampa del Indio, generated major changes in the rural dynamics of the area. In this case, the scarce demand for labor has forced the Moqoit to go farther afield in search of work. Usually they travel to other provinces such as Santiago del Estero, where they work clearing land. The distances to their work sites have driven Moqoit to rent their lots or just give them to someone who can work them (interviews, 2010–2012). Generally, they receive a percentage of the sales of the production in payment for the use of the land. While revenues are small, most do this because, as stated by one, "If we leave it unworked, the roots will take hold again, and it'll be twice the work because we'll have to clear the trees out again. So we give it to someone else to work on it. Sometimes they give us something. When they sell, half a hectare is for us. That's our payment" (2012).

In addition to the lack of employment, the advance of soybean cultivation, increased deforestation, agrochemical spraying, and denial of entry to private properties have decreased the practice of *marisca*. Despite these problems, Colonia Cacique Catán did not organize any mobilizations to protest these issues. What factors explain the different positions of the Qom versus Moqoit communities in response to processes of dispossession?

Memories of Past Experiences

The migration from Santa Fe Province prior to the foundation of their current settlement was a watershed between the "ancient Moqoit" and the "new Moqoit." Rodolfo described the foundation of Paraje Las Tolderías: "When they were in Santa Fe, our grandparents didn't work; they were very poor. They didn't have anything to plough the land or any of that. And then when they came here, they decided to change" (2012). The persecution they suffered, their status as forced migrants for more than twenty years, the scarcity of free land, and the subsequent need to engage in paid work resulted in the suppression of their cultural traits and the assimilation of a wider range of criollo cultural practices (Citro 2006; López 2009).

The settlement in the colony and the "start of the new era" coincide with the prelude to the cotton cycle. This period was remembered by most as an era of happiness and abundance, when there "was more life and movement" (interviews, 2010–2012). The memories of happiness are closely associated with the family unit. Most interviewees stated that in that era the family stayed together, in clear contrast to the present situation, in which the men migrate to other provinces in search of work while the women stay behind. Pablo recalled the era as follows: "Cotton meant something special before today. Cotton motivated the family; it's what kept the family happy. During harvest time, the father, the son, and the grandson and everyone would join in the harvest, and it was money that came every weekend; it was a tiny salary. At its best, it was a party" (2012).

In most accounts, the wages obtained from working on the cotton harvest explained the general well-being during this period. Money allowed people to survive but also gave them access to certain goods as they came into closer contact with criollos. The prosperity of these years is also associated with the help that the *patrones*, the criollo colonists, gave them. Fernando said,

> At first you don't have anything; to get what you want, you have to work. I was raised like my mother, as a harvester. Labor for cotton. Before it was easier for us to live because with a proper little job, you could survive and earn what our work was due in a dignified manner. And it was also little because we never gave up on the food from the bush. That helped us a lot because there was a lot of bush, and the producers, who knew us, allowed us to go onto their lots to hunt the animals. (2012)

The so-called *ayuda* (help) they received from the criollos was not limited to the opportunity for *marisca* on the property of the colonists; it also refers to loans or donations of different objects and supplies, as described in the following account by Pedro:

> I got here in the 1920s or 1930s. Other people were here—they're not any more—we were new. Before, we were naked. . . . I didn't have anything. When they saw me, some of the colonists gave me shirts and old jackets. I had a lot of gringo friends. I worked with them a lot. People bought [hired] me to plough the fields in the colony. Fernández, a colonist, helped me in the large field close to the school. He came and asked me, and I said I didn't have anything, not a plow or horses, nothing. "Then, we'll help you with the tractor," he said. He helped me. I had a few hectares of cotton. And when the cotton came, I sold it and earned money. A lot of money! And I asked how much they charged for the tractor, and they said, "No, no, no, we won't charge. We just wanted to help." They told me that I should buy horses with the money. And I bought two mules. I finished the harvest, and they helped me again. (2012)[16]

In this colony, wage labor was not just a complement to production; rather, it was work that allowed the Moqoit to get the *ayuda* they needed—from criollos, not from the state—to practice agriculture on their own lots.

Actual Experiences of Power and Dispossession and Their Perceptions

During my visits to Colonia Cacique Catán to discuss the changes that have occurred due to the expansion of soybean production in the region, the main topics of conversation were the "depeasantization" (Araghi 1995) caused by the debt colonists incurred and the subsequent crisis of cotton cooperatives. José explained, "What's happening is that the small colonists who harvested with the help of extra labor sold everything to the large colonists. The small colonists have now left because they got into debt or something and because bigger ones came and bought everything. Today, the owners of the fields aren't in the fields either. No one lives in the fields any more; the only person in the field is the manager, and the owners are the big colonists" (2012).

Narciso and Fernando used very similar terms in describing the changes that took place over the previous decade. Narciso said, "Before, we had neighbors. There was one called Mansilla; he was criollo, a poor *santiagueño* like us.[17] He had to sell, and then the *cordobés* man came and bought everything and left the countryside.[18] Many had to sell their lots" (2012). Fernando said, "People sold their fields; they left. The ones planting now are from Córdoba, and when they plant they use their cure [agrochemicals]. How can we defend ourselves if they're the owners?" (2012). Fernando's question expresses the sense of inevitability that characterizes almost all the accounts of this period. That sense constitutes a key element in understanding the lack of mobilization in the community. James Scott has argued that "resignation to what seems inevitable is not the same as according it legitimacy, although it may serve just as efficiently to produce daily compliance. A certain tone of resignation is entirely likely in the face of a situation that cannot, in the short run, be materially altered" (1985, 324). Although sometimes the process was criticized, it was not challenged.

The neoliberal restructuring and new agricultural model for the Moqoit has meant above all the loss of their previous employers and the whole set of relationships associated with them. To some degree, the fact that the criollo colonists were the first to be affected means that the process and its consequences are perceived by the Moqoit as being beyond their power to change. As Ángel said, "You saw that today, you can't farm like before.

Today, it's more to do with agrochemicals. Progress ate us up as it went along" (2012).

Just as important is that the consequences are seen as something that does not affect just them. Regarding unemployment, for example, the majority said that the criollos were suffering just as much. José observed, "The other sad thing for us is that every fortnight, trucks arrive full of people, and other groups leave. Poor indigenous people and criollos have to travel for ten hours to Santiago. Around Santiago, they're clearing forest to an incredible extent" (2012).

The inability to conceive of an alternative scenario is not the only explanation for the group's lack of mobilization. The greater presence of the state is undoubtedly another variable that should be considered. In this colony, in contrast to Pampa del Indio, many said that although there was less work at the moment, there isn't as much poverty as before because now they receive state help. The help they refer to is mainly social security and pensions given to retired rural laborers.

In addition to unemployment, the expansion of soybean production has caused major changes in the environment. As in other cases, the increased crop spraying and deforestation that come with this form of production created new problems and challenges for the community. Marcelo was the first to note the impact of agrochemical spraying: "The poisons hurt you because now everyone is spraying by plane, and it goes into the water. The animals eat the plants, and they die. Because it's all poisoned. But now, when they cure [spray] the crops, they let us know, and then people take precautions, tie up the animals. They all come with respect" (2010). Other residents of San Lorenzo neighborhood said agrochemical spraying had contaminated the water they drank every day from a well. A resident explained, "The manager always warns the families before spraying that they need to get enough water to last the month. Therefore, we do" (2010).

What all these accounts have in common is the contrast to Pampa del Indio, where the Qom said the company and the government had ignored their complaints. Instead, the Moqoit continued to see the producers as good neighbors. Therefore, the consequences of the fumigations were seen as accidents caused by working people and thus were not a motive for confrontation. Mariana said, "You can't say, 'Hey! I'm going to report you because you're using planes.' That's their job. They do their job and also take care of the *paisanos*.[19] Because we're very small and depend on them" (2010).

Position of Subalternity

Although in the Moqoit community most people perceived a greater presence of the state, this perception was not homogeneous, which has created certain tensions. In general, the interviewees observed that the Santa Rosa neighborhood received more help from the state.

Members of the Santa Rosa community said the reason for less *ayuda* for the San Lorenzo community was because it was known to be "a little bit more rebellious," which made the authorities consider it "more difficult" (interviews, 2012). The inhabitants of San Lorenzo, meanwhile, also stated that they received less *ayuda* and that their differences with the Santa Rosa community arose because they have sustained more autochthonous practices. Rosa of San Lorenzo said, "They [in Santa Rosa] don't speak the language like our children. Our children only speak Spanish at school. They speak their own language at home. They say San Lorenzo is here, and Santa Rosa is there. The community has two names. Here, we maintain the customs more; here, we never changed our minds about how to bring up our children" (2011). The differences between the two neighborhoods seem to have contributed to the idea that those who are more assimilated to the criollo culture will get more support and that confrontation or differentiation is not a beneficial mechanism.

The Moqoit' positioning as a minority indigenous group in Chaco Province vis-à-vis the Qom also seems to have favored greater acquiescence. Many interviewees placed an emphasis on the differences that existed between the work culture of the Moqoit and the political culture of the Qom, and these comments were accompanied by heavy criticism of the forms of struggle that the political culture represented. In Pampa del Indio, a Qom stated that "in a system such as this, one has to hold marches, block roads, and present petitions to be heard." In contrast, interviewees in Colonia Cacique Catán said protests are not necessary. One of the leaders explained,

> I know communities that don't do anything but block roads. If I go to the colony and call for a roadblock, they'll reject it. As an indigenous leader, I don't agree with roadblocks. My point of view today is that my work is to knock on the doors of all the government offices. If I can opt for dialogue, I'll choose dialogue, and if I have to come back later, I'll come later, so the minister will meet me. That's my objective as a leader, not going to the road with my brothers and saying, "No, the minister doesn't want to hear me." And that's what I do, put myself

on the white man's level, use the same strategies so that my people can have something without having to block roads. (2012)

Final Remarks

Although studies on accumulation by dispossession have been very important in expounding on the links between global and local processes, the role of subalterns in those processes has barely been acknowledged. Undoubtedly, dominant groups and states "play a crucial role in both backing and promoting these processes" (D. Harvey 2003, 145). However, to consider the political nature of the processes is not to limit them to the actions of these sectors. The processes also require the participation, resistance, or acquiescence of the subaltern groups.

Local rationalities provide a more suitable starting point for understanding the new rural dynamics. They are the basis from which subalterns develop their positions not just of resistance but also of acquiescence and negotiation (Nilsen and Cox 2013). The three aspects of local rationalities on which I have focused on are memories of past periods, actual experiences of dispossession, and a position of subalternity.

In the case of the Qom, memories of the cotton-growing period centered on the presence of the state, as reflected by training policies, support, and the provision of work tools. In contrast, in the case of the Moqoit, memories of the period prior to neoliberalism centered primarily on wage labor for small producers and the absence of the state. Once the process of neoliberal transformation, which involved an increase in soybean production, had begun, these different memories of the prior period played an important role in the formation or lack of formation of resistance movements. Therefore, in the case of the Qom, the restructuring of the state, budget cuts, and the removal of incentives for cotton production were perceived as policies of dispossession and created foundations for social protest. In contrast, for the Moqoit, the neoliberal transformations were not perceived as dispossession because those initially affected were the people's former patrons who were forced to sell their land to larger producers. Since the state did not have an important role in their memories, its restructuring and shrinking did not have an apparent impact on the community.

Regarding the actual experiences of dispossession in the cases analyzed here, it is important to take into account that in Pampa del Indio, these changes occurred and became apparent after the establishment of a large company with the backing of the state. Despite numerous complaints and reports of violations of different regulations, Don Panos continued its operations but also received state loans to expand its production at the same time that the state was reducing help to small producers. All these elements have contributed to the emergence of resistance in the community. In Colonia Cacique Catán, the new rural dynamics appeared slowly through the gradual arrival of various different mid-size producers who rented or bought land from the existing farmers. Insofar as wage labor had been the main form of subsistence since the 1920s, the new rural dynamics, although they caused significant changes, did not entirely alter the indigenous people's practices or greatly affect their identity. Essentially, even though they needed to migrate to other provinces, they were still seasonal workers. The absence of the state during the cotton period also was partially reversed through the implementation of some social subsidies and benefits that served to supplement monetary income. These characteristics make it possible to explain to a great degree why the Moqoit have been more acquiescent.

Finally, the greater degree of mobilization observed in Pampa del Indio must be seen in the context of the greater influence of leftist political parties and during the early years of the struggle, the presence of a charismatic leader, Mártires López, the first president of the Unión Campesina. Also important was the weakening of resistance in the area after a change in the UC's position. The relative acquiescence observed on the part of the Moqoit seems to have been influenced both by the local divisions and by the differences between this group and the Qom at the provincial level.

The comparison of these two cases shows that the process of accumulation by dispossession should be understood not as a project uniformly implemented from above, imposed upon people who resist more or less successfully, but as a process that is perceived, experienced, and acted upon diversely by different groups according to their local rationalities. The local rationalities perspective allows us to understand what types of resistance arise, why some groups do not try to limit their exposure to the market, and why some groups do not mobilize to prevent or reverse the new dynamics.

Acknowledgments

I am especially thankful to the Qom and Moqoit families whose hospitality and patience made this research possible. For their friendship and support, I would like to extend my deepest thanks to Silvia Hirsch and Paola Canova.

Notes

1. I carried out in-depth interviews in Spanish on multiple trips to Chaco Province between 2010 and 2016, employing both semistructured and open formats. In the majority of cases the talks took place in the homes of indigenous families; so, although they were initially planned to be held with individuals, many often ended up being collective. In these situations, the men generally took the lead, while women gradually got involved in the conversation. The names of the interviewees have been changed except for the subjects who occupy public roles and whose opinions are a matter of record.

2. Braunstein (2008) defines a *banda* as a group of relatives without a unilinear or local focus; that is, the members live together in the same place, be it stable or not. *Bandas* are described as bilateral or nonunilinear because no distinction is made between maternal or paternal lines.

3. Several documents testify to the immobilization of indigenous groups by the government of the national territory of Chaco due to increasing competition for labor (Cordeu and Siffredi 1971; Miller 1979).

4. Forty square leagues is approximately 100,000 hectares; however, some of my informants stated that the area granted by Yrigoyen was 220,000 hectares rather than 100,000. The decree granting this land has never been found, so it is impossible to know the exact figure.

5. "Criollo" refers to a person of mixed racial background, generally of European ancestry.

6. The term "clearance" refers to the processes of deforestation, derooting, and slash and burn for leaving the plot free of weeds.

7. The Forestry Department provided authorization to clear 1,000 hectares, but the company exceeded that limit, clearing more than 1,600 hectares. Following this, the Forestry Department fined the company, which would violate regulations again a few months later. On that occasion, the company cleared 2,500 hectares without receiving official authorization (Greenpeace 2006). Some informants claim that the company did not pay the fine.

8. The purpose of the latter construction was to feed water to the modern irrigation system required by soybean cultivation.

9. The so-called countryside conflict started in March 2008 after Resolution 125/08 was announced by the Ministry of the Economy, increasing the percentage of taxes on exports on certain commodities. More specifically, this resolution established a structure of mobile values that changed in accordance with international prices over a four-year period. In the case of soybeans, the increase in the share rose from 35 percent to 44 percent. This measure was immediately rejected by the representatives of the traditional organizations in the sector (Petras and Veltmeyer 2016).

10. The Comisión Zonal de Tierras and the Asociación Civil Cacique Taigoyik were founded in the early 1990s. The groups were originally linked to ENDEPA (National Team of Pastoral Aborigines) and INCUPO (Institute of Popular Culture), a Christian nonprofit civil association. The Unión Campesina was founded in 2001 and is linked to the Revolutionary Communist Party.

11. See Darío Aranda, "La lluvia es un agrotóxico," *Página 12*, January 24, 2011, https://www.pagina12.com.ar/diario/sociedad/3-161022-2011-01-24.html.

12. Colonia Cacique Catán, named in honor of the man who is considered the last of the great Mocoví cacique, is also known as Paraje Las Tolderías.

13. This account of colonization differs markedly from the memories of the Qom, as related by Mariana from Pampa del Indio after the death of cacique Taigoyik: "Strange people came from everywhere looking for land. Nobody knew where they came from."

14. When the accounts gathered from the Moqoit feature the word "help," it is sometimes used as a synonym for "support," referring to training activities and tools linked to production, but more generally it is associated with money and goods obtained through the charity of other actors.

15. Córdoba is a province in the Pampeana region, a central nucleus of the production of soy in Argentina. Córdoba province is approximately 670 kilometers southwest of Chaco Province.

16. While Pedro shared his memories in the Moqoit language, one of his grandchildren simultaneously translated them into Spanish.

17. A *santiagueño* is someone born in Santiago del Estero Province.

18. A *cordobés* is someone born in Córdoba Province.

19. In Chaco Province, *paisano* is a term used to describe indigenous peoples. Seen as inoffensive, it is used by the indigenous community to describe people of their own and other indigenous ethnicities and by nonindigenous peoples indiscriminately to describe an indigenous group or person.

7

Infrastructures of Settler Colonialism

Geographies of Violence, Indigenous Labor, and Marginal Resistance in Paraguay's Chaco

JOEL E. CORREIA

Ruta 5 connects the towns of Pozo Colorado and Concepción, Paraguay, while simultaneously bisecting Yakye Axa and Sawhoyamaxa, two Enxet indigenous communities.[1] The road passes a few other smaller communities nestled into the highway's margin; most are comprised of a handful of houses made of faded gray palm wood with tin roofs. Palm trees and cattle pastures dominate the landscape as one travels down the highway, save for the chance that a freshly skinned animal, honey in repurposed plastic soda bottles, or fans woven from palm leaves might be hanging from a stake set near the highway's edge, advertising their sale to passersby. The goods serve as markers that call to the eye because they break with a landscape otherwise defined by seemingly continuous cattle ranches and the remnants of a transitional palm and scrub brush forest. Makeshift memorials commemorating lives lost to traffic accidents or due to an inability to access transportation to the nearest medical post are other markers that break the pattern of fence rows and signs that announce *propiedad privada* (private property). However, it seems likely that many people pass by without taking notice of the homes, people, and lives on the margin of the highway.

From the side of the road, it is difficult not to notice each passing car and bus or the trucks carrying cattle to the slaughter. The vehicles are loud and interrupt sounds of kids playing, people talking during community meetings, and the shrill songs of countless locusts in the afternoon sun of summer. I can recall from one of my first visits to Yakye Axa sleeping in my tent, then waking in the night, startled by the rumble of cargo trucks lumbering over the road's many potholes. The heavy trucks make the ground tremble like a low-grade earthquake as they pass, to say nothing of the sounds of their creaking chassis, loud music, and cattle mooing in protest of the rough ride. The traffic passes day and night while most people in Yakye Axa and Sawhoyamaxa have little to no access to transportation other than their feet, often referred to as *línea once*. *Línea once* literally means "line 11," a metaphor for bus route 11 that also evokes the shape of two parallel legs in the number 11. Instead of taking a bus, *línea once* means the person will be walking.

Life on the side of the road is pedestrian. In contrast to the traffic, the pace of life is slow. Kids play on the cracked, dry earth or in the mud, depending on the season. Families go to the small Pentecostal church, while some still practice what many refer to as *cultura indígena* (indigenous culture).[2] Women wash clothes in a pond dug into the margin. Men often look for scarce day-labor opportunities on nearby ranches. In many ways, everyday life on the margin of the highway is not unusual in comparison with that in other rural communities across the region that are subject to the challenges and opportunities posed by the large-scale cattle ranching; wage labor is sparse, as is access to state services, and struggles for land rights abound.

*   *   *

The political economy of cattle ranching in the Bajo Chaco and its interplay with Enxet life resonates with the friction between indigenous peoples and agro-extractivism across the settler colonial frontiers in Latin America. Such forms of friction are often mediated through infrastructural components upon which systems operate, be they the bodies of laborers or the roads, fences, and stock ponds. Through ethnographic attention to Enxet struggles for land rights from the margin of Ruta 5 and attention to the histories of ranching in the Bajo Chaco, I find that settler colonialism operates through material and embodied forms of infrastructural violence. Drawing from research with members of Sawhoyamaxa and Yakye Axa,[3] I trace contemporary infrastructural violence to its historical roots in the establishment of settler ranching systems in the Bajo Chaco.

Settler colonialism, understood as a structure of social-spatial relations (Speed 2017; Wolfe 2006), is mediated through material objects such as fences and embodied infrastructure such as labor. Enxet lands and labor have become central infrastructural components for the establishment and spread of cattle ranching. Penelope Harvey's analysis (2014, 281) informs my approach: "Infrastructures can orient research to particular relational

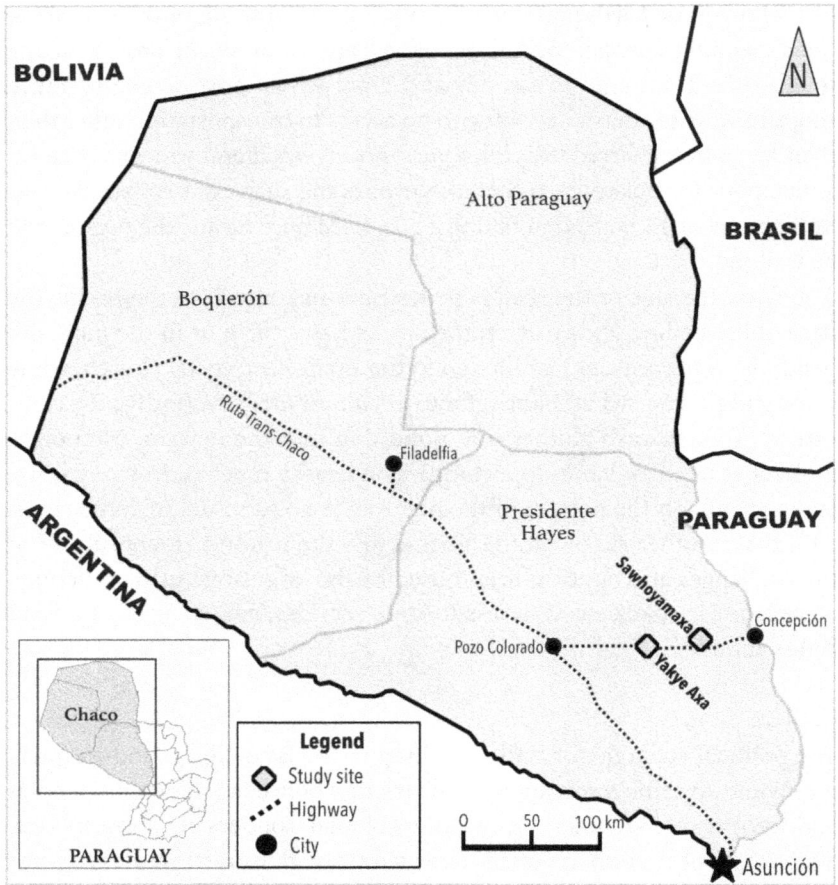

Map 7.1. Sawhoyamaxa and Yakye Axa study sites and major regional roads. Map by Joel Correia.

dynamics that tend to be taken for granted, but at the same time they reveal the creative possibilities that emerge even when systems seem to be at their most limiting. They are material, social, and ideational conditions that configure lifeworlds, *constraining but not determining* how people live" (my emphasis). While the structures of settler colonialism conditions Enxet life on the margin, they do not determine the outcomes of Enxet resistance from those spaces.

Of Land and Dispossession

Nearly 95 percent of the land in the Bajo Chaco is private property, and of that virtually all is used for cattle ranching (Vásquez 2010).[4] The Paraguayan state sold its Chaco landholdings in the late 1800s to finance debts incurred during the War of the Triple Alliance against Brazil, Argentina, and Uruguay in 1864–1870 (Kleinpenning 2003). The establishment and imposition of private property in the Bajo Chaco set forth a process of land dispossession materially reinforced by fences that limit Enxet peoples, among others, access to their traditional territories (Kidd 1992; Leake 1998; Villagra Carron 2010).

Dispossession is not a uniform process, however, and has occurred in different ways across Enxet territories due to the varying practices of landholders and their approach to indigenous peoples. In some cases, communities were forced to live on the margins of ranches, and in other cases, entire families would move from one ranch to another to join extended family groups or to Anglican mission stations (IACHR 2005, 2006; Kidd 1992). In other cases, English and U.S. ranch owners "ordered the indigenous [sic] into different villages in the area to integrate and go live near the core of the ranch in order to have more control" over the indigenous population (IACHR 2010, 24; Renshaw 2002). Thus, the establishment of private property and cattle ranches in the Chaco removed many indigenous communities from land and fixed them in place by enclosing communities within ranches. Stephen William Kidd argued (1992, 67),

> By the 1950s the landowners' control of Enxet territory was total, and the Enxet themselves had been almost entirely deprived of their freedom. They could only reside where they were given permission to by the owner of the land and were therefore restricted to villages next-door to the Paraguayan ranch settlements. Economically, they were completely dependent on the will of the landowners who severely restricted their freedom of movement and frequently denied them permission to hunt, gather, fish, garden, or keep livestock.

The process of dispossession Kidd describes is all too familiar across the Bajo Chaco. Many Enxet peoples with whom I have spoken recall strikingly similar histories, histories that shape present-day marginalization and ongoing struggles for territorial rights.

The people of Yakye Axa and Sawhoyamaxa lived and labored for generations on the ranches established in their traditional territories. Both

Figure 7.1. Yakye Axa, July 2016, seen from Ruta 5. The homes on the left abut a fence on the property line of a ranch that occupies ancestral territories claimed by the community. Photo by Joel E. Correia.

communities came to occupy the margin of Ruta 5 after they initiated legal claims for land rights, calling for the restitution of their lands via norms established in Paraguayan law during the 1980s and early 1990s.[5] Ranch owners responded by denying community members permission to continue living and laboring on the ranches, while the Paraguayan state did little to enforce laws outlining legal protections for indigenous peoples. As a result, Enxet peoples established Yakye Axa and Sawhoyamaxa in the only publicly available lands in the area, a 30-meter-wide strip of land between Ruta 5 and the ranch fences built upon the very lands that both communities claim (figure 7.1). The occupation of the highway's margin was intended to be brief while each community navigated the legal process for land restitution.

However, state inaction and rancher resistance to the land claims generated a fraught legal process that has spanned nearly three decades and been adjudicated before both national and international courts (Correia 2018a). The Inter-American Court of Human Rights (IACHR) issued judgments on behalf of both communities that recognize the human rights violations caused by land dispossession and challenge the settler colonial territoriality in the Bajo Chaco. As a result, the IACHR has demanded that Paraguay restitute land to Yakye Axa and Sawhoyamaxa (IACHR 2005, 2006). Despite these legal victories, implementation of the rulings, particularly regarding land restitution, has been excruciatingly slow and incomplete.

Throughout much of their legal struggles, members of Sawhoyamaxa and Yakye Axa have occupied the political geographic manifestation of the gap between de jure and de facto rights, living on the literal margin of the highway and figurative margins of citizenship as people simultaneously are bestowed and denied rights. Lack of access to reliable and clean sources of drinking water and state services, as well as the deadly threat of vehicular traffic are but some of the factors that inflict forms of violence that are infrastructural. Such violence is built into the everyday geographies of the margin and has caused many of the human rights violations that propelled each community's case to the IACHR in the early 2000s. Though assessing the implementation politics is important to ensuring that the IACHR judgments contribute to indigenous peoples' justice, the imbrication of infrastructure, settler colonial territoriality, and Enxet resistance are equally important. Those considerations inspire the following question: What are the relations between indigenous labor, infrastructure, and settler colonialism, both historically and in the present? Answering this question invites engaging debates in recent work on the "infrastructural turn" in human geography and cultural anthropology, particularly the notion of infrastructural violence (Li 2018; Rodgers and O'Neill 2012).

On Infrastructure and Violence

Infrastructure studies in anthropology and geography grapple with spectacular development projects as well as mundane objects that condition everyday life (Ferguson 2012; Anand, Gupta, and Appel 2018). If "infrastructure is always about the future, or distant futures" (Hetherington and Campbell 2014, 193), one must always question whose vision of that future is advanced and with what effects on social difference. Gastón Gordillo's (2014, 14) brilliant ethnography of rubble in Argentina and efforts to "politicize object-oriented approaches through an attentiveness to destruction, violence, and reification" provides a helpful analytical framework to evaluate the imbrication of infrastructure and injustice. I engage everyday objects of ranching and histories of Enxet labor to center on *infrastructural violence*. Dennis Rodgers and Bruce O'Neill (2012, 405) note, "The notion of infrastructural violence seeks to squarely identify the political economy underlying the socio-spatial production of suffering." While their focus is on urban design and justice in the city, I shift the analysis to South America's rural heartland to show how ranching infrastructures disproportionately shape, discipline, and facilitate violence against indigenous peoples.

Infrastructural violence operates in mundane and spectacular ways. Kregg Hetherington (2014) details how one key actor who facilitates the promise of infrastructure—a land surveyor—yields his power in relation to campesinos seeking his services to demean their material poverty and threaten to displace them in efforts to create more legible, "modern" landscapes, thus creating uncertainty that undermines campesino well-being. Tania Li (2018) maintains a focus on materiality of infrastructure but also highlights unseen elements of system operations, building from Susan Star's (1999, 380) theorization of infrastructure as the "underlying features of system organization," or a "'system of substrates' that underlies the built phenomenal world." In doing so, Li shows how corruption shapes Indonesian palm oil plantations and enables their function as systems that exact social-ecological violence. These studies examine how infrastructure mediates tensions between notions of the future perfect while often exacerbating social inequality or producing new forms of violence.

Therefore, I use the term "infrastructural violence" to shift the analysis of structural violence to material forms through which it operates within geographies of power. Johan Galtung (1969) and Paul Farmer (1996, 2004) paved the way for studies of *structural violence*, though I build from Akhil Gupta's approach in *Red Tape* (2013). Such violence, Gupta contends, is "built into the structure of power," manifest as a "constant rather than episodic, and, far from disrupting actors' understandings of their social worlds, it provides them with *a particular kind of situated knowledge with its own epistemic certainties*" (20, my emphasis). Simon Springer (2011) has warned that the term "structural violence" runs the risk of losing analytical precision because it is often widely applied or used to reference acts that some may not consider violent because they do not entail physical violence. I am aware of that potential. Yet, I engage the intersection of structural violence and infrastructure because it allows my analysis to focus on how violence with no precise locus still has an undeniable impact on suffering and mortality via material objects and their effects. While the Paraguayan state is culpable of human rights violations against members of Yakye Axa and Sawhoyamaxa (IACHR 2005, 2006), much of the violence experienced in both communities is diffuse, without a clear perpetrator though often mediated by infrastructure. Thus things like fences that reinforce dispossession become sites to understand material manifestations of violence and the trauma of epistemic violence that results from settler colonialism (Fanon 1961; Rifkin 2013; Tuck and Yang 2012).

In this case, roads, fences, and stock ponds can therefore draw attention to how the amorphous nature of structural violence operates across multiple registers—from material to epistemic—in Yakye Axa and Sawhoyamaxa. Through attention to infrastructural violence, I shift focus between such material structures and those that are the underlying features of settler colonialism, such as land dispossession and environmental racism, that function through cattle ranching as a system of extraction and capitalist accumulation. Infrastructure has facilitated human rights abuses in the Yakye Axa and Sawhoyamaxa cases by starkly delimiting which bodies benefit from state services and which do not (Biehl 2016). A focus on infrastructure can thus enunciate which lives are rendered expendable, left on the side of the road in biopolitical acts intended to manage indigenous dispossession through legal abandonment (Correia 2018a; Li 2010b). The same infrastructures that enunciate injustice for Yakye Axa and Sawhoyamaxa also serve to advance state territoriality by rendering frontiers sites amenable to economic production (P. Harvey 2014) vis-à-vis infrastructures that protect cattle life and facilitate the transportation of beef and dairy commodities to domestic and external markets.

Shaylih Muehlmann (2019) avers that infrastructure is always multiple; it transcends any particular road's or fence's material traces to shape relations between people, place, and the more-than-human world. I think with the multiple meanings and manifestations of infrastructure in Paraguay's Bajo Chaco to move beyond a base or superstructure analysis and consider the contingencies of infrastructure as an analytic (Hetherington 2019; Anand, Gupta, and Appel 2018). Brian Larkin (2013) argues for evaluating infrastructure relationally, as comprised of material things such as roads or fences that mediate relations between different actors, places, and processes. Gordillo (2014) and Li (2018) also direct attention to the symbolic and unseen facets of infrastructure that play central roles in the organization and operation of oppressive *systems*. The system in question here is cattle ranching as a constituent element of settler colonialism in the Bajo Chaco. Thus, I use infrastructure as a lens to examine racialized inequalities that threaten Enxet human rights by destabilizing the mundane sites through which settler colonial power is given form and contingency (Anand, Gupta, and Appel 2018, 14). Examining infrastructural components of Bajo Chaco cattle ranches, I reconsider Patrick Wolfe's notion of settler colonialism as "a structure rather than an event" (2006, 390) by taking seriously material elements of that structure and their relation to violence. Building from these works, I contribute to an emergent if not undertheorized aspect of the infrastructural turn—the material and symbolic relations of infrastructure and settler colonialism (Bosworth 2018; Fanon 1961; Povinelli 2002; Wolfe 2016). How do historical infrastructures condition contemporary political struggles and social relations in the context of cattle ranching and indigenous territorial struggles in Paraguay's Bajo Chaco?

Cattle Ranching in Paraguay's Chaco and Settler Colonial Infrastructures

The cattle ranch is a system, not entirely unlike palm oil plantations that Li (2018) critiques, one specifically designed to extract economic value from the environment by manipulating life and landscapes to ensure specific economic outcomes. Ranching functions as a system of control that has become the predominant economic activity in the Paraguayan Chaco and requires a constellation of infrastructural components to operate effectively: specific varieties of pasture grasses that withstand the seasonal heat and precipitation variation in the Chaco, the strategic location of water sources such as *tajamares* (stock ponds), corrals for the application of vaccines and brands, ear tags that render each cow life legible and traceable to ensure biopolitical control for a disease-free industry, miles of fences, and more. The cattle ranch is ostensibly a site of order where laborers, cattle, and the biophysical environment must be disciplined to ensure expected outcomes and return on investment. Larkin (2013, 328) theorizes infrastructure as "built networks that facilitate the flow of goods, people, or ideas and allow for their exchange over space." In this way, ranches are made of "infrastructural components" (Muehlmann 2019, 49) such as fences and stock ponds that facilitate social-spatial relations and are also fundamental to the system of settler colonialism in the Bajo Chaco. Understanding these relations is a matter of scale that requires shifting from the ranch as a specific site of analysis to considering how ranching across the region functions as a system that structures social-spatial relations in specific ways with direct effects on indigenous life.

Large-scale cattle ranching like that found in the Bajo Chaco requires a particular production of space that renders social-environmental relations governable through practices that ensure sustained economic production (Gardner 2009; Hecht 1985). Land enclosure, deforestation, and indigenous dispossession have been the hallmarks of ranching's expansion across the Chaco since inception alongside Anglican missionization in the late 1800s. From humble beginnings, beef production in the Chaco has steadily risen in recent decades with Paraguayan state policy now promoting industry efforts to join the top five beef exporters globally. The roots of ranching are often closely associated with Mennonite immigrants' arrival in the Central Chaco in the 1920s and 1930s (Caldas et al. 2013; Canova 2015). And, without question, Mennonite settlers have been fundamental in establishing the cattle ranching industry via the cooperatives that they founded.[6] However, little attention has been placed on the crucial historical role that Anglican missionaries played in establishing the Paraguayan Chaco as a site of cattle capitalism.

There is an important geographic differentiation between cattle-ranching trajectories in the Central and Bajo Chaco of Paraguay. Mennonites helped pave the way for the large-scale ranching operations found across the Central Chaco today and have undeniably transformed Paraguayan cattle ranching from a market based on domestic demand to a major export industry. However, Anglican missionaries preceded the Mennonite arrival by more than thirty years and introduced ranching to the Bajo Chaco to sustain their mission stations and support the incursion of British and Paraguayan ranchers. The Anglican arrival and missionizing efforts among Enxet, Sanapaná, and Maskoy peoples were fundamental to establishing cattle ranching in the Bajo Chaco through the appropriation of an indigenous labor force that was used to build the basic infrastructures upon which settler colonialism has since operated in the region. Therefore, ranching in the Chaco has mediated social-spatial relations through the land dispossession and labor dynamic that Shannon Speed (2017) posits as central to the enduring structure of settler colonialism in Latin America.

Land, Labor, and Anglican Mission Ranches

The British Anglican mission began working in Paraguay in the late 1800s shortly after the establishment of the once-extensive tannin industry that operated north of the Bajo Chaco along the banks of the Paraguay River.[7] Colonizing the Bajo Chaco and establishing cattle ranching required extensive manual labor—indigenous labor. The British missionary Barbrooke Grubb was charged with establishing the Anglican Church in the Bajo Chaco and led the church's efforts there from 1889 to 1919 (Powell 2007). As the first state-recognized general commissioner of the Chaco, Grubb saw his role as one of bringing indigenous peoples to Christianity while also

creating a labor force that would support the Church's cattle ranches to ensure the sustainability of the missionizing efforts (Grubb 1993 [1911], 1914).
Cattle sales helped generate income that supported the Anglican missionary effort in Paraguay. Anglican missionaries primarily operated in areas
where British citizens had their most significant financial interests, in the
current-day Presidente Hayes Department.

Over the course of its one hundred years of work in the Bajo Chaco, the
Anglican South American Missionary Society (SAMS) established twelve
mission stations with ranches from the Paraguay River southeast toward
the Pilcomayo River; a network of roads and paths connected the missions
and later served as the trajectory upon which Ruta 5 would eventually be
constructed. Makxawáya, also known as Mission Station, was the core of
the Anglican presence in Paraguay's Chaco, yet another smaller mission
station, El Paso, established in the Yakye Axa territories functioned as the
primary cattle ranch that supported the missionary activity. By 1949 cattle
ranching became the main income source to support the Anglican mission
in the Bajo Chaco (Anglican Church 1979).

With the expansion of the mission system, the need for labor increased.
Using donations from British benefactors, Grubb and colleagues established the Paraguayan Chaco Indian Association to "enable the [indige-
nous] people to obtain profitable work and industrial training, and thus
to localize them at the mission stations, where they could be more efficiently dealt with" (Grubb 1993 [1911], 140). Given Grubb's writings as the
predominant accounts of missionary activities at the time, the Anglican
mission had a dual purpose. The first purpose was salvation; the second
was to create a labor force to support British business interests through the
establishment and operation of cattle ranches. SAMS, which supported the
Anglican missions, stated in a 1909 report on mission activities, "Those
who have an interest in Chaco lands can surely not fail to see the benefit of
a numerous, trained and willing population of workers with whom to develop the lands in which they have placed their capital" (in Kidd 1992, 64).
Indigenous labor cleared the forest, established fence lines, built roads, dug
stock ponds, planted grasses for cattle forage, and participated as scouts
on survey crews to demarcate land for investors (Grubb 1993 [1911], 1914).
The Anglican Church used the mission as a conduit to govern and produce
indigenous subjects amenable to capital accumulation: Christian laborers
with "a desire for culture and progress" (Grubb 1914, 218).

Anglican-operated industrial schools located on the mission ranches were used to educate Enxet in "proper" moral conduct and support the mission ranches through their labor (SAMS 1909, cited in Kidd 1992). In this case, Grubb and his colleagues understood "useful" indigenous people as those who abandoned their ancestral lifeways and adopted settler governmentalities predicated on Christianity and capitalism. Therefore, the missionary efforts were part of a governmental project that sought to expand the Anglican Church and establish a settler colonial society in the Bajo Chaco. If government is the "'art' of acting on the actions of individuals, taken either singly or collectively, so as to shape, guide, correct and modify the ways in which they conduct themselves" (Bruchell 1996, 19), then the mission advanced governance through assimilation. Grubb's efforts embody the coupling of indigenous land dispossession and indigenous labor exploitation on the very lands taken from them that Speed (2017) argues is a definitive attribute of settler capitalism in Latin America. In this way, Enxet labor became an infrastructural component of settler colonialism.

Throughout the missionizing process, the Paraguayan state tacitly relied on populating the Bajo Chaco to ensure its tenuous territorial claims to that region. The emergence and spread of cattle ranching in the Bajo Chaco, first through the missions and shortly after that through private investments, produced distinct social, spatial, and power relations that influenced how the Paraguayan state has come to govern that region and the indigenous peoples who live there. Therefore, Anglican missionary activities and infrastructures provided a foundation for Paraguay's establishment as a settler colonial state in the region. The Anglican missionary efforts were the first non-indigenous occupation of the Paraguayan Chaco, aside from the tannin logging communities to the north (Borrini 1997; Vázquez Recalde 2013). The mission stations relied on ranching for subsistence and income generation, which ultimately facilitated the spread of commercial cattle ranching by preparing a workforce and establishing the necessary infrastructure to transport cattle from interior ranchlands east to the Paraguay River. As Kidd notes (1992, 63), road networks developed by the Anglicans to support their mission stations became "the main artery along which colonization of the Chaco progressed." With the expansion of the ranching industry, more lands were enclosed by non-indigenous peoples, and more indigenous peoples were drawn into the ranching economy as laborers on those ranches, often with close connections to the Anglican Church (Villagra Carron 2010). That some twenty-three ranches either housed Anglican pastors or held formal church services through the 1970s indicates the strong linkages between the missionary efforts and establishment of the lasting cattle ranching activities (Powell 2007).

Indigenous labor has long functioned as a central underlying feature upon which settler colonialism in the Bajo Chaco was established and continues to operate. The history I briefly discuss here illustrates the conjoined, simultaneous acts of indigenous dispossession *and* labor exploitation fundamental to settler colonialism in Latin America. Speed observes, "Labor regimes were often the very mechanisms that dispossessed indigenous peoples of their lands forcing them to labor in extractive undertakings on the land that had been taken from them" (2017, 784). Settler colonists used indigenous labor to create the very ranching infrastructures that maintain indigenous dispossession. Thus, while there is a land dispossession and labor exploitation relation fundamental to the "structures of settler capitalism" in Latin America (Speed 2017), the material infrastructures that indigenous peoples were conscripted to build also played a pivotal role in the establishment and endurance of settler colonial geographies. The history of land dispossession and the exploitation of indigenous labor initiated by the Anglican missionaries created a structure of social-spatial relations that persists across the Bajo Chaco, serving as the basis for settler colonialism and infrastructural violence that condition many of the challenges that Enxet peoples confront in their ongoing struggles for self-determination with regard to land rights.

Infrastructural Violence and the Margins of Cattle Ranches

The margins have long held a contradictory and tenuous relation in anthropological and geographic inquiry, seen as sites of exploitation and oppression by some while as generative sites of resistance, innovation, and hope for others (hooks 1990; Das and Poole 2004; Korf and Raeymaekers 2013, Tsing 1994). Rather than an either/or proposition, I understand the margin as a liminal space (Correia 2018a) better captured by a both/and relation (Ybarra 2018), something hooks (1984) captures by stating "to be in the margin is to be part of the whole but outside the main body." Cattle ranch infrastructures create the geographic margins that Enxet peoples have long occupied, exemplifying how settler colonial structures *both* enroll indigenous peoples as the subjects of rights *and* dispossess them of those rights simultaneously. Roads, stock ponds, and fences are material infrastructures that underscore the social-political, and geographic marginalization of Yakye Axa and Sawhoyamaxa in relation to the Paraguayan state and area cattle ranchers. Roads provide a critical link to necessary services, but the presence or absence of transportation can also prove deadly and tormenting. Stock ponds built to sustain cattle lives have become critical water sources for humans, sustaining human life while harboring intestinal parasites that threaten those lives. Fences that once provided labor to the Enxet "employed" to build them now restrict their access to ancestral territories and define a settler colonial grid of property in land that reiterates dispossession.

Roads make an easy foil with which to consider infrastructure in relation to dispossession and violence in these cases. Ruta 5, the road that bisects Yakye Axa and Sawhoyamaxa, is one of two paved roads that transect the Paraguayan Chaco. The *ruta* is thus a crucial transportation artery that facilitates the circulation of Mennonite and other ranchers' goods, mainly cattle and dairy products. Rather than mere conduits of transportation, the highways are intimately bound with an ongoing project to modernize and settle Paraguay's frontier spaces by establishing extractive economic activities. As I write this chapter, a third major paved route, the Bioceanic Highway, is under construction and promises to transform Paraguay's Chaco into a site of strategic importance for agro-export industries. The Paraguayan Chaco's transformation to a site of extensive cattle production helps construct an image of the region as a space produced by industrious white settlers who tamed the country's western frontier and turned it into a central node in the global political economies of cattle production.

Due to Mennonite settlers' predominant role and their successful dairy cooperatives and ranching operations in the Central Chaco, they are colloquially credited with bringing order to the region and igniting its economic potential. Mennonite settlers were instrumental in lobbying the Paraguayan state to construct and pave the Trans-Chaco and Ruta 5 highways to facilitate their access to markets to sell goods produced by their cooperatives (Ratzlaff 1999). While Mennonite influence helped ensure the paving of Ruta 5, the current road follows the course of old Anglican mission station supply lines created by Enxet laborers. Therefore, the road connects sites of cattle production and exchange, but it also connects experiences of indigenous exploitation and dispossession across time.

Ruta 5 enables mobility, but its function to facilitate the transport of cattle is realized in quiet tandem with a patchwork of barbed-wire fences that run parallel to the road and refract outward to trace the property lines of seemingly innumerable cattle ranches. In the Bajo Chaco the fences dissect a vast floodplain and semi-arid palm forest into pasturelands where cattle are confined to graze on ranches owned by Paraguayan, Uruguayan,

Brazilian, Mennonite, US, English, and Korean cattle ranchers. Since the arrival of the Anglican missionaries in the last decade of the 1800s, the Paraguayan Chaco has turned into a region of vast cattle ranches, with the largest spanning more than a million hectares (Vázquez Recalde 2013). If private property in land facilitates "the white possessive" upon which settler colonialism operates (Moreton-Robinson 2015), the fences that demarcate property lines and pastures are core infrastructural components that materially score settler colonial structures into the landscape. Ranches materially operate on a dialectic of mobility and containment (Murton 2017) enabled by the relations between roads and fences; the former facilitate the transportation of cattle products, laborers, and capital (Harvey and Knox 2015), while the latter ensure that cattle stay where they should and enforce the exclusionary logics of private property in land (Blomley 2003; Moreton-Robinson 2015).

As numerous people from Yakye Axa and Sawhoyamaxa told me, the Chaco was open to the movement of indigenous peoples before the establishment of cattle ranches. Andrew Leake, in expert-witness testimony to the IACHR, describes the enclosure of the Bajo Chaco in the following terms: "The fencing in of the fields, together with the authority of the new owners, who enjoyed the support of government officials, had the effect of restricting, and eventually stopping, residential mobility [of indigenous peoples]. The last hunting grounds reserves of the Enxet were fenced in at the beginning of 1940" (IACHR 2006, 18). Through their ability to restrict movement for some (Enxet peoples) while facilitating movement for others (cows), the cattle ranches utilized indigenous labor to build and maintain the material infrastructural components of settler colonialism in the Bajo Chaco. The conjoined relation of indigenous dispossession and labor exploitation found across Paraguay's Chaco (Renshaw 2002; Tauli-Corpuz 2015; UNHRC 2018) builds from the historical social-spatial relations established by Christian missionaries and reiterated through different missionizing work that has sought to transform indigenous peoples into "productive" members of society through religion and labor (Bessire 2014).[8] While this process has been distinct in every instance, the land dispossession–labor exploitation dynamic (Speed 2017) provides the infrastructure upon which cattle ranching-based settler colonialism has continued to operate in the Paraguayan Chaco through the marginalization of indigenous peoples, which brings us back to the margins of cattle ranches.

Located on the margin of Ruta 5, people from Yakye Axa and Sawhoyamaxa have had a tenuous relationship with mobility and containment. The road promises mobility, but the lack of transportation ensures that most people spend their days between the highway and the fences that delimit ranch boundaries. This situation limits Enxet access to necessary resources, particularly access to hunting grounds or reliable water sources. Consequently, community members have had to cross onto ranch lands to access the only reliable water sources in the area—stock ponds. A primary infrastructural element of *chaqueño* cattle ranches, stock ponds are excavated from the earth to collect rainwater in pools for cattle to drink.

Water is always problematic in the Bajo Chaco. Due to seasonal and interannual fluctuations between flood and drought, there is usually either too much or too little water. When rains are abundant, large areas flood and fill the stock ponds with whatever floodwaters pick up as they flow across the landscape: latrine waste, household trash, animal feces, sediment, and more. During times of drought, water levels drop, and the water turns red, brown, or green from concentrated sediments, suspended particulates, and algae blooms. Water reveals an important gendered dimension of infrastructural violence, as collection and use disproportionately affect women whose customary role is to supply it for households (Bennett, Dávila-Poblete, and Rico 2005). An elderly woman from Sawhoyamaxa discussed such gendered effects of infrastructural violence with me in 2016. Reflecting on seasonal droughts, she stated that when "times are bad," she and others used old T-shirts to strain the water from mud at the bottom of nearly dry ponds because no other water sources were available. She also recalled that strained water "smells and tastes bad" and that "it is hard to drink, but sometimes it's all we have."

Land dispossession exacerbates the problem of limited water access in Yakye Axa and Sawhoyamaxa because the prevalence of saline soils and subsurface water supplies forecloses the possibility of digging wells in the margin and many streams flow with brackish water. As a result, most ranches utilize rainwater-collection systems for potable water on their ranches. Building such a system in the margin would require scant resources including water storage tanks, gutter systems, and adequate roofing material. With no other viable option, stock ponds serve as the main water source for people in Yakye Axa and Sawhoyamaxa. Limited water access not only is a product of the physical geography but is built into the landscape because ranch fences limit free access to naturally occurring water sources. The water quality from the stock ponds is highly variable and often produces intestinal illness and preventable disease.

According to the IACHR (2005, 2006) and testimonies I gathered from numerous people in Yakye Axa and Sawhoyamaxa, many deaths have been attributed to preventable water-borne diseases since the occupation of the margin began in the early 1990s. Most of the water-borne illnesses found in stock ponds are relatively benign. Parasites like giardia are generally only deadly when people lack access to basic sanitation and medical care. Due to logistical and financial constraints, I was unable to test the quality of stock pond water. Yet, judging from the effects of that water on my body and results of medical analyses performed to identify what was responsible for the symptoms I experienced, many types of amoebas, protozoa, and bacteria live in the stock ponds.[9] When I conducted household questionnaires in Sawhoyamaxa, 95 percent of respondents reported that stock ponds were their primary water sources. Seventy percent of those peoples reported that the water was a source of illness, closely linked to seasonal wet and dry periods. Stock ponds and the issue of water access help reveal the infrastructural violence of life on the margin of cattle ranches and in the margin of Ruta 5.

Li (2018, 332) suggests that although the Indonesian palm-oil plantation system intends to be a "total institution," its actual function relies on a "mafia system" of corruption and adaptations by those involved in the system. In this way, she shows that seemingly total, oppressive systems are always challenged by actors within them. Given the predominance of ranching in Paraguay's Chaco and settler land control, there are significant parallels with Li's study, especially regarding popular notions that settler colonialism is a total system with no outside. Despite this seeming totality, the Yakye Axa and Sawhoyamaxa communities are using the margin to take back territories once lost, recalling Penelope Harvey's (2014, 281) charge that creative possibilities emerge "even when the systems seem to be at their most limiting." The process is under way in Sawhoyamaxa, which utilized an IACHR judgment in the community's favor to justify their reoccupation of ancestral territories in 2013 even as legal battles continue to ensure the issuance of title. Per a second IACHR judgment, the Paraguayan state purchased lands for Yakye Axa in 2012; nevertheless, the community awaits the construction of an access road to one day leave the margin of Ruta 5 and occupy the lands purchased for them. Despite all that remains to be done, the promise that each community will soon regain their lands continues to animate their struggles from the margin, something that resonates with indigenous resistance across the Gran Chaco.

Dreaming of Justice on Extractive Frontiers

Extractive frontiers across the Americas are marked by radical environmental transformation, the dispossession of land and livelihoods through myriad forms of violence, and the imposition of new infrastructures to facilitate resource extraction, be that from labor or natural resources. As others have noted, infrastructure facilitates the function, social-spatial governance, and political economy of states (Anand, Gupta, and Appel 2018; Campbell 2015; Harvey and Knox 2015; Hetherington 2014; Larkin 2013). By focusing on infrastructural components used in ranching, I have shown that material infrastructures and labor as embodied infrastructure are central to the operation of settler colonial systems and the production of racialized geographies that reiterate indigenous dispossession. Ranches and cattle advance state territoriality in the Chaco frontier while simultaneously coding the "productive" spaces as white, nonindigenous, and oriented toward capital accumulation (Moreton-Robinson 2015).

The production of the Bajo Chaco as a space of white possession and a system of cattle ranching required materially transforming the landscape and establishing a structure to support the reiterated dispossession of indigenous peoples and create a reserve labor force. The simultaneous act of dispossessing indigenous peoples within the region was part and parcel to the new spatial ordering of private property that facilitated the emergence and spread of cattle ranching as a foundational settler colonial project. The expansion of Anglican missionary work in the service of British economic interests helped draw the Chaco into the Paraguayan national imaginary through the lives and labor of countless indigenous people whose stories are all too often erased from histories of this region. The way cattle ranching has advanced across the Chaco produced a system of racialized social-spatial relationships—indigenous labor exploitation and land dispossession for the benefit of nonindigenous landholders—that persist to the present day. The present-day sites of Yakye Axa and Sawhoyamaxa are a direct product of a settler colonial project that began with Anglican missionaries yet has helped transform the region into a cattle-based economic system. In Paraguay's Chaco, roads and fences are two material infrastructural components that provide daily reminders that the region is Paraguayan state territory, despite many critiques that the state is, by and large, absent in this vast frontier. Instead of state officials or an official state presence, one more often sees countless cattle grazing on pastures and among palm forests that lie behind or within the confines of barbed-wire fences that correspond with the private property rights of ranchers, and other settlers as well as investors who have endeavored to transform the Chaco into a platform for cattle production. The ranching industry's ongoing expansion continues to draw spaces once on the Paraguayan state's margins into the logics of capital accumulation and settler colonialism.

As a result, cattle ranching is driving some of the world's fastest rates of deforestation in the Chaco through a process that replicates many of the dynamics that Enxet people experienced in the turn of the twentieth century—the dispossession of indigenous peoples from the land, exploitation of their labor, and expansion of export-oriented agrarian extractivism. Recognizing the role of ranching and its relation with settler colonialism in Paraguay is crucial to understanding how historical material and discursive processes shape the present and future politics of indigenous environmental justice, not only in Paraguay but across the Gran Chaco. Given that more than four million hectares have been deforested for ranching in Paraguay since 2000 (Veit and Sarsfield 2017) and that similar dynamics are turning much of Argentina's Chaco forests to "rubble" (Gordillo 2014) in the name of settler capitalism (Speed 2017), indigenous peoples across the region disproportionately bear the effects of infrastructural violence. Continued prioritization of agro-export-oriented industrial development and renewed emphasis on regional integration to facilitate trade with projects like Paraguay's Bioceanic Highway project that promises to connect the Atlantic and Pacific Oceans by transecting the Paraguayan Chaco, suggest that the indigenous peoples will continue to face significant challenges as settler colonialism expands in the region through new infrastructures. Resistance to such systems are marginal only insofar as they often literally are waged from the margins, from the side of Ruta 5 in Paraguay, the edge of soybean fields in Argentina, or the shadow of natural gas flares in Bolivia. Yet it is precisely from the margin that many indigenous communities continue to resist infrastructural violence in pursuit of justice.

Acknowledgments

I would like to extend my sincere gratitude to the members of the Yakye Axa and Sawhoyamaxa who accompanied me throughout the research that informs this chapter. Several people commented on different phases of this work whose insights I appreciate: Joe Bryan, Kregg Hetherington, Emily Yeh, Tim Oakes, Mario Blaser, Paola Canova, Mercedes Biocca, Silvia

Hirsch, and students in my 2019 infrastructure seminar at University of Florida. Thanks are also due to two anonymous reviewers.

Notes

1. The Enxet peoples of Yakye Axa and Sawhoyamaxa are members of the Maskoy language family that spans much of the Bajo Chaco in Paraguay. In 2020 Yakye Axa comprised approximately 30 families, though it was much larger at the onset of their land claim; many people have left due to the hardships on the margin of the highway. Sawhoyamaxa in 2020 was comprised of approximately 160 families. While scholars debate the naming of Enxet peoples (Kalisch and Unruh 2003), I maintain usage of "Enxet" because it was used by the people with whom I worked in Yakye Axa and Sawhoyamaxa to self-identify. "Enxet-Sur" is also commonly used.

2. Throughout my research, both indigenous and nonindigenous peoples often used this phrase to refer to traditional indigenous practices, particularly spirituality, and it was often seen at odds with evangelical Christian religions.

3. I draw from sixteen months of ethnographic research conducted from 2013 to 2017 with Enxet peoples in Paraguay's Chaco. I do not claim universal knowledge about Enxet lifeways, struggles, or life. Instead, this work is written in solidarity with their ongoing efforts to secure land. I recognize the partial and situated perspective I write from and take responsibility for any errors in my analysis.

4. The Bajo Chaco is the southeastern, humid portion of the Chaco that lies in Paraguay, primarily in the Presidente Hayes Department.

5. See Correia 2018b for a detailed discussion.

6. Mennonite cooperatives and producers are key actors in the contemporary deforestation rates that accompany the expansion of the cattle-ranching industry across the Paraguayan Chaco (Baumann et al. 2017; Veit and Sarsfield 2017).

7. The expansion of quebracho logging and the tannin industry was a significant extractive force to the north of Enxet territories that I discuss in this chapter. While I do not have space to address the impacts of the tannin industry and its role in colonizing the Paraguayan Chaco, Kleinpenning 2003, Blaser 2010, and Villagra and Bonifacio 2015 provide helpful analyses.

8. This phenomenon is much more extensive than merely the Anglican Church's activities and can be seen in the efforts of the New Tribes Mission, Mennonites, and Pentecostals, among others.

9. I would often drink water from the stock ponds while sharing *tereré*, cold yerba mate tea, with people or during mapping and hunting trips with community members.

8

Tense Territories

Negotiating Natural Gas in Weenhayek Society

DENISE HUMPHREYS BEBBINGTON AND GUIDO CORTEZ

Since the mid-1990s, investment in extractive industries in Latin America has grown at a remarkable rate (Bebbington 2012; Bebbington and Bury 2013).[1] Much of this expansion has occurred on lands historically occupied and claimed as territory by indigenous and campesino populations and has frequently involved real and perceived processes of dispossession as well as significant socioenvironmental conflict (Bebbington 2007; Bebbington et al. 2008; Bury and Kolff 2003; De Echave et al. 2009; Garibay et al. 2011; Perreault 2008). These processes of dispossession and conflict pit "companies," "states," and "communities" against each other in broader struggles over the governance of territory, but the extractive economy also creates new and significant disparities and conflicts *within* local populations, strengthening some local political economic projects and weakening others. Such internally differentiated dimensions of conflict and inequality have received much less analytical attention than have the broader processes of dispossession (Galeano 1973). Yet their implications for populations affected by extraction can be critical because they elicit new patterns of social differentiation and identity formation, and they affect the nature of and possibilities for any future collective action.

In this chapter we trace the interactions between the broad conflicts among companies, states, and communities and the dynamics that these conflicts can trigger within indigenous populations in the Chaco. We focus on the ways consultation and compensation have been used to try and mediate state-company-community relations and how these very processes of consultation and compensation can create new sources of tension within populations and between them and the state. A detailed case study of natural gas extraction in the part of the Bolivian Chaco occupied by the Weenhayek people offers insight into these relations and the ways actual consultation processes unfolded during 2008–2009. These experiences are located within longer histories of Weenhayek livelihood, organization, and dispossession to draw attention to the types of transformation that natural gas extraction has triggered in Weenhayek society. In this sense, contemporary consultation and territorial consolidation processes involving the Weenhayek need to be understood as products of relations across time and space, particularly between the highlands and lowlands and between the central government and subnational authorities in the department of Tarija. It is not possible to develop these connections more fully here, but it is important to recognize that they have been inherent to negotiations over natural gas since the turn of the millennium. The material for this chapter comes from the first author's nine months of fieldwork in the Bolivian Chaco and subsequent, shorter field visits, all of which allowed for the observation of consultation processes at close quarters. The second author has a long engagement with Weenhayek communities and ORCAWETA (Organización de Capitanías Weenhayek de Tarija, Organization of Weenhayek Captaincies of Tarija), first as a researcher and staff member and later as director of a regional nongovernmental organization (NGO).[2]

We examine elements of Weenhayek history, dispossession, livelihood, and social organization. These histories and organizational dynamics are important to understanding the lenses through which contemporary hydrocarbon development is experienced in Weenhayek territory. In particular, repeated Weenhayek efforts to secure revenue from hydrocarbons must be understood as a response to a long-term "reproduction squeeze" (Bernstein 1977) on livelihoods, and the gravity of contemporary conflicts triggered by natural gas expansion should be viewed in the light of the evolution of Weenhayek settlements and organization and longer-standing tensions within Weenhayek society (map 8.1). Within these points of reference hydrocarbon development unfolded in Weenhayek territory between 1960 and 2015, and the nature of this development and the broader context in which it unfolds structure how the Weenhayek interact with the sector.

Those interactions are seen in the case of a consultation and participation process through which British Gas (BG) Bolivia and the Bolivian government sought to arrive at a compensation agreement that would allow extraction to proceed in Weenhayek territory.[3] Based upon the right of indigenous peoples to prior consultation and to informed consent, consultation processes have come to be constitutive of Bolivian society and of the

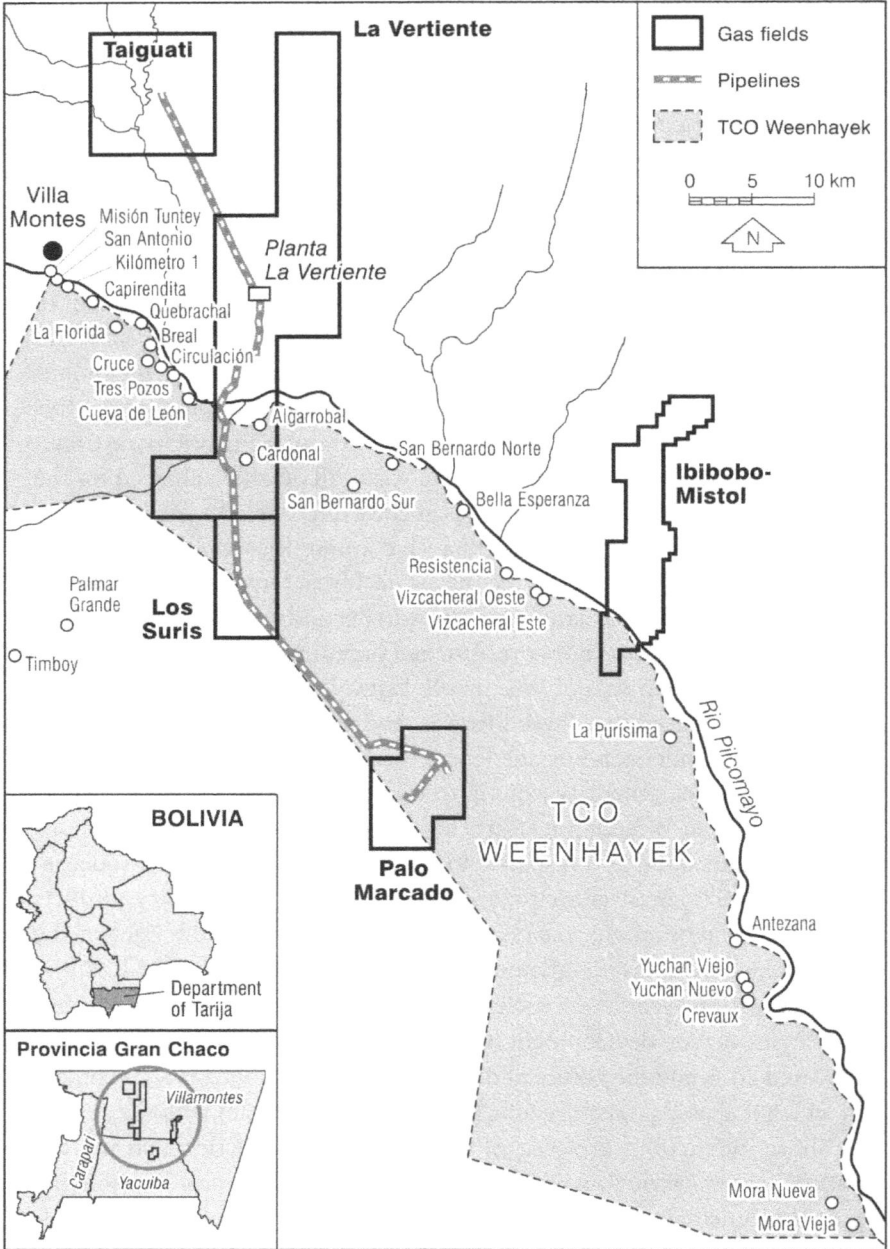

Map 8.1. Weenhayek TCO and surrounding hydrocarbon operations. M. Perez, CER-DET, Department of Tarija, Bolivia. Map by Denise Humphreys Bebbington and Guido Cortez.

groups that participate in them. For members of Weenhayek society, consultation and participation was much more than a simple negotiation over a specific project at a given point in time. To the contrary, the outcomes of this process continue to define just how far the Weenhayek can fulfill their long-standing dream of territorial consolidation.

A Brief History of Weenhayek Livelihood and Organization

Dispossessions and Pressures on Livelihood

The Weenhayek and the Wichí belong to the same ethnic group and were known as *matacos* (a name imposed by the Spanish) in the colonial period. They were recognized in three subgroupings: the Vejoz, who live along the Bermejo River; the Guisnay in the lower part of Pilcomayo River, both in the Chaco of Argentina; and the *matacos noctenes*, a Guaraní term referring to the Weenhayek, of the Bolivian Chaco (Ortiz 1986).[4] They live in a string of some sixty separate settlements that run along the Pilcomayo River in the semiarid lowlands of southeastern Bolivia, extending from the town of Villa Montes in the north to the border with Argentina in the south.[5] Another two settlements are located farther inland, at the base of the Aguaragüe mountain range, where they live alongside Guaraní and campesino communities. Together these settlements accounted, in a 2010 BG Bolivia–commissioned study, for a population of some 4,818 persons grouped into 1,050 families. The Weenhayek have continued to fish and collect fruits and honey from the forests for their subsistence, but their livelihoods have grown more reliant on financial resources that are external to their territory.

Although there is a sense that the younger generation is more open to change through education and external employment, the Weenhayek have remained firmly apart from other segments of society, maintaining their language and preferring to live among themselves. Isabelle Combès writes that "the sine qua none of the group's survival—distribution—is also a social value in which no one should stand out, no one should eat if the neighbor has nothing to eat, and no one should stand above the rest" (2002, 14). Nonetheless, after 2009, with the incorporation of indigenous representatives into national and subnational politics, a small but powerful Weenhayek leadership emerged that is at least temporarily seen as different from other families, as it administers financial resources from gas companies and from government projects and investments.

As with other indigenous groups of the Chaco, the Weenhayek have experienced a long history of dispossession and persistent discrimination that has extended up to present times. As the Weenhayek are highly mobile, scholars suggest that the group was able to avoid much contact with the Spanish until well into the eighteenth century.[6] Despite the growing presence of soldiers and mestizo settlers and the diversity of lowland indigenous groups in the Chaco that often led to warfare and the domination of some groups over others, Jan Ake Alvarsson (2007) sustains that the *matacos* were able to maintain their independence and cultural sovereignty within their traditional lands until the twentieth century, when actions by the Bolivian military resulted in progressively violent confrontations. The coup de grace came with the Chaco War (1932–1935), ostensibly fought over oil reserves in the subsoil, during which Bolivian troops occupied nearly all of the territory considered to be Weenhayek.[7] The army forced them to settle into camps and there are accounts that Weenhayek men were forced to serve as guides through the dry Chaco forest and as *chalaneros* (rowers or boatmen) transporting soldiers and goods in small boats and rafts across the Pilcomayo River. Some Weenhayek today interpret these experiences as early dispossessions driven even then by the hydrocarbon economy: "Our grandfathers supported the army during the Chaco War as guides and *chalaneros*, but they are not [considered] excombatants. In order to eat they have worked every day until the day of their death because they were never recognized for having defended oil" (Lucas Cortez, former *capitán grande* of ORCAWETA, cited in Castro 2004).[8]

After the Chaco War, soldiers-turned-ranchers occupied Weenhayek lands and introduced extensive cattle ranching, forcing the Weenhayek to settle on the banks of the Pilcomayo River on ever smaller and poorer strips of land. The forests, fruits, and wild animals that underlay their subsistence were progressively destroyed by uncontrolled grazing and hunting, and as ranchers reduced their access to the forests, the Weenhayek were forced to collect fruits and honey from farther afield and turned to fishing, part-time wage labor,[9] and begging in town (Combès 2002). It was during this period that a group of Pentecostal Swedish missionaries settled in Villa Montes and began ministering to the Weenhayek. The Free Swedish Mission in Bolivia (Misión Sueca Libre en Bolivia) was established in 1948, and it has been the single most important external institution among the Weenhayek for nearly five decades.[10]

Until 1960, fishing was a subsistence activity for Weenhayek families. Subsequently, with the introduction of refrigeration, fishing became central to the Weenhayek economy. Fresh fish could be transported to markets in Santa Cruz, Camiri, and Tarija, and for the Weenhayek fishing season became known as a time of plenty.[11] Attempts to calculate the composition of Weenhayek household income expenditure suggest that fishing may constitute as much as 50 percent of family resources, though intra- and inter-community differences make any attempt to calculate average income very difficult. One consequence of this dependence upon the fishing economy is that outside of the fishing season or during a prolonged drought, as experienced in 2010,[12] few other local economic opportunities can provide sufficient resources to sustain families. This often leads to food crises in communities and especially in those more remote from the town of Villa Montes.

Weenhayek Structure and Organization

Weenhayek Wiky'i is the term designating a unit of families who together formed a clan that was recognized as such by other Wiky'i and moved about within a fixed territory, hunting, harvesting, and fishing (Alvarsson 2007, 2–3). The impulse to create a second level of political organization of Wiky'i appears to have been a direct result of the organizing activity carried out by the national Confederación de Pueblos Indígenas de Bolivia (CIDOB, Confederation of Indigenous Peoples of Bolivia) in the 1980s, a period of heightened organization and mobilization among lowland indigenous groups in Bolivia (Yashar 2005). These second-level organizations also responded to the needs of national government and subnational authorities to have a single interlocutor to facilitate negotiations and agreements.[13] ORCAWETA was created in 1989 as a supracommunal organization, bringing together both Weenhayek communities and the one remaining Tapiete community to recover and consolidate ancestral lands and to improve the economic and cultural conditions of its members.[14] Its structure consists of a *capitán grande* (big captain), a *segundo capitán* (second captain), a directorate with secretariats based on specific issues or themes such as health and land, and community *capitanes*; the structure was borrowed from the Guaraní, whose forms of consensual decision making significantly differ from those of the Weenhayek. José Braunstein (2006) notes the dissonance between this form of modern representation and more traditional forms of group representation and how this has often resulted in debilitating intra- and intergroup struggles.

Written accounts as well as author interviews with leaders and NGO advisers reflect a difficult first decade for ORCAWETA, one characterized by prolonged conflict and crisis. In 2000–2005, under new leadership and with greater involvement and preparation of younger members who had finished their high school studies, ORCAWETA began a process of organizational consolidation supported by the Swedish missionaries, CIDOB, and several local NGOs. ORCAWETA paid for the construction of two hundred modest homes, the drilling of a dozen freshwater wells, and educational stipends in addition to actively pursuing efforts to recover territory. The leaders who followed abandoned that path and began focusing on securing and distributing compensation payments from oil companies and forging relations with the government of President Evo Morales, who took office in 2006, and his Movimiento al Socialismo (MAS) party. Soon afterward, divisions within ORCAWETA resurfaced.

Much of this conflict appears to have been the product of opaque negotiations conducted with outsiders (development projects, transnational gas companies, political parties, and local authorities) and centers on perceptions of ORCAWETA leaders acting independently and secretively, withholding information, and perhaps enriching themselves and their clans in the process. They are seen as abrogating Weenhayek values, violating the ways decisions are made by communities, and failing to distribute resources in a generous and fair manner, ultimately provoking internal conflict and division.[15]

The growing dependence on ORCAWETA to represent and negotiate on behalf of member communities by engaging with a complex array of external actors has given rise to an ongoing crisis of internal governance. Community members have grown ever more annoyed and restless with the lack of information and significant quantifiable products, the violation of the principle of distribution, and the slow but sure destruction of their territory. Up to the early 2010s, the crisis would usually come to a head once the fishing season was over and different groups would turn their attention to controlling ORCAWETA. The organization has been seen as an alternative source of resources as well as, by some at least, a vehicle that might more effectively defend the interests of Weenhayek communities against outsiders who should not be trusted. If one group was unable to unseat the group in power, the tendency was to simply announce that it was now the representative leadership, giving rise to confusion for outsiders and a further undermining of ORCAWETA's credibility. This pattern changed somewhat when ORCAWETA's leadership became more closely tied to the Morales government, which reduced the scope to create parallel leaderships and rendered ORCAWETA more dependent on its *capitán grande*.

This history and evolution of Weenhayek organization is marked by the evolving crisis of governance experienced by the communities despite long-term efforts to build organizational and political capacity. Internal conflict among the Weenhayek is not new, but the conflict has grown more complex and chronic and is in large part fueled by efforts to consolidate access to the flows of hydrocarbon and other rents. These sources of income have become increasingly important since the 2010s and are part of the longer, continuous history of struggle to identify and secure access to resource flows to ensure Weenhayek reproduction.

National Hydrocarbon Development in Weenhayek Territory, 1960–2015

It is not entirely clear when exploration for hydrocarbons first impinged upon Weenhayek lands and livelihoods. Various reports and studies (Centeno 1999; Combès 2002; Gutiérrez and Rodríguez 1999; Mamani 2005; Ribera 2008); suggest that Weenhayek territory has long been a site of hydrocarbon exploration and exploitation, albeit sporadically, with periods of intense activity followed by prolonged spells of neglect and abandonment.

Almost certainly the state hydrocarbons agency, Yacimientos Petrolíferos Fiscales de Bolivia (YPFB), was the first to conduct exploratory activity in this area sometime between 1950 and 1960. In the decades between the 1950s and 1990s, hydrocarbon operations in the Chaco were conducted on a fairly limited scale. Within Weenhayek territory, important reserves of natural gas were discovered. However, bringing these reserves into production was constrained by Bolivia's reliance on a single and somewhat unreliable buyer, Argentina. In the 1990s the situation changed drastically with the opening up of the Brazilian market and the subsequent acquisitions of gas reserves by large transnational firms. The natural gas boom that began in the mid-1990s developed in a significantly different way than in previous decades. This gas boom has complicated Weenhayek efforts to reconstitute their territory, shaping both their strategies and success in this endeavor.

First, rather than engaging with a single company, the Weenhayek have had to negotiate and manage a wide range of projects and relationships simultaneously with a series of transnational companies (table 8.1). These projects include exploratory drilling and the reactivation of wells held in reserve, the construction of access roads, pumping stations, and a network of pipelines, environmental impact assessments and baseline studies conducted by consultancy companies, and the installation of work camps by contractors. During the late 1990s and early 2000s, the heart of the boom period, Weenhayek leaders were engaged in negotiations with BG Bolivia in 1999, now Shell Oil, over expanded operations in the Block XX-Tarija Este; with the then privatized Chaco company in 1997 and 2001 over exploratory drilling in the Timboy-Palmar Grande area;[16] with Transierra in 2001 over the construction of a major north-south pipeline (GASYRG); and in 2002 with Transredes, another gas transport firm. By 2010 there were some fifteen wells operating within Weenhayek lands in addition to two major pipelines, a separation plant for liquids, a series of pumping stations, and an extensive network of feeder (collector) lines and access roads to provide maintenance services to the wells, plants, and gas lines.

Second, the larger social and legal context in which this boom developed changed in ways that influenced how companies and communities interacted. Indigenous groups were now organized with recognized legal claims to ancestral lands, and the government of Bolivia was signatory to international conventions protecting indigenous rights and habitats. Multilateral agencies providing financial backing to extractive projects such as the Inter-American Development Bank, the Overseas Private Investment Corporation, and the World Bank Group were now obliged to require social and environmental policies and practices that included public consultations and the granting of environmental licenses while ensuring that the rights of indigenous peoples would be respected. This context was shaped by persistent socioenvironmental conflict involving transnational companies and local communities and high-profile cases of human rights abuses linked to extractive activity in indigenous territory elsewhere in the Amazon in the 1970s and 1980s (Fontaine 2007; Sawyer 2004). Transnational alliances of civil society actors played key roles in bringing public attention to bear on the unfolding dramas involving transnational firms and vulnerable indigenous groups in the Americas.[17]

Third, in response to rising criticism, transnational firms adopted policies of corporate social responsibility, elaborated guidelines on environment and indigenous peoples, and made commitments to finance local development in an effort to cast themselves as good corporate citizens (O'Faircheallaigh and Ali 2008). The oil and gas sector and its financial backers had come under significant pressure from transnational civil society and political networks of activist shareholders to change the way they conducted business.[18] In Weenhayek territory, however, the industry encountered a particularly challenging operational environment that has

Table 8.1. Hydrocarbon companies and projects affecting Weenhayek territory, 1960–2010

Period of activity	Company	Block/activity	Field/area affected
1960–1961	YPFB	Exploration	La Vertiente
1960	Chaco Petroleum	Exploration	Palo Marcado Los Monos
1970s–1998	Andina	Exploration of Capirenda block 96,000 hectares	Crevaux Yunchan
1972–1999	Tesoro Bolivia Petroleum Company	Exploration/exploitation XX Tarija Este block 161,000 hectares	Los Suris La Vertiente Escondido Ibibobo Palo Marcado
1999–present	British Gas–BG Bolivia (now Shell Oil Company)	Exploration/exploitation of XX Tarija Este block 161,000 hectares. Construction/amplification of gas line under Pilcomayo River	Los Suris La Vertiente Escondido Palo Marcado Ibibobo
1997–2006	Chaco (BP-Amoco)	Exploration/exploitation of Aguaragüe block 2,500 hectares	Los Monos
2001–present	Transierra	Construction/operation of 24 km pipeline and compression station	Affecting communities Timboy, Palmar Grande, Kilometro 1, Capirendita, San Antonio
2002	Petrobras	Construction of 5 km feeder line to Transierra pipeline	Timboy
2002–present	Transredes	Construction of replacement pipeline under Pilcomayo, operation of pipelines	Affecting fishing concessions
2010	Petroandina	Exploration/exploitation of Aguaragüe Centro and Aguaragüe Sur blocks Timboy-X1 and Timboy-X2	Affecting communities Timboy, San Antonio, Capirendita, Kilometro 1

Sources: YPFB, BG Bolivia, Shell Bolivia, Transierra, Transredes, and Petroandina.

required significantly more corporate time and resources to obtain both environmental and social licenses and secure the necessary conditions for extraction to go forward.[19] These corporate efforts have affected dynamics within Weenhayek communities and ORCAWETA as well as attempts to consolidate Weenhayek territory.

Hydrocarbons and Territory

ORCAWETA and Weenhayek Claims for Territory

The creation of ORCAWETA was followed by Weenhayek claims for collective land rights (known as Tierras Comunitarias de Origen, TCOs) to 195,659 hectares. In 1993 the government formally recognized the Weenhayek TCO claim in Supreme Decree 23500 and indicated that it would move quickly to demarcate the lands and proceed with formal titling. In the face of the third-party presence of more than one hundred privately owned parcels, resistance from the ranching community, and corruption within the Tarija office of the Land Reform Agency, it was only in September 2008 that titling began. When Capitán Grande Moises Sapiranda attended a private meeting of indigenous leaders with President Evo Morales, more than 20,000 hectares were formally titled in favor of the TCO. Sapiranda later explained, "After waiting nearly fifteen years for legal title, one conversation with Don Evo, and twenty-five days later the TCO had 25,000 hectares."[20] A similar negotiation would be repeated during the final stage of the July 2009 consultation process when another 8,206 hectares were titled.

Land and territorial consolidation have been the single overarching objective of Weenhayek society. Figure 8.1 presents a timeline of the evolution of Weenhayek social organization and territorial claims and contrasts this evolution with the expanding presence of natural gas extraction in Weenhayek territory. Other than a small donation of land by the municipal government of Villa Montes in 1948 (used by the Free Swedish Mission to establish a settlement adjacent to the mission, a church, and a boarding school), Weenhayek families were not given titles to their plots of land. Only in 2008 did they gain legal possession of their homes. In the 1990s, with support from European governments, efforts to reclaim ancestral lands culminated in state authorization of the Weenhayek TCO. The government resolution Supreme Decree 23500 of 1993 recognized Weenhayek sovereignty over the territory. However, it also established a precedent, as it

Weenhayek Agency and Organization

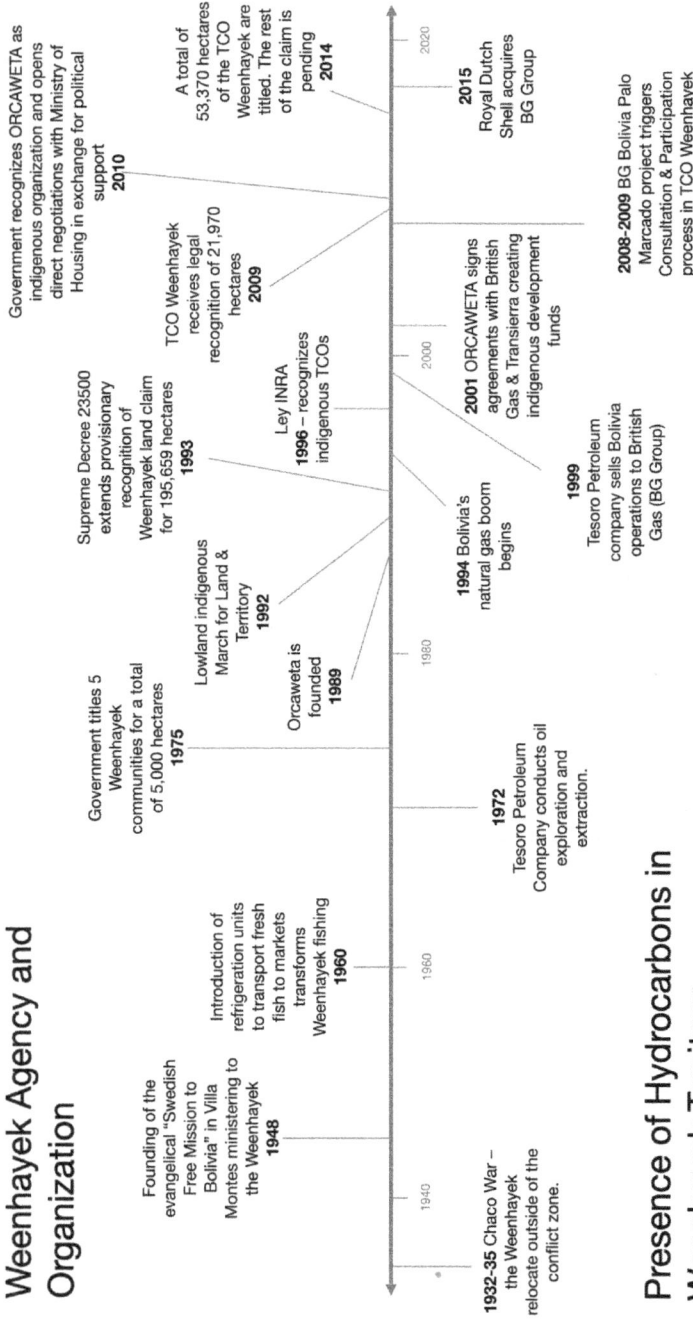

Founding of the evangelical "Swedish Free Mission" in Villa Montes ministering to the Weenhayek 1948

Introduction of refrigeration units to transport fresh fish to markets transforms Weenhayek fishing 1960

Government titles 5 Weenhayek communities for a total of 5,000 hectares 1975

Lowland indigenous March for Land & Territory 1992

Supreme Decree 23500 extends provisionary recognition of Weenhayek land claim for 195,659 hectares 1993

Government recognizes ORCAWETA as indigenous organization and opens direct negotiations with Ministry of Housing in exchange for political support 2010

TCO Weenhayek receives legal recognition of 21,970 hectares 2009

A total of 53,370 hectares of the TCO Weenhayek are titled. The rest of the claim is pending 2014

2015 Royal Dutch Shell acquires BG Group

Presence of Hydrocarbons in Weenhayek Territory

1932-35 Chaco War – the Weenhayek relocate outside of the conflict zone.

1972 Tesoro Petroleum Company conducts oil exploration and extraction.

Orcaweta is founded 1989

1994 Bolivia's natural gas boom begins

Ley INRA 1996 – recognizes indigenous TCOs

1999 Tesoro Petroleum company sells Bolivia operations to British Gas (BG Group)

2001 ORCAWETA signs agreements with British Gas & Transierra creating indigenous development funds

2008-2009 BG Bolivia Palo Marcado project triggers Consultation & Participation process in TCO Weenhayek

1940   1960   1980   2000   2020

Figure 8.1. Timeline of natural gas development and territorial recognition in Weenhayek lands.

allowed ranchers to maintain their presence and activity within the Ween-hayek TCO. This has effectively stifled the consolidation of the TCO.

The relationship between the presence of hydrocarbons in TCOs, the overlap of third party interests in these same spaces, and the agonizingly slow progress in titling TCO lands suggest that where there are hydrocarbon reserves, TCO efforts to claim those lands systematically fail to advance.[21] The Weenhayek case is an extreme example of this source of territorial fragmentation. One hundred percent of Weenhayek territory lies within an area classified as having hydrocarbon potential, more than 50,000 hectares are under contract for hydrocarbon exploration and exploitation, the ter-ritory has been penetrated and crisscrossed by pipelines and access roads, and 80 percent of the TCO is controlled by nonindigenous ranchers and farmers.[22] Under these circumstances an effective consolidation of territory and control of resources will not form the basis of livelihoods for future generations. The history of the evolving presence and impacts of one par-ticular transnational firm in Weenhayek territory, BG Bolivia, illuminates this dilemma and the conflicts catalyzed by its efforts to secure gas.

BG Bolivia in Weenhayek Territory

During the gas rush of the late 1990s, the BG Group,[23] based in the United Kingdom, became active in the Bolivian gas market, successfully obtaining licenses for six exploration/exploitation blocks as well as securing partici-pating interest in two of the country's most important gas fields, Itaú and Margarita. In late 1999, BG Bolivia acquired the Tesoro Bolivia Petroleum Company, which had carried out exploration and exploitation of gas on Weenhayek lands since the early 1970s and held the rights to explore and exploit gas fields in the area (Centeno 1999).

BG Bolivia found itself operating in a context of greater indigenous re-sistance and demands for compensation linked to its activities. Like other energy firms, BG Bolivia sought to smooth the negotiation of its projects by offering to support local development projects. As part of its negotia-tions with ORCAWETA, BG Bolivia instituted a program of support to the Weenhayek. This included short-term interventions (the Program of Community Relations and Support) and a mechanism to guide support for longer-term initiatives (the Indigenous Development Plan), though in practice it is difficult to distinguish between the two and between these instruments and other agreements over rights of way and compensation for damages.[24] The Indigenous Development Plan is a framework or open agreement between the company and the indigenous group in which financial contributions can be negotiated and channeled to support a series of activities and projects during the company's operations, usually twenty to thirty years. BG Bolivia's Indigenous Development Plan directs support to communities most affected by its operations but also responds to activities proposed by the *capitán grande* and ORCAWETA's directorate while retaining say over what will and will not be funded as well as administrative control over the funds. Both negotiations and administration of the development plan have tended to be closed, and the information is not made public at the preference of ORCAWETA leaders. There is no system to monitor the results of the plan or to establish if both sides have complied with their responsibilities, even when disbursements can reach US$250,000 per year.[25]

It was in this context that BG Bolivia sought to expand its operations in the Weenhayek TCO by initiating the Palo Marcado project.[26] The proposal would bring into production three existing wells held in retention since the 1990s and allow for the drilling of a fourth well. It would also construct a pumping station and twenty-three kilometers of feeder gas lines. Palo Marcado is not a particularly large project, at a total investment of US$30 million, or a controversial one, as exploratory drilling has taken place on Weenhayek lands since the 1960s. Still, in accord with governmental decrees passed in the latter 2000s to safeguard the rights of indigenous peoples, the project was required to carry out an additional process with the affected indigenous group prior in the elaboration of an environmental impact assessment. Specifically, the company had to conduct a consultation and participation process with the representative organization of the Weenhayek TCO in order to obtain an environmental license.

Consultation, Compensation, and Disputes over Representation

In early August 2008, the leadership of ORCAWETA received a fax from the Ministry of Hydrocarbons and Energy notifying them of the government's intent to conduct a consultation and participation process in relation to a proposal to develop the Palo Marcado gas field affecting the Weenhayek TCO. Consultation and participation was originally included in the Hydrocarbons Law 3058 of 2005, which grew out of Bolivia's "gas wars" (Perreault 2006) and the prolonged social conflict over how the country's hydrocarbon resources were to be exploited, a conflict that in large measure set the stage for the subsequent election of Evo Morales's MAS government. Indeed, it was only under the MAS government that the enabling law was promulgated that made Law 3058 operational. This law, together with Su-preme Decree 29103, which regulates the law for carrying out participatory socioenvironmental monitoring on indigenous and campesino territories, represented the culmination of years of mobilization, lobbying, and nego-tiation with executive and legislative officials, bringing indigenous lowland groups closer to their goal of effective control over their territories. These mechanisms were also of enormous symbolic importance to the Morales government, which heralded them as being of universal importance to in-digenous societies faced with extractive activity in their territories.

Yet, despite these important legislative gains, the MAS government showed a persistent tendency to disregard social and environmental safe-guards and participatory procedures (Bebbington and Humphreys Beb-bington 2011; Yrigoyen 2009). Indigenous groups found themselves im-mersed in increasingly acrimonious debates with government bureaucrats to ensure that the law be respected. The way the state carried forward its program of extraction clashed head-on with the discourse of a sympathetic state as well as with indigenous expectations for greater say in how ex-traction was to proceed. This led to tensions between the Weenhayek and the state while also creating and aggravating conflicts within Weenhayek society.

After some delays and false starts, by late 2008 the government appeared ready to carry out the consultation announced in the fax. As envisaged by its promoters, the consultation process would be administered by the Min-istry of Hydrocarbons with support from YPFB and the Ministry of Rural Development and Ministry of Environment and Water; representatives of the agencies would form a government team to provide information about the project and conduct negotiations with indigenous groups.[27] The pro-cess was to be relatively straightforward. However, its logic of narrowly focusing on the proposed activity did not allow for a more general treat-ment of indigenous concerns regarding previous or unresolved interven-tions elsewhere in their territory; for the Weenhayek, the very way the state viewed Weenhayek territory became an important point of contention. For their part, Weenhayek leaders were concerned about a number of unre-solved issues regarding ongoing hydrocarbon activity within their terri-tory, and they sought to use the consultation process to seek remedy for these broader issues. This situation was aggravated by confusion about the documentation provided, complaints that the information was incomplete, and questions about the ownership of the lands affected by the proposed activity. The consultation process offered the Weenhayek the opportunity to gain access to a range of technical information about the BG Group's operations within the TCO that had not been available previously, and it empowered ORCAWETA and the *capitanes* by providing them with historical information and a broader understanding of the rules of the game around hydrocarbon operations. However, it also fueled growing concern among leaders that there would be insufficient time and resources to ensure respect for the Weenhayek way of consultation and decision making. Government representatives emphasized time frames and the need to make progress, while Weenhayek leaders insisted that unresolved issues be included in negotiations and that the whole TCO be considered the unit of analysis, not just the lands affected by the Palo Marcado project.

The series of meetings conducted with government representatives, led by officials from the Ministry of Hydrocarbons and YPFB, revealed that the government team had limited knowledge about the history of the Weenhayek TCO or the cumulative impacts of decades of hydrocarbon activity on their territory and culture. The absence of BG Bolivia in the negotiations, initially viewed favorably by ORCAWETA, became an obstacle when discussion turned to the specifics of the proposed project. Rather than representing a state now legally in control of the hydrocarbons sector, the government team's role in the process seemed to be that of an intermediary, presenting a PowerPoint of the proposed project that had been prepared by BG Bolivia and providing documentation obviously prepared by the company but without any analysis by ministry officials. Weenhayek leaders and advisers grew tense, sensing that the TCO might be forced into accepting a project by a state that claimed to be defending its interests. Gauging the sentiment of the *capitanes*, Sapiranda asked for breaks during which he consulted with them to determine if the process should move forward. Finally, he and the *capitanes* decided to suspend further meetings after disagreements arose over how to proceed, with complaints that BG Bolivia had drilled a well and laid large pipelines under the Pilcomayo River without consulting ORCAWETA. At this point ORCAWETA called for a suspension of the consultation process.

In addition to creating tensions with the state, the consultation process was also aggravating tensions among the Weenhayek. The Palo Marcado project straddles two municipalities, Villa Montes and Yacuiba, each keen to see hydrocarbon projects within their jurisdictions and each looking to influence decision-making within the TCO by establishing and funding relations with rival Weenhayek leaders. These rival leaderships spilled into the open, as reflected in a moment in the consultation and participation process described in the text from one author's field notes.

The patio of Moises Sapiranda, Capirendita, Weenhayek TCO, 27 November, 2008:

The Consultation and Participation meeting has reconvened in the patio of the house of Moises Sapiranda, Capitán Grande of OR-CAWETA where a representative of the Ministry of Hydrocarbons and Energy, along with various government officials from other ministries and YPFB have come in an attempt to revive the lagging process. At the last meeting, Weenhayek leaders voted to suspend the Consultation and Participation process after confusion arose about the process itself and the completeness of informational documents that had been given to ORCAWETA by the Ministry of Hydrocarbons and Energy. Today, at this informal, informational meeting in Capirendita, government officials hope to jump start talks.

I am late in arriving after spending over an hour trying to find the exact location of the meeting. There are some one hundred people gathered in the patio of Sapiranda, among them the leaders of the twenty-two Weenhayek settlements, members of the ORCAWETA directorate, advisors and staff from the NGO CER-DET [Centro de Estudios Regionales para el Desarrollo de Tarija (Center of Regional Studies for the Development of Tarija)] and from the lowland indigenous organization, CIDOB, as well as former leaders now advisors of ORCAWETA. In one corner of the patio, near the house, is a group of women peeling and cutting vegetables for today's lunch. They talk among themselves but do not interact with the larger group.

One of the Weenhayek promoters, Saul, tells me that there will be problems today. There are growing tensions between Moises and a rival leadership that has not been part of the Consultation and Participation process. Saul tells me they fear being left out of negotiations over compensation—believing that the presence of government officials signals that such a negotiation is about to take place.

The meeting begins with a presentation by a representative from the Ministry of Hydrocarbons and Energy who talks of the government's goodwill in carrying out the Consultation and Participation process. The first Consultation and Participation meeting between the government and ORCAWETA ended rather abruptly after the capitanes decided to suspend the meeting and the process for what they perceived to be duplicitous negotiations on the part of the Ministry of Hydrocarbons and Energy. At that meeting ORCAWETA expressed concern that not all informational documents were made available to leaders and advisors and there was confusion about the actual process as well (indeed this was among the first Consultation and Participation processes in the country following the new regulations). The capitanes are still cross with government officials from the last meeting and their comments reflect their impatience and frustration with the incompetency shown in the first meeting.

During the course of the morning, rival leader Pablo Rivero and his followers arrive uninvited to the meeting. They are immediately challenged by some of the capitanes loyal to Sapiranda and the rebel group is told to leave. They refuse and an argument ensues with pushing, shoving, and kicking among the two groups. The rebel band shouts out that Sapiranda and his capitanes are cutting deals with the government and BG Bolivia behind their backs, that they are corrupt and will keep all the money for themselves. The pushing and shoving eventually stop, but the heated verbal exchange goes on as the rebel band adamantly refuses to leave. Sapiranda is angry and overwhelmed and paces nervously as he makes phone calls on his mobile. He complains to a group of us standing nearby that Pablo Rivero and his followers have come to his home, his own patio, to confront him and embarrass him in front of government officials. Moises continues making phone calls (one of which I am told later is to the head of YPFB who told him to alert the colonel at the local military base in Villa Montes). Sometime later a military transport vehicle arrives with twenty or so well armed soldiers in the back. The rival group stands to one side. The Colonel says he will accompany the Ministry representatives away from the meeting and warns that violence will not be tolerated. But violence is not necessary now. The rebel band has succeeded in preventing the meeting from going ahead. The ministry officials leave with the soldiers, with the representative from the Ministry of Hydrocarbons murmuring that the situation requires a political solution. Rivero and his capitanes satisfied that they have kept any negotiations from taking place, talk among themselves and eventually leave. The women who have been preparing food throughout the morning, undeterred by the violence unfolding around them, pour the thick chicken and vegetable stew onto paper plates and the remaining leaders eagerly tuck into their dinner.

Following the intervention of the rival band on the patio of Moises Sapiranda, the rebel leader Pablo Rivero pursued a campaign to further undermine Sapiranda's leadership. Rivero faxed a letter to YPFB, BG Bolivia, and CIDOB claiming to be the legitimate *capitán grande* of ORCAWETA and accusing BG Bolivia of intending to "once again trick the Weenhayek people with false promises of social and economic development as a consequence of environmental damage caused by its hydrocarbons operations." The letter specifically condemned ORCAWETA–BG Bolivia talks around compensation for an unauthorized well and threatened to organize a roadblock if his leadership was not recognized within seventy-two hours. Unable to recruit a sufficient number of *capitanes* to unseat Sapiranda, Rivero and his band could not make good on their threat.

By early December 2008, ORCAWETA and BG Bolivia were able to resolve the impasse and agree on compensation for the unauthorized well. This allowed for the next stage of the consultation and participation process to move forward, though it too would suffer even more delays. ORCAWETA prepared a plan and budget and organized a technical team to conduct Consultation and Participation activities with the then twenty-two communities of the TCO over a three-month period that was later reduced to two months and a smaller budget by ministry officials.[28] After gaining state approval of the plan, ORCAWETA leaders and the team traversed the TCO, communicating the content of the proposed Palo Marcado project to the Weenhayek. The team was under enormous pressure to finish the work within the allotted time while traveling to communities, holding workshops, and analyzing a large amount of data. A general assembly disseminated the results of the workshops and discussed the content of the final proposal. Following a review by the Vice Ministry of the Environment, ORCAWETA and that agency's officials signed the validation agreement (*acta de validación*). The team managed to finish the consultation process and present a proposal to the government by late April 2009.

In its proposal to the Vice Ministry of the Environment, ORCAWETA argued that BG Bolivia has a nonindigenous vision of Weenhayek territory in that it, like the state, did not recognize privately held land within the TCO as constituting part of Weenhayek territory and thus excluded this land, 80 percent of the TCO, from compensation negotiations. OR-CAWETA also argued that BG Bolivia's vision did not take into consideration the combined impact of its and other companies' operations on the TCO and its members' livelihoods or consider the impact population growth might have on the availability of resources for future generations.

ORCAWETA's proposal included a table of impacts grouped into the categories cultural, social, psychological, economic, and environmental (flora and fauna) and the subcategories cultural values, social-internal/external conflict, psychological self-esteem, and more. For each category and subcategory, the table listed whether the impacts would be positive or negative, short- or long-term, direct or indirect, and acute or cumulative. A set of activities was then recommended to avoid, mitigate, or control impacts. The table would come to form the heart of the discussion over which impacts would be defined as ones that could be managed or moderated (*mitigable*) and which impacts would be considered unmanageable (*no mitigable*) and whether they would be subject to compensation or not. By late May 2009, the government indicated it was time to allow its partner BG Bolivia and ORCAWETA negotiate the final compensation package based on a reworked list of impacts.

Negotiations to agree on the compensation package were held in the community of Capirendita and drew significant interest. In attendance were the *capitanes* from communities directly affected by the project but also members of the fishing syndicates based in Capirendita as well as OR-CAWETA leaders and advisers. A team of representatives from BG Bolivia was present, as was a representative of YPFB. When the BG Bolivia representative attempted to explain the project, he was stopped cold by the *capitanes*, who argued that they were quite familiar with the project. Calling for a break, the *capitanes* agreed to refuse to allow BG Bolivia to engage in what they perceived as stalling tactics, and they insisted that the meeting proceed on the basis of the validation agreement signed with the Vice Ministry of the Environment. The BG Bolivia representative attempted to continue with his explanation to highlight the company's planned efforts to avoid damaging areas of natural and cultural importance to the TCO. The *capitanes* insisted on focusing on compensation. This prompted the BG Bolivia representative to present the company's proposal; it would only compensate impacts that could not be managed and would offer interventions to address the impacts that could be managed or moderated. Social and cultural impacts were generally ignored. The BG offer, a one-off payment of US$185,000 and an additional annual contribution of US$50,000 to the Indigenous Development Plan budget for twenty years, was deemed unacceptable.

ORCAWETA's counterproposal called for a compensation package of US$11 million, with an additional US$550,000 per year over twenty years for the Indigenous Development Plan. At an impasse, BG threatened to turn over negotiations to YPFB, suggesting that ORCAWETA could end up with nothing at all. Perhaps fearing that they would lose rights to compensation, the *capitán grande* accepted a revised BG offer. The final negotiation was conducted behind closed doors. Despite efforts to democratize and transform negotiations around hydrocarbon operations within the TCO, the final negotiation thus retreated to a well-known pattern of secretive discussions and the consolidation of asymmetries of power.

In the weeks and months following the final negotiation with BG Bolivia, there was an abundance of both cash and conflict within the TCO. Rival leaders and followers besieged the *capitán grande*, and he responded with offers of cash and motorcycles. Unable to pay them outright, he resorted to borrowing from local loan sharks at interest rates of 10–20 percent monthly, and this led to a deeper crisis. Anger over the agreement and the distribution of monies triggered a new round of debilitating internal conflict including episodes of sporadic intracommunal violence, challenges to ORCAWETA leadership, accusations of corruption, and a general breakdown in the social order.

Conclusion

This historicized and ethnographic analysis shows how hydrocarbon expansion has interacted with and affected the Weenhayek and points to the sorts of tension the hydrocarbon economy has produced both within Weenhayek society and between the Weenhayek, the state, and one particular hydrocarbon company. The consultation and participation process oriented toward identifying compensation presents a means to explore these issues in some detail. The patterns that emerged are illustrative of a larger phenomenon of indigenous-state negotiations over expanding the extractive frontier in the Chaco and elsewhere.

In the case of the Weenhayek TCO, the tensions surrounding hydrocarbon expansion and processes of consultation must be understood in light of the particular economic calculations, territorial experiences, and organizational dynamics of the Weenhayek. The calculations are heavily marked by the logic of collection and the overriding importance of securing livelihoods in general but also from season to season. These imperatives and logics clearly affect what they negotiate for and how the dynamic of negotiation will vary across the annual cycle.

Meanwhile, Weenhayek territorial integrity has been historically compromised first by soldiers, then by ranchers, and more recently by hydrocarbon actors. In the face of this historical experience, the Weenhayek consistently seek to reconsolidate territory. The collective aspiration to restore territorial wholeness affects what is negotiated for and how. It reflects a group who, because of this history, is quick to distrust the government, including a MAS one, meaning that as soon as a government team acts in ways suggesting duplicity, negotiation becomes harder to conduct. Where the MAS government saw excessive demands for compensation, the Weenhayek leadership argued that they were merely asking for what is owed to them and what had been promised to them by MAS.

The Weenhayek have been called *inmediatistas* (immediatists), a reflection of the strong instinct to collect that characterizes much of their interactions with outsiders. While this characterization might be descriptively true, at least in part, it is analytically misleading because it suggests only opportunism and short-sightedness. Yet the immediate compensation that the Weenhayek demand reflects a clear understanding and awareness of the very limited and fragile nature of what is on offer and the weak ties they have with those who are making the offer as well as their own limited bargaining position.[29]

On the other hand, the short-term bargaining positions adopted by the state and hydrocarbon companies are reflected in a consultation and participation process intended to obtain local agreement for a specific project through selective offerings of financial compensation in the form of direct payment or through programs for indigenous development. The time span for conducting a consultation and participation process is condensed, and this fosters a sense of uncertainty and vulnerability. The climate of tension and distrust that characterizes negotiations around extraction weakens already fragile local organizations as well as efforts to build more participatory institutions.

In this way, consultation and participation processes come to constitute the society of the groups who participate in them. The hydrocarbon extraction that drives consultation and participation changes landscapes in ways that alter livelihood practices forever, albeit in ways that reflect historical continuities. Among the Weenhayek, this combination of transformation and continuity is exemplified by the maintenance of the logic of collection but in a context in which the practices of collection are changed in profound ways. The consultation and participation process also becomes part of internal sociopolitical dynamics in ways that can strengthen or weaken the indigenous group. Among the Weenhayek the process has caused great stress to the supracommunal organization ORCAWETA as well as to intracommunal relations. And the extent to which the Weenhayek succeed or fail in negotiating their larger concerns around territory through consultation and participation will determine how far they are going to be able to fulfil their aspiration to consolidate their territory. In this regard, the consultation and participation process constitutes a critical moment for the group and is much more than a simple negotiation at a point in time; rather, its outcomes will determine, for the foreseeable future, the ability of the Weenhayek to fulfill or not fulfill their historical project of territorialization.

Over the years of the Morales MAS government (2006–2019), efforts to consolidate Weenhayek territory through further land titling processes were uneven. After some initial progress in 2008–2010, the period on which I have focused, the bulk of Weenhayek territory remains under non-Weenhayek control.

From 2013 onward, interest in recovering territory was gradually replaced with struggles to access monetary resources from hydrocarbon companies. But there have also been internal struggles over TCO lands. Since 2017 more than eight complaints, filed by a handful of *capitanes*, warned of the illegal sale of TCO land by ORCAWETA leaders. The sale of TCO lands is illegal. These land deals were strongly rejected by Weenhayek families who wanted to occupy the plots to establish family settlements. This sale of TCO lands, now occupied by nonindigenous persons, was prevented neither by the former ORCAWETA leadership nor by state authorities. In the end, the scandal led to the February 2019 election of a new *capitán grande*. ORCAWETA is trying to recover the sold lands. The lack of progress in consolidating TCO lands confirms earlier observations (Humphreys Bebbington and Bebbington 2010) that as long as a natural resource extraction-based economic model remained in place, the government will privilege hydrocarbon investments over the territorial claims and projects of indigenous peoples.

Also confirming earlier concerns (Humphreys Bebbington and Bebbington 2010), initial hopes that consultation and participation would rectify power asymmetries between communities and companies in Bolivia have turned to alarm over the exacerbation of internal divisions within and between communities and the debilitating impacts on indigenous institutions throughout the lowlands (Schilling-Vacaflor and Eichler 2017). Between 2012 and its fall in November 2019, the Morales MAS government doubled down on natural resource extraction. In the process, MAS deployed tactics to control indigenous organizations and divide and conquer critical voices (Fabricant and Postero 2019; Schilling-Vacaflor and Eichler 2017) in order to control dissent and allow resource extraction to proceed. This strategy is seen both in the hydrocarbons sector and the mining sector, where consultation is described as "regimented, choreographed, and formalized" and devoid of meaningful participation (Perreault 2015, 434).

These patterns have been clear in Weenhayek territory and in the government's relations with ORCAWETA leadership. After the fallout of a 2012 conflict in which lowland indigenous organizations were feeling pressure to fall in line with the MAS Morales government,[30] the *capitán grande* of ORCAWETA introduced a series of changes that would consolidate his leadership and reduce tensions between the Weenhayek, gas companies, and the state. ORCAWETA's new bylaws that called for elections every five years instead of every two years were sent to CIDOB (by then also subject to MAS influence) for approval without being vetted at the community level. At the same time, consultation and participation processes linked to hydrocarbon projects turned into massive events with the presence of many dozens of leaders. With a handful of loyal leaders, the *capitán grande* would negotiate final agreements that would later be announced to community leaders. The contents of such agreements, subject to confidentiality clauses as part of company practice that remains unchallenged, are not divulged to the population. This meant that only the ORCAWETA leadership is party to the amounts transferred and the projects for which such resources are ostensibly intended.

In addition to overseeing the distribution of company compensation funds packaged as Indigenous Development Plans, the *capitán grande* accumulated more power through influencing the flow of resources from central government and subnational authorities. Once understood as a spokesperson for Weenhayek communities, the *capitán grande* became a broker with external actors and determined who would benefit from projects, who would receive the monies from BG/Shell, who would gain employment opportunities, and who would receive the support of ORCAWETA. Just as access to these benefits could be provided, access could be withheld. This meant that leaders who disagreed with the *capitán grande* or questioned the hierarchical form in which monies were redistributed were then excluded from receiving funds and other perks, imitating the tactics used by Morales and MAS to control dissent.

Nonetheless, the payments sustaining relations between the *capitán grande* and the *capitanes* were increasingly challenged by younger and disaffected community leaders. Rising tensions produced five internal rebellions from 2009 to 2019, each calling for the *capitán grande* to be stripped of power and replaced with a new, elected leader. None of these efforts was successful until early 2019 when, after multiple complaints were lodged, elections were held. The results of the election, supported by CIDOB, were denounced by the deposed *capitán grande*, who by 2019 had occupied this position for twelve years. In October 2019, shortly before presidential elections, Morales signed an agreement with this same longtime *capitán grande*, recognizing his authority. After a highway blockade in Villa Montes that kept Morales from visiting Weenhayek communities during the electoral campaigns, Morales and MAS ultimately backed down and acknowledged the newly elected leadership. Following reports that the presidential elections had been fraudulent (OAS 2019), only the former *capitán grande* responded to MAS's call to support the return of Morales to power.

At the time of writing, the former *capitán grande* remained "former," while Evo Morales, together with his Vice President Alvaro García Linera, returned to Bolivia following a period of exile and the election of Luis Arce (MAS) as president in October 2020. Without exaggerating the comparison, the standing of the leadership of MAS and ORCAWETA had become linked through relations of mutual support and networks of patronage sustained by hydrocarbon revenues. The ultimate benefits from this for the consolidation of Weenhayek territory and organization have been partial at best.

Meanwhile the gas keeps flowing.

Notes

1. An earlier version of this chapter was first published as "Consultation, Compensation, and Conflict: Natural Gas Extraction in Weenhayek Territory, Bolivia," *Journal of Latin American Geography* 11, no. 2:49–71, https://muse.jhu.edu/article/488196.

2. Fieldwork for the first author was supported by the Economic and Social Research Council of the United Kingdom and later by a Ford Foundation grant. Both authors would like to thank Anthony Bebbington for his guidance and support.

3. British Gas, the owner of BG Bolivia, was acquired by Royal Dutch Shell in February 2016.

4. Alvarsson (2007) describes the Weenhayek's decision to reject the term *mataco* (used pejoratively by whites and mestizos) and refer to themselves as Weenhayek Wiky'i as part of a long and ongoing process of ethnoregeneration, in which a group attempts to define or recover an identity that has been submerged. In this chapter, we use the singular term "Weenhayek." The term *mataco* appears only when used by the author being cited.

5. In May 2008 there were twenty-two Weenhayek communities. In 2010, however, the number of settlements swelled to thirty-six after disputes arose among clans linked to a negotiated agreement between ORCAWETA and BG Bolivia in 2009–2010. Over the next decade the number of settlements continued to grow and in 2020 stood at sixty. The settlements are represented by nearly 180 community leaders, with multiple leaders representing the various clans within a single settlement. The advantage of this organizational model is that there is more direct representation to ORCAWETA and what is seen as a more equitable distribution of resources. The disadvantage is that coming to consensus over how to address problems requires more time. The forming of new settlements also reflects the strategy of clan members to gain additional access to financial resources from subnational and national authorities but also from negotiated agreements around gas.

6. The earliest encounters between Spanish soldiers and Wichí occurred in 1626 in a locality known as Ledesma in Jujuy Province, Argentina. Attempts by Jesuit missionaries in 1638 and by Franciscan priests in 1865 to evangelize and settle the Wichí-Weenhayek failed. Franciscans established their first Weenhayek and Guaraní mission in San Antonio, Villa Montes, Bolivia, but after some years the Weenhayek abandoned the mission. With the arrival of the Swedish Evangelical Mission in 1948 the Weenhayek joined the Pentecostal Church.

7. Bolivian scholars link the causes of the Chaco War to an emerging conflict between Standard Oil of New Jersey, a US-based firm with operations in Bolivia, and Royal Dutch Shell, a British firm with interests in Paraguay, for control over what were thought to be significant hydrocarbons reserves. Other historians (e.g., Klein 1992) dispute this view. What is important is that the majority of Bolivians, among them President Evo Morales, contend that the Chaco War was the result of transnational oil companies' greed and duplicitous dealings. Since 2016 the Bolivian subsidiary of Royal Dutch Shell returned to the Chaco to play an important role in the development of potential natural gas reserves ("Drilling Begins at a Natural Gas Field in Southern Bolivia," EFE, May 22, 2018, https://www.efe.com/efe/english/business/drilling-begins-at-natural-gas-field-in-southern-bolivia/50000265–3623162).

8. *Capitán grande* (big captain) is a title conferred on the top leader of ORCAWETA.

9. Some migrated to northern Argentina to work cutting cane.

10. The Free Swedish Mission established a mission in Tuntey on the outskirts of Villa Montes. Despite its withdrawal in 2006, the organization has continued to exert significant influence in local affairs.

11. Fishing season generally extends from May to August or September, though the Weenhayek continue to fish for household consumption during the off season.

12. In 2011 there was a near collapse in the sábalo (a ray-finned fish species native

to South America) population, with a 95 percent decline in landed fish from the previous year. The apparent trigger of the collapse was Paraguay's decision to dredge a canal that led to a change of course in the Pilcomayo River that in turn affected the flow of sediments in the upper basin ("Informe final: Evaluación de la situación de la seguridad alimentaria de comunidades indígenas del rio Pilcomayo, Provincia Gran Chaco del Departamento de Tarija," October 2011).

13. Such authorities preferred to negotiate with a single representative organization rather than with dozens of local leaders who had distinct opinions and positions in meetings that could last for days with unpredictable outcomes.

14. The Tapiete have since withdrawn from ORCAWETA.

15. Here we draw on interviews with indigenous leaders and promoters.

16. A small portion of the Weenhayek Tierra Comunitaria de Origen (TCO) is located farther inland, at the foot of the Aguaragüe mountain range, and is thus affected by the Aguarague hydrocarbon block, at the time operated by Chaco, an area covering nearly 64,000 hectares.

17. Among these groups are Acción Ecológica, Amazon Watch, Cultural Survival, Friends of the Earth, Oilwatch Rainforest Action Network, and Survival International.

18. Interview with Hugh Atwater, social performance manager, BG Group PLC, November 10, 2008.

19. Interview with Jose Magela Bernardes, general manager, BG Bolivia, January 22, 2009.

20. Interview with Moises Sapiranda, December 16, 2008. The area of land titled was actually 21,190 hectares.

21. Interviews with Erick Araoz and Nolberto Gallardo.

22. Many of these ranches are owned by absentee landlords. Compensation settlements with hydrocarbon companies then provide important resources that permit an otherwise unprofitable and unsustainable activity to continue. There is an interesting similarity here to arguments made most of all in Brazil that ranching in the Amazon was often a strategy for gaining fiscal benefits rather than for producing cattle (Binswanger-Mkhize 1991; Hecht 1985).

23. Information about BG Group's operations in Bolivia are from the BG website http://www.bg-group.com/OurBusiness/WhereWeOperate/Pages/Bolivia.aspx, now https://www.shell.com. Information about Royal Dutch Shell's operations in Bolivia can be found at https://www.shell.com.bo/.

24. This ambiguity serves a useful purpose in that companies can engage in short-term negotiations linked to specific problems or activities linked to projects without having to renegotiate the larger program of support. ORCAWETA does not maintain a single register of agreements negotiated with BG Bolivia, Shell, or other companies.

25. The Bolivian government does not have a mechanism in place to oversee fulfilment of these negotiated agreements.

26. Proyecto Desarrollo del Campo Palo Marcado, BG Bolivia, "Información sobre el proyecto 'Desarrollo del Campo Palo Marcado' proceso de consulta y participación, Ministerio de Hidrocarburos y Energía, Bolivia," PowerPoint presentation, 2008.

27. Originally YPFB was not involved in the process; the government modified the consultation and participation process in 2008 to include YPFB.

28. The costs related to consultation and participation processes are covered by the company.

29. Alvarsson (2007) has made similar comments in regard to Weenhayek relations with the city and with missionaries. See also Stuart Kirsch 2006 on indigenous peoples' relations with mines in Melanesia.

30. Lowland groups, under the leadership of CIDOB, staged two marches to contest Morales and MAS plans to open TIPNIS (Territorio Indígena y Parque Nacional Isiboro Sécure, Isiboro Sécure Indigenous Territory and National Park) to extraction and infrastructure development. Nicole Fabricant and Nancy Postero (2019) refer to the confrontation over TIPNIS as "a watershed moment for the Morales government: the government's ethical and political commitments to bettering the lives of all indigenous peoples came into question" (248).

9

The Guaraní People's Struggle for Indigenous Autonomy in Bolivia

NANCY POSTERO

In 2005 Bolivia elected its first indigenous president, Evo Morales. Morales, who came to power vowing to enact indigenous rights, presided over a 2006–2007 Constituent Assembly of popularly elected delegates, many of them indigenous people, who rewrote the constitution to refound Bolivia as a new "plurinational" state. The resulting 2009 Constitution declares the fundamental goal of the state to be decolonization, recognizes indigenous peoples and their cultures and values as central to the new state, and grants them important new rights, echoing the language of the UN Declaration of the Rights of Indigenous Peoples. Article 2 of the Bolivian Constitution declares:

> Given the precolonial existence of the indigenous originary peasant nations and peoples and their ancestral dominion over their territories, their self-determination is guaranteed within the framework of the unity of the State and consists of their right to autonomy, to self-government, to their culture, to the recognition of their institutions, and to the consolidation of their territorial entities, in conformity with this Constitution and the law. (Bolivia, Congreso Nacional 2009)

The intervening years have brought enormous debates about the meaning of these constitutional rights, especially as Bolivia has continued its full-on dedication to a development model based on natural resource extraction. In my recent book (Postero 2017), I trace the arc of the first ten years of the Morales regime, analyzing what many have called an "indigenous state." At the beginning of the Morales regime, indigeneity and decolonization formed the basis of an emancipatory politics aimed at overturning colonial and neoliberal legacies. However, over the following decade, Morales and his MAS (Movimiento al Socialismo, Movement toward Socialism) party moved away from that early commitment to indigenous rights toward a policy of "economic liberation" based on resource extraction and limited redistribution of its profits. In the process, for many urban indigenous people linked to the global market through commerce or for those hoping to improve their living standards, indigeneity began to take a back seat to class, as they worked to climb the ladder to the middle class. For them, decolonization has more to do with national sovereignty than local autonomy.

Here, I take up a very different situation: the case of Charagua, where indigenous Guaraní activists in this municipality in the Bolivian Chaco have won an important political victory, establishing their city as the country's first—and only, so far—indigenous autonomous municipality. The Guaraní of Charagua are strategically using the rights established in the new constitution to move towards their long-term goal of reconstituting a Guaraní nation. For the Guaraní, decolonization is an important goal and discourse and a set of juridical tools they utilize in their own struggle for local autonomy.

The victory in Charagua in 2015 was the first step in what is likely to be a long process of seeking autonomous status for indigenous lands; many more communities are in the pipeline, preparing for autonomy. It was also a very significant accomplishment, bringing the Guaraní of Charagua one step closer to their goal of autonomy. I focus on how Guaraní leaders managed to overcome local tensions to win the election through their pragmatic politics as they negotiated in the spaces between national, departmental, and local sovereignties. While still subsumed within the liberal nation-state, this new form of local government offers the first institutionalized vision of indigenous alternatives to liberalism, a first glimpse of what the "indigenous state" could mean at the local level. The case shows that political reforms can result not only from disagreements or contestation but also from the hard work of consensus building.

Autonomía Guaraní Charagua Iyambae

Charagua is a small town in the Chaco region of the department of Santa Cruz. It is high desert, a dry forest crossed by occasional rivers and streams. It is Bolivia's largest municipality in terms of size, at 74,000 square kilometers, and in the 2012 census had about 35,000 inhabitants. Xavier Albó (2012) estimates that about 60 percent of the population is indigenous

Guaraní. The Guaraní are organized into four *capitanías*, local federations, made of two groups of Guaraní: the Avas of Charagua Norte and the Para-petiguasu of Charagua Sur, and the Isoseños from the more remote Bajo and Alto Isoso zones. These groups live in small, dispersed communities throughout the large municipality, mostly growing corn and raising small herds of cattle and other livestock. Their organizations are part of the larger national Guaraní organization, the Asamblea del Pueblo Guaraní (APG, Assembly of the Guaraní People), founded in 1987. Throughout the zone, mestizo families have large landholdings where they raise cattle for sale. These families are the traditional elites who since colonial times have ex-ercised economic and political power over the Guaraní (Albó 2012, Pifarré 1989, Postero 2007). Guaraní have worked on their haciendas and in some sectors were held in a form of slavery. The *hacendados* (large landholders) live in the pueblo, where they have run the municipality until recently. The *hacendados* have traditionally been allied with the conservative mestizo political party of Santa Cruz, the Verdes (Greens, for the green and white colors of the party), now officially called Demócratas. As in Santa Cruz, the civic committee, run by the elites and their families, has been a central site of local politics. The other important organization is the *junta vecinal* (neighborhood association), which represents the urban residents and is run mostly by mestizo schoolteachers. These groups have overtly fought the autonomy process.

There are two other major sectors. One is a large group of Mennonites who have established large *colonias* (colonies) in the region. Although they make up about 20 percent of the region's population, they do not vote be-cause their religion requires them to stay out of political debates. The other group is made up of highland Andean migrants who have moved to the zone in recent decades and established an urban settlement a few kilome-ters outside town near the old train station. The residents of this sector, La Estación, are farmers, merchants, and *transportistas* (truck drivers). Most speak Quechua and are supporters of Morales and his MAS party. So, al-though they make up a large majority of the population, the Guaraní activ-ists pushing indigenous autonomy are forced to negotiate with the rest of the people living in the municipality.

Over the six years of struggle to bring autonomy into being—what Guaraní leaders call a *peregrinación* (pilgrimage), given the endless trips and meetings with state and judicial officials—leaders have maintained a dogged commitment to gaining state recognition for their autonomous government, which their statute calls Autonomía Guaraní Charagua

Iyambae. *Iyambae* is a Guaraní term often translated as freedom or without owners. I have been observing their process since 2010, when they held an assembly to draft an autonomy statute, essentially a new constitution for the community. In August 2010 I asked René Gómez, the president of the assembly, to explain the goals of their efforts. What did they mean by autonomy? Patiently, with smiling eyes, he explained.

> We understand autonomy as being free [*ser libre*]. . . . Not that we aren't already. We, the Guaraní nation, have always been autonomous, free. But there are no laws or norms that say we are autonomous. So for us, autonomy consists of when one can govern oneself [*uno gobierne por sí solo*], that is self-government [*autogobierno*], without political parties. . . . What we are doing here in Charagua with our assembly is the fruit of decolonization and its transversal themes of racism, discrimination, and dependence. . . . We are decolonizing because we are thinking from another world [or space, *en otro ámbito*]. These are new forms of thinking, seeing things in another way, as we indigenous peoples have always done.

Don René is saying what I heard over and over during my visits to Charagua, that the Guaraní believe that they are already autonomous and have always been so. Their goal with the assembly and with using the autonomy law was to make their autonomy visible and functional in the world of liberal laws and norms. Don René hoped the process of decolonization begun by the Constituent Assembly and the new constitution would provide an opportunity for them to articulate their understanding of sovereignty with that of the rest of the people in the country. "Every pueblo has its culture," he said, "its form of living, its *ñandereko* [way of being]." Here he used a complex term that has multiple meanings. *Ñandereko* is sometimes translated as "the harmonious life" (Bolivia, Congreso Nacional 2009). However, Bartolomeu Meliá, the most important historian of the Guaraní, makes clear that it refers not only to the Guaraní way of being, culture, and customs but also to the place and medium that make that way of being possible: the interrelated cultural, economic, social, religious, and political spaces linking land, beings, and people (cited in Medina 2002, 100–101).

Don René's statement here echoes what the Catalán anthropologist Pere Morrel i Torra suggests in his excellent 2013 analysis of the autonomy process in Charagua: for the Guaraní, autonomy is a set of intersecting meanings (2013, 11). First, it is an existing set of social practices that have emerged over hundreds of years. Drawing on historical archives, especially the work of Isabelle Combès (2005), Morrel i Torra describes the ways differing sectors of Guaraní in the *cordillera* region have long maintained autonomy from each other. Each community has made its own decisions except during times of war. Even in the past fifty years, as these autonomous communities formed the Asamblea del Pueblo Guaraní federation to push for territorial rights, in practice each *capitanía* has maintained its decision-making power. This is what Don René means when he says, "We, the Guaraní nation, have always been autonomous, free."

Second, autonomy is a political discourse used by Guaraní leadership to push towards their goal of a united Guaraní nation. As Morrel i Torra makes clear, unity is a relatively new goal, given the long history of independence and the underlying tensions between Avas and Isoseños (2013, 51). These two groups have long been at odds with each other and have exercised very different strategies in their relations with the dominant politicians. Albó asserts (2012) that the Isoseños have more often allied with the Cruzeño elite. Yet, since the multicultural era and the formation of the APG, the Guaraní have been working together consistently toward the control of their territory and the formation of an indigenous-led government. Albo's comprehensive history of the Guaraní's efforts demonstrates a careful and determined strategy of using every possible political opening to do so. He shows how the APG worked with various NGOs to create development projects for their communities. In the multicultural era, the APG claimed millions of hectares under the Ley INRA, the 1997 Agrarian Reform law. By 2011 they had successfully gained title to more than 800,000 hectares plus two large protected areas, one of which was named a national park (Albó 2012, 98). This new limited form of territorial titling allowed local communities to negotiate with the transnational oil companies that were pumping oil and gas from under their lands. The funds they obtained from this went directly to the individual *capitanías* to be used for local development (84–85). Albó also documents the ways the Guaraní took up the Law of Popular Participation, which channeled state funds to municipalities. Beginning in 1995 the Guaraní began participating in municipal politics and putting up their leaders to run in city council and mayoral elections. Tracing their progress election by election, Albó argues that this strategy consolidated the Guaraní as mature political actors able to articulate their demands for autonomy. Don René knows this *en carne propia* (in his own flesh), as he served several terms on Charagua's city council in the 1990s.

Finally, Morrel i Torra suggests, indigenous autonomy is a status of juridical recognition by the state. It was this that René meant when he explained that "there are no laws or norms that say we are autonomous." At Bolivia's Constituent Assembly in 2006–2008, indigenous activists and their allies proposed new forms of self-government that would return to indigenous communities both territorial control and traditional forms of governance as part of their centuries-old demands for self-determination. The Guaraní of Charagua participated in these debates. Don Abilio Vaca, from Charagua Norte, was a delegate to the assembly and served on the Commission on Autonomies. Yet, the form of indigenous autonomy in the final constitution is a substantially watered-down version of what activists had proposed. Instead of the far-reaching self-determination indigenous activists had longed for since the conquest and for which they fought in insurrections up until the twentieth century, indigenous autonomy is not significantly discernable from a local administrative entity within a liberal centralized state. There are some meaningful changes, but this form of governance continues to be embedded within a strong centralized state model. Despite this, however, the Guaraní hoped they could use the political opening to advance their long-term goals.

Thus, instead of a radical challenge to liberalism, Bolivia's indigenous autonomy may be closer to what Audra Simpson calls "nested sovereignties." Given the continuing monopoly of military and institutional power held by settler states, she suggests that "like indigenous bodies, indigenous sovereignties and indigenous political orders prevail within and apart from settler governance" (2014, 11). "Sovereignty may exist within sovereignty. One does not entirely negate the other, but they necessarily stand in terrific tension and pose serious jurisdictional and normative challenges to each other," she finds (10). Simpson shows how the Mohawks negotiate these tensions, often "refusing" the gift of citizenship from the United States and Canada, bearing their own passports across national borders they find illegitimate. The Guaraní I describe here also find themselves in a complex set of nested sovereignties crossing national, departmental (state), and local levels. Yet, they do not operate through refusal. Instead, they have used the resources of the plurinational constitution and alliances with multiple political factions to press forward toward self-determination.

The Pilgrimage toward Autonomy

The path to autonomy was long and complex. The Bolivian Constitution (Article 2) establishes the rights of indigenous people to self-government through what are called Autonomías Indígenas Originarias Campesinas

(AIOCs, Indigenous First Peoples Peasants Autonomies). In 2009 Morales began the process of autonomy with Decree Law 231, which set up a complex system of requirements for local communities seeking conversion to this status. There are three possibilities: the conversion of existing municipalities; the conversion of indigenously held territories; and the creation of new regional autonomies composed of two or more converted municipalities (Tockman and Cameron 2014). The government then put out a formal call for municipalities to apply for the status. Then, in 2010, Congress passed an enabling law, the Ley Marco de Autonomía y Decentralización (Framework Law on Autonomies and Decentralization), which formalized all the requirements for creation and operation of the autonomies. The second path, that of converting indigenous territories, opened in 2012 and would arise not from a referendum but by consultation based on norms and procedures. In 2014 that process was under way in about ten indigenous territories; more have begun the process since then (Tockman 2014, 248–249).

The first step of the complex autonomy process was to apply to hold a public referendum to begin the conversion process. As Jason Tockman and John Cameron report (2014), the bureaucratic requirements were onerous. Those who wanted to begin the autonomy process had to collect the signatures of 10 percent of the municipality's voting population, provide evidence of precolonial occupation of the municipality, and secure from the municipal council ratification of an ordinance supporting conversion by two-thirds of the council's members. Besides that, the deadlines were tight, and only twelve communities managed to file these documents in time (Tockman and Cameron 2014, 53). Since the state did not provide funding or administrative help, the communities had to rely on technical help from local nongovernmental organizations (NGOs). The first round of referenda was held in 2009, and only eleven communities were successful in their bids. Charagua was one of only two lowland communities to pass this step, with 55.7 percent voting yes (Albó 2012, 125). The second step was to convene a representative assembly to elaborate formal autonomy statutes. This was a time-consuming process in which the differing sectors and interests debated whether and how autonomy might serve the community's interests. In several cases, the tensions proved insurmountable.

In Charagua the Guaraní held an assembly to draft the autonomy statute, bringing elected delegates from various sectors to the table. In an assembly that met for several months and was overseen by the central government's Ministry of Autonomies, the delegates drafted a statute establishing a new form of municipal government based on Guaraní norms and procedures. Once written, these statutes were submitted to Bolivia's Plurinational Constitutional Tribunal to ensure that they complied with constitutional requirements. Charagua's statute was presented to the high court in Sucre in October 2012, and in December 2013 the Plurinational Constitutional Tribunal issued its ruling of constitutionality. This ruling was provisional, pending several required revisions, the most significant of which was the ruling that the statute's investment of broad oversight powers in the *ñemboati guasu*, the highest deliberative assembly, was unconstitutional. After the assembly revised the statute on these and several other issues, the statute was approved in June 2014. The final step was a second referendum. If a majority of the public in the municipality approved, the process of conversion could commence (Tockman and John Cameron 2014, 53). In September 2015 two communities, Totora Marka in the highlands and Charagua in the lowlands, had passed all these requirements and put their new statutes to the test in referenda. Only Charagua won, with a slim but important margin of 53 percent (Colque 2015, Portugal 2015).

Thus, Charagua's new statute is a historic document, one that moves the country forward in terms of what local autonomy might look like in practice. It is the result of a long deliberative process of local democracy. The proponents of the conversion process organized the assembly in 2010 with help from local NGO Centro de Investigación y Promoción del Campesinado (CIPCA, Center for Investigation and Promotion of Peasants) and with oversight from the national Ministry of Autonomies. The minister of autonomies personally came to town several times at key moments to encourage participation, and the ministry did provide some minimal help printing posters and copies of the statutes. Nevertheless, the Guaraní relied instead on CIPCA, which had grants from private and public Spanish foundations, for most of the logistical help necessary to move the process forward (Morrel i Torra 2013, 84).

The Guaraní designed an assembly with delegates from all the sectors of Charagua's population. The Guaraní delegates attended regularly, although the length of the assembly sessions made it hard for everyone, as they had to leave their jobs or their farms for weeks at a time. Yet, there was very little attendance by the mestizo members. In 2011 and 2012 I interviewed *vecinos* (neighbors) from the pueblo and found they had opted not to be part of the process. These elites acknowledged their fears. They did not participate in the assembly because they felt it was illegal or useless since they were the minority, but they raged against the process as having been imposed from the outside. One Verde city councilor told me the autonomy process was a MAS government project "intended to knock us over" (*tumbarnos*), meaning to overturn elite power in the region. The people of the pueblo also openly expressed a deep racism when they spoke of a possible future under indigenous autonomy. One cattle rancher called the idea of indigenous autonomy "retrograde, it takes us back to ancestral times" of using ancient customs. "Imagine, our grandchildren living in an indigenous municipality. . . . This is a dark and uncertain future, because I know them. They have lots of land, but they do not know how to produce." Relying on classic tropes of the corrupt, lazy, or backward Indian, these mestizo leaders could not imagine ceding or even sharing power with their indigenous neighbors.

In 2011 I attended the autonomy assembly that took place in the Arakuaarenda Cultural Center at the edge of town. The meeting had a decidedly historic feeling. Section by section, the delegates put forward their ideas, drawn from commission meetings and discussions with local base communities. Long debates in Guaraní and Spanish followed as the delegates considered the structure of the new form of government they wanted to create. The technical team from CIPCA sat in the back with their laptops, recording and systematizing the material. The long, hot days in the hall were broken up by shared lunches and coffee breaks, where discussions continued. Over the process, the delegates designed a new system of local governance based on Guaraní values and notions of autonomy.

Because I had followed the negotiations at the Constituent Assembly and seen how this new legal status was so embedded within the liberal structure of the nation-state, I wondered how this new system could actually accomplish any real change. In my discussions with delegates then and in the visits that followed in 2012 and 2015, I asked everyone I met, "How would this new system of governance change things? What would autonomy mean in the light of the constitutional constraints?" They returned to several themes again and again. Guaraní told me they wanted a system that prevented political parties from monopolizing power. At first I did not understand the depth of this concern. I assumed it was an expression like that I had heard all over Bolivia, a distrust of the corrupting power of traditional political class, which was dominated by mestizos. Yes, it was that, people said, but it was also the result of their own experiences in Charagua over the previous twenty years. Although they had been able to get Guaraní elected to the city council and even as mayor, often those leaders had been coopted by the political parties and betrayed the Guaraní project. This had caused enormous discord within the communities, and they wanted to avoid that. "*Tenemos que ser unidos, hermanos*" (We have to be unified, brothers and sisters), they said frequently to each other and to me.

People also said they wanted to find a way of getting resources directly, without the mediation of the mayor's office, political parties, or the departmental government. The funding process required indigenous groups to present proposals to the governor and the mayor for any development projects they might be trying to implement. Not only was this a tiresome and uncertain process, it put them in the position of supplicants begging for resources. They asserted that the resources flowing from the national government to the departments were the result of extractivist projects carried out on indigenous territories. "These are our resources," said one delegate. "We should control them and decide what kind of development we need." The *capitanías* have experience with administering development projects, as they have been receiving monies directly from some of the petroleum companies for some time, so this is not a surprising demand.

The final revised statute organizes municipal government in a radically decentralized manner. Each of the six sectors (the four Guaraní *capitanías*, the pueblo, and La Estación) is an autonomous entity with the right to elect its own representatives according to the community's *usos y costumbres* (traditional customs). For the *capitanías*, this means elections made by consensus at public assemblies. For the other two, elections can be by secret vote according to liberal notions of democracy or however they decide to do it. Each zone sends representatives to collective decision-making bodies at the communal, zonal, and municipal levels as well as to a legislative body. There is an executive body, but rather than a mayor and council, it is a body made up of representatives from each zone. Is this new system actually different, or is this another example of indigeneity as emancipatory politics ceding to indigeneity as symbolic window dressing for a continuation of liberalism?

I agree with Morrel i Torra that while this statute is in fact "very distant from the discourse of ancestrality that prevails in the usual theoretical approaches to indigenous autonomy" (2013, 96), it could bring about some important transformations in the relations of power, forms of territorial control, and sociocultural dynamics in Charagua. Morrel i Torra points to three specific changes. First, he signals the way the statute decentralizes or disperses power from a political institution to a collective body (98). This follows the indigenous model Pierre Clastres (1989) has described as "societies against the state," in which no one leader holds the power of violence over others. Instead, society as a whole is the site of political power, and leaders act as mediators to promote harmony rather than to exercise command over others. Individual people and communities maintain autonomy, only giving power to leaders in emergencies such as times of war. The Charagua autonomy statute continued this logic by separating power from a mayor and dispersing it throughout a series of collective decision-making bodies in which positions are rotated across time and communities. It is worth noting again, however, that this effort to disperse power was diminished by the Plurinational Constitutional Tribunal's 2013 rulings (Tockman 2014, 182–183). In 2015 Mayor Belarmino Solano explained it to me this way: "Before, the mayor was above everyone and important. Now we want the leaders to be in contact with everyone, to come down to society. This is a way to decolonize, with open doors."

Second, Morrel i Torra suggests that, like the Bolivian Constitution, the Charagua statute has inserted within it indigenous values such as *iyambae* (freedom, without owners) and *yaiko kavi pave*, a Guaraní notion often translated as *vivir bien* (living well). This is a form of hybridity in which indigenous logics are inserted into the liberal text as a non-Western and decolonizing resource (2013, 107). Finally, Morrel i Torra suggests that the statute goes beyond multiculturalism by including all the other sectors and allowing the groups the right to organize and represent themselves. This was an important selling point in all the public events I attended, as non-Guaraní expressed their fears of having to conform to Guaraní customs. The statute incorporates others but does not subordinate them (131).

From Aspiration to Recognition

While the delegates to the Charagua autonomy assembly were busy formulating a new way to govern their local communities, politics as usual were continuing around them in the nation, department, and municipality. That is, at the same time they were planning a future of autonomy, they were also living and working in the old system, in which political parties and discourses were holding sway. To move from their aspirations as expressed in the statute, they had to work in the existing system to assure their rights and get the referendum passed to make the conversion to autonomy a reality.

During the six years the Guaraní of Charagua worked on the autonomy process, the political landscape changed radically. When the Guaraní leaders began the autonomy assembly in 2010, the mayor and the majority of the city council members were conservative Verdes, aligned with and representing the views of mestizos of the city center who were firmly opposed to autonomy. They saw it as a clear threat to their traditional control over the mayor's office and the funding from the state that flowed to the city. They also saw autonomy as part of the larger MAS project to overturn traditional elite power. This was not an accurate assessment; in Charagua, conversion to autonomy was not a MAS project at all. Most MAS supporters in Charagua were Aymara and Quechua immigrants from the highlands who were opposed to the Guaraní-led process. For the Guaraní of Charagua, this was not just a MAS project; it was a centuries-long project of territorial self-determination. They were, however, able to use the dominant MAS discourse of decolonization and indigenous rights to legitimize their struggle. In 2010 the narrative of indigenous rights, *vivir bien*, and preservation of Mother Earth was on everyone's tongues, especially the president's, and the Guaraní of Charagua took advantage of it to push their local demands onto the national agenda, moving their project through the national-level courts.

But by 2011 the president's commitment to indigenous rights began to be called into question. Controversy arose over a proposed highway segment through an indigenous territory and national park called the Territorio Indígena y Parque Nacional Isiboro Sécure (TIPNIS).[1] Lowland communities opposed to the project met severe government repression, demonstrating that Morales was willing to sacrifice indigenous lands to extractivist development (Postero 2017, Chapter 5). The transformation from decolonization to development had begun. The APG supported the 2011 march for TIPNIS, and many Guaraní from Charagua participated. The way Morales dealt with the marchers and particularly the violent repression during that march still counts for many as the biggest betrayal of their political lives. Those government actions made MAS an unsavory ally. Yet, with the autonomy process slowed down and not certain to win, the Guaraní decided to keep pushing that long-term strategy but with a variety of tactics: they would work with the Verdes (Demócratas) and MAS at the same time at very different levels of government.

At the departmental level they took advantage of the new electoral scheme that guaranteed each of the five indigenous groups in the department of Santa Cruz one *asambleista* (representative) to the department legislature. These *asambleistas* were elected according to *usos y costumbres*, that is, not as part of any political party. This allowed them to form pacts with any party. Under the fiscal structure of Bolivia, gas rents and royalties are collected by the central government and distributed to departments, universities, and a development fund for indigenous people. The department then distributes the funds to municipalities. So, to get these monies flowing to their municipality and to get the governor and legislature to approve projects, the indigenous *asambleistas* had to work with the Verdes in power. MAS saw this as a betrayal. How could indigenous people work with lowland elites instead of the indigenous MAS party? But Ruth Yarigua, then a Guaraní *asambleista* and a former *capitana grande* (leader) of Charagua Norte, explained that her loyalty was to her people. Their dream for centuries has been to "occupy these spaces of power, at all levels, without regard for political colors. . . . This is just what autonomy in Charagua will also provide: the liberty to decide for ourselves, without conforming ourselves to any political party" (interview, July 27, 2015). She and her fellow *asambleistas* put forward development projects to be approved for the annual operating budgets and convinced their fellow legislators to approve them.

More importantly, though, the five indigenous *asambleistas* collaborated with Demócrata *asambleistas* to pass a departmental autonomy statute. (Departments have a similar constitutional requirement to pass their statutes.) Their goal was to make sure that indigenous rights, especially autonomy, were inserted into the department statute. This was critical for the long-term strategy of autonomy, but it positioned them right between MAS and the Verdes. It is clear that Ruben Costas, the powerful mestizo governor of Santa Cruz, did not support indigenous autonomy because it would take away some of his territorial and fiscal power. On the other hand, by taking a public position allying with local indigenous peoples, Costas offered a slap in the face to Morales. The indigenous representatives invited the MAS delegates to collaborate with them in making amendments to the proposed statute, but the MAS delegates refused. Verdes, on the other hand, were eager to work with them to include their amendments.

The resulting legislative session to approve and amend the statute was an amazing event. The hall was filled with elites of Santa Cruz, there to witness the historic victory for departmental (regional) autonomy for which their movement had struggled so long. Yet the indigenous delegates were also winning an important victory. As the president of the assembly called for approval of each article, it was the Verde representatives—mostly rich, white members of the traditional political class—who put forth amendments recognizing indigenous peoples' languages, territories, and the rights to autonomy. When the votes were called, all seventeen representatives on the Verde side of the hall raised their hands in assent, along with all five indigenous representatives beside them. The dramatic physical act of actually choosing sides reinforced the political decisions being made there. The pattern continued for many hours as hundreds of articles were approved one by one. On each vote, the president registered the twenty-two votes in favor, enough to create the two-thirds majority of the twenty-seven total votes. The MAS delegates abstained on each vote.

The next day, the legislators presented the approved statute to Governor Costas in an even more spectacular event. At the governor's office on the main plaza, the hall was filled with press, legislators, and the public there to celebrate departmental autonomy. Governor Costas came down the stairs accompanied by the leaders of the five indigenous groups and their assembly representatives. Costas said he was sorry to make everyone wait, but he had to meet with these important indigenous leaders to assure them that Santa Cruz's departmental autonomy "was not just for some, but for all." He said the indigenous peoples are *iyambae*, using the Guaraní word for freedom that has been claimed by the departmental autonomy movement (Lowrey 2006). "They have no fear, no owners, so they are part of this process of autonomy," Costas declared. Then he acknowledged that without the five indigenous votes, the Verdes could not have passed the new departmental autonomy statute. "Thank you!" he roared, bringing the crowd to their feet. "We will continue to coordinate with you, to help meet your demands (*reivindicaciones*), you who have been here even before the republic was formed." He turned to the crowd and said, "Now we are working on basic services, with women and youth, to create a better society. I told our indigenous brothers and sisters, 'Don't worry: now there will be development for all! Let us prepare to keep moving forward!'"

Strategies at Home

While there were both risks and benefits to working with the Verdes at the departmental level, at home in Charagua, things were different. To get the autonomy statute passed in town, the Guaraní chose another path: an alliance with MAS. Belarmino Solano, then mayor of Charagua, explained their tactical decision. In 2010, he said, the APG wanted to make alliances with other parties, especially MAS, but the Guaraní were divided among themselves, some with the Verdes, some with other particular interests. "And this was a crucial moment for autonomy!" he said. "We always had indigenous autonomy as plan A, but this had been delayed, so we went for plan B, making an alliance with MAS and the APG." They began with the 2014 national-level elections, putting forward a Guaraní candidate, Abilio

Vaca, as a MAS congressman to the national legislature. Their campaign was successful. Morales and Vaca won. Then, in the March 2015 municipal elections, they tried the same tactic, all the while knowing the alliance might prove transitory.

This was also a beneficial alliance for MAS. Having seen the lowland indigenous groups migrate toward the Verdes at the departmental level, MAS leaders considered it was a way to exert influence in Charagua and have a hand in the autonomy project. Mayor Belarmino said the national-level elections had shown that the APG could bring out the vote:

> They can see we have the power of convoking people here. With the win for Vaca and Evo, they can see that we are part of the *proceso de cambio* [process of change] that our brother Evo began. We are indigenous people like him, we are brothers and sisters. . . . We didn't want to lose this space and this means to move together toward equality. (personal communication, August 2015)

So the APG-MAS candidates campaigned with the blue banner of MAS and handily won the mayor's position and four city council seats, to hold a majority. This was a savvy tactic for a number of reasons but most importantly because the highland residents of La Estación, who were leery of the autonomy statute, were strongly MAS voters. By wearing the colors of Morales's party, the Guaraní hoped to convince their Quechua migrant neighbors that they were on the same path. Rosa Mamani, one of the leaders of Bartolina Sisa, a highland women's organization aligned with the MAS, told me that this alliance would make the town better. Previous mayors ignored highland demands, like the one her group is pushing for: a new municipal marketplace to sell their products. But when Belarmino came to see their association during his campaign, he was listening, she said. While she was still not convinced about the autonomy statute, she was opening up to it. Perhaps, she said, she would just leave the ballot blank and not oppose it now.

This strategy did not impress everyone, however. The *junta vecinal* and the civic committee, made up of mestizos who lived in the pueblo, still had strong objections to the statute. One afternoon in August 2015 I went to talk with them as they finished their meeting in the schoolhouse. Sitting in an empty classroom, we talked for hours about their fears. The president of the civic committee, María Antonia Arancibia, with whom I had talked on each of my visits, was the most vehement. Her family has raised cattle in the region for generations. She argued that the statute was an invention that had nothing to do with the real issues of social relations in town. "This whole thing is just made up," she told me. "It is copied from the Andeans and from Evo Morales." She suggested that the NGO CIPCA, had written it, and not the Guaraní delegates. "Moreover," she said, and here they all agreed, nodding their heads vigorously, "this new statute excludes us. We don't even appear in the prologue. We too are ancestral here. We, too, care for the fauna and the space, but in the statute prologue, only Guaraní appear. We also live here!" The leader of the junta, a schoolteacher named Jorge, said, "Look, we aren't against autonomy, just not with this statute. It doesn't recognize us as mestizos."

A second teacher, Lilly, a young woman with a worried look, said, "We are not against the conversion. After all, they are our ancestors. It is that they brought us the statute all finished, without letting us intervene." This did not square with the facts. In 2011 María Antonia told me they had been invited, but they refused to be involved. Now, in 2015, they were faced with their worst fears. Lilly continued, "We all know what is going to happen. The community leaders are going to benefit from this, and they won't share the money with the town or even their own communities." Jorge added, "No, it will create a Guaraní upper caste, and we will end up paying the bill." María Antonia argued that the statue would allow the autonomous government to establish new tax measures. "Who has the money to pay taxes? We, of the pueblo, will be taxed, and we will lose our lands." They all remained unmoved by the repeated declarations that the statute would allow each sector to govern itself. María Antonia declared with disgust: "The statute requires that all representatives [to the decision-making bodies] speak Guaraní! That excludes us all."

The Guaraní had heard these objections since they began their push for autonomy, and they were not deterred. Instead, they used their political control of the mayor's office to push toward approval of the autonomy statute in the September 2015 referendum. This was evident at a summit meeting in July 2015 organized by the mayor's office, the Ministry of Autonomies, and the Electoral Tribunal, the national entity responsible for organizing elections. The summit brought together protagonists for indigenous autonomy from municipalities all over the Chaco region with officials from various government ministries, cities, and funding institutions. The meeting was a powerful way to raise issues and provoke discussion among Charagua's many sectors. The Ministry of Autonomies and the Ministry of Health pooled money to be able to make the event happen, and so there were commissions on health, agrarian development, indigenous justice, and education. Staff members of the Ministry of Autonomies came from La Paz, and they grumbled openly about how little support the central government was giving to this project. These were young anthropologists and social scientists dedicated to social change who were holding on to the one space within the government apparatus where they thought they could make a difference. Pointing their fingers at the more conservative agencies such as the Hacienda (Treasury) and the State Department, they said it was only a matter of time before their work supporting autonomy would be stymied. Until then, they worked creatively to find money for printing, per diems for leaders, and publicity.

The meetings demonstrated the social complexity of the region. My Guaraní friends from Santa Cruz had arrived to support the process and learn how they might use this experience to move their own demands forward. Sitting next to their aunts and uncles from small villages in Charagua, they caught up with family gossip and compared political strategies. I had encouraged María Antonia and the *junta vecinal* members to participate. She and Jorge, the schoolteacher, pushed into the crowded room, listening with frowns on their faces. There were representatives from communities all over the Chaco region, several of them in the process of petitioning for conversions of their municipalities.

At the inauguration, Mayor Belarmino introduced the ministers of autonomies and defense, who had arrived from La Paz, along with indigenous and union leaders who came from across the region to support the process. Local NGOs and church people mixed with ministry staff. Representatives from the four *capitanías* arrived on trucks sent to fetch them from the outlying villages. Children ran around and babies cried, while this amazing mix of people and interests debated the intersecting needs of the region: infrastructure, health programs, better education, and most importantly, control over profits from the hydrocarbon industry. In the commission on autonomy, which I attended, the young *capitán* (leader) of Charagua Norte gave an impassioned speech about how the statute would include all sectors of the Charagua community and how this united community would benefit from development projects and more direct flow of funds to the town. At a break, María Antonia continued her disapproval, saying she was not moved. Jorge, on the other hand, was impressed with the commissions and the many important projects he was hearing about in the works. He seemed much more open to working together. "I'm surprised," he said.

On the final afternoon of the summit, the participants delivered the results of their deliberations to the ministers in a public display in the town's open-air coliseum. A huge poster with government logos declared "Guaraní autonomy will benefit all the population, without excluding or discriminating against anyone." Many of the town's residents trickled in, curious to see what the Guaraní mayor could extract from the two MAS ministers. The many guests—among them senators, union leaders, and a priest—all affirmed that the Charagua autonomy process was historic and would serve as an example across the country and even internationally. Finally, the mayor made his tactical move, linking autonomy with getting new development projects. Belarmino addressed the ministers: "Before, our authorities could never get any projects from the government, but now we are working with Evo. You ministers are the spokespeople now, to witness that Charagua is with Evo and that we will get projects." He delivered the proposals from the autonomy summit, and using the language of MAS, he declared, "We are going to continue the process of change right here. You can't be plurinational without indigenous autonomy. Here we will practice interculturality every day, defending democracy and promoting development for all. This is autonomy!" He began bringing out binders bulging with the projects his staff had prepared for presentation to the ministers. Handing a binder to each minister, he called out the projects, including the completion of the paved highway to the town (to huge applause from everyone); construction of a new coliseum in the rural Isoso zone, a new school building, a bus terminal (applause from the *transportistas*), and a municipal market (high-pitched shouts from the highland market women, waving their banner). Entrusted to take the enormous stack of projects back to La Paz, the ministers were covered with Guaraní textiles and sent on their way.

First Steps toward an Indigenous State?

The pragmatic politics carried out by the Guaraní of Charagua were successful. Only a few weeks after the summit, a majority of the residents of the city voted yes in the 2015 referendum. In 2016 the Guaraní leaders began the process of implementing the new statute, converting the municipality into an indigenous autonomous government.

The first few years have shown just what is at stake. The margin was slim, declining slightly from the 55.7 percent the proponents of autonomy won in the first referendum to 53.3 percent. The autonomy project declined in votes most in the city centers, from 38 percent in 2009 to 33.6 percent in 2015. This includes La Estación, so perhaps Rosa Mamani, the Quechua market vendor, was not so convinced in the long run. The vote also declined slightly in Bajo and Alto Isoso, where it had received 53 percent in 2009 but managed to hold 51 percent of that critical electorate. That means that although the Guaraní won, they were implementing the new structure of governance with a host of people who opposed it and were determined to make it fail. In September 2016 the town held elections for the various new assemblies, putting the autonomy status into force and constituting the country's first indigenous self-governed municipality. The new officials began their terms in January 2017.

The fact that each sector chose its own way of electing their representatives by secret vote or in assemblies led some to see this as the first example of an "intercultural public institution" (Villagomez Guzmán 2016). Yet, there were all kinds of accusations and disputes, mainly from the people of the pueblo. Then, in a shocking move, the *comité cívico* (civic committee) made threats to CIPCA, the NGO that had assisted in the autonomy process, calling for it to be expelled from town. The UN High Commission on Human Rights in Bolivia had to intervene, protecting the NGO's rights (*El Deber* 2016). Yet, the Charagua autonomous government has the legal and institutional support of the Bolivian Constitution and the Constitutional Tribunal, even if MAS's political support is grudgingly given.

Conclusions

The Charagua autonomy project illustrates the many meanings decolonization and a focus on indigeneity can have at the local level. One the one hand, Mayor Belarmino's performance at the summit demonstrates how powerful the developmentalist discourse put forward by the Morales government had become and how local actors, indigenous and nonindigenous, were forced to utilize that discourse to gain support from their constituencies. Local governments have always lived or died on the basis of public works (Postero 2007), but this took on a particular tone in the Morales era. Here, Belarmino tied indigenous autonomy to economic development in the same way Morales did in his new discourse of economic liberation. Morales linked "liberation" to successful management of international hydrocarbon markets; Belarmino linked "autonomy" to successfully channeling the profits from that resource exploitation to his community in the form of development projects. This is not merely mimicry or instrumental pandering. Rather, local politics are part of these national-level transformations. Thus, Morales argued that the national extractivist development project is liberating and decolonizing because it is under the control of a sovereign plurinational state instead of foreign transnational corporations. Similarly, the Guaraní of Charagua pushed for an autonomy that will be funded by oil and gas rents that they control.

The Charagua case study shows something else as well: the complex negotiations Guaraní actors carry out in the *spaces between* nested sovereignties. The Guaraní politicians Belarmino Solano in Charagua and Ruth Yarigua in the capital were trying to make visible their own indigenous notion of autonomy in the interstices of liberal politics, all the while taking advantage of the ambiguities to make both political and material gains. When Governor Costas used the Guaraní word for freedom and insisted the indigenous "brothers and sisters" were part of departmental autonomy, he was referring to a very different understanding of autonomy. His notion implied regional administrative power in a liberal-neoliberal state system. For many Guaraní, however, autonomy is something entirely different, linked to the Guaraní way of being in the world or a set of historical organizing practices. The Guaraní did not contest Costas's use of this word but rather forged an alliance on the basis of it.

Similarly, in Charagua, Belarmino articulated his local autonomy demands in terms understandable in relation to the national MAS discourse: decolonization, plurinationalism, interculturality, and most of all, development. Again, these terms have radically different meanings for the various actors who use them, but it is this ambiguity, this ability to project various meanings onto them, that makes them such useful tools. The ambiguities also make possible consensus within the Guaraní communities, where there are also significant debates over visions for the future. For some, autonomy is most important because it will bring more development in the form of economic resources and educational opportunities for their children. For others, autonomy is closer to that articulated by Charagua's autonomy assembly president René Gómez: a recognition of the reciprocal relationships with each other and their land and a call to live their own Guaraní way of life. This vision promotes a form of equality in which sovereign actors speak nation to nation. For still others, these goals overlap. The Guaraní leaders' political negotiations have managed to create spaces for all these visions as they come together and swerve apart in the "partial connectedness" that is indigenous life in settler societies (Cadena 2015).

When I asked my indigenous collaborators in Charagua how they managed the dizzying dance between political parties and ambiguous meanings, they shook their heads, trying to make me understand. One said, "We have always lived this way, in this space. This is how we work." They are used to holding in tension conflicting meanings, the sort of cohabitation Silvia Rivera Cusicanqui (2010) calls "ch'xi." This Aymara concept illuminates the way a color can be simultaneously white and not white and black and not black, the juxtaposition producing the illusion of gray. It is very different from hybridity; it is a matter of experiencing both colors at the same time. Historians have shown that since colonial times, indigenous groups have managed this multiplicity, living and working between partially connected worlds of rural collective communities on the one hand and mines and markets on the other (Harris 1995). The Guaraní, especially, have always been good at this, forging temporary alliances with different groups to ensure their survival but not disappearing in the process. Francisco Pifarré has argued that their central strategy over time was to "make pacts without selling themselves to the *karais* (whites)" (1989, 295–297). This "Guaraní diplomacy" (294) has given them a practical historical understanding of how to negotiate nested sovereignties.

In this most recent iteration of Guaraní diplomacy, the leaders of Charagua have accomplished something they proudly declare to be *inédito* (unprecedented). Although the Morales government's discourse and practices moved away from indigenous rights, these local politicians doggedly pushed the "indigenous state" to acknowledge their rights to create one at the local level in Charagua. Granted, it is not as radical as it could be, but these new institutions are incorporating collective decision-making practices into the liberal state structure in a new way. In 2015 Charagueños put the new government, the Gobierno Autónomo Guaraní Charagua Iyambae, into place, electing officials to fill the newly formed governing bodies. By 2019, tempers had settled, and for the most part the different sectors of the community were participating in government affairs. As hoped, the deliberative organ, the Ñemboati Guasu, made up of community representatives, was exercising a significant amount of power. Decisions made there are drafted into laws by the legislative body and then implemented by the executive branch, in a sense reversing the structure of power in traditional liberal systems (Postero and Tockman 2020).

Furthermore, municipal revenue is divided and spent by each of the six zones according to the wishes expressed in their assemblies. Naturally, this experiment in indigenous self-governance has produced new debates. If the funds go to the six local zones, who manages the whole territory, including the protected areas? Moreover, who is the "authentic" government, the traditional leaders or the newly elected officials, who are in many senses part of the central state bureaucracy? Like many conflicts facing the Guaraní, these issues will be negotiated in practice as the new government moves forward. As my colleague Jason Tockman and I have described (2020), however, a fundamental challenge to a robust form of autonomy remains: the government's ability to control the extraction of natural resources, especially hydrocarbons, from its territory. Going forward, the young autonomous government will have to negotiate with the central state over these critical issues. As a pilot case, it will be carefully watched and if successful, emulated. Here at least, indigeneity and indigenous practices remain useful as the basis of emancipatory politics. Whether they remain such will have to be seen.[2]

Notes

1. In 2010 Bolivian President Evo Morales announced that the government would construct a highway through the Territorio Indígena y Parque Nacional Isiboro Sécure (Isiboro Sécure Indigenous Territory and National Park), commonly called by the acronym TIPNIS. The road would pass through the tropical region of the Beni to connect Bolivia's capital to the Brazilian border. Lowland indigenous communities organized a march to protest the road, which they feared would result in environmental damage, and the fact they had not been consulted as required by the constitution. The national police met the march with brutal measures in September 2011 in the small town of Chaparina. While the highway plans were halted in 2011, the government continues to say the project will continue.

2. This chapter is a slightly shortened and revised version of chapter 7 of Postero 2017, *The Indigenous State: Race, Politics, and Performance in Plurinational Bolivia* (Oakland: University of California Press, 2017). That book is available at http://www.luminosoa. org/site/books/10.1525/luminos.31/. This version is published as part of the Attribution-Non-Commercial-Share-Alike license (CC BY-NC-SA) held by the author.

10

Ayoreo Women and Access to Health Care

Negotiating the Multicultural Reform of the State in Paraguay

PAOLA CANOVA

Vaela Picanerai, a young Ayoreo woman, had been living since 2015 with her family in Guidai Ichai, the new Ayoreo neighborhood established in Filadelfia, the main urban center of the Mennonite colonies in Paraguay's central Chaco region. Before then, like many Ayoreo families, she had squatted for years in plastic tents on the outskirts of the city. Ever since I met her, Vaela had been suffering from high blood pressure, which ran in her family. After years of intermittent treatment she wasn't feeling any better. Like most indigenous people living in town, she had three available options to access health services. The first was the Clínica Indígena Filadelfia (indigenous clinic) administered by the Mennonites' private Hospital Filadelfia. By law, all employers in Paraguay are required to enroll their employees in governmental health insurance; Mennonites, however, enforce their own health care system for indigenous people since 1992 known as Ayuda Mutua Hospitalaria.[1] According to officials of the Mennonite colonies, indigenous people can participate in this system if they acquire a certain number of uninterrupted hours of work for Mennonite employers.

This health care system has no legal status within Paraguayan laws, and although national government officials are aware of this extralegal status, they overlook it, arguing that it supports the indigenous peoples in the region. Mennonites argue that this system was created because of the absence of state services in the region. However, when Congress tried to cancel the Mennonite health system in place in 2006 for being unconstitutional, Mennonites mobilized indigenous peoples to keep the system in place (Duerksen 2006). In order to receive health care and medications at a reduced rate at the Clínica Indígena Filadelfia, one has to show proof of employment. Because Vaela's husband was employed by a Mennonite, when she had money she would go there to avoid the long wait at the public health services in town.

Her second option was the Puesto de Salud Amistad, a health clinic that the municipality of Filadelfia has been operating since 2008 or earlier with the support of a local health council; the council is part of a decentralized modality that resulted from the reform of the national health care system. While this public clinic, which has served 10,000 low-income individuals yearly, does not charge for medical exams, getting there was a problem for Vaela, as she had to walk two kilometers and often wait for hours before seeing a physician. Her final option was the only public hospital nearby, the Hospital Materno-Infantil Villa Choferes del Chaco, fifteen kilometers away on the Trans-Chaco Highway. This hospital is dependent on funds provided by the regional administration, the Gobernación de Boquerón, and while the hospital is staffed with a permanent rotating team of doctors, medication and means of transportation for patients are a continuing problem. Like most indigenous peoples in town, and against the advice of health officials, Vaela would often alternate between these three places. However, the high cost of medications at the Clínica Indígena Filadelfia, the mistreatment that she frequently experienced at the Puesto de Salud Amistad, and the burdensome travel costs to the Hospital Materno-Infantil, as well as a lack of understanding of the risks of her health problem, did not motivate her to follow indicated treatment for high blood pressure as advised by physicians.

In 2019 she experienced an acute complication and was taken to the only public urgent care facility available, at the Hospital Materno-Infantil. With no intensive care unit in the entire Chaco, where more than 46 percent of the total indigenous population of the country lives, she had to be transferred to Asunción, the capital, 450 kilometers away. To complicate matters, as could be expected, an ambulance was not immediately available to transport her. Eventually she reached a public hospital on the outskirts of Asunción, where she lay in a coma for almost a month. Chomai, her younger brother who was fluent in Spanish, made the trip with her. At the request of the hospital's social services office, Chomai commuted downtown once a week to the Instituto Nacional del Indígena (INDI, National Institute for Indigenous Affairs), the institution in charge of indigenous affairs, to request funds to help pay for the costs of his sister's medication and medical supplies. I had followed Vaela's case closely, and one Monday morning in August 2019, I accompanied Chomai to INDI offices, hoping we could find the means to fulfill the doctor's requests of medical supplies for her much-needed intubation, as the respirator she was using was starting to damage her throat. At the time, the INDI office was temporarily stationed at a military post. It had been moved there after continued confrontations between the president of INDI and members of various indigenous groups who sought her resignation.[2] The complaint was that she had no previous experience working with indigenous peoples but was given the position as a political favor for collaborating with the election campaign of President Mario Abdo Benítez in 2018. In a move to protect herself from these mobilizations, the president requested that INDI's offices be temporarily housed at the army's Intendencia del Ejército.

There, the entrance was guarded and protected by a tall metal gate. Past the entrance, a decommissioned guard office had been converted into INDI's main reception area. Four improvised tables and six agents with unclear roles occupied the reception area, where complaints were filed and requests brought by members of diverse indigenous groups. Outside this small room, the only place to sit was a long wooden bench or outside the building. With frustrated faces individuals squeezed into the guard room or onto the outside bench, as Javier Auyero (2012) puts it, waiting as good "patients of the state." Chomai and I had been there since 8:30 a.m., when we presented the detailed prescription prepared by Vaela's doctor to one of the officials. After a seemingly interminable wait, by 12:30 p.m. Chomai was finally called in. He was told that there was no budget for the intubation supplies, and he was given a pack of adult diapers with the equivalent of ten dollars cash, which required signatures on multiple documents. A week later, still on the same respirator, Vaela succumbed to heart complications. In a twist of irony, the ambulance that was nowhere to be found to transport her to Asunción was readily available to take her back to the Chaco, this time in a black plastic body bag.

The health problems and complications experienced by Vaela that led to her premature death at age thirty-five, along with the experiences of Chomai in Asunción to access basic supplies and health support for his sister, are not isolated instances but rather a reality frequently experienced by many indigenous people from the Chaco seeking access to health services. This situation demands a critical evaluation of the much-celebrated "intercultural" reform of the health system in Paraguay, an ongoing process that began in the early 2000s. Unlike other Latin American countries, Paraguay experienced its first multicultural reforms almost a decade after the wave

Figure 10.1. Indigenous people waiting outside the INDI office in Asunción, 2019. Photo by Paola Canova.

of reforms in the 1990s. Interrogating how multiculturalism is articulated and experienced as a contemporary form of governance in Paraguay reveals that multicultural citizenship is constructed by colliding agendas that ultimately reproduce colonial hierarchies, hierarchies that in turn continue to exclude indigenous people from accessing state resources and services. Neoliberal state reforms of governmental institutions were initiated after the fall of the thirty-five-year dictatorship of Alfredo Stroessner in 1989; these reforms were introduced alongside multicultural programs. In Paraguay, this imbrication has generated a contradictory model of governance in which multicultural reforms were set in motion following a neoliberal logic of implementation. In this way, multiculturalism was constituted through state-civil alliances, decentralization, and the deployment of rights-based discourses of access to state services. While the state recognized and incorporated, for the first time, the cultural rights of indigenous peoples into their policies and programs, the ways these were operationalized ultimately deepened the legacies of colonial hierarchies.

Focusing on the experiences of Ayoreo women in the Paraguayan Chaco shows how the state-sponsored multicultural health system reforms play out at the local level. While health care policies promote ethnic diversity and inclusion, the experiences of Ayoreo people living in the context of the Mennonite colonies reveal how providers engage in discourses and practices that aim at regulating indigenous women's bodies and ultimately limit their access to prevention and treatment programs. Moreover, interactions between government health professionals and young Ayoreo women in Filadelfia reveal how biomedical discourses and practices perpetuate disparities in the exercise of multicultural citizenship by indigenous women as proclaimed by the state.

Indigenous Peoples and the Neoliberal Reform of the State in Paraguay

A broad anthropological scholarship on indigeneity has focused on the ways indigenous groups have experienced multicultural reforms of the state in many Latin American countries, a process that started in the 1980s (Cadena and Starn 2007; Greene 2009; Jackson 2019; Warren and Jackson 2002). Several authors have drawn attention to how these reforms have been closely linked to a larger neoliberal political and economic project (Gustafson 2009; Hale 2004; Povinelli 2002; Sieder 2002). This intimate relationship between new cultural rights and neoliberal political-economic reforms has been known as "neoliberal multiculturalism" (Hale 2004). The early 2000s were marked by yet another phase of sociocultural and economic transformations in Latin America that emerged with the so-called Pink Tide, that is, the establishment of left-wing governments in countries including Bolivia, Ecuador, and Venezuela.

These new forms of governance were read as "interruptions" to the neoliberal order (Goodale and Postero 2013), and a new wave of social movements created a phenomenon by which indigenous peoples began to draw on some of the rationalities of neoliberalism to articulate their demands in terms of citizenship, a shift that Postero (2007) has labeled the "post-multicultural" turn drawing on the case of Bolivia. Arturo Escobar (2010, 11) has described the social and political effervescence of the region as marked by projects of "alternative modernizations based on an anti-neoliberal development model" and "decolonial projects based on a different set of practices (communal, indigenous, hybrid, and above all, pluriversal and intercultural), leading to a post-liberal society (an alternative to euro-modernity)." But these broader regional shifts and processes played out at a different pace in Paraguay. Specifically, the introduction of multicultural reforms was initiated relatively late compared to other Latin American countries, hindered in part by Stroessner's prolonged dictatorial regime, which persisted until the late 1980s. Neighboring countries like Brazil had already introduced multicultural reforms to their constitutions by the 1980s (Chernela 2015; Ramos 1992); in Bolivia, the failure of multicultural policies was already being felt in the 1990s as indigenous peoples were mobilizing against its tenets (Gill 2008; Goldstein 2004). At the same time, however, Paraguay was only just beginning its transition to democracy, a time when neoliberal state reforms were being embraced and promoted with the strong support of international financial institutions such as the World Bank and the Inter-American Development Bank (Borda and Masi 1998).

The first step toward recognizing the cultural rights of indigenous peoples in Paraguay was through the constitutional reform of 1992 in which, for the first time, indigenous rights were included in the constitution. This was in part the result of intense lobbying of indigenist nongovernmental organizations (NGOs) that played a major role in defending indigenous rights during the dictatorial regime of Stroessner (Harder Horst 2007). As an early sign of the fragmented role that neoliberal multiculturalism was to offer indigenous peoples, they participated in the constitutional assembly with voice but were not given vote. Nevertheless, the recognition of indigenous rights at the constitutional level marked a significant moment in the establishment of policies protecting the rights of indigenous peoples. Throughout the 1990s the Paraguayan state continued to restructure its economy and institutions following neoliberal tenants through the shrinking of state institutions and privatization. A peculiar aspect of multicultural state reforms was that it was furthered by nongovernmental organizations working with indigenous peoples with the support of international cooperation agencies. No multicultural policies would, however, be implemented in state agencies for at least another decade.[3]

By 2004, INDI was the first target of reforms through the project Modernización Institucional del INDI (Institutional Modernization of INDI). A highly corrupt and inefficient institution, INDI was established in 1981 as an autonomous entity by Law 904/81, dependent on the executive branch. Prior to that, beginning in 1958, it functioned within the Ministry of Defense (Berajano 1977). To date, in its sixty years of existence, it has had twenty-five presidents, none of whom completed their mandated period; of these twenty-five, only two were indigenous. In 2004, under the presidency of Nicanor Duarte Frutos, the Inter-American Development

Bank, a key player in the introduction of neoliberal institutional reforms throughout Latin America, provided a grant of US$150,000 to further this reform. A much-needed and major component envisioned for INDI was the decentralization of the institution. The goal was to open regional offices and involve local governmental institutions such as the *gobernaciones* (equivalent to a US state's administrative offices) that were expected to play an active role in the outline and application of programs and projects for indigenous peoples. INDI would take the role of coordinator to assure that different public institutions provided adequate financial resources in their programs related to indigenous issues (Fogel 2003). This process stimulated the political participation of representatives of indigenous organizations in outlining a new structure for the institution. However, due to a lack of strategic alliances and their still fragile political bargaining power vis-à-vis international institutions, scarce tangible progress was made, and the funds were quickly drained.

Since then, the restructuring of INDI has not happened. INDI was neither reformed nor closed, and the new trait of multicultural state reforms in Paraguay would be that of decentralizing indigenous affairs. Under this new model, several ministries would have their own offices to handle indigenous issues. In 2007 the Ministry of Education would become the first to adopt this model by issuing Law 3231/2007 and establishing the Dirección General de Educación Escolar Indígena (General Office of Indigenous Schooling and Education) (CONAPI 2017). A push for a multicultural reform of the education system by mostly Catholic NGOs began in 1990. With few advances on the part of the national government, this dynamic shifted by the first decade of 2000, when most governmental institutions had offices on indigenous affairs, based on principles of "interculturality" in an effort to recognize the autonomy and cultural rights of indigenous peoples.

While this approach has been celebrated by many, on the ground the decentralized institutional structure has created an overlap of programs run by different public institutions, often working with colliding agendas and little coordination. This situation has also fostered the formation of a new category of "experts" (Mitchell 2002) on indigenous topics not only within public institutions but in cooperation with the private sector, a late liberal strategy of government. Moreover, access to services and resources are now dependent on essentialized constructions of what it means to be indigenous according to governmental officers, perceptions based on what Francesca Merlan (2009, 305) has termed "criterial" definitions of indigeneity, that is, definitions based on a "set of criteria, or conditions, that enable identification of the 'indigenous' as a 'global kind.'" Ultimately, these are perceptions that shift according to the dependencies and the level of training of the personnel.

In 2008 another relevant reform of the state concerning indigenous affairs was set in motion. This time it took place in the context of the brief turn to the left experienced by Paraguay, when the socialist ex-bishop Fernando Lugo took power, ending sixty-one years of unbroken domination by the conservative Colorado Party. His regime was short-lived, as he was impeached in 2012. Lugo fostered a series of broad social reforms, of which the restructuring of the health care system was one of the priorities of his government. When he became president, attending to the demands of indigenous peoples became an important aspect of his political agenda. When asked about his goal of inclusive health reform in an interview with a Spanish newspaper, he stated, "We aim for a universal health care plan. Our main priority is that indigenous peoples stop dying due to lack of health services. We hope that in five years, no Paraguayan citizens will be excluded from accessing basic public health" (in Carracedo 2008).

With that focus in mind, in 2008 the Ministry of Public Health launched its Política Nacional de Salud Indígena (National Policy on Indigenous Health), the plan envisioned for a national indigenous health system. This plan was elaborated by a Mesa Interinstitutional de Salud (Inter-Institutional Health Committee) made up of health care representatives of indigenous groups and organizations, NGOs, and international cooperation agencies. The plan was approved for implementation in 2009, with the objectives of better understanding perceptions of health problems, improving patient-physician interactions, and applying culturally sensitive treatments. Various internal offices of the Ministry of Public Health were in charge of the national plan until 2016, when the ministry created an agency to attend to indigenous affairs, the Dirección Nacional de Salud de los Pueblos Indígenas (National Office for the Health of Indigenous Populations). The agency is intended to operate according to principles of "universality, integrality, equity, participation, gratuity, and interculturality" (Paraguay, MSPBS 2019).

Interculturality here is conceived as the application of the notion of cultural differences to the realm of health, that is, incorporating the "culture of the beneficiaries to the process of health attention" (Paraguay, MSPBS 2010, 13). In this health paradigm, discourses on cultural rights collide with the promotion of individual values of late liberalism. One of the trademarks of this new model of governance is that indigenous peoples, rather than being passive beneficiaries, are considered active members with the right to decide on their well-being and fully participate in the outline and implementation of health-related programs and projects. Law 5469 on indigenous health care states that indigenous people have the right to participate "in an autonomous and organized way in the planning, organization, management, execution, and enforcement of the services of the National Health System for Indigenous Peoples" (Paraguay, MSPBS 2019, 14).

Since its inception, the official national policy on indigenous health care has been a collaborative effort in consultation with members of different indigenous groups and nonindigenous representatives from civil society. Representatives of international cooperation agencies and at least seven NGOs also participated in this process, with a strong presence of the Catholic Church, which had a firm influence on indigenous affairs during the dictatorship and continues to have leverage on indigenous affairs in the country. While neoliberalism values the strengthening and participation of civil society that is seen as compatible with indigenous cultural priorities, in the Paraguayan case, this type of multisectoral collaboration has the detrimental effect of fostering high levels of dependency of indigenous peoples on NGOs, which since the 1990s have also expanded significantly in the country. These NGOs have taken over control of funds and resources, forcing indigenous peoples into a patron-client relationship and precluding the claimed autonomy celebrated in policies and laws. This dynamic has strengthened the ability of the professional middle class to speak for impoverished groups, having a particularly harmful impact on the autonomy of indigenous organizations that continue to function in dependency to NGOs. In this way, and unlike its neighbors Bolivia and Brazil, which have long histories of indigenous activism (Chernela 2015; Jackson 2019; Ramos 1992), indigenous participation in state affairs in Paraguay continues to be highly mediated by nonindigenous members of civil society.

Decentralization of state institutions has been another trademark of structural adjustment reform throughout Latin America (Cerruti and Grimson 2013; Perreault and Martin 2005), a process that urges citizens to participate in the process of solving their own problems in collaboration with nonstate civil society. Paraguay initiated a program called Decentralization of Health and Community Participation with funding from US Aid for International Development (USAID). A joint report states that in the program, "civil organizations, in a participatory way, design and implement basic local programs of access to health to consolidate the national health

Figure 10.2. Amistad Health Clinic in Filadelfia, Paraguay, 2020. Photo by Paola Canova.

program" (USAID and CIRD 2012). The initiative fostered the formation of *consejos locales de salud* (local health councils) through which local authorities can receive and manage state or private funds to implement governmental health policies. In the Chaco, since 2008 the municipality of Filadelfia has operated a *consejo de salud* to establish the Amistad clinic, which offers subsidized health care services and medical supplies for the local indigenous and nonindigenous population. The construction, equipment, and training of personnel were funded by the Japan International Cooperation Aid and USAID. The clinic is run with some funding from the Paraguayan government and some from member organizations of the *consejo local de salud*, local governmental and private institutions. The *consejo* and the municipality manage the funds and revenues received by the clinic. While participation is local rather than centralized in the nation's capital, it does not include representation of local indigenous organizations in any way as stipulated in the law on indigenous health. The clinic does not hire indigenous peoples. Other agencies of the Ministry of Public Health have strived toward incorporating indigenous peoples in their work units; these numbers, however, remain very low, and due to lack of appropriate training, those hired perform only basic procedures.

Finally, although the collective rights of indigenous peoples have been recognized through the intercultural approach promoted by the state through public policies and laws, the focus on "cultural difference" takes priority only in its performative role. It is not uncommon to have representatives of indigenous groups opening workshops or conferences with their traditional ceremonies. These apparently culturally sensitive initiatives do not always fit the self-representation that several indigenous peoples have of themselves, although supposedly they follow tenets of respect for cultural and ethnic difference. This became evident to me in a conference sponsored by officers of the Ministry of Public Health, a meeting organized to share and explain their policies among indigenous health care providers shortly after the national policy on indigenous health was promulgated. Participating in the conference were representatives of the Ayoreo, among other indigenous people. For Ayoreo health care providers present at the event, the incorporation of traditional notions of health care into the practices of indigenous health care providers turned out to be a major point of debate.

After five decades of intense Christian missionization by the New Tribes Mission, most Ayoreo self-identify as Christians and emphatically reject advocating for the revival of local shamanic knowledge, arguing that it is no longer part of their culture. Their rejection was such that at the opening ceremony of the event, when shamans were invited to stand up and perform, the Ayoreo representatives refused to participate. Such a response drastically challenges essentialized state-sponsored conceptualizations of multicultural citizenship. Moreover, under this tenet, indigenous culture is authorized as long as it does not disrupt *universalizing* moral values and agendas. Some of these contradictions surface when Ayoreo women seek access to health care services in the Mennonite colonies.

The multicultural governmental regime established in Paraguay since the 2000s reveals a system that, while including indigenous peoples' cultural rights into state projects, has simultaneously deployed neoliberal logics as a means of implementing these policies. In doing so, the system has established a racialized politics in which state institutions, rather than empowering indigenous peoples, have led to a fractured process of participation that is highly dependent on nonindigenous members of civil society and on international funding sources to fight for their rights. This reproduces colonial hierarchies that continue to grant the state and its allies the power to define the terms inclusion/exclusion and ultimately gives them the sovereign power to decide "who may live and who must die" (Mbembe 2003, 11).

Ayoreo Women and Access to Health in the Mennonite Colonies

With the transition to a democratic regime in Paraguay, the Chaco region underwent an important process of decentralization. Until 1945 the area had been geographically divided into three military command districts administered by the Ministry of War and Marines. By 1973 these *comandancias* had been turned into five *departamentos*, although they remained under military control. With the transition to democracy and as part of the state reform in 1992, the *departamentos* were merged and reduced to three (Villa Hayes, Boquerón, and Alto Paraguay), each with political autonomy. Of the total indigenous population in Paraguay, 47.2 percent live in the Chaco, distributed as follows: Villa Hayes 3.5 percent, Boquerón 21.6 percent, and Alto Paraguay 22.1 percent (Paraguay, DGEEC 2012).

Adequate access to health services is one of the major challenges today for indigenous peoples in the country. In 2011 the Ministry of Public Health conducted the first national survey on risk factors for nontransmissible diseases among indigenous populations, based on interviews of 1,057 individuals at the national level whose ages ranged between fifteen and seventy-four years old (Paraguay, MSPBS 2014). According to this study, about 75 percent of the indigenous population in the country had never measured their cholesterol, more than 39 percent of the population was overweight or obese, and 75 percent had never tested their blood glucose, an indicator of diabetes or disposition toward diabetes. Indigenous women found themselves in an even more vulnerable situation, as 74 percent never had a Papanicolaou exam, and more than 96 percent had never had a mammogram (Paraguay, MSPBS 2014). These numbers substantiate the lack of access to and awareness of basic health services among indigenous peoples. In the Chaco, access to health services becomes more complicated due to the long distances, poor road conditions, and lack of frequent public transportation to reach urban centers.

The Ayoreo people, foragers until the mid-1960s when they were sedentarized, had a population of about 2,600 until 2012 when the last national indigenous census was recorded, and most live in villages in the Departamento de Boquerón near the Mennonite colonies. Between 1926 and 1947, Dutch and German descent Mennonites migrating from Russia formed three *colonias* (settlements) there: Fernheim, Menno, and Neuland. These populations remained geographically and ideologically isolated until the Trans-Chaco Highway was constructed in the 1960s. By the 1990s the regional economy greatly accelerated, attracting an ever-increasing flow of labor (Canova 2015). A concomitant phenomenon that has taken root among Ayoreo is the commodification of the sexuality of young single women known as *curajodie*. This term is used by the Ayoreo to refer to single women who monetize sexual liaisons with non-Ayoreo men, mostly in the Mennonite colonies. These women approach intimate liaisons on their own terms; they initiate courting and flirting, and they do not see the involvement of money as morally problematic but rather as constitutive of sexual encounters. Non-Ayoreo people perceive women's practices as sex work. However, the monetization of women's sexuality is neither new nor understood by Ayoreo as sex work; it has been constitutive of the sexuality of young women since the 1990s. While the intimate practices of these women are embedded in customary systems of exchange, they have undergone transformations and now operate alongside newer notions of racialized desire as a result of the introduction of money into the realm of intimacy. That the Ayoreo people do not see this as a moral issue creates tensions with the local nonindigenous community, more specifically with local health care officials, most of whom belong to the Christian Mennonite community.

In 2009, while the multicultural reforms to the health care system implemented by the Paraguayan state began to reach the local level, a municipal officer in Filadelfia commented to me, "We need these girls out of the streets. They give a negative image to our city. Other indigenous women at least stay in their villages or hide at night, but not the Ayoreo girls." When I asked about possible health support programs for these young women, she mentioned that they were considering opening a "red zone" on the outskirts of the city where they could receive health cards and be periodically checked for sexually transmitted diseases. This project, far from trying to engage in an intercultural approach to understanding women's practices, was being promoted by a local Paraguayan physician working at the Amistad clinic administered under the decentralized model of local health councils. With more than twenty years of experience working on health issues among indigenous populations, he remarked to me, "People might criticize me, but I told the Mennonite colony several times we should do a whorehouse, get them all inside, and get them controlled every week. Right now, we don't even know who they are." The reactions of both of these public officers stemmed in part from their frustration in trying to resolve what they have come to label "the Ayoreo problem," an issue that they perceive is not being tackled by the Mennonite community. The discourses of these health officials, rather than promoting the principles of inclusion, interculturality, and access to services, resemble nineteenth-century Victorian constructions of the "prostitute body" as a category that needs to be medically and spatially surveilled and contained (Levine 2002; Walkovitz 1980).

By 2017 the same physician, by then a board member of the local municipality, was still pushing for a local ordinance to regulate the practices of Ayoreo young women in the streets of Filadelfia. Although he had garnered some support, most members of the board rejected this initiative, concerned not necessarily about the discriminatory nature of the idea but because it would create clashes with the local Christian community, as the board would be officially supporting what the Christians perceived as prostitution. This is the same reason that despite concerns about the health conditions of these young women, no local government institution since 2009 had engaged in any programs to support the well-being of *curajodie* in the streets of Filadelfia.

These young women, mostly between the ages of fourteen and twenty-eight, enter into temporary intimate liaisons with multiple partners, and as a result they are constantly exposed to sexually transmitted infections including HIV/AIDS and other health problems as well as rape and other forms of violence. Unwanted pregnancies are also a major social problem, as most young women do not use contraceptives. A generalized lack of information drives the women to circulate rumors about consequences of using condoms. *Curajodie* I interviewed shared that they were afraid of using condoms. One said, "It can stay inside and never come out again." Another reason is that male liaisons often requested not to use them. With lack of educational opportunities on the topic, unwanted pregnancies have become common, and since Ayoreo perceive pregnancy without a permanent partner as morally fraught, the women give their newborn children in adoption to relatives.

Because the health care system does not have a strong preventive medicine program, like most indigenous people, young women only visit the clinic when their cases become urgent. Many of them reported that "shyness" prevents them from seeking help sooner. However, as narrated by most of the young women, interaction with medical staff is actually one of the main reasons they avoid visiting the clinic on a regular basis. After several trips accompanying some of them to the municipal health post and the Mennonite clinic, I witnessed multiple occasions when the women faced explicit practices of racism and discrimination. For example, in daily encounters with health care providers, stereotypical perceptions of indigenous cultural traits were deployed to manipulate and replace Ayoreo notions of self-care and health.

Hygiene was a major point of contention frequently mentioned by the staff. In addition to openly making discriminatory remarks that constructed women as "ignorant" and "dirty," health care providers also repeatedly encouraged women to become responsible and engage in basic hygiene practices as a prerequisite to receiving medical attention. This insistence on self-discipline is consistent with new forms of neoliberal citizenship (Rose 1999). To become what Charles Briggs and Daniel Hallin (2007) have termed "sanitary citizens"—individuals who discipline their own bodies and become actively aware of the health and disease of their bodies, in terms of medical epistemologies—Ayoreo women were required not only to follow routines of hygiene but also to undergo regular checkups, medication, and family planning instruction. A nurse at the Hospital Materno-Infantil Villa Choferes shared with me, "We don't like to have Ayoreo as patients because they never follow the rules. Once I asked a woman who was accompanying a patient to change the sheets of the bed where her sister was lying because she would hardly bathe. But the lady simply refused to do so, telling me it was my job to do it."

This type of confrontation is not rare and often drives Ayoreo to escape from the hospital. This happened to Loida. She had been injured but did not seek help in Filadelfia. Her lungs became infected, and she eventually had to be taken to the hospital as an emergency. There she was given antibiotics and had to stay under observation for a few days, but she left suddenly, saying that she would not be able to find transportation back to her village if she were to stay. A typical response of physicians to such reactions by Ayoreo is to tell patients that if they leave, they should not come back when things get worse. This candid response, which triggers anxiety among Ayoreo patients, unveils a lack of understanding regarding the precarious context in which individuals have to make decisions regarding access to health services. Rather, control of the medical staff over the terms of access to health care and practices gives them the power to decide who deserves to receive medical attention and who does not. This power was poignantly evidenced in the case of Ijoya.

Ijoya, one of several *curajodie* in her early thirties, was diagnosed with a lung tumor in 2013. This was shortly after having had an operation to have her breast removed due to cancer. Although the doctor who saw her at the clinic was aware of her medical condition, Ijoya was never referred to undergo required treatments at the National Cancer Hospital near Asunción where patients are usually transferred. Instead, and not by mistake, she was given oral medication for gastrointestinal problems rather than medication to treat her cancer. When her pain became unbearable and she finally decided to go back to the clinic, she was given ibuprofen pills. Finally, a former employer of her father took her to the capital to receive adequate treatment. But it was too late. I accompanied her on one of her last visits to the clinic before she died. There, the same physician who had failed to treat her adequately now demonstrated pity for her and gave her the equivalent of five dollars so she could "enjoy a good meal." His display of such an attitude reveals how, while multicultural reforms can be well-intended in their objectives, their implementation at the local level is tangled in the stereotypes and discrimination by those in charge of putting the reforms into practice.

In addition to their control over the terms of access to care, local health care providers mingle medical concerns with moral debates of what they consider proper relations of gender. They do this unaware of the cultural nuances and larger socioeconomic processes that drive young women to engage in the commodification of their sexuality. The sexuality of *curajodie* is constructed as out of place and therefore as needing to be constrained. Such gender and racial anxieties regarding Ayoreo sexuality were revealed to me in a discussion I had with a physician who admitted that he did not grant exceptions to Ayoreo women, whom he considered "prostitutes," from paying the costs of clinical analysis. To justify his position, he blatantly argued, "They make lots of money in the streets and should be able to pay for the services provided." In another instance, when discussing the health situation of young Ayoreo women with the director of the *health post*, he contended, "I'm in favor of developing a comprehensive program if it would include having the young women identify themselves as sex workers so that we can actually keep track of their whereabouts."

This view was shared by health care providers from the local private clinic, one of whom confessed that he would not know what to do to "contain" patients with HIV. In an earnest tone he said, "The first thing that comes to my mind is to lock the person up in a room. I honestly don't know how to proceed, as we have not had such cases yet." By 2017, UN Women had initiated, following an "intercultural approach," consultations with indigenous women in the Chaco to draft a report about HIV/AIDS in the region. However, the so-called intercultural frameworks never usually move beyond the production of reports and focus-group meetings with indigenous women.[4] This becomes a major failure of multicultural health care in the region; the programs only target indigenous peoples rather than health officials; the latter do not benefit from adequate training in cross-cultural health-related aspects in order to offer better and more comprehensive treatments.

A lack of such broad initiatives is evidenced in the way local health officials are approaching important issues such as HIV. By 2017, HIV among indigenous peoples in the colonies had increased significantly since 2009, when it was last assessed by local health providers, yet no data had been published on the topic. The national government provides free medication through its National AIDS Program, local health officers say a considerable obstacle is that patients are not consistent in taking their medications. A physician in Filadelfia told me about the case of an HIV-positive Ayoreo male patient with whom he had decided not to share that diagnosis because, the doctor said, this patient was known for not taking his medication: "I know him, because he always comes to the clinic. He never took any of his previous medicines regularly, so if we give him the treatment, he won't complete it, and we'll lose the opportunity to give it to someone who will actually complete the treatment." This up-front decision by the medical staff shows how access to health care for Ayoreo is defined in terms of their moral worth, reproducing a colonial logic in which indigenous peoples are literally left to die based on individual decisions made by health care providers on a daily basis. These are ways the clinic and hospital become sites where Ayoreo are introduced to the rules and rights of expected norms of behavior not only of the medical establishment per se but of local society as well.

The local construction of indigenous citizenship through the health care establishment in the Chaco becomes a key site to produce "biopolitical subjects" (Ong 1996) that reflect and respond to the state's logic of ethnic citizenship being constructed under a multicultural paradigm. Ayoreo in general and Ayoreo women in particular, aware of the expectations, navigate on their own terms the discrimination they experience when seeking access to health services. Responses such as that of Vaela, who would constantly change physicians and often took recommended medicines only intermittently, are common to many Ayoreo I have interviewed and accompanied to health services over the years. Individual acts of refusal, in this case to comply with the medical establishment, could be read as expressions of political assertion (Simpson 2004); however, at the same time, the refusal to engage the health care system in place is having deadly consequences for Ayoreo individuals, who are dying of treatable diseases such as tuberculosis and syphilis.

The Biopolitics of the Multicultural Health Reform

The new health care structure in place, part of the multicultural reform of the state in Paraguay, has involved important progress at the level of policy making. In this sense, the creation of a specific health office for indigenous issues and the elaboration of a comprehensive national indigenous health care plan with indigenous participation are noteworthy advances. Their application, however, is still fractured and incomplete. Indigenous participation is welcomed only as long as it does not alter established governmental models of ethnic participation, usually expressed by having indigenous people attend workshops to craft diagnostic reports and perform their dances and rituals at conferences and events. Beyond this level of inclusion and participation, indigenous people have not become active participants in and enacters of the health care system. Rather, health officials and NGOs continue to mediate that role and define access to services at the local level. These are processes that take place often to the detriment of indigenous organizations that have not participated beyond surface-level consultations regarding multicultural policies.

The multicultural discourses of citizenship articulated at the national level to integrate indigenous peoples as ethnic minorities plays out in a unique way in the Mennonite colonies. The promotion of an ethnic citizenship in this region is mediated not only by regional representatives of the national health care system but also by Mennonites themselves. The latter, with a strong Christian influence, construct Ayoreo practices by drawing on moral judgments that leave Ayoreo women and indigenous women in general in a particularly vulnerable situation. The ways local health care providers implement state policies promoted by the health reform show how the internal logics of governmental reforms involve unexpected and sometimes contradictory effects. What is clear is that the multicultural reforms have in no way *yet* altered the racialized power structures in place, an unavoidable reality in the day-to-day relations between health care providers and indigenous patients. Institutionalized hierarchies of power deem health care professionals appropriate to decide who is worth receiving medical treatment and who is not. Repeated failed attempts at turning Ayoreo women into biomedical subjects translates into ostracizing and discriminatory practices against them in health services locales. The end result is that 25 percent of the total indigenous population in the country gets treated at health posts, according to the Ministry of Public Health (Paraguay, MSPBS 2014).

While health care providers insist on disciplining Ayoreo bodies, young *curajodie* engage in diverse practices to circumvent control and hierarchical medical regimes. Some of them tactically seek medical attention in other clinics when they feel mistreated or are unhappy with the attention given to them. Others deflect doctors' authority by not adhering to medication compliance. In doing so, these young women, amid constant discrimination, are challenging established power dynamics and in the process are rethinking on their own terms what they consider their rights regarding access to health services. The role of public health workers is critical in embracing structural changes at the local level to improve health services. However, interactions between Ayoreo *curajodie* and governmental health care providers evidences how the state, through its interlocutors, continues to articulate universalizing discourses of moral imperatives as a way to justify discriminative practices toward Ayoreo women that deflect their proposed participation in constructing a multicultural indigenous citizenship.

The reform of the health care system reveals how the Paraguayan state's construction of multicultural citizenship is being deployed as a sophisticated form of biopolitical regulation that is meant to domesticate the different ways indigeneity is experienced in contemporary Paraguay. Medical discourses play a crucial role in defining and naturalizing social inequality in relation to Ayoreo women and indigenous women in general in the Mennonite colonies. Even as the local debate between health care providers and local authorities on what should be done with Ayoreo young women continued in 2020, the health situation of Ayoreo women continued to deteriorate due to exclusionist attitudes and practices that remain unattended under the banner of multicultural reforms being fostered by the Paraguayan state.

Acknowledgments

The data presented in this article are based on interviews collected among health providers and Ayoreo individuals in Filadelfia and Ayoreo villages of the Departamento de Boquerón during sixteen months in 2009–2011 and thereafter in several visits in 2012–2019. I acknowledge the kind support of the Wenner-Gren Foundation and the College of Liberal Arts, University of Texas at Austin.

Notes

1. Since the national governmental insurance system for workers, the Instituto de Prevision Social, does not have its own health care institutions in the Chaco, Mennonites have created their own health insurance for indigenous peoples that is autofinanced through the contributions of employers (10 percent) and employees (5 percent) from their pay. In Fernheim, by 2004 this system was supporting about 24,000 indigenous individuals, half of the indigenous population in the Chaco (Duerksen 2006).

2. For details on this confrontation see *Última Hora* 2018.

3. Influenced by the UN summit, in the 1990s the Paraguayan government created the following state agencies: Infancy (1990), Environment and Development (1992), Human Rights (1993), Population and Development (1994), Women and Social Development (1995), and Habitat (1995) (Borda and Masi 1998).

4. Initiatives with indigenous women in the Paraguayan Chaco led to reports such as "Desde el saber de ellas construimos ciudadanía" by Paraguay's Secretaría de la Mujer in 2010 and "Strengthening Integrated Services for Indigenous Women Affected by HIV and Violence: Boquerón Paraguay" (UN Women 2016).

11

Multiterritoriality and the Tapiete Trinational Experience in the Chaco

SILVIA HIRSCH

In 1990 I visited for the first time the Tapiete Indian community in the northwestern Argentine province of Salta. In order to get there, I took a taxi from the center of the town of Tartagal, a distance of a kilometer or so, which took no more than ten minutes to cross. Despite the short distance, the cab driver did not know where the community was located; in fact, he had never heard of it. More remarkably, neither had I. This was indeed noteworthy; I had spent many years conducting fieldwork in the area in Guaraní communities, but this group was also unknown to me.

Located on the edge of town, the Tapiete community consists of five contiguous city blocks, surrounded by criollo neighborhoods and farther away by six indigenous groups: Guaraní, Chorote, Chulupi, Wichí, Chané, and Qom. Although they have lived in the town for decades, local residents regularly confuse indigenous groups. What made the Tapiete invisible to their neighbors? Was it the result of a long history of discrimination by criollo neighbors to their presence? Or perhaps the Tapiete's own strategy and ability to blend in, adapt to local circumstances, and disguise themselves as generic *aborigen*, as indigenous peoples are called in the country? Indigenous groups have been historically invisibilized in Argentina, a country that still claims its European heritage and where indigenous peoples are frequently labeled as being foreigners, meaning from Chile or Bolivia (Gordillo and Hirsch 2011). Even so, the invisibility of the Tapiete was particularly striking. I found few ethnographic accounts of the Tapiete of Argentina; those few were written between 1912 and 1936, then a long absence of studies ensued until the first decade of the twenty-first century, when the linguists Hebe González (2005, 2009, 2017) and Florencia Ciccone (2012,

2015; Ciccone and Hirsch 2016) and I as an anthropologist (Hirsch 2006a,b) began to conduct research among the Tapiete.[1] I also found a muddling of ethnonyms, a blurred ethnogenesis and history that meant disentangling layers of experiences of displacements, migrations, and tense interethnic relations.

During the initial stage of research in 2002 I learned that the Tapiete had a high rate of interethnic marriages with members of other Indian communities, that few families spoke the language, but that most in the community identified as Tapiete and were definitely identified by their neighbors as *aborígenes*, Indians. In the course of many conversations and visits with Tapiete families, I realized that the Tapiete had crafted a distinct identity largely due to unique transnational relations they had forged with relatives, fictive and real, who lived across the Bolivian and Paraguayan Chaco. During recent years, ongoing contacts and repeated visits among them have intensified, broadened, and deepened their interactions and contributed to consolidating their Tapiete identity. In 2001 they created the Tapiete Trinational Organization to strengthen their transnational links, develop a common agenda, and advance their shared interests in access to land, cultural and educational rights, and development projects. Given the many differences among the Tapiete communities of Argentina, Bolivia, and Paraguay, by employing the common idiom of evangelism they reach consensus over a broad range of issues, enabling them to underscore their commonalities for the collective construction of identity and community.

Democratization and activism of indigenous groups in Argentina paved the way for major legislative and constitutional reforms granting rights to native peoples. Furthermore, there has been a growing presence of state institutions and programs in indigenous communities throughout the country. Ethnic reemergence and claims for legal rights have, in ways both tense and tranquil, reshaped indigenous relations with the state and its institutions (Gordillo and Hirsch 2011). Various agencies, among them the municipality,[2] the Indigenous Peoples Institute,[3] CAPI,[4] and the National Insurance Agency,[5] have provided social subsidies, built housing, and developed agricultural projects among the Tapiete Indians in northwestern Argentina. This heterogeneous set of interventions has not been continuously sustained; the presence of state projects and assistance has been intermittent. Since 2002 there have been unprecedented political, social, and economic transformations in Argentina. At the turn of the twenty-first century, an economic and political crisis as a result of failed economic policies, hyperinflation, contraction of the state, and increased poverty led to the demise of the government of President Fernando de la Rúa (1999–2001), who resigned amid civil unrest, rioting, and violence. Under the administrations of Néstor Kirchner (2003–2007) and Cristina Kirchner (2007–2015), new social policies aimed at poverty alleviation and inclusion increased the distribution of social subsidies and development of economic projects. In a few years the economic situation of indigenous groups such as the Tapiete improved, although an unstable and precarious situation persisted.

Their settlement in northern Argentina in the 1930s was marked by forced displacements caused by urbanization that drove them to build, move, and rebuild their community. Like other groups, the Tapiete have experienced diasporic displacements, and their sense of indigeneity is grounded on living in a borderland and undergoing processes of invisibilization and reemergence (Hirsch 2006b). Their current and permanent location is called Misión Los Tapietes; although they lost part of their territory in the 1970s, orally transmitted memories longingly refer to a larger geographic space. The majority of the inhabitants of this community were born and raised in an urban environment, which creates new identities and subjectivities in particular among the youth and provides greater access to infrastructure, jobs, and consumer culture, differing from the lives of the Tapiete who live in rural areas. The Tapiete recurrently mention that Spanish has displaced their language and that most families are formed by members of six other indigenous groups settled in the region. Likewise, Tapiete of this community frequently mention their transnational trips and contacts with Tapiete of Bolivia and Paraguay, their massive evangelical campaigns on both sides of the border, and their notion of a vast territory undeterred by geopolitical boundaries.

Like many indigenous groups throughout the Americas that have undergone massive displacements and interventions, the Tapiete are resilient and malleable in their ways of responding to changes and to the presence and at times absence of the state and other institutions. What narratives, imaginaries, and practices have they forged as a group to maintain a sense of collectivity? In what ways have their transnational relations with Tapiete of Paraguay and Bolivia expanded their sense of territory and strengthened their internal cohesion? And what is the role of the state and its institutions in guaranteeing the livelihood of the Tapiete? Have the Tapiete gained greater visibility?

The Tapiete have claimed space, recognition, and participation, and in so doing they have articulated transnational connections that strengthen their identity. Faced with an intermittent presence of the state and its institutions and an unstable economic and social context, the Tapiete have resorted to the evangelical church as a source of support and community cohesion. Evangelism provides a sense of continuity in a context of disruptive political practices and loss of legitimacy undergone by political leaders of the community throughout the years, and it provides a common idiom in Tapiete transnational and trinational connections.[6] The transnational dimension of Tapiete life can be better understood by examining their multiterritoriality.

When the Tapiete of the Bolivian Chaco were forced to migrate and leave their territory, they created and settled in new communities, some of which were dispersed and smaller. They became a deterritorialized people, although as Rogério Haesbaert suggests, deterritorialization cannot be disassociated from reterritorialization: "Territory must be considered the product of the combined movement of deterritorialization and reterritorialization, in which power relations are built in and with space, considering space as something constitutive and not as something that can be separated from social relations" (2013, 26, my translation).

In this sense, the settlement of Tapiete in three countries involves a multiterritoriality, "the possibility of having simultaneous or successive experiences of different territories, constantly rebuilding their own" (Haesbaert 2013, 34). Multiterritoriality involves different scales that range from the micro level such as individual property of the land to communal, municipal, provincial, or national territories. Historically, Chaco indigenous peoples were not sedentary, but as the result of colonization, their territories were reduced, and they were forced to settle permanently in small spaces, both rural and urban, and in some cases traversing the regional and national boundaries. Haesbaert suggests that in the case of small indigenous groups in border areas, their processes of territorialization involve fragmented territories in which they reterritorialize and constitute network territories that ignore the international border (2013, 36).

The Tapiete construct diverse territorial forms of settlement and identities; for many of them their origin is in Bolivia, but they were raised and live in Argentina and have an extended kinship network residing in Paraguay. What strengthens their collective identity is precisely their multiterritorial articulation, knowing that there are more of them on the other side of the border.

A brief history of the Tapiete people and their multiple displacements conveys how they constitute transborder communities linked by historical processes by complex political contingencies under three different nation-states. In the transnational practices link the Tapiete of three countries, Evangelism plays a distinctive role. Although the focus here is on the Tapiete of Argentina, their counterparts in Bolivia and Paraguay also form part of the trinational dimension of their social, cultural, and geographic processes.

The Tapiete as an Invisibilized People in a Multiethnic Context

The Gran Chaco has a complex ethnic cartography of indigenous groups that have interacted with each other through wars, alliances, and exchanges before and after colonization. While the ethnic origins of the Tapiete are uncertain, some ethnographers indicate that they were either Zamuco or Mataco-Mataguayo groups who were "guaranized" and adopted the Guaraní language (Métraux 1946; Nordenskiöld 2002 [1912]; Schmidt 1938). Isabelle Combès (2004b) notes that the Tapiete were differentiated from the Guaraní and Ayoreo groups, and their territory was to the south of the Isoso region in southeastern Bolivia.[7] Their territory prior to the Chaco War (1932–1935) extended from the eastern margin of the Parapetí River to the Pilcomayo River to the south; they were referred to by several ethnonyms in documents, as Yanaigua (those who come from the bush) and Tapii (confusingly referred to as "slave"). Some sources say that part of the group was bellicose and attacked criollo ranches, while others have depicted them as "tame" people who worked for criollos and other Guaraní groups (Combès 2010).

The Tapiete population prior to the Chaco War was significantly larger than what is reported in censuses of this century; prior to the war only one village was reported as having more than two hundred people (Combès 2010, 45), more than the total current population of Tapiete in Bolivia. What is known and certain is that the Tapiete speak a language that belongs to the Tupí-Guaraní linguistic family; that they share material aspects with other lowland groups such as the Wichí, Qom, Chorote, and Nivaclé; and that they have adopted and share cultural and religious practices from the Guaraní (also referred to as Chiriguano) and other Chaco groups such as the Wichí, Chorote, and Qom with whom they have intermarried. Tapiete history is characterized by interaction and intermarriage with other Chaco indigenous peoples, and their multiple territorial displacements have allowed them to survive in a social environment marked by territorial dispossession.

Misión Los Tapietes, in the city of Tartagal, Salta Province, shares the name *misión* with many indigenous neighborhoods and communities in Argentina that were at some point under the custody of the Franciscans or Anglicans or evangelical denominations, but the term is more a marker of ethnic boundaries. Those who live in a *misión* are indigenous, although many of them might not identify as such. The term is both self-ascribed and ascribed by the local criollo population. The mission is an administrative and ethnic category also used by the municipality to regulate, delimit, and control indigenous lives. But for the Tapiete as well as other indigenous groups, the mission, village, or barrio transcends these delimited borders; it incorporates communities along the Pilcomayo River, 160 kilometers away, and crosses the geopolitical borders of the Paraguayan and Bolivian Chaco. Still, the Tapiete as well as their criollo neighbors are well aware of the ethnic, class, and racialized borders that separate them; in Argentina local notions of alterity are ever present and separate the indigenous and non-indigenous (Briones 2008). The notion of mission stigmatizes and at the same time protects;[8] the mission is a space where indigenous people feel at home and where their religious practices such as massive outdoor evangelical campaigns, meetings, trinational gatherings, and interethnic marriages take place.

What Shaped Tapiete History

Four turning points have shaped Tapiete history and social life in Argentina, affected their families in Bolivia and Paraguay, and are reiterated in their oral histories and conversations. First, the Tapiete began to migrate from Bolivia to Argentina initially in the beginning of the twentieth century. The Swedish ethnographer Erland von Nordenskiöld (2002 [1912]) mentions the presence of Tapietes as early as 1908 on the sugarcane plantations of the Ingenio La Esperanza, where they were recruited as temporal workers. The Argentine anthropologist Enrique Palavecino (1930) met Tapiete in 1927 in the province of Salta. By the 1920s numerous Tapiete families were traveling to the sugarcane plantations and agricultural farms of northwestern Argentina in search of work. Together with other indigenous groups of lowland as well as highland Bolivia and Paraguay, they worked during the harvests, and these interactions led to the formation of interethnic marriages among indigenous groups of the region. By the 1940s, at the end of the sugarcane harvest several families decided not to return to Bolivia and to settle permanently in the town of Tartagal.

Second, the Chaco War between Bolivia and Paraguay had a most profound impact on almost all of the indigenous groups of the Chaco (Capdevila, Combès, and Richard 2008). It led to the displacement of hundreds of Tapiete and was a turning point in the multiterritoriality of the Tapiete. It meant the desolate exodus of the villages in Bolivia and marked the settlement of hundreds of Tapiete in western Paraguay and in Argentina. In 1935 the German ethnographer Max Schmidt traveled to the Chaco of Paraguay and encountered Tapiete families who had suffered the impact of the Chaco War and were in dire situations of poverty and hunger. Schmidt "was struck by the interethnic fluidity that characterized the region, where intermarriage, multilingualism, cultural loans, and exchange networks were typical features of social reality" (Bossert and Villar 2013, 39). During the first decades of the twentieth century, the Tapiete were settled in an extended territory in southeastern Bolivia, in the departments of Tarija and Santa Cruz. During battles in this region many of them were taken to Paraguay as prisoners by the Paraguayan army or migrated on their own, escaping from the ravages of the war. Many settled permanently in the department of Boquerón in western Paraguay, and others migrated to Argentina. Hence, work and war migration provoked a diaspora of Tapiete to the town of Tartagal and a few families to the village of La Curvita on the banks of the Pilcomayo River, where they initially settled in precarious camps in what is now the center of the town. As Tartagal became more urbanized they were pushed to its outskirts where they now live (Hirsch 2006a).

The third turning point was the massive conversion to evangelism that began in 1955 in Bolivia with the arrival of the Swedish missionaries Rudolf Jalmar Olsson and his wife, who founded the first mission among the Tapiete of Bolivia. The missionaries rapidly and successfully preached the gospel and tenaciously converted the majority of the Tapiete. Another missionary, Olof Jonsson, and his wife settled in Argentina in 1945 in the town of Embarcación; there they met Horacio Martínez, the first Tapiete evangelical convert. Jonsson went to Sweden and returned to Argentina in 1951; he worked intensely in a village on the banks of the Pilcomayo River and later bought land and created an interethnic indigenous community formed by Wichí, Qom, Chorote, and Tapiete. The village, six kilometers east of the town of Tartagal, is named Kilómetro 6 for its location. Martínez began to preach in numerous indigenous communities and among his family and friends, and he generated a mass conversion. Evangelism gradually permeated everyday life. Oral narratives emphasize the problems generated by alcoholism and violence since the 1950s and in particular after the work experience on the sugarcane plantations. In the 1970s the mayor of Tartagal helped finance the construction of an evangelical church because he wanted the "Indians sober so they could work at the local timber mills and farms," he told me in an interview in 1989. Evangelism became a dominant narrative of modernization, pacification, and cohesion among the Tapiete. Evangelism enhanced literacy and new cultural practices such as modern clothing, disciplined work, and abandonment of alcoholic beverages, dances, and non-Christian festivities.

The fourth turning point was the community's urbanization, which meant access to infrastructure including running water, electricity, and housing but also a dramatic reduction of space. In the 1970s the mayor of Tartagal wanted to "modernize" indigenous communities and develop criollo neighborhoods and housing projects in the area. This led to a significant reduction of Tapiete territory and the loss of their agricultural fields near their homes that allowed them to practice agriculture and complement their meager incomes based on wage labor. Loss of part of their territory drastically reduced hunting, gathering, and agricultural practices, though the Tapiete continued going to the bush nearby to search for firewood, hunt, collect honey, visit their relatives, and fish in the Pilcomayo River. Misión Los Tapietes became a small enclave, a crowded community surrounded by criollo neighborhoods. In the mission, few families have permanent jobs; most are temporarily employed as wage laborers and depend on government social programs and subsidies. The Tapiete have flexible ethnic boundaries with other indigenous groups, and although discursively they argue against interethnic marriages, 70 percent of families are formed by individuals belonging to different indigenous groups (Hirsch 2015). That shortage of marriageable partners who are not relatives in their small community has reinforced the formation of interethnic families, especially as the Tapiete live in a multiethnic milieu surrounded by different indigenous groups.

Although the Tapiete were invisibilized and remained a small enclave, reduced to five blocks surrounded by criollo neighborhoods, their leaders participated actively in the 1980s and 1990s in the struggle for indigenous rights in the legal and constitutional reforms in Argentina. In 1985 the Argentine government passed Law 23.302, on indigenous policies and support to indigenous communities (Ley sobre política indígena y apoyo a las comunidades aborígenes). This law ensured collective ownership of the land as well as legal recognition and cultural and linguistic rights. Another landmark in relations between indigenous peoples and the state was the

1994 Constitutional Convention held to debate and reform the Argentine Constitution. The indigenous political lobby actively participated in demanding the reform of Article 75, which held that the state would promote peaceful relations with indigenous peoples, conversion to Catholicism, and secure borders. It was replaced with subsection 17, which grants recognition of indigenous peoples as preceding the Argentine nation and legal recognition of communities, leading to land titling. Two Tapiete leaders were delegates at this convention. One of them told me that his life changed forever after his participation, that he "gained political consciousness." These same Tapiete representatives were later involved in founding the Tapiete Trinational Organization. Even in their invisibilized presence, the Tapiete managed to have representation in the political lobby for indigenous rights and have been dexterous at gaining access to political spaces for claiming rights and resources.

At a more local level, the government of Salta Province passed Law 6373 for "development of the indigenous peoples"; it created the Provincial Institute of the Aborigen (Instituto Provincial de la Aborígen), now named Provincial Institute of Indigenous Peoples (Instituto Provincial de los Pueblos Indígenas de Salta). The institute was created to represent the indigenous communities, coordinate activities and programs, and oversee relations and programs developed by the government. It is formed by a board with representatives of the different indigenous groups of the province. These leaders are in office for two years; Tapiete representatives have held positions for many years in the institute, and one of them is a permanent employee. Holding a position at the institute provides a venue, though limited to resources. Morita Carrasco (2005) provides a critical assessment of the laws enacted in Salta Province for indigenous peoples, arguing that initially legislation was aimed at integrating the native population, and later on the provincial government developed a discourse of recognition of cultural differences. However, indigenous peoples were treated as beneficiaries of programs and projects and made responsible for implementing public policies in a system based on clientelistic forms of politics; such approaches led to greater dependence on local politicians.

Guillermo Wilde and Matthias vom Hau (2010) compare two indigenous groups in Argentina and the ways they have mobilized and organized to defend their lands and territory. In the article the authors suggest that "the current politics of recognition in Argentina plays a central role in deepening cultural and political rights, while its impacts remain limited in addressing broader issues of social justice. The constitutional recognition of communal lands only gained traction once indigenous social movements actively pursued formal titling. Similarly, ethnic mobilization around communal lands introduced a new language of 'rights,' used even by communities without property titles to protect their access to land" (1288). Access to titling of land is a long and complex process depending not only on a corpus of laws but also on the political will of elected officials and those in government institutions. In this sense, the Tapiete have claimed land outside of their small urban community and have acquired 259 hectares fifteen kilometers from the town of Tartagal; however, they share the property, called Colonia 15, with five urbanized indigenous communities, and very few Tapiete reside there because of the distance and a lack of access to water and electricity.

In 2011 a group of Tapiete settled on a plot of twenty-two hectares that they named Tapiete IV. Juan Vega, one of the founders of this new settlement, told me their motives for settling there: "We can't live there [Misión Los Tapietes] any longer. There is no space, we used to live from our crops, [and] we have a lot of family. Some have eight or ten children. Before we lived dispersed and not crowded." Vega and the families who have settled in Tapiete IV imagine a place unsullied by drugs and alcoholism where they can live healthy, evangelical lives and practice agriculture. And lastly, several Tapiete families reside in the interethnic village of La Curvita on the banks of the Pilcomayo River, where most of them engage in fishing and agriculture and have temporary jobs. These heterogeneous settlements depict the multiterritoriality of Tapiete displacements, their diverse ways of building, negotiating, and occupying territories that are not necessarily ancestral but are construed as places to live in a rural milieu, with a desire to forge a subsistence with greater independence and fewer restrictions, away from the urban milieu.

Transnational and Territorial Connections

Small indigenous groups such as the ones who live along the borders between Brazil, Paraguay, and Argentina have defied the geopolitical borders, and although forced to settle in reserves or small territories, they have constantly moved across boundaries. Haesbaert (2013, 36) states that these groups have

> ignored their reclusion in the microterritories of the "reserves" and
> even ignored the existence of the international border—some of them

> spend 60 to 90 days in one side of the border (these are the same
> Guaraní Indians on both sides) and 60 to 90 days on the other. Their
> territorialization in terms of fragmented territories is reterritorial-
> ized in the form of network territories that ignore the international
> border, and currently the official documents of the Guaraní specify
> that condition and demand the recognition of their "transterritorial
> condition." (My translation)

While the Tapiete do not make this demand, crossing the borders of the
countries in which they live does not pose a problem or a restriction as long
as they carry with them their identity cards. Multiterritorial practices allow some of the less numerous indigenous groups to develop alliances and
networks across borders in order to articulate efforts to strengthen their
organizations or simply engage in economic practices, find marriageable
partners, and fortify their presence in a context of subalternity.

While the Tapiete of Tartagal are confined to five blocks, their sense
of experienced space transcends rigid geopolitical borders; their territoriality incorporates a vast geography that includes not only the village of
La Curvita and the new settlements but also the numerous villages of the
Paraguayan Chaco, where more than two thousand Tapiete families live,[9]
and the sparsely populated villages of the Bolivian Chaco. Their diasporic
experience became visible in the 2000s when they organized transnational
and trinational evangelical campaigns and political meetings that brought
them together from their dispersed localities. The chronology of these encounters begins in 1995 when a group of Argentine Tapiete rented a truck,
crossed the Pilcomayo River, and entered the Paraguayan Chaco to contact
relatives they had never met and conduct an evangelical campaign. Miguel
Arias, the pastor of Misión Los Tapietes, told me that his father always mentioned their family in Paraguay and said that one day they should go there
and reunite with them. This initial trip was a turning point. The Tapiete
of Paraguay arrived from different villages to meet their Argentine relatives, trace their kinship descent, and share stories of their past in Bolivia
and their settlement in Paraguay. They experienced a rural environment, a
common language, and a shared religion. Later trips led to a few marriages
between Tapiete men from Argentina and Tapiete women from Paraguay,
and several families migrated to Argentina.

In Paraguay the Tapiete are self-denominated Guaraní Ñandeva. They
live in the department of Boquerón in five areas: the small community
of Barrio Obrero Colonia 5 that is seven kilometers from the town of

Figure 11.1. Entrance to Guaraní Ñandeva community, 2018. Colonia 5 Barrio Obrero is outside Filadelfia, Paraguay. Photo by Silvia Hirsch.

Filadelfia; fourteen villages on 7,500 hectares in the area known as Laguna Negra; five settlements in the multiethnic area of Santa Teresita; the village of Pikasu, also known as Fortín Infante Rivarola, thirty kilometers from the border with Bolivia; and Pedro P. Peña, on the border with Argentina. These missions and settlements are examples of the reorganization of space and the reterritorialization that occurred during and after the Chaco War. Santa Teresita was founded as a mission in 1942 by the Catholic order Oblates of Mary Immaculate and was initially formed mostly by Guaraní originally from Bolivia (locally known as Guaraní *occidentales*), Guaraní Ñandeva, and Nivaclé. Most Guaraní Ñandeva are agriculturalists, raise animals, work in temporary jobs, and live in rural areas. In the 1980s the Indigenist Association of Paraguay sponsored Proyecto Ñandeva Guaraní, which led to the resettlement of numerous families on the Laguna Negra property of 7,500 hectares jointly purchased by the Association of Indigenous Mennonite Cooperation Services,[10] the Catholic Equipo Nacional de Misiones (National Missionary Team), and the Indigenist Association of Paraguay. This land was also shared with the Guaraní Occidentales (Renshaw 2002). The indigenous Organización Guaraní Ñandeva claims access to water, among other demands, and is under the leadership of women. That organization, in turn, is a member of the umbrella Federation of Indigenous Peoples and Organizations of the Paraguay Chaco (Federación de Pueblos y Organizaciones Indígenas Chaco del Paraguay). While most people living in Laguna Negra are evangelical, this is not the case in Santa Teresita, which has a strong Catholic presence.

In Paraguay the development of indigenous political organizations has been delayed compared with other Latin American countries. The long dictatorship of Alfredo Stroessner, which ended in 1989, aimed toward the integration of the native population, and those policies had a deleterious effect on indigenous people. In 1981 the Stroessner government passed Law 904/81 of indigenous rights; it promised to respect indigenous cultures and native people's rights to own ancestral lands. Despite this law, the loss of indigenous territory all over Paraguay is astounding; deforestation, pressure from agribusiness, and livestock production have reduced indigenous territories and in many places forced them to move. While the Guaraní Ñandeva of Paraguay are the more numerous group and in Laguna Negra they have access to land, the expansion of the agricultural frontier, livestock production, and climate change have had dramatic impacts on sources of water and threaten the possibility of subsistence (Skjerping 2011).

In Bolivia the Tapiete live in the villages of Samuwate and Capirenda and the towns of Crevaux and Villamontes; their total population is less than two hundred. Paradoxically, despite their low population they obtained 21,840 hectares of land in 2001 on which to cultivate, hunt, and gather. The small Tapiete community is formed by intermarriage with Guaraní and Weenhayek people. The access to a large territory is the result of a political process in Bolivia that culminated in the 1996 law of agrarian reform and establishment of TCOs (Tierras Comunitarias de Origen), a designation of autonomous and communally owned indigenous land. Under the Evo Morales government in 2015, the Plurinational Institute of Culture and Language created the Tapiete Institute of Culture and Language, directed by a Tapiete teacher. In Bolivia, the small Tapiete community has larger landholdings than those in Argentina and Paraguay and an institute to promote the Tapiete language and cultural practices. At play here are the political and public policies of indigenous recognition and autonomy supported by the notion of a plurinational government.

In 1994 the Tapiete and Weenhayek people jointly formed the Organización de Capitanias Weenhayek y Tapiete (ORCAWETA, Organization of Weenhayek and Tapiete Captaincies) to advance the interests and demands of both groups. ORCAWETA forms part of the Confederation of Indigenous Peoples of Bolivia, which represents lowland indigenous groups nationally. The Tapiete have since diverted from ORCAWETA their joint organization with the Weenhayek to join the pan-Guaraní Asamblea del Pueblo Guaraní, formed in 1987; that group has a larger constituency and a long history of struggle for lands, cultural, linguistic rights, and national recognition (Martínez and Villegas 2005). When the Tapiete of Argentina and Paraguay visit Bolivia, they can hear children speaking in their native language, and they observe a vast territory and a consolidated political organization. Their memories are activated in narratives expressed by them as "our place of origin," "where our ancestors came from," and "indigenous peoples do not have borders." The Bolivian case shows that despite numerous political problems, the context is one of greater recognition, rights, and autonomy for indigenous groups.

The Evangelical Connection

Evangelism became a growing force among the Tapiete at a time when they faced social problems such as alcoholism, violent contact with national society, and territorial displacements. Several authors (Ceriani Cernadas 2013; Gordillo 2004; Wright 2002b, 2008) argue that the presence of missions was perceived by indigenous Chaco people in contradictory ways. On the one hand, missions were seen as places of domination and profound change. On the other hand, they were seen as places of refuge from the violence exerted by the state (through the military) and the colonists, places where they were provided resources such as food, shelter, access to medicine, and schooling. Some missions purchased lands to promote the settlement of indigenous peoples in concentrated spaces, while in other cases indigenous people sought missionaries to fund missions. Horacio Martínez, the first Tapiete convert in Argentina, returned to his community to evangelize his people and in doing so cleared the way for a collective conversion process.

César Ceriani Cernadas and Hugo Lavazza (2013) contend that missions were established in criollo towns as a way of facilitating the integration of native peoples to the nation-state. Missionaries prohibited feasting, dancing, shamanism, and other cultural practices, but they provided a sanctuary, protection from military incursions, exploitive work, and greater loss of territory. In a similar way, among the Tapiete, evangelism protected them from violent relations with the national society; it was a civilizing project somewhat less violent than public education and everyday relations with the larger society. Pastors taught the people how to dress, behave, maintain a schedule, abandon chewing coca leaves and drinking alcohol, and

Figure 11.2. Young women in an evangelical campaign, Tartagal, Argentina, 2019. Photo by Silvia Hirsch.

incorporate hygienic practices. Literacy was strongly enhanced as well as Bible study. Elderly women told me how distressing it was to see the men drunk and the children abandoned with no food or support, especially during traditional celebrations. I was also told how gendarmes entered the community and abused women. Hence, the conversion to evangelism and the presence of foreign missionaries reorganized everyday life and social relations amid territorial displacements but also mitigated internal conflicts and tense relations with the surrounding society.

In 1955, Swedish missionaries arrived in Bolivia, causing apprehension among the Tapiete. Reynaldo Balderas from Samuwate explained to me, "Most people didn't want to hear the message, didn't like religion, and wanted the missionary to leave; they weren't interested." This was the general attitude until Olsson and his wife arrived and provided protection from the abuses by the colonists and the military. The Tapiete became members of the Assembly of God Church, and some of the elderly men attended biblical seminaries and courses in which they were taught the scriptures and how to preach in their communities. By the 1980s the presence of the church was consolidated, although several young people discontinued attending and opted for participating in what they call "mundane" activities and celebrations such as the carnival, when drinking, dancing, and playing music are at the core of the sociality.

Although transnationally evangelical campaigns have increased, the trinational organization meetings have not continued regularly, and some members indicate that this is the result of funding and internal political differences. At least twice a year the Tapiete from Argentina cross the border to participate in evangelical campaigns in Bolivia and Paraguay. Several Tapiete have told me that what they mostly have in common with the Tapiete of Paraguay and Bolivia besides their origins, their kinship ties, and the language they speak is that they are all members of evangelical churches, and these massive gatherings generate a sense of strength and belonging to a group that is growing and not circumscribed to a small community.

In Bolivia the Tapiete acknowledge that the Swedish Free Mission has helped them improve their education and provided resources for the communities, while in Laguna Negra in Paraguay, the Mennonites have been involved in improving agricultural practices, commercializing the Tapiete's produce, and helping them settle in a larger territory. Edward Cleary and Timothy Steigenga assert (2004, 77), "Religion forms a major component of indigenous life and culture, provides resources and motivations for public action, and serves as a transnational link to state and non-state actors who can advocate for indigenous causes."

The Tapiete Trinational Organization across Borders

In 2001 the Tapiete of Paraguay held the I Encuentro Trinacional Tapiete, which led to the formation of the Ñandereta Mbajape Tenta Tappii (Tapiete Trinational Organization) with the objective of consolidating ties and developing projects between Tapiete in the three nations. The guiding principles of the Tapiete Trinational Organization are to maintain unity and solidarity, improve living conditions, obtain a common fund to develop activities, promote bilingual intercultural education, and support the cultural identity of the Tapiete people. This first meeting set the guidelines for future encounters across boundaries. The second trinational meeting was held in 2004 in Argentina, in Misión Los Tapietes, with resources and assistance from the Bolivian nonprofit Ecovia and meager support granted by the municipality of Tartagal. Delegations arrived from Bolivia and Paraguay, and the Argentine gendarmerie band played the national anthems of the three countries at the inauguration, while the leaders raised the flags of three

Figure 11.3. Trinational Tapiete meeting, 2004. Delegates from Argentina, Bolivia, and Paraguay raise the flags of their countries at the meeting in Tartagal, Argentina. Photo by Silvia Hirsch, author.

countries. I read in these symbolic gestures a recognition of the diasporic indigenous experience as one that transcends national borders. What also caught my attention was that in the evenings the organization held long religious services at the evangelical church; the organization has a religious commission headed by a pastor, and at the commission's sessions, political and religious leaders gave passionate speeches that integrated identity, belonging, and biblical messages. The late Tomás Ferreyra, a seasoned Tapiete leader of Bolivia, said, "We are trinationally united, three flags that we see, this is what these three flags are saying. When they say 'trinational' I am amidst my people. This trinational organization will not come to an end in three or four years; it will go deeper and deeper. I am the founder of this trinational Tapiete." Reynaldo, from Samuwate, Bolivia, mentioned that God has designated the authorities of the organization.

Until then, I had not witnessed political indigenous meetings held at a church, but here I saw the fluidity between religious and political practices, and the strengthening of transnational bonds enhanced by the Church. At the core of these trinational meetings, was the effacement of geopolitical boundaries and the strengthening of Tapiete identity and kinship ties. These meetings allow time for the interaction between friends and relatives, where people strengthen their transnational connections. When I visited Guaraní Ñandeva communities in Paraguay, in August 2018, I was introduced and asked to present myself in the church, then I met with a group of elderly men who welcomed me warmly, I was bringing news of their family and friends in Argentina, most of them had visited Misión Los Tapietes, and referred to them as their relatives, and jointly participated in the Evangelical campaigns. I was particularly welcomed as someone who knew and understood the historical ties that connected them across borders.

Françoise Morin and Roberto Santana (2003, 10) suggest, "The transnational practice constitutes for autochthonous groups a positive aspect of globalization because it allows them to form alliances to constitute pressure groups and compensate their political weakness in the heart of the nation-states that marginalize them. This instrument may favor the reunification of groups divided over one or more national borders, and it also recomposed the collective identities that have been fragmented by migratory processes" (my translation). It is important to emphasize that the Argentine Tapiete are considered by some of their neighbors as Bolivian nationals, which is locally a disparaging ethnic marker associated with a stigmatized population and lack of access to rights and territory. Nonetheless, for the Argentine Tapiete, their sense of citizenship and national identification lie within Argentina. They say, "We don't have borders, but we are Argentines" as well as Salteños, from Salta Province. The Guaraní who live in the same region as the Tapiete and have strong bonds to the Bolivian Guaraní articulate an identity that is strengthened by the transnational dimension of their history and kinship ties. This transterritorial articulation does not reduce or blur an identity that is locally grounded as being Argentine; it coexists with an identification that goes beyond the border. The Guaraní express a discourse of recognition of their pan-Guaraní identity and refer to their transnational identity, although grounded in local geographies where borders did not exist prior to the formation of nation-states (Hirsch 2000, 2003). The Tapiete are aware of being a small group and of being encroached upon territorially and culturally; they recognize that their political organizations are not as strong as those among the Guaraní. Identifying with Bolivia and Paraguay also generates ambiguous feelings, a sense of transterritorial belonging and kinship bonds, but also a differentiation in terms of national affiliation. Hence, being from Salta Province and from Argentina also lies at the core of their identity.

James Clifford (1994) observes how indigenous populations sustain "diasporic borderlands" as those spaces of displacement from a place of origin but where communications shorten distances and create spaces of greater contact and frequency. This Tapiete community is located in a multiterritorial space, along the Pilcomayo River in the Paraguayan Chaco and among communities in southern Bolivia. Kinship and bonds of common religion are held in practice in these transnational locations. Though borders are sites of deployment of state control, of military presence, of enforcement of security measures against smuggling, and commerce of all sorts, these trinational borders are not an obstacle to cross. Visitors are required to carry identity cards, and when asked the motive of their trips, the Tapiete mention they will visit their relatives or belong to an evangelical church and are visiting their religious "brothers and sisters."

The Tapiete of Argentina frequently mention their historical and kinship bonds with Bolivia and Paraguay and say that in Bolivia, the Tapiete are "purest," as they speak the language fluently, maintain several traditional practices, and have a larger territory, although they are more intermixed with Weenhayek and Guaraní people. The Paraguayan Tapiete (Guaraní Ñandeva) are much more numerous, and they are seen as also retaining the language and living in rural communities but with a weaker sense of political organization and less support from the government. What they all share is an origin, a language, and participation in the evangelical church. This last common denominator grants visibility, fosters encounters, exchanges, and trips beyond the organization of trinational meetings, which wait for external funding to be organized.

Tropes That Bind across Boundaries

In the diverse territorial and political situations of the Tapiete in the Gran Chaco, three different geographical, political, and social contexts have greater or lesser recognition, more or less land, and differentially enforced cultural and linguistic rights. In Argentina, with reduced access to land but with access to rights and recognition, the Tapiete receive social subsidies from the state, and their location, near the center of town, has allowed them access to health care and education, although with certain limitations. Nonprofit organizations (NGOs) have less of a presence in Argentina, and the Tapiete look for resources to the municipal and state levels and to local politicians.

Similar to what occurred in other Latin American contexts where indigenous identities went through an effacement and deindigenization, the Tapiete were invisiblized by others and by themselves. The subalternity of living in town, being a small group, and experiencing everyday discriminatory practices are some of the factors that have impinged on their personal lives. A civilizing project enforced in schools, churches, public spaces, and workplaces has been a dominant cultural and social force. It is in this context that the Tapiete extend their kinship, religious, and political ties across the border; they travel to participate in evangelical campaigns and indigenous political organizations, and they find in Bolivia and Paraguay a strengthening of their identity. René Harder Horst (2004, 77) indicates that in the case of religious conversion of indigenous peoples in Paraguay, participation in evangelical churches strengthened the ethnic identity and the communal and political fabric and even helped in reclaiming tribal territories. Ceriani Cernadas and Lavazza (2014) find that among the Qom of Argentina, the church became a space for the emergence of leadership and new forms of authority; this is a common trend throughout the Gran Chaco. Among the Tapiete, the leadership of the church holds prestige and is able to mobilize community resources more than any state or nongovernmental project has ever achieved. While legislation and state social policies have created a greater sense of inclusion of indigenous peoples, the presence of the Argentine state is defined by its intermittent character and gradual withdrawal of subsidies and programs.

Participating in transnational meetings and evangelical campaigns creates a sense of belonging to a greater territory and to a larger group; participation reinforces kinship and friendship bonds and becomes instrumental in learning about new forms of organization and negotiating with the state and NGOs. On this geopolitical border of Argentina, ethnic and class differences marginalize indigenous peoples, and there is constant tension between everyday forms of exclusion and public policies of inclusion. The Tapiete are aware of the signals sent by the state and its agencies that at times are inclusive and promote well-being and at other times exclude and are absent. The Tapiete find in their transnational connections, in their multiterritorial ways of life, a source of reaffirmation of their diasporic indigeneity and a reinforcement of their kinship ties, and in the evangelical church they find a constant source of support and cohesion. It remains to be seen what new forms of community cohesion and identity politics the younger generations will develop in the future.

Notes

1. For an updated bibliography on the Tapiete see Hirsch, González, and Ciccone 2019.

2. Municipalidad de Tartagal, Acción Social y Desarrollo Comunitario (Municipality of Tartagal, Social Affairs and Community Development).

3. Instituto Nacional de Asuntos Indígenas (National Institute of Indigenous People).

4. The Componente de Atención a la Población Indígena (CAPI, Development Program for the Indigenous Population) was developed between 1998 and 2005. It was part of an agreement between the Ministerio de Desarrollo Social and the Inter-American Development Bank.

5. Administración Nacional de la Seguridad Social (ANSES, Social Security Administration).

6. The presence of the evangelical church and its numerous denominations among indigenous Chaco groups has been thoroughly studied by numerous scholars in Argentina (Ceriani Cernadas 2011a,b; 2017a,b; Ceriani Cernadas and Citro 2005; Gordillo 2004; Wright 2002a,b, 2008).

7. Ethnohistorical documents and evidence on the ethnogenesis of the Tapiete is scarce. For more information see Combès 2004b, 2007, 2008.

8. For an analysis of the missions as places of protection as well as ambiguity see Gordillo 2004.

9. According to the Paraguayan census published in 2012, the Guaraní Ñandeva population was approximately 2,393 (Paraguay, DGEEC 2012).

10. Asociación de Servicios de Cooperación Indígena Menonita (ASCIM, Association of Indigenous Mennonite Cooperation Services) is a nonprofit organization formed by Mennonites in Paraguay.

Afterword

The Contested Terrain of the Gran Chaco

GASTÓN GORDILLO

What type of place is the Gran Chaco? Or to be more precise, what type of places constitute, in their diversity, this vast and transnational spatial entity in the tropical lowlands of South America? This book gives a rich and thought-provoking overview of the fraught, vibrant, emergent but also violent and damaged geography of the Gran Chaco in the early twenty-first century. It does so by capturing the most constitutive rupture that has historically defined the region, as it went from being one of the last autonomous indigenous territories in the Americas to becoming a sacrifice zone for extractive industries in three nation-states: Argentina, Paraguay, and Bolivia. The once-mysterious Gran Chaco, renowned and mythologized for its impassable forests and swamps and its rebellious inhabitants, now generates soybeans, beef, oil, and natural gas to the supply chains of globalized capitalism. Yet the book also shows that despite these dramatic transformations and the violence and dispossession that made them possible, the descendents of the people who once controlled the Gran Chaco continue being crucial actors in shaping and contesting the sociospatial configuration of the region. The counterpoints brought forth by the book invite examination into what the Gran Chaco teaches more broadly about places as contested processes that are also part of the planet's terrain, which in this region is a flat, semiarid, partly forested, and tropical plain traversed by roads, fences, and pipelines.

The question of the spatiality of the Gran Chaco is in my case insepa-rable from my experience of doing ethnographic research in various areas of the Argentine Chaco for more than three decades. When I first visited western Formosa Province in 1987 as an anthropology undergraduate so-cialized in the city of Buenos Aires, what struck me about this region were the (back then) vast and dominant presence of thick forests (*el monte*) and how the local indigenous villages exuded a distinct social and historical texture through the stories that my Qomle'ec (Toba) hosts began sharing with me. I was particularly captivated by the memories of elders who described how back in the 1910s and 1920s that same terrain on the Pilcomayo River was a radically different place under the control of their ancestors, whom they described as proud, egalitarian people who moved freely over a wide area and did not recognize the Argentine state (Gordillo 2004). Those were memories, in short, about what today seems unthinkable: a territory "outside" of the state. This autonomy was ended by the Argentine army and its superior firepower. In listening to those stories I was apprehending a constitutive spatial and territorial feature of the Gran Chaco: that it is a place-region where state power is a relatively recent and violent imposition.

That until not too long ago the Gran Chaco was among the last autonomous indigenous territories in South America has defined many dimensions of its sociospatial specificity. The book amply documents the many ways in which the practices, memories, perceptions, and imaginaries of indigenous people continue shaping local places, for instance through their sensibility toward the presence and agency of invisible nonhuman beings (Kalisch), their shamanic visions (Villagra Carron), and the memories of their engagement with the state (Bossert, Biocca). Some chapters capture that the social memory of those days of autonomy before the arrival of the state is still fresh in current spatial perceptions. As Hannes Kalisch shows, the Enlhet people in Paraguay refer to their traditional territory as "the space in which we move" (*nengeleyvomaklha'*), making clear that they experienced it not as a bounded, controllable object but as the medium of their freedom of mobility. Also in the Paraguayan Chaco, Rodrigo Villagra Carron notes a similarly flexible pattern of spatial appropriation among the Angaité people, who are now immersed in a landscape of cattle ranches but whose ethnogenesis was defined by the dynamic fusion and fission of different groupings organized around a charismatic shamanic leader.

The book confirms that in most areas of the Gran Chaco the land encroachment and dispossession by settlers, corporations, and state agencies have been profound and that many indigenous people have been confined to shrinking and crammed spaces in rural and urban areas (Correia, Bossert, Biocca, Hirsch). In some of these places, people are subjected to high levels of toxicity created by the fumigation of soy fields with pesticides (Biocca) or by the contaminated water of stock ponds on cattle ranches (Correia). This territorial rearrangement was also structured in the twentieth century by the action of Protestant missionaries. As César Ceriani Cernadas shows, missionization reorganized indigenous populations around mission stations, creating new places structured by notions of "hygiene" and "development" and significantly redefining indigenous subjectivities and identities—to the point that in many cases an evangelical identity is felt as stronger than other attachments, as Silvia Hirsch notes among Tapiete people.

The book also brings to light that the conditions of domination currently faced by indigenous people in relation to settlers, officials, ranchers, or corporations are not part of a rigid, top-down structure but a complex field of disputes and adaptations that are often decided by the deployment of bodies on the ground. In the heavily privatized lands of the Paraguayan Chaco, this involves a microphysics of indigenous people navigating both their confinement on small plots surrounded by cattle ranches and the ongoing power of racist and gendered discourses about their primitivism (Correia, Kalisch, Canova). As Joel Correia argues, the confinement imposed on the Enxet-Sur people is made possible by the "infrastructural violence" of roads, fences, and contaminated ponds. The estrangement from the land has been so intense among the Enlhet people that the roads, Kalisch notes, are "the only spaces they know." These roads are also feared spaces dominated by the speed of long-distance traffic, which as Correia demonstrates contrasts with the slower, local pace of Enxet-Sur people's mobility. But roads are also contested spaces that indigenous people regularly use to their advantage. In Paraguay, Paola Canova reveals, the same roads that have brought economic growth to the Mennonite colonies allow young Ayoreo women to assert their own forms of mobility and sexuality in relation to the attempts by Mennonite settlers to control them. And in the case of Argentina, Mercedes Biocca analyzes how the organization of road blockades by Qom people became central to their political agency, something influenced by the salience of this tactic elsewhere in the country. Yet she also warns that not all indigenous people resist the conditions of their domination and that some Moqoit people are wary of disruptive forms of protest and have adopted an attitude of relative acquiescence. Because fences are the material embodiment of the expropriation of indigenous land and of the new boundaries created by private property, they are particularly contested infrastructures. Federico Bossert shows in the example of the Chané people of the Itiyuro basin in Argentina that efforts by indigenous people to defend their land often involve their capacity to physically challenge and stop the attempts by intruders to set up fences on the terrain.

Contestations over territory also adopt more institutional channels, often involving extralocal agencies and actors as well as national media. These include demands to government officials for state resources (Biocca), legal disputes (Bossert), negotiations over compensations for resource extraction (Bebbington and Cortez), and struggles that involve electoral politics and complex negotiations with rival political parties (Postero). Nancy Postero reveals a particularly novel and radical type of activism among Guaraní people in Bolivia that, drawing from the "pro-indigenous" momentum of the early years of Evo Morales's government (2005–2019), managed to create the first "autonomous indigenous municipality" in the country. But she also shows that, far from being opposed to the state or to extractivism, this is an autonomy imagined as existing within the plurinational Bolivian state and funded by oil and gas rents. The power of extractive industries in the Bolivian Chaco is also documented by Denise Bebbington and Guido Cortez, who show how the efforts by Weenhayek people to be compensated for the extraction of natural gas and for the expansion of access roads, pumping wells, and pipelines on their land ended up creating numerous divisions and disputes as well as class differentiation. They reveal, in short, that the consultation and compensation implemented by officials and corporations are often a source of conflict that further new forms of domination.

The book also illustrates that the sociopolitical character of places in the Gran Chaco is never purely local but shaped by the regional and national territories they are part of. As the previous examples show, in the Bolivian Chaco the political experiences and strategies of indigenous people became inseparable from the impact that Evo Morales's government had on Bolivia as a whole and in the Santa Cruz and Villa Montes regions in particular. Biocca shows that a similar national and province-specific territoriality involved the Argentine Chaco with the rise of Peronism and later with the center-left governments of Néstor Kirchner (2003–2007) and Cristina Kirchner (2007–2015), for indigenous political identities and subjectivities were strongly influenced by them and by the impact of neoliberal reforms in this country in the 1990s. Canova reveals that in Paraguay the legacy of Alfredo Stroessner's long dictatorship meant that discourses of multiculturalism and indigenous rights were popularized much later than in neighboring Bolivia and Argentina. Bossert adds a notable twist to the territorial impact of borders, for he focuses on a region, the Itiyuro basin, which used to be part of Bolivia but was handed over to Argentina at the turn of the twentieth century. Bossert shows that while Bolivian officials protected the Chané from land encroachment, under the Argentine government these protections disappeared and a rapid land privatization ensued. Hirsch, in her chapter on Tapiete people in Argentina, confirms that despite these national differences, borders are also porous spaces of connectivity that generate novel identites and multiterritorialities. In particular, she brings to light how Tapiete people have created diasporic identities and forms of mobility that connect them with Tapiete groups in Bolivia and Paraguay and that they experience through their shared evangelical rather than purely ethnic positioning.

Bret Gustafson covers a different type of contestation, this time among the academics who have long sought to make sense of the complex and dynamic ethnic landscape of the Gran Chaco. In particular, he challenges a well-known interpretation of the history of the Guaraní of southestern Bolivia, called Chiriguano by the Spanish, according to which these people emerged from the *mestizaje* between local Chané people and Guaraní newcomers from the east. For Gustafson, this is a "colonial fabrication" that reads too much into scant historical and linguistic evidence and has the problematic effect of suggesting that the westernmost Guaraní speakers are not, in fact, Guaraní, but something else. This debate reminds us that discourses produced by scholars have long shaped imaginaries about the Gran Chaco, often oscillating between essentializing and historically grounded perspectives (Bessire 2014; Gordillo 2006).

What type of place is the Gran Chaco? The book helps answer this question by presenting a fascinating, tense constellation of different and often contradictory places, constituted by local, regional, and transnational connections and by political contestations and experienced locally through distinct cultural habits, memories, and aspirations. The book also shows that the Gran Chaco is also more than how these diverse human actors have experienced and remade it, for the region has a nonhuman materiality that is part of the texture of terrain in this tropical area in the heart of lowland South America.

This terrain has been a palpable, often hard-to-represent constant in my stays in different parts of the region: the hardness of the soil; the brightness of the sunlight; the dust blown by the wind across soy fields; the size and texture of the many tree and plant species that define the remaining forests of the Chaco; the unique animal and insect wildlife and its lively soundscapes; the wetlands of the Pilcomayo or the meandering waters of the Bermejo; the density of air in the summer that oscillates between the dry heat of the north wind, *el viento norte*, and the refreshing arrival of cool air and rainstorms with the south wind; the stunningly clear nights where the galaxy forms a continuum of stars. Beyond local specificities, this is a terrain that I encountered in places hundreds of kilometers away from each other and that you also can find in the Bolivian and Paraguayan Chaco. In each place, residents experience this terrain differently depending on their own cultural habits, practices, and memories. But as the climate crisis worsens and the deforestation of the Gran Chaco continues, this is also a terrain increasingly affected by cycles of droughts, heat waves, and floods created by the absence of the forests that once provided humidity and shade. The Gran Chaco, in this regard, is one of the areas in the world where the impact of global warming is being amplified and made more severe by deforestation. Hence the urgency to support the struggles against ecocide currently taking place in the region.

This peripheral region in the heart of South America is a prism through which experiences, contestations, and disruptions taking place elsewhere in the world acquire a particular clarity and intensity. Hence the paradox that the Gran Chaco evokes one of the most extraordinary and mythologized geographies of the planet and also a microcosm of the wider experiences and challenges that define our world. And this is also the region that taught me to appreciate that places are made, disputed, destroyed, and remade by human actors as part of the terrain.

The political agency of indigenous people in the Gran Chaco, documented in this book and a rich literature, may lack the radicalism and level of organization one can find among other indigenous people elsewhere in Latin America, such as the Mapuche in Chile or the Zapatista collectives in their autonomous territories in rebellion in Chiapas, Mexico. Yet it is worth remembering that this often-neglected region of South America once embodied like few others and for several centuries a geography "against the state," as Pierre Clastres (1987) has put it (inspired by the former Nivaclé combatants he met in the Paraguayan Chaco). As I learned in the Andean foothills that formed the Chaco frontier during colonial times, that history of defiance lives on in the rubble of Spanish towns and forts destroyed by indigenous and mestizo insurrections (Gordillo 2014). The current marginalization of the Gran Chaco and its multiple and contested inscriptions in the terrain have been, in many ways, the price that its original inhabitants were made to pay for their practices of freedom.

Works Cited

Adorno, Rolena. 2007. *The Polemics of Possession in Spanish American Narrative*. New Haven, CT: Yale University Press.

Aguirre, Juan Francisco. 2017 [1948]. *Diario y observaciones de Juan Francisco de Aguirre en el Paraguay 1784–1796*. Asunción: Academia Paraguaya de la Historia and Tiempo de Historia.

Aikhenvald, Alexandra. 1999. "The Arawak Language Family." In *The Amazonian Languages*, edited by Robert M. W. Dixon and Alexandra Aikhenvald, 65–106. Cambridge, England: Cambridge University Press.

———. 2002. *Language Contact in Amazonia*. Oxford, England: Oxford University Press.

Albó, Xavier. 2012. *El Chaco Guaraní, camino a la autonomía originaria*. La Paz: Centro de Investigación y Promoción del Campesinado.

Almirón, Alejandro A. 2014. "La ocupación del territorio nacional del Chaco: Empresarios, agricultores y el rol de los expertos estatales (1926–1935)." *Anuario de Historia Regional y de las Fronteras* 19, no. 1:139–163.

Altman, Agustina. 2017. La disolución de Nam Cum en perspectiva: Contextos globales de la menonita en el Chaco Argentino. In *Los evangelios chaqueños: Misiones y estrategias indígenas en el siglo XX*, edited by César Ceriani Cernadas, 117–143. Buenos Aires: Rumbo Sur.

Alvarsson, Jan Ake. 1988. *The Mataco of the Gran Chaco: An Ethnographic Account of Change and Continuity in Mataco Socio-Economic Organization*. Uppsala Studies in Cultural Anthropology, 11. Uppsala: Acta Universitatis Upsaliensis.

———. 2007. "The Process of Ethno[re]genesis among the 'Weenhayek' of the Gran Chaco (1976–2006)." *Revista del Centro para los Estudios Latinoamericanos/International Latin American Studies Review*, no. 10:139–156. Redalyc, https://www.redalyc.org/articulo.oa?id=243316417008.

Anand, Nikhil, Akhil Gupta, and Hannah Appel. 2018. "Introduction: Temporality, politics and the Promise of Infrastructure." In *The Promise of Infrastructure*, edited by Nikhil Anand, Akhil Gupta, and Hannah Appel, 1–40. Durham, NC: Duke University Press.

Anglican Church. 1979. *Paraguayan Chaco Indian Colony: Project Presented by the Anglican Church in Paraguay*, November 1979. Report. Asunción: Anglican Church.

Anthias, Penelope. 2014. "The Elusive Promise of Territory: An Ethnographic Case Study of Indigenous Land Titling in the Bolivian Chaco." PhD diss., University of Cambridge.

———. 2016a. "Ch'ixi Landscapes: Indigeneity and Capitalism in the Bolivian Chaco." *Geoforum* 82 (June): 268–275. http://dx.doi.org/10.1016/j.geoforum.2016.09.013.

———. 2016b. "Indigenous Peoples and the New Extraction. From Territorial Rights to Hydrocarbon Citizenship in the Bolivian Chaco." *Latin American Perspectives* 20, no. 30:1–18.

Araghi, Farshad A. 1995. "Global Depeasantization, 1945–1990." *Sociological Quarterly* 36, no. 2:337–368.

Aráoz, Guillermo. 1884. *Navegación del Río Bermejo y Viajes al Gran Chaco*. Buenos Aires: Imprenta Europea and Taller de Grabados en Madera.

Asad, Talal. 2003. *Formations of the Secular: Christianity, Islam and Modernity*. Stanford, CA: Stanford University Press.

Auyero, Javier. 2012. *Patients of the State: The Politics of Waiting in Argentina*. Durham, NC: Duke University Press.

Ávalos, Sonia E., María de las Nieves Montiel Domínguez, and Matías Ever Medina. 2018. *Koahlvo: El pueblo angaité en la recuperación de su lengua*. Asunción: Paraguái Ñĕenguéra Sãmbyhyha, Secretaría de Políticas Lingüísticas.

Azara, Félix de. 1850. *Viajes por la América del Sur: Desde 1789 a 1801*. Montevideo: Imprenta del Comercio del Plata.

———. 2003 [1943]. *Descripción e historia del Paraguay y el Río de la Plata*. Alicante, Spain: Biblioteca Virtual Miguel de Cervantes.

Bailey, Geoff. 2014. "Accumulation by Dispossession: A Critical Assessment." *International Socialist Review* 95, no. 1. https://isreview.org/issue/95/accumulation-dispossession.

Ballantyne, Tony. 2011. "Humanitarian Narratives: Knowledge and the Politics of Mission and Empire." *Social Sciences and Missions* 24:233–264.

Ballvé, Teo. 2017. "Frontiers: Remembering the Forgotten Lands." In *Other Geographies: The Influence of Michael Watts*, edited by Shared Chari, Susanne Freidberg, Vinay Gidwani, Jesse Ribot, and Wendy Wolford, 169–183. Newark: John Wiley and Son.

Barabas, Alicia. 2001. "Territorialidad, santuarios y peregrinaciones." *Diario de Campo, Boletín Interno de los Investigadores del* Área *de Antropología, INAH* 34:16–18.

———. 2004. "La territorialidad simbólica y los derechos territoriales indígenas: Reflexiones para el estado pluriétnico." *Alteridades* 14, no. 27:105–119.

Barroso, Maria. 2009. *Fronteiras étnicas, fronteiras de estado e imaginação da nação: Um estudo sobre a cooperação internacional norueguesa junto aos povos indígenas*. Rio de Janeiro: E-papers.

———. 2015. "Lógicas de espacialização missionária e agendas da cooperação internacional: Uma perspectiva multisituada a partir de ações junto aos povos indígenas." *Religião e Sociedade* 35, no. 2:189–212.

Bartolomé, Miguel. 2010. "Interculturalidad y territorialidades confrontadas en América Latina." *RUNA* 31, no. 1:9–29.

Barúa, Guadalupe, and Javier Rodríguez Mir. 2009. "Introducción: El área cultural del Gran Chaco; dossier etnología del Chaco." *Revista Española de Antropología Americana* 39, no. 2:139–149.

Baumann, Matthias, Cristoph Israel, María Piquer-Rodríguez, Gregorio Gavier Pizarro, José Norberto Volante, and Tobias Kuemmerle. 2017. "Deforestation and Cattle

Expansion in the Paraguayan Chaco 1987–2012." *Regional Environmental Change* 17:1179–1191.

Bebbington, Anthony. 2007. *Minería, movimientos sociales y respuestas campesinas: Una ecología política de transformaciones territoriales.* Lima: Instituto de Estudios Peruanos.

———, ed. 2012. *Social Conflict, Economic Development, and Extractive Industries: Evidence from South America,* London: Routledge.

Bebbington, Anthony, and Jeffrey Bury, eds. 2013. *Subterranean Struggles: New Geographies of Extractive Industries in Latin America.* Austin: University of Texas Press.

Bebbington, Anthony, and Denise Humphreys Bebbington. 2011. "An Andean Avatar: Post Neoliberal and Liberal Strategies for Securing the Unobtainable." *New Political Economy* 16, no. 1:131–145.

Bebbington, Anthony, Denise Humphreys Bebbington, Jeffrey Bury, Jeannet Lingan, Juan Pablo Muñoz, and Martin Scurrah. 2008. "Mining and Social Movements: Struggles over Livelihood and Rural Territorial Development in the Andes." *World Development* 36, no. 12:2888–2905.

Bedoya Silva-Santisteban, Álvaro, and Eduardo Bedoya Garland. 2005. *Servidumbre por deudas y marginación en el Chaco de Paraguay.* Working paper no. 45, Declaration/WP/45/2005. Geneva: International Labour Organization.

Bello Maldonado, Alvaro, and José Aylwin Oyarzún. 2008. *Globalización, derechos humanos y pueblos indígenas.* Temuco, Chile: Observatorio de Derechos de Pueblos Indígenas.

Bennett, Vivienne, Sonia Dávila-Poblete, and María Nieves Rico. 2005. *Opposing Currents: The Politics of Water and Gender in Latin America.* Pittsburg, PA: University of Pittsburg Press.

Berajano, Ramón. 1977. *Solucionemos nuestro problema indígena con el INDI.* Serie Estudios Antropológicos 6. Asunción: Instituto Nacional del Indígena.

Bernard, Carmen. 1973. "La Fin des capitaines." *Bulletin de l'Institut Français d'Études Andines* 2, no. 1:72–82.

Bernstein, Henry. 1977. "Notes on Capital and Peasantry." *Review of African Political Economy* 4, no. 10:60–73.

Bessire, Lucas. 2014. *Behold the Black Caiman: Chronicles of Ayoreo Life.* Chicago: University of Chicago Press.

Bialet Masse, Juan. 1986 [1904]. *Informe sobre el estado de las clases obreras argentinas.* Vol. 1. La Plata: Ministerio de Trabajo de la Provincia de Buenos Aires.

Bianchi, Susana. 2001. *Catolicismo y Peronismo: Religión y política en la Argentina 1943–1955.* Buenos Aires: Trama and Prometeo.

Biehl, João. 2016. "The Postneoliberal Fabulation of Power: On Statecraft, Precarious Infrastructures, and Public Mobilization in Brazil." *American Ethnologist* 43, no. 3:437–450.

Binswanger-Mkhize, Hans. 1991. "Brazilian Policies That Encourage Deforestation in the Amazon." *World Development* 19, no. 7:821–829.

Biocca, Mercedes. 2016. "Más allá de las letras de sangre y fuego: Trayectorias de desposesión en Chaco, Argentina." *Población y Sociedad* 23, no. 2:61–90.

Blaser, Mario. 2009. "The Threat of the Yrmo: The Political Ontology of a Sustainable Hunting Program." *American Anthropologist* 111, no. 1:10–20.

———. 2010. *Storytelling Globalization from the Chaco and Beyond.* Durham, NC: Duke University Press.

———. 2013. "Notes towards a Political Ontology of 'Environmental' Conflicts." In *Contested Ecologies: Nature and Knowledge,* edited by Lesley Green, 13–27. Cape Town: HSRC.

Blomley, Nicholas. 2003. "Law, Property, and the Geography of Violence: The Frontier, the Survey, and the Grid." *Annals of the American Association of Geographers* 93, no. 1:121–141.

Boggiani, Guido. 1900. "Compendio de etnografía paraguaya moderna." *Revista del Instituto Paraguayo,* no. 25:141–144; no. 27:145–189.

Bolivia, Congreso Nacional. 2009. Constitución Política del Estado Plurinacional de Bolivia. La Paz.

Bolivia, Ministerio de Desarrollo Rural y Tierras, Ministerio de Salud y Deportes, and Ministerio de Defensa. 2011. *Informe final de evaluación de la situación de la seguridad alimentaria de comunidades indígenas del Rio Pilcomayo Provincia Gran Chaco del Departamento de Tarija.* La Paz: Ministerio de Desarrollo Rural y Tierras.

Bonifacio, Valentina. 2009. "The Passion of Civilization: Encounters between Paraguayan and Maskoy People in Puerto Casado, Paraguayan Chaco." PhD diss., University of Manchester.

———. 2017. *Del trabajo y vacas ariscas: Puerto Casado, genealogías (1886–2000).* Asunción: Centro de Estudios Antropológicos de la Universidad Católica.

Borda, Dionisio, and Fernando Masi. 1998. *Los límites de la transición: Economía y estado en el Paraguay en los años 90.* Asunción: Centro Interdisciplinario de Derecho Social y Economía Política, Universidad Católica de Asunción.

Borras, Saturnino M. Jr., and Jennifer C. Franco. 2013. "Global Land Grabbing and Political Reactions 'from Below.'" *Third World Quarterly* 34, no. 9:1723–1747.

Borrini, Héctor R. 1997. *Poblamiento y colonización en el Chaco Paraguayo (1850–1990).* Resistencia, Argentina: Instituto de Investigaciones Geohistóricas.

Bossert, Federico. 2008. "Los chané a través del Gran Chaco (siglo XVI)." *Suplemento Antropológico* 43, no. 1:283–338.

———2013. "Ingenios azucareros y relaciones interétnicas." In *Al pié de los anges: Estudios de etnología, arqueología e historia,* edited by Pablo Sendón and Diego Villar. Cochabamba: Instituto de Misionlogía.

Bossert, Federico, Isabelle Combès, and Diego Villar. 2008. "La Guerra del Chaco entre los chané e isoseños del Chaco Occidental." In *Mala guerra,* edited by Nicolas Richard, 203–233.

Bossert, Federico, and Diego Villar. 2005. "Aproximación al problema de la historia oral entre los chané." *Actas del Quinto Congreso Argentino de Americanistas* 3:41–62. Buenos Aires: Sociedad Argentina de Americanistas.

———. 2007. "La etnología chiriguano de Alfred Métraux." *Journal de la Société des Américanistes* 93, no. 1:127–166.

———. 2013. *Sons of the Forest: The Ethnographic Photography of Max Schmidt.* Santa Monica, CA: Perceval.

Bosworth, Kai. 2018. "'They're Treating Us Like Indians!': Political Ecologies of Property and Race in North American Pipeline Populism." *Antipode* (September). https://doi.org/10.1111/anti.12426.

Braticevic, Sergio. 2009. "Metamorfosis de los modelos evangelizadores en el Chaco Central: Las ONGs para el "desarrollo" y su "razón intervencionista" en un espacio de expansión productiva reciente." *Papeles de Trabajo* 17:1–21.

Braunstein, José. 1981. "El problema de la significación de la cultura material de los maká." PhD diss., Universidad de Buenos Aires.

———. 2006. "El signo de agua: Formas de clasificación étnica wichí." In *Definiciones étnicas, organización social y estrategias políticas en el Chaco y la Chiquitanía*, edited by Isabelle Combès, 145–154.

———. 2008. "'Muchos caciques y pocos indios': Conceptos y categorías del liderazgo indígena chaqueño." In *Liderazgo, representatividad y control social en el Gran Chaco*, edited by José Braunstein and Norma. C. Meichtry, 3–30. Resistencia, Argentina: Universidad del Nordeste Argentino.

———. 2016. "Núcleos culturales del indio colonial en el Gran Chaco: El digesto etnográfico de los expulsos de Faenza." In *Entre los Jesuitas del Gran Chaco: Compilación de Joaquín Camaño S.J. y otras fuentes documentales del S. XVIII*, edited by José Braunstein, Julio Folkenand, Ernesto Maeder, and María Laura Salinas, 55–195. Buenos Aires: Academia Nacional de Ciencias de Buenos Aires.

Braunstein, José, and Elmer Miller. 1999. "Ethnohistorical Introduction." In *Peoples of the Gran Chaco*, edited by Elmer Miller, 1–23. Westport, CT: Bergin.

Bray, David B. 1989. *El estado, los donantes extranjeros y los pueblos indígenas de la provincia del Chaco, Argentina: De la subyugación al comienzo de la autodeterminación, 1884–1988*. Buenos Aires: Grupo de Análisis, Desarrollo Institucional y Social.

Brenner, Robert. 2007. "What Is, and What Is Not, Imperialism?" *Historical Materialism* 14, no. 4:79.

Briggs, Charles, and Daniel Hallin. 2007. "Biocommunicability: The Neoliberal Subject and Its Contradictions in News Coverage of Health Issues." *Social Text* 25, no. 4:44–66.

Briones, Claudia, ed. 2005. *Cartografías argentinas: Políticas indigenistas y formaciones provinciales de alteridad*. Buenos Aires: Antropofagia.

———. 2008. "Formaciones de alteridad: Contextos globales, procesos nacionales y provinciales." In *Cartografías argentinas: Políticas indigenistas y formaciones provincials de alteridad*, edited by Claudia Briones, 11–44. Buenos Aires: Antropofagia.

Briones, Claudia, and Carlos del Cairo. 2015. "Prácticas de fronterización: Pluralización y diferencia." *Universitas Humanística*, no. 80:13–52.

Bruchell, Graham. 1996. "Liberal Government and Techniques of the Self." In *Foucault and Political Reason: Liberalism, Neo-liberalism, and Rationalities of Government*, edited by Andrew Barry, Thomas Osborne, and Nikolas Rose, 19–36. Chicago: University of Chicago Press.

Brunn, Augusto, Miguel Chase Sardi, and Miguel Á. Enciso. 1990. *Situación sociocultural, económica, jurídico-política actual de las comunidades indígenas en el Paraguay*. Asunción: Centro Interdisciplinario de Derecho Social y Economía Política.

Buckwalter, Albert, and Lois Buckwalter. 2009. "Misión a las comunidades indígenas:

Un testimonio personal." In *Misión sin conquista: Acompañamiento de comunidades indígenas autóctonas como práctica misionera alternativa*, edited by Willis Horst, Ute Mueller Eckhardt, and Frank Paul, 193–203. Buenos Aires: Kairós.

Bury, Jeffrey, and Adam Kolff. 2003. "Livelihoods, Mining, and Peasant Protests in the Peruvian Andes." *Journal of Latin American Geography* 1:3–17.

Cáceres, Daniel M. 2015. "Accumulation by Dispossession and Socio-Environmental Conflicts Caused by the Expansion of Agribusiness in Argentina." *Journal of Agrarian Change* 15, no. 1:116–147.

Cadena, Marisol de la. 2010. "Indigenous Cosmopolitics in the Andes: Conceptual Reflections beyond 'Politics.'" *Cultural Anthropology* 25 (2): 334–370.

———. 2015. *Earth Beings: Ecologies of Practice across Andean Worlds*. Durham, NC: Duke University Press.

Cadena, Marisol de la, and Orin Starn. 2007. *Indigenous Experience Today*. Book 2, Wenner-Gren International Symposium Series. New York: Berg.

Caimari, Lila. 1995. *Perón y la Iglesia Católica*. Buenos Aires: Ariel.

Caldas, Marcellus M., Douglas Goodin, Steven Sherwood, Juan M. Campos Krauer, and Samantha M. Wisely. 2013. "Land-Cover Change in the Paraguayan Chaco: 2000–2011." *Journal of Land Use Science* 10, no. 1 (July): 1–18. http://dx.doi.org/10.1080/1747423x.2013.807314.

Camaño y Bazán, Joaquín. 1931. "Etnografía rioplatense y chaqueña." Edited by Guillermo Furlong Cardiff. *Revista de la Sociedad de Amigos de la Arqueología* 5:309–343.

Campanella, Andrés. 1935. "Algunas observaciones sobre el indio americano." *Revista Geográfica Americana* 19:257–262.

Campbell, Jeremy. 2015. *Conjuring Property: Speculation and Environmental Futures in the Brazilian Amazon*. Seattle: University of Washington Press.

Canclini, Santiago. 1970. *Los evangélicos en el tiempo de Perón: Memorias de un pastor Bautista sobre la libertad religiosa en la Argentina*. Buenos Aires: Mundo Hispano.

Canova, Paola. 2015. "Los ayoreo en las colonias menonitas: Análisis de un enclave agroindustrial en el Chaco paraguayo." In *Capitalismo en las selvas*, edited by Lorena L. Córdoba, Federico Bossert, and Nicolás Richard, 271–286.

———. 2018. "Reflexiones sobre el proceso de consulta previa y la participación indígena en proyectos gubernamentales en el Chaco Paraguayo." *Suplemento Antropológico* 53, no. 1:9–58.

———. 2019. "La urbanidad de los guaraní occidentales en el Chaco Paraguayo." In *Indígenas en las ciudades de las Americas: Condiciones de vida, procesos de discriminación e identificación y luchas por la ciudadania* étnica, edited by Jorge Enrique Horbath, 117–136. Buenos Aires: Miño Davila.

Capdevila, Luc, Isabelle Combès, and Nicolás Richard. 2008. "Los indígenas en la Guerra del Chaco: Historia de una ausencia y antropología de un olvido." In *Mala guerra*, edited by Nicolás Richard, 13–66.

Capdevila, Luc, Isabelle Combès, Nicolás Richard, and Pablo Barbosa. 2010. *Los hombres transparentes: Indios y militares en la Guerra del Chaco (1932–1935)*. Cochabamba: Instituto de Misionología.

Carracedo, José David. 2008. "Fernando Lugo: 'La prioridad es que los indígenas no sigan muriendo de hambre.'" *Público*, April 30. https://www.publico.es/internacional/fernando-lugo-prioridad-indigenas-no.html.

Carrasco, Morita. 2005. "Política indigenista del estado democrático salteño entre 1986 y 2004." In *Cartografías argentinas políticas indigenistas y formaciones provinciales de alteridad*, edited by Claudia Briones, 253–292. Buenos Aires: Antropofagia.

———. 2009. *Tierras duras: Historias, organización y lucha por el territorio en el Chaco Argentino*. Copenhagen: International Work Group for Indigenous Affairs.

Carvalho, Fernando O. de. 2016. "Terena, Chané, Guaná and Kinikinau Are One and the Same Language: Setting the Record Straight on Southern Arawak Linguistic Diversity." *Liames* 16, no. 1:39–57.

Casaccia, Gladys, and Mirna Vázquez. 1986. *La lucha para la tierra en defensa de la vida: El Pueblo Maskoy frente a Carlos Casado S.A. Relatorio del Caso*. Asunción: Equipo Nacional de Misiones de la Conferencia Episcopal Paraguaya.

Castellanos-Navarrete, Antonio, and Kees Jansen. 2015. "Oil Palm Expansion without Enclosure: Smallholders and Environmental Narratives." *Journal of Peasant Studies* 42, no. 3–4:791–816.

Castelnuovo Biraben, Natalia. 2010. "Tensiones, contradicciones y disputas en el encuentro de los guaraníes con las ONG´s de desarrollo en el Noroeste Argentino." *Avá* 18:43–59.

———. 2015. *Mujeres guaraníes y procesos de participación política en el Noroeste Argentino*. Buenos Aires: Antropofagia.

———. 2017. "Collaborations in Faith: NGO Development Policies in Northern Argentina." *Urban Anthropology and Studies of Cultural Systems and World Economic Development* 46, no. 3–4:333–373.

———. 2019. "Mujeres indígenas ¿Un actor político? ¿Una fórmula neoliberal?" *Journal of Latin American and Caribbean Anthropology* 24, no. 1:203–220.

Castro, Miguel. 2004. *Memorias de un caminar*. Tarija, Bolivia: Centro de Estudios Regionales para el Desarrollo de Tarija.

Centeno, Daniel. 1999. *Reservas posibles de gas y condensado en el departamento de Tarija*. Tarija, Bolivia: Luis de Fuentes.

Cepeda, Lic. 1914 [1584]. "Carta de Licenciado Cepeda dando cuenta de la Guerra á los Chiriguanae." In *Bolivia-Paraguay: Exposición de los títulos que consagran el derecho territorial de Bolivia, sobre la zona comprendida entre los Ríos Pilcomayo y Paraguay*, edited by Ricardo Mujía, supplement to volume 2, Época colonial, 254–270. La Paz: El Tiempo.

Ceriani Cernadas, César. 2005. "Conflicto sociorreligioso y representaciones simbólicas entre tobas mormones y evangélicos." *Avá: Revista de Antropología* 7:45–69.

———. 2006. "El general y el profeta: Acomodación social del mormonismo durante el régimen peronista (1946–1954)." *Entrepasados* 30:29–46.

———. 2007. "El tiempo primordial: Memorias tobas del pastor Chur." *Revista de Ciencias Sociales* 18:71–86.

———. 2009. "Las enseñanzas de don Juan Chur entre los toba de Formosa (Argentina), 1937–1950." *Papeles de Trabajo* 5:1–20. Instituto de Altos Estudios Sociales. http://revistasacademicas.unsam.edu.ar/index.php/papdetrab.

———. 2011a. "Evangelio, política y memoria en los toba (qom) del Chaco Argentino."

Nuevo Mundo Mundos Nuevos, Cuestiones del Tiempo Presente (March). https://journals.openedition.org/nuevomundo/61083.

———. 2011b. "La misión pentecostal escandinava en el Chaco Argentino: Etapa Formativa, 1914–1945." *Memoria Americana* 19:117–141.

———. 2013. "Entre la confianza y la sospecha: Representaciones indígenas sobre las experiencias chaqueñas de misionalización protestante." In *El Gran Chaco: Ontologías, poder, afectividad,* edited by Florencia Tola, Cecilia Medrano, and Lorena Cardín, 297–320, Buenos Aires: Rumbo Sur.

———. 2014. "Configuraciones de poder en el campo evangélico indígena del Chaco Argentino." *Sociedad y Religión* 41:13–42.

———. 2015. "Flujos teóricos y transformaciones empíricas en el estudio de los pueblos indígenas del Chaco Argentino." *Papeles de Trabajo* 9:110–141.

———. 2017a. *Los evangelios chaqueños: Misiones y estrategias indígenas en el siglo XX.* Buenos Aires: Rumbo Sur.

———. 2017b. "Misión, nación y religión: Las fronteras del dios Chur entre los toba formoseños." In *Los evangelios chaqueños: Misiones y estrategias indígenas en el siglo XX,* edited by César Ceriani Cernadas, 71–89. Buenos Aires: Rumbo Sur.

Ceriani Cernadas, César, and Silvia Citro. 2005. "El movimiento del evangelio entre los toba del Chaco Argentino: Una revisión histórica y etnográfica." In *De indio a hermano: El pentecostalismo indígena en América Latina,* edited by Bernardo Guerrero Jiménez, 11–170. Iquique: Universidad Arturo Prat.

Ceriani Cernadas, César, and Hugo Lavazza. 2013. "Fronteras, espacios y peligros en una misión evangélica indígena en el Chaco Argentino (1935–1962)." *Boletín Americanista* 67:143–162.

———. 2014. "Inestables reputaciones: Liderazgo y conflicto en una misión evangélica indígena del Chaco Argentino." In *Experiencias plurales de lo sagrado: La diversidad religiosa argentina en perspectiva interdisciplinaria,* edited by Fabian Flores and Paula Seguer, 3–18. Buenos Aires: Imago Mundi.

Ceriani Cernadas, César, and Alejandro López. 2017. "Introducción: Una antropología comparativa sobre las misionalizaciones chaqueñas." In *Los evangelios chaqueños: Misiones y estrategias indígenas en el siglo XX,* edited by César Ceriani Cernadas, 19–36. Buenos Aires: Rumbo Sur.

Cerruti, Marcela, and Alejandro Grimson. 2013. "Neoliberal Reforms and Protest in Buenos Aires." In *Neoliberalism, Interrupted: Social Change and Contested Governance in Contemporary Latin America,* edited by Mark Goodale and Nancy Postero, 109–136. Palo Alto, CA: Stanford University Press.

Chernela, Janet. 2015. "Directions of Existence: Indigenous Women Domestics in the Paris of the Tropics." *Journal of Latin American and Caribbean Anthropology* 20, no. 1:201–229.

Chico, Juan, and Mario Fernández. 2011. *Napa'lpí: La voz de la sangre.* Resistencia, Argentina: Instituto de Cultura de la Provincia del Chaco.

Ciccone, Florencia. 2012. "Contacto del tapiete (tupí-guaraní) con el español: Cambio de código y préstamo gramatical en contextos de desplazamiento lingüístico." In *Prácticas y repertorios plurilingües en Argentina,* edited by Virginia Unamuno and Ángel Maldonado, 31–55. Bellaterra: GREIP, Universidad Autónoma de Barcelona.

———. 2015. "Contacto, desplazamiento y cambio lingüístico en tapiete (tupí-guaraní)." PhD diss., Universidad de Buenos Aires.

Ciccone, Florencia, and Silvia Hirsch. 2016. "El pueblo tapiete de argentina: Historia, prácticas y cambios culturales." In *Ecos del mundo vegetal entre los tapietes de Argentina: Diccionario etnobotánico*, edited by Hebe González, 7–21. Munich: LINCOM.

Citro, Silvia. 2006. "Tácticas de Invisibilización y estrategias de resistencia de los mocoví santafesinos en el contexto postcolonial." *Indiana* 23:139–170.

———. 2009. *Cuerpos significantes: Travesías de una etnografía dialéctica*. Buenos Aires: Biblos.

Clastres, Pierre. 1987. *Society against the State: Essays in Political Anthropology*. New York: Zone Books.

Cleary, Edward L., and Timothy J. Steigenga. 2004. *Resurgent Voices in Latin America: Indigenous Peoples, Political Mobilization and Religious Change*. New Brunswick, NJ: Rutgers University Press.

Clifford, James. 1994. "Diasporas." *Cultural Anthropology* 9, no. 3:302–338.

Cobos, Norberto B. 1926. "Límite argentino-boliviano." *Boletín del Instituto Geográfico Argentino* 1 (Segunda Época): 19–31.

CODEHUPY (Coordinadora de Derechos Humanos del Paraguay). 2013. *Situación de los derechos a la tierra y al territorio de los pueblos indígenas en el Paraguay*. Asunción: CODEHUPY.

———. 2017. *Derechos Humanos 2017*. Asunción: Arandurá.

Colque, Gonzalo. 2015. "El punto de quiebre de las autonomías." October 11. La Paz: Fundación Tierra. http://www.ftierra.org/.

Comajuncosa, Antonio. 1884 [1810]. "Manifiesto histórico de lo que han trabajado los misioneros de tarija así entre los fieles como entre los Infieles desde el año 1755 hasta el 1810, escrito por el P. Fr. Antonio Comajuncosa." In *El Colegio Franciscano de Tarija y sus misiones*, edited by Alejandro Corrado, 75–278. Rome: Colegio de San Buenaventura.

Comajuncosa, Antonio. 1971 [1800]. "Descripción de las Misiones, al cargo del Colegio de Nuestra Señora de los Ángeles de la Villa de Tarija." In *Obras y documentos relativos a la historia antigua y moderna de las provincias del Río de la Plata* VII, edited by Pedro De Ángelis, 97–166. Buenos Aires: Plus Ultra.

Comaroff, John, and Jean Comaroff. 1992. *Ethnography and the Historical Imagination*. Oxford, England: Westview.

———. 1997. *Of Revelation and Revolution*. Vol. 2: *The Dialectics of Modernity on a South African Frontier*. Chicago: University of Chicago Press.

Combès, Isabelle. 1992. *La tragédie cannibale chez les anciens tupí-guaraní*. Paris: Presses Universitaires de France.

———. 2002. "El pueblo weenhayek y las actividades de transredes." Mimeo.

———. 2004a. "Chindica y guaricaya, capitanes chané 'ynfieles de las montañas.'" In *Anuario del Archivo y Biblioteca Nacional de Bolivia*, no 10,223–240. Sucre, Bolivia.

———. 2004b. "Tras la huella de los ñanaigua: De tapii, tapiete y otros salvajes en el Chaco Boliviano." *Bulletin de l'Institut Français d'Études Andines* 33, no. 2: 255–269.

———. 2005. *Etno-historias del Isoso: Chané y chiriguanos en el Chaco Boliviano (siglos*

XVI a XX). La Paz: Instituto Francés de Estudios Andinos, Fundación para la Investigación Estratégica en Bolivia.

———, ed. 2006. *Definiciones étnicas, organización social y estrategias políticas en el Gran Chaco y la Chiquitania*. Vol. 2 of *Actes et mémoires*. Santa Cruz de la Sierra, Bolivia: IFEA.

———. 2007. "De Sanandita al Itiyuro: Los chanés, los chiriguanos (¿y los tapietes?) al sur del Pilcomayo." *Indiana* 24:259–289.

———. 2008. "Los fugitivos escondidos: Acerca del enigma tapiete." *Boletín del Instituto Francés de Estudios Andinos* 37, no. 3:511–533.

———. 2009. *Zamucos*. Cochabamba, Bolivia: Nómades.

———. 2010. "El coronel Ayoroa y los indios del lugar. In *Los hombres transparentes: Indígena y militares en la Guerra del Chaco (1932–1935)*, edited by Luc Capdevila, Isabelle Combès, Nicolás Richard, and Pablo Barbosa, 33–82. Cochabamba, Bolivia: Instituto de Misionología.

———. 2014a. "Como agua y aceite: Las alianzas guerreras entre tobas y chiriguanos en el siglo XIX." *Indiana* 31: 321–349.

———. 2014b. *Kuruyuki*. Cochabamba, Bolivia: Itinerarios.

———. 2015. "Historia franciscana y etnografía chiriguana." *Boletín Americanista* 70:57–72.

Combès, Isabelle, and Kathleen Lowrey. 2006. "Slaves without Masters? Arawakan Dynasties among the Chiriguano (Bolivian Chaco, Sixteenth to Twentieth Centuries)." *Ethnohistory* 53, no. 4:689–714.

Combès, Isabelle, and Thierry Saignes. 1991. *Alter Ego: Naissance de L'identité Chiriguano*. Paris: École des Haute Études en Sciences Sociales.

Combès, Isabelle, and Diego Villar. 2004. "Aristocracias chané: "Casas" en el Chaco Argentino y Boliviano." *Journal de la Societé des Américanistes* 90, no. 2:63–102.

———. 2007. "Os mestiços mais puros. Representações chiriguano e chané da mestiçagem." *Mana* 13, no. 1:41–62.

Combès, Isabelle, Diego Villar, and Kathleen Lowrey. 2009. "Comparative Studies and the South American Gran Chaco." *Tipiti: Journal of the Society for the Anthropology of Lowland South America* 7, no. 1:69–102.

Cominges, Juan de. 1892. *Exploraciones*. Madrid: Juan A. Alsina.

CONAPI (Coordinación Nacional de Pastoral Indígena). 2017. *Educación indígena: Antecedentes y alcances de la Ley N 3.231/07 'Que Crea la Dirección General de Educación Escolar Indígena.'* Asunción: Coordinación Nacional de Pastoral Indígena.

Cordeu, Edgardo, and Alejandra Siffredi. 1971. *De la algarroba al algodón: Movimientos milenaristas del Chaco Argentino*. Buenos Aires: Juárez.

Córdoba, Lorena, Federico Bossert, and Nicolás Richard, eds. 2015. *Capitalismo en las selvas: Enclaves industriales en el Chaco y Amazonía indígenas (1850–1950)*. San Pedro de Atacama, Chile: Ediciones del Desierto.

Córdoba, Lorena, and José Braunstein. 2008. "Cañonazos en 'La Banda': La Guerra del Chaco y los indígenas del Pilcomayo Medio." In *Mala guerra,* edited by Nicolás Richard, 125–147.

Corrado, Alejandro. 1884. "Continuación de la historia del Colegio Franciscano de Tarija y de sus misiones desde el año 1810 hasta el de 1882." In *El Colegio Franciscano de*

Tarija y sus misiones, edited by Alejandro Corrado, 1–74, 279–506. Rome: Colegio de San Buenaventura.

Correia, Joel E. 2018a. "Indigenous Rights at a Crossroads: Territorial Struggles, the Inter-American Court of Human Rights, and Legal Geographies of Liminality." *Geoforum* 97:73–83.

———. 2018b. "Adjudication and Its Aftereffects in Three Inter-American Court of Human Rights Cases Brought against Paraguay: Indigenous Land Rights." *Erasmus Law Review* 11, no. 1:43–56.

Cortez, Guido. 2006. "Cambios sociales y culturales en el pueblo indígena weenhayek en los últimos cien años." In *Definiciones étnicas, organización social y estrategias políticas en el Chaco y la Chiquitanía*, edited by Isabelle Combès, 163–178.

Cote, Stephen. 2013. "A War for Oil in the Chaco, 1932–1935." *Environmental History* 18 (October): 738–759.

Coulthard, Glenn S. 2014. *Red Skin White Masks: Rejecting the Colonial Politics of Recognition*. Minneapolis: University of Minnesota.

Cox, Laurence. 1999. "Power, Politics, and Everyday Life: The Local Rationalities of Social Movement Milieu." In *Transforming Politics*, edited by Jeff Hearn and Paul Bagguley, 46–66. London: Palgrave Macmillan.

———. 2011. *Building Counter Culture: The Radical Praxis of Social Movement Milieux*. Helsinki: Into-ebooks.

Dalla-Corte, Gabriella. 2012. *Empresas y tierras de Carlos Casado en el Chaco Paraguayo*. Asunción: Intercontinental.

———. 2014. *San Francisco de Asís del Laishí: Sensibilidades tobas y franciscanas en una misión indígena (Formosa, 1900–1955)*. Rosario, Argentina: ProHistoria.

Dalla-Corte, Gabriela, and Fabrizio Vázquez Recalde. 2011. *La conquista y ocupación de la frontera del Chaco entre Paraguay y Argentina*. Barcelona: Universitat Autònoma de Barcelona.

Das, Veena. 1997. "Sufferings, Theodicies, Disciplinary Practices, Appropriations." *International Social Sciences Journal* 49, no. 154: 563–572.

Das, Veena, and Deborah Poole. 2004. "State and Its Margins: Comparative Ethnographies." In *Anthropology in the Margins of the State*, edited by Veena Das and Deborah Poole, 3–34. Santa Fe, NM: School for Advanced Research Press.

Dasso, María Cristina, and Zelda Alice Franceschi. 2015. "La representación wichí del trabajo y el ingenio azucarero." In *Capitalismo en las selvas*, edited by Lorena Córdoba, Federico Bossert, and Nicolás Richard, 65–92.

De Echave, José, Alejandro Diez, Ludwig Huber, Bruno Revesz, Xavier Ricard Lanata, and Martín Tanaka. 2009. *Minería y conflicto social*. Lima: Instituto de Estudios Peruanos, Centro de Investigación y Promoción del Campesinado, Centro Bartolomé de las Casas, and Consorcio de Investigación Económica y Social.

De Souza, Ilda. 2008. "Koenukunoe emo'u: A lingua dos índios kinikinau." PhD diss., Universidade Estadual de Campinas.

Delporte, Joseph. 1992. *El choco o el baile de los toba maskoy*. Master's thesis. Universidad Técnica Particular de Loja.

———. 1998. "Los angaité en las estancias." *Suplemento Antropológico* 34, no. 1:235–274.

Descola, Philippe. 2004. "Las cosmologías indígenas de la Amazonía." In *Tierra adentro:*

Territorio indígena y percepción del entorno, edited by A. Surrallés y P. García Hierro, 25–36. Copenhagen: International Work Group for Indigenous Affairs.

DGEEC. See Paraguay, DGEEC.

Dietrich, Wolf. 1986. *El idioma chiriguano: Gramática, textos, vocabulario.* Madrid: Instituto Cooperación Iberoamericana.

D'Orbigny, Alcide. 1835–1837. *Voyage dans l'Amerique méridionale.* Paris: Pirous Levarault.

Duerksen, Marvin. 2006. "Indígenas exigen aprobación de ley sobre ayuda mutual hospitalaria." *Diario ABC Color*, October 3. https://www.abc.com.py/.

EFE. 2018. "Bolivia y Paraguay repasan avances del proyecto del tren bioceánico." November 9. https://www.efe.com/efe/america/politica/bolivia-y-paraguay-repasan-avances-del-proyecto-tren-bioceanico/20000035-3807768.

Ekdahl, Muriel, and Joseph Grimes. 1964. "Terena Verb Inflection." *International Journal of American Linguistics* 30, no. 3:261–268.

El Deber. 2016. "Alto comisionado rechaza amenazas contra 'CIPCA.'" October 4. https://eldeber.com.bo/.

Elizeche, José A., dir. 2007. *Waika.* Film. 29 minutes. Visión Documenta, Grupo SUNU, and CEADUC.

Engle, Karen. 2010. *The Elusive Promise of Indigenous Development: Rights, Culture, Strategy.* Durham, NC: Duke University Press.

Escobar, Arturo. 1996. *La invención del Tercer Mundo: Construcción y deconstrucción del desarrollo.* Bogotá: Norma.

———. 2010. "Latin America at a Crossroads. Alternative Modernizations: Post-Liberalism, or Post-Development?" *Cultural Studies* 24, no. 1:1–65.

Escobar, Ticio. 1988. *Misión: Etnocidio.* Asunción: Comisión de Solidaridad con los Pueblos Indígenas and RP.

Fabre, Alain. 2005. "Los pueblos del Gran Chaco y sus lenguas, primera parte: Los enlhet-enenlhet del Chaco Paraguayo." *Suplemento Antropológico* 40, no. 1:503–569. http://www.academia.edu/3611583/Dic_Enlhet_Enenlhet.

Fabricant, Nicole, and Bret Gustafson. 2016. "Revolutionary Extraction? Mapping the Political Economy of Gas, Soy, and Mineral Production in Evo Morales' Bolivia." *NACLA Report on the Americas* 48, no. 3:271–279.

Fabricant, Nicole, and Nancy Postero. 2019. "Performing Indigeneity in Bolivia: The Struggle over the TIPNIS." In *Indigenous Life Projects and Extractivism: Approaches to Social Inequality and Difference,* edited by Cecilie Vindal Ødegaard and Juan Javier Rivera Andía, 245–276. Cham, Switzerland: Palgrave Macmillan.

Fanon, Frantz. 1961. *The Wretched of the Earth.* New York: Grove.

Farmer, Paul. 1996. "On Suffering and Structural Violence: A View from Below." *Daedalus* 125, no. 1:261–2813.

———. 2004. "An Anthropology of Structural Violence." *Current Anthropology* 45, no. 3:305–325.

Farrow, George R. 1914. "Account of a Shor Evangelistic Trip in the Sanapana Country." *SAMS Magazine* 48 (September): 146–148.

Fassin, Didier. 2012. *Humanitarian Reason: A Moral History of the Present.* Berkeley: University of California Press.

Ferguson, James. 1994. *The Anti-Politics Machine. Development, Depoliticization, and Bureaucratic Power in Lesotho*. Cambridge, England: Cambridge University Press.

———. 2012. "Structures of Responsibility." *Ethnography* 13, no. 4:558–562.

Fernández, Analía, and José Braunstein. 2001. "Historias de Pampa del Indio." *IV Congreso Argentino de Americanistas*, no. 2:161–193.

Fifer, J. Valerie. 1976. *Bolivia: Territorio, población y política desde 1825*. Buenos Aires: Francisco de Aguirre.

Figallo, Beatriz J. 2003. "Espacios nacionales y espacios regionales: Conflictos y concertaciones en las fronteras chaqueñas de Argentina, Bolivia y Paraguay." *Anuario de Estudios Americanos* 60, no. 1:183–212.

Fogel, Augusto. 2003. "Una propuesta de reestructuración institucional del INDI." *Población y Desarrollo* 24:36–42.

Fontaine, Guillaume. 2007. *El precio del petróleo: Conflictos socio-ambientales y gobernabilidad en la región Amazónica*. Quito: Facultad Latinoamericana de Ciencias Sociales.

Foster, Robert. 2002. Bargains with Modernity in Papua New Guinea and Elsewhere. *Anthropological Theory* 2, no. 2:233–251.

Franco, Mariana, and Gladys Imaz. 2006. *Angaité Koalhvok: Las voces de un pueblo*. Asunción: Centro de Estudios Antropológicos de la Universidad Católica.

Fritz, Miguel. 2011. *Nunca me voy a olvidar de los ojos: Derechos humanos en el Paraguay, como los viví*. Asunción: ServiLibro.

Furlong Cardiff, Guillermo. 1936. "Cartografía jesuítica sobre el Río de la Plata." Vol. 2, no. 71. Buenos Aires: Instituto de Investigaciones Históricas.

Fuscaldo, Liliana E. 1982. *La relación de propiedad en el proceso del enfrentamiento social: De propiedad comunal directa a propiedad privada burguesa*. Serie Estudios, No. 42. Buenos Aires: Centro de Investigación de Ciencias Sociales.

Fuss, Max, and Juergen Riester. 1983. *Vocabulario español-chiquito y chiquito-español*. Cochabamba, Bolivia: Los Amigos del Libro.

Galeano, Eduardo. 1973. *Open Veins of Latin America*. New York: Monthly Review.

Galtung, Johan. 1969. "Violence, Peace, and Peace Research." *Journal of Peace Research* 6, no. 3:167–191.

Galvão, Rufino E. G. 1875. *Relatório da Repartição dos Negocios Estrangeiros apresentado á Assambléa Geral Legislativa*. Rio de Janeiro: Repartição dos Negocios Estrangeiros.

García Hierro, Pedro, and Alexander Surrallés. 2004. "Introducción." In *Tierra adentro: Territorio indígena y percepción del entorno*, edited by Alexandre Surrallés and Pedro García Hierro, 9–22. Copenhagen: International Work Group for Indigenous Affairs.

Gardner, Benjamin. 2009. "Are Livestock a Troublesome Commodity?" *Geoforum* 40: 781–783.

Garibay, Claudio, Andrew Boni, Francesco Panico, Pedro Urquijo, and Dan Klooster. 2011. "Unequal Partners, Unequal Exchange: Goldcorp, the Mexican State, and Campesino Dispossession at the Peñasquito Goldmine." *Journal of Latin American Geography* 10, no. 2:153–176.

Giannecchini, Doroteo. 1996 [1898]. *Historia natural, etnografía, geografía, lingüística del Chaco Boliviano*. Tarija, Bolivia: Fondo de Inversión Social, Centro Eclesial de Documentación.

Gill, Lesley. 2008. "Power Lines: The Political Context of Nongovernmental Organization (NGO) Activity in El Alto, Bolivia." *Journal of Latin American Anthropology* 2, no. 2:144–169.

Giordano, Mariana. 2004. *Discurso e imagen sobre el indígena chaqueño.* La Plata, Argentina: Al Margen.

Girbal-Blacha, Noemi M. 2010. "El cooperativismo agrario en regiones marginales: Aciertos y fracasos en el Nordeste Argentino (NEA), 1920–1960." *Investigaciones de Historia Económica* 6, no. 17:39–64.

Giudicelli, Cristophe. 2005. "Pacificación y construcción discursiva de la frontera: El poder instituyente de la guerra en los confines del imperio (siglos XVI-XVII)." In *Máscaras, tretas y rodeos del discurso colonial en los Andes,* edited by Bernard Lavallé, 57–176. Lima: Pontificia Universidad Católica del Perú, Instituto Riva-Agüero, and Instituto Francés de Estudios Andinos.

Glassman, Jim. 2006. "Primitive Accumulation, Accumulation by Dispossession, Accumulation by 'Extra-Economic' Means." *Progress in Human Geography* 30, no. 5:608–625.

———. 2009. "The Ongoing (Ir)relevance of Primitive Accumulation." *Human Geography* 2, no. 3:94–97.

Glauser, Marcos. 2009. *Extranjerización del territorio paraguayo.* Asunción: Base Investigaciones Sociales.

———. 2018. "Entendiendo las respuestas de un pueblo indígena a la desposesión territorial." *Gestión y Ambiente* 21, no. 1:86–94.

———. 2019. *Angaite's Responses to Deforestation: Political Ecology of the Livelihood and Land Use Strategies of an Indigenous Community from the Paraguayan Chaco.* Curupira Series, Book 30. Berlin: LIT.

Glauser, Marcos, and Igor Patzi. 2014. *Indígenas en contextos urbanos de la región del Chaco sudamericano.* Asunción: Interkerkelijke Coordinatie Commissie Ontwikkelingssamenwerking (ICCO).

Goldstein, Daniel. 2004. *The Spectacular City: Violence and Performance in Urban Bolivia.* Durham, NC: Duke University Press.

Gómez, Mariana. 2016. *Guerreras y tímidas doncellas del Pilcomayo: Las mujeres qom del oeste de Formosa.* Buenos Aires: Biblos.

Gómez, Mariana, and Silvana Sciortino. 2015. "Mujeres indígenas, derechos colectivos y violencia de género. intervenciones en un debate que inicia." *Entramados y Perspectivas: Revista de la carrera de Sociología* 5, no. 5:37–63.

González, Hebe. 2005. "A Grammar of Tapiete (Tupí-Guaraní)." PhD diss., University of Pittsburgh.

———. 2009. "Una aproximación a la fonología del tapiete (tupí-guaraní)." *Llames* 9:7–43.

———2017. "Ecos del mundo vegetal entre los tapietes de Argentina." *Diccionario etnobotánico,* vol. 64. Muenchen: LINCOM.

Goodale, Mark, and Nancy Postero, eds. 2013. *Neoliberalism, Interrupted: Social Change and Contested Governance in Contemporary Latin America.* Palo Alto, CA: Stanford University Press.

Gordillo, Gastón. 2003. "Shamanic Forms of Resistance in the Argentinean Chaco: A Political Economy." *Journal of Latin American Anthropology* 8, no. 3:104–126.

———. 2004. *Landscapes of Devils: Tensions of Place and Memory in the Argentinean Chaco*. Durham, NC: Duke University Press.

———. 2006. *En el Gran Chaco: Antropologías e Historias*. Buenos Aires: Prometeo.

———. 2011. "Longing for Elsewhere: Guaraní Reterritorializations." *Comparative Studies in Society and History* 53, no. 4:855–888.

———. 2014. *Rubble: The Afterlife of Destruction*. Durham, NC: Duke University Press.

Gordillo, Gastón, and Silvia Hirsch. 2011. "La presencia ausente: Invisibilizaciones, políticas estatales y emergencias indígenas en la Argentina." In *Movilizaciones indígenas e identidades en disputa en la Argentina: Historias de invisibilización y re-emergencia*, edited by Gastón Gordillo and Silvia Hirsch, 15–39. Buenos Aires: La Crujía.

Grant, Suzanne. 2006. "Becoming Similar: Knowledge, Sociality, and the Aesthetics of Relatedness amongst the Nivaclé of the Paraguayan Chaco." PhD diss., University of St. Andrews.

Greene, Shane. 2009. *Customizing Indigeneity: Paths to a Visionary Politics in Peru*. Palo Alto, CA: Stanford University Press.

Greenpeace. 2006. "Desmontes S.A. Quiénes están detrás de la destrucción de los últimos bosques nativos de la Argentina, parte 1." Buenos Aires: Greenpeace. https://www.greenpeace.org/archive-argentina/es/informes/desmontes-s-a/.

Grubb, W. Barbrooke. 1914. *A Church in the Wilds: The Remarkable Story of the Establishment of the South American Mission amongst the Hitherto Savage and Intractable Natives of the Paraguayan Chaco*. Edited by H. T. M. Jones. London: Seeley, Service.

———. 1993 [1911]. *Un pueblo desconocido en tierra desconocida. un relato de la vida y las costumbres de los indígenas lengua del Chaco Paraguayo, con aventuras y experiencias de veinte años de trabajo pionero y exploratorio entre ellos*. Asunción: Iglesia Anglicana Paraguaya and Centro de Estudios Antropológicos de la Universidad Católica.

Gupta, Akhil. 2013. *Red Tape: Bureaucracy, Structural Violence, and Poverty in India*. Durham, NC: Duke University Press.

Gustafson, Bret. 1995. *Ñee: Introducción al estudio lingüístico del idioma guaraní, para guaraní hablantes*. La Paz: UN Children's Fund and Agencia Global para la Paz.

———. 2009. *New Languages of the State: Indigenous Resurgence and the Politics of Knowledge in Bolivia*. Durham, NC: Duke University Press.

———. 2014. *Guaraní: Lenguas de Bolivia*. Edited by Milly Crevels. Nijmegen, Netherlands: University of Nijmegen.

Gutiérrez, Marín, and Rosario Rodríguez. 1999. *Situación del territorio indígena weenhayek y sus actores*. Report. Tarija, Bolivia: Centro de Estudios Regionales para el Desarrollo de Tarija.

Guy, Donna, and Thomas E. Sheridan. 1998. *Contested Ground: Comparative Frontiers on the Northern and Southern Edges of the Spanish Empire*. Tucson: University of Arizona Press.

Guyra Paraguay. 2018. Executive summary, *Informe de deforestación Junio 2018*. http://guyra.org.py/informe-de-deforestacion-2018/.

Haesbaert, Rogério. 2013. "Del mito de la desterritorialización a la multiterritorialidad." *Cultura y Representaciones Sociales* 8, no. 15:9–42.

Hald, Margrethe. 1962. *An Unfinished Tubular Fabric From the Chiriguano Indians, Bolivia*. Stockholm: Ethnographical Museum of Sweden.

Hale, Charles. 2004. "Rethinking Indigenous Politics in the Era of the 'Indio Permitido.'" *NACLA Report on the Americas* 38, no. 2:16–21.

———. 2008. "Neoliberal Multiculturalism: The Remaking of Cultural Rights and Racial Dominance in Central America." *PoLAR Political and Legal Anthropology Review* 28, no. 1:10–28.

Hall, Ruth, Marc Edelman, Saturnino M. Borras, Ian Scoones, Ben White, and Wendy Wolford. 2015. "Resistance, Acquiescence, or Incorporation? An Introduction to Land Grabbing and Political Reactions 'from Below.'" *Journal of Peasant Studies* 42:467–488.

Hannah, Matthew G. 2002. *Governmentality and the Mastery of Territory in Nineteenth-Century America*. Cambridge, England: Cambridge University Press.

Harder Horst, René. 2003. "Consciousness and Contradiction: Indigenous People and Paraguay's Transition to Democracy." In *Contemporary Indigenous Movements in Latin America*, edited by Eric Langer and Elana Muñoz, 103–132. Wilmington, DE: Scholarly Resources.

———. 2004. "Breaking Down Religious Barriers: Indigenous Peoples and Christian Churches in Paraguay." In *Resurgent Voices in Latin America Indigenous Peoples, Political Mobilization and Religious Change*, edited by E. Clearly and T. J. Steigenga, 65–92. New Brunswick, NJ: Rutgers University Press.

———. 2007. *The Stroessner Regime and Indigenous Resistance in Paraguay*. Gainesville: University Press of Florida.

Harris, Olivia, 1995. "Ethnic Identity and Market Relations: Indians and Mestizos in the Andes." In *Ethnicity, Markets, and Migration in the Andes: At the Crossroads of History and Anthropology*, edited by Brooke Larson and Olivia Harris, 21–40. Durham, NC: Duke University Press.

Hart, Gillian. 2006. "Denaturalizing Dispossession: Critical Ethnography in the Age of Resurgent Imperialism." *Antipode* 38:977–1004.

Harvey, David. 2003. *The New Imperialism*. Oxford, England: Oxford University Press.

———. 2006. "Neo Liberalism as Creative Destruction." *Geografiska Annaler: Series B, Human Geography* 88, no. 2:145–158.

———. 2007. *A Brief History of Neoliberalism*. Oxford, England: Oxford University Press.

Harvey, Penelope. 2014. "Infrastructures of the Frontier in Latin America." *Journal of Latin American and Caribbean Anthropology* 19, no. 2:280–283.

Harvey, Penelope, and Hannah Knox. 2015. *Roads: An Anthropology of Infrastructure and Expertise*. Ithaca, NY: Cornell University.

Hecht, Susana B. 1985. "Environment, Development, and Politics: Capital Accumulation and the Livestock Sector in Eastern Amazonia." *World Development* 13, no. 6:663–684.

Heckenberger, Michael. 2002. "Rethinking the Arawakan Diaspora: Hierarchy, Regionality, and the Amazonian Formative." In *Comparative Arawakan Histories: Rethinking Language Family and Culture Area in Amazonia*, edited by Jonathan Hill and Fernando Santos-Granero, 99–122. Urbana-Champagne: University of Illinois Press.

Hermitte, Esther. 1995. *Estudio sobre la situación de los aborígenes de la provincia del*

Chaco y políticas para su integración a la sociedad nacional. Vol. 3. Edited by Alejandro Isla. Posadas, Argentina: Editorial Universidad Nacional de Misiones.

Hertz, Robert. 1960 [1909]. *Death and the Right Hand.* Translation by R. N. Needham. Aberdeen, Scotland: University Press Aberdeen.

Hetherington, Kregg. 2014. "Waiting for the Surveyor: Development Promises and the Temporality of Infrastructure." *Journal of Latin American and Caribbean Anthropology* 19, no. 2:195–211.

———. 2019. "Keywords for the Anthropocene." In *Infrastructure, Environment, and Life in the Anthropocene,* edited by Kregg Hetherington, 1–16. Durham, NC: Duke University Press.

Hetherington, Kregg, and Jeremy M. Campbell. 2014. "Nature, Infrastructure and the State: Rethinking Development in Latin America." *Journal of Latin American and Caribbean Anthropology,* 19, no. 2:191–194.

Hirsch, Silvia. 2000. "Misión, nación y región entre los chiriguanos de Argentina: Procesos de integración y de re-etnización en zonas de frontera." In *Fronteras, naciones e identidades: La periferia como centro,* edited by Alejandro Grimson, 278–298. Buenos Aires: CICCUS.

———. 2003. "The Emergence of Political Organizations among the Guaraní Indians of Bolivia and Argentina: A Comparative Perspective." In *Contemporary Indigenous Movements in Latin America,* edited by Erick Langer and Elana Muñoz, 81–102. Wilmington, DE: Scholarly Resources.

———. 2006a. *El pueblo tapiete de Argentina: Historia y cultura.* Buenos Aires: Universidad de Buenos Aires.

———. 2006b. "¿Aborigen, tapiete o tapii? Procesos de construcción de la identidad Tapiete en Argentina." In *Definiciones étnicas, organización social y estrategias políticas en la chiquitanía y el Chaco,* edited by Isabelle Combès, 181–188.

———. 2014. "Mujeres guaraníes, vínculos transnacionales e identidades en la frontera argentino-boliviana." *Transfronteras: Las fronteras del mundo y procesos culturales,* edited by José Manuel Valenzuela Arce. Tijuana, Mexico: Colegio de la Frontera Norte.

———. 2015. "Familias interétnicas y fronteras étnicas entre los tapiete de Argentina." Paper presented at "Tierras Bajas, II Jornadas de Antropología, Historia y Arqueología." Museo de Historia de la Universidad Autónoma Gabriel René Moreno, Santa Cruz de la Sierra, October 14–16.

Hirsch, Silvia, Hebe González, and Florencia Ciccone. 2019. "Los tapietes y guaraníes ñandeva del Gran Chaco." Reseña bibliográfica. *Suplemento Antropológico* 54, no. 1:9–32.

Hirsch, Silvia, and Mariana Lorenzetti. 2016. *Salud pública y pueblos indígenas en la Argentina: Encuentros, tensiones e interculturalidad.* Buenos Aires: Universidad de San Martín.

Hirsch, Silvia, and Adriana Serrudo. 2010. *Educación intercultural bilingüe en Argentina: Identidades, lenguas y protagonistas.* Buenos Aires: Novedades Educativas.

hooks, bell. 1984. *Feminist Theory from the Margin to the Center.* Boston: South End.

———. 1990. "Marginality as Site of Resistance." In *Out There: Marginalization and Con-*

temporary Cultures, edited by Russell Ferguson, Martha Gover, Trinh T. Min-ha, and Cornel West. 341–343. New York: Massachusetts Institute of Technology.

Hornborg, Alf. 2005. "Ethnogenesis, Regional Integration, and Ecology in Prehistoric Amazonia: Toward a System Perspective." *Current Anthropology* 46, no. 4:589–620.

Horst, Willis. 2001. "Spirituality of the Toba/Qom Christians of the Argentine Chaco." *Missiology: An International Review* 29, no. 2:166–184.

Horst, Willis, Ute Mueller Eckhardt, and Frank Paul. 2009. *Misión sin conquista: Acompañamiento de comunidades indígenas autóctonas como práctica misionera alternativa*. Buenos Aires: Kairós.

Howe, James. 2009. *Chiefs, Scribes, and Ethnographers: Kuna Culture from Inside and Out*. Austin: University of Texas Press.

Hugh-Jones, Stephen. 1994. "Shamans, Prophets, Priests, and Pastors." In *Shamanism, History, and the State*, edited by Caroline Humphrey and N. Thomas, 32–75. Ann Arbor: University of Michigan Press.

Humphreys Bebbington, Denise, and Anthony Bebbington. 2010. "Extracción, territorio e inequidades: El gas en el Chaco Boliviano." *Umbrales* 20:127–160.

Hunt, Richard J. 1932. *The Livingstone of South America: The Life and Adventures of W. Barbrooke Grubb among the Wild Tribes of the Gran Chaco in Paraguay, Bolivia, Argentina, the Falkland Islands, and Tierra del Fuego*. London: Seeley, Service.

IACHR (Inter-American Court of Human Rights). 2005. *Case of Yakye Axa Indigenous Community v. Paraguay: Judgment of June 17, 2005 (Merits, Reparations and Costs)*. http://www.corteidh.or.cr/docs/casos/articulos/seriec_125_ing.pdf.

———. 2006. *Case of the Sawhoyamaxa Indigenous Community v. Paraguay: Judgment of March 29, 2006 (Merits, Reparations, and Costs)*. http://www.corteidh.or.cr/docs/casos/articulos/seriec_146_ing.pdf.

———. 2010. *Case of the Xákmok Kásek Indigenous Community v. Paraguay: Judgment of August 24, 2010 (Merits, Reparations, and Costs)*. http://www.corteidh.or.cr/docs/casos/articulos/seriec_214_ing.pdf.

Ingold, Tim. 2010. *The Perception of the Environment: Essays on Livelihood, Dwelling, and Skill*. London: Routledge.

IWGIA (International Work Group for Indigenous Affairs). 2009. *El caso ayoreo*. Informe IGWIA 4. Asunción: IWGIA, Unión de Nativos Ayoreo de Paraguay, and Iniciativa Amotocodie.

Jackson, Jean. 2019. *Managing Multiculturalism: Indigeneity and the Struggle for Rights in Colombia*. Palo Alto, CA: Stanford University Press.

Jensen, Cheryl. 1999. "Tupí-Guaraní." In *The Amazonian Languages*, edited by R. M. W. Dixon and A. Aikhenvald, 125–164. Cambridge, England: Cambridge University Press.

Johnson, Jean Dye. 1988. *God Planted Five Seeds*. Sanford, FL: New Tribes Mission.

Jolis, Giuseppe. 1789. *Saggio sulla Storia Naturale della provincia del Gran Chaco: E sulle pratiche e su' costumi dei populi che l'abitano insieme con tre giornali*. Faenza, Italy: Lodovico Genestri.

Joy, Juan Carlos. 1992. *Los fortines de la guerra: Toponimia chaqueña*. Asunción: Estudio Gráfico.

Julien, Catherine. 2006. "Descripción de la población del oriente boliviano en el siglo

XVI." In *Definiciones étnicas, organización social y estrategias políticas en el Chaco y la Chiquitanía*, edited by Isabelle Combès, 49–67.

Kalisch, Hannes. 2010. "Nengelaasekhammalhkoo: La Paz 'enlhet' y su reciente reconfiguración." *Suplemento Antropológico* 65:343–392.

———. 2011. "Nengelaasekhammalhkoo: An Enlhet Perspective." In *The Palgrave International Handbook of Peace Studies: A Cultural Perspective*, edited by Wolfgang Dietrich, Josefina Echavarría Álvarez, Gustavo Esteva, Daniela Ingruber, and Norbert Koppensteiner, 387–414. London: Palgrave McMillan.

———. 2012. "Lectura de las fiestas enlhet." In *La belleza de los otros*, edited by Ticio Escobar, 349–465. Asunción: ServiLibro.

———. 2018a. "Observaciones." In *¡No llores! La historia enlhet de la Guerra del Chaco*, edited by Hannes Kalisch and Ernesto Unruh, 141–193.

———. 2018b. "Los relatos enlhet y el Paraguay." In *¡No llores! La historia enlhet de la Guerra del Chaco*, edited by Hannes Kalisch and Ernesto Unruh, 195–282.

———. 2018c. "Espacio, memoria y los discursos que los engloban. marcar el espacio propio entre los enlhet del Chaco." *A Contracorriente: Una Revista de Estudios Latinoamericanos* 15, no. 2:167–192.

Kalisch, Hannes, and Ernesto Unruh. 2003. "Enlhet-enenlhet: Una familia lingüística chaqueña." *Thule: Rivista Italiana di Studi Americanistici* 14/15:207–231.

———, eds. 2014. *Wie Schön ist deine Stimme. Berichte der Enlhet in Paraguay zu ihrer Geschichte*. Asunción: Centro de Artes Visuales Museo del Barro.

———, eds. 2018. *¡No llores! La historia enlhet de la Guerra del Chaco*. Asunción: ServiLibro and Centro de Artes Visuales Museo del Barro.

Kam'aatkok Ketsek. 2018. "Los hombres de arriba." In *¡No llores! La historia enlhet de la Guerra del Chaco*, edited by Hannes Kalisch and Ernesto Unruh, 117–119.

Kasmir, Sharryn, and August Carbonella. 2008. "Dispossession and the Anthropology of Labor." *Critique of Anthropology* 28:5–25.

Keane, Webb. 2007. *Christian Moderns: Freedom and Fetish in the Mission Encounter*. Berkeley: University of California Press.

Khotari, Uma. 2005. *A Radical History of Development Studies: Individuals, Institutions, and Ideologies*. London: Zed.

Kidd, Stephen William. 1992. "Religious Change: A Case-Study Amongst the Enxet of the Paraguayan Chaco." PhD diss., Durham University.

———. 1995. "Land, Politics, and Benevolent Shamanism: The Enxet Indians in a Democratic Paraguay." *Journal of Latin American Studies* 27, no. 1:45–73.

———. 1999a. "The Power of the Lord: The Transformation of Anglican Missionaries into Indigenous Leaders." Paper presented at the Society for Latin American Studies Annual Conference, University of Cambridge.

———. 1999b. "Love and Hate among the People without Things: The Social and Economic Relations of the Enxet People of Paraguay." PhD diss., University of St. Andrews.

Kirsch, Stuart. 2006. *Reverse Anthropology: Indigenous Analysis of Social and Environmental Relations in New Guinea*, Stanford, CA: Stanford University Press.

Klassen, Pamela. 2011. *Spirits of Protestantism. Medicine, Healing, and Liberal Christianity*. Berkeley: University of California Press.

Klassen, Peter P. 2002. *Mennonites in Paraguay*. Vol. 2: *Encounter with Indians and Para-guayans*. 2nd edition. Translation by Gunther Schmitt. Kitchener, Canada: Pandora.

———. 2004. *Mennonites in Paraguay*. Vol. 1: *Kingdom of God and Kingdom of This World*. 2nd edition. Translation by Gunther Schmitt. Hillsboro, OR: Print Source Direct.

Kleinpenning, Jan M. G. 2003. *Rural Paraguay 1870–1963: A Geography of Progress, Plun-der, and Poverty*. Madrid: Iboamericana Vervuert.

Knauft, Bruce, ed. 2002. *Critically Modern: Alternatives, Alterities, Anthropologies*. Bloomington: Indiana University Press.

Korf, Benedikt, and Timothy Raeymaekers. 2013. "Introduction: Border, Frontier, and the Geography of Rule at the Margins of the State." In *Violence on the Margins*, edited by Benedikt Korf and Timothy Raeymaekers, 3–27. New York: Palgrave.

Krebs, Edgardo, and José Braunstein. 2011. "The Renewal of Gran Chaco Studies." *History of Anthropology Newsletter* 38, no. 1:9–19.

Lagos, Marcelo, and Ana Teruel. 1991. "Conformación del ingenio-plantación en el ám-bito regional." *Cuadernos de Humanidades* 4:131–138.

Langer, Erick L. 1987. "Franciscan Missions and Chiriguano Workers: Colonization, Ac-culturation, and Indian Labor in Southeastern Bolivia." *The Americas* 63, no. 3:305–322.

———. 2009. *Expecting Pears from an Elm Tree: Franciscan Missions on the Chiriguano Frontier in the Heart of South America, 1830–1949*. Durham, NC: Duke University Press.

Lapegna, Pablo. 2016. *Soybeans and Power: Genetically Modified Crops, Environmental Politics, and Social Movements in Argentina*. Oxford, England: Oxford University Press.

Laqueur, Thomas. 1987. "Bodies, Details, and the Humanitarian Narrative." In *The New Cultural History*, edited by Lynn Hunt, 176–204. Berkeley: University of California Press.

Larkin, Brian. 2013. "The Politics and Poetics of Infrastructure." *Annual Review of An-thropology* 42:327–343.

Leake, Andrew Paul. 1998. "Subsistence and Land-Use amongst Resettled Indigenous People in the Paraguayan Chaco: A Participatory Approach." PhD diss., University of Hertfordshire.

Lebowitz, Michel A. 1982. "The One-sidedness of Capital." *Review of Radical Political Economics* 14, no. 4:40–51.

———. 1997. "The Silences of Capital." *Historical Materialism* 1, no. 1:134–145.

———. 2003. *Beyond Capital*. London: Palgrave Macmillan.

———. 2007. "The Politics of Beyond Capital." *Historical Materialism* 14, no. 4:167–183.

Lefebvre, Henri. 2009. *State, Space, World: Selected Essays by Henri Lefebvre*. Edited by Neil Brenner and Stuart Elden. Minneapolis: University of Minnesota Press.

Leguizamón, Amalia. 2016. "Environmental Injustice in Argentina: struggles against Ge-netically Modified Soy." *Journal of Agrarian Change* 16, no. 4:684–692.

Lenton, Diana. 2005. "De centauros a protegidos: La construcción del sujeto de la políti-ca indigenista argentina desde los debates parlamentarios (1880–1970)." PhD diss., University of Buenos Aires.

Leone, Miguel 2016. "De 'pueblo pobre' a "pueblo indígena': 'Pastoral aborigen' y saberes antropológicos en la región chaqueña argentina 1970–1985." *Quinto Sol* 20, no. 3:1–23.

Leone, Miguel, and Crístian Vázquez. 2016. "La pastoral rural en formosa y el surgimiento de una pastoral aborigen (c. 1960–1980)." *Itinerantes: Revista de Historia y Religión* 6:89–114

Le Polain de Waroux, Yann, Matthias Baumann, Nestor Ignacio Gasparri, Gregorio Gavier Pizarro, Javier Godar, Tobias Kuemmerle, et al. 2018. "Rents, Actors, and the Expansion of Commodity Frontiers in the Gran Chaco." *Annals of the American Association of Geographers* 108, no. 1:204–225.

Lévi-Strauss, Claude. 1963 [1958]. *Structural Anthropology*. New York: Basic Books.

Levien, Michael. 2011. "Special Economic Zones and Accumulation by Dispossession in India." *Journal of Agrarian Change* 11, no. 4:454–483.

———. 2013. "Regimes of Dispossession: Special Economic Zones and the Political Economy of land in India." *UC Berkeley*. http://escholarship.org/uc/item/4t30m658.

———. 2015. "From Primitive Accumulation to Regimes of Dispossession: Six Theses on India's Land Question." *Economic and Political Weekly* 50, no. 22:146–157.

Levine, Phillipa. 2002. *Prostitution, Race, and Politics*. New York: Routledge.

Li, Tania M. 2000. "Articulating Indigenous Identity in Indonesia: Resource Politics and the Tribal Slot." *Comparative Studies in Society and History* 42, no. 1:149–179.

———. 2010a. "To Make Live or Let Die? Rural Dispossession and the Protection of Surplus Populations." *Antipode* 41, no. 1:66–93.

———. 2010b. "Indigeneity, Capitalism, and the Management of Dispossession." *Current Anthropology* 51, no. 3:385–414.

———. 2014. *Land's End: Capitalist Relations on an Indigenous Frontier*. Durham, NC: Duke University Press.

———. 2018. "After the Land Grab: Infrastructural Violence and the 'Mafia System' in Indonesia's' Oil Palm Plantation Zones." *Geoforum* 96:328–337.

Lida, Miranda. 2012. "Catolicismo y sensibilidad anti burguesa: La Iglesia Católica en una era de desarrollo, 1955–1965." *Quinto Sol* 16, no. 2:1–20.

Lista, Ramón. 1881. "El Gran Chaco." *Boletín de la Sociedad Geográfica Argentina* 1, no. 1:4–31.

Lizárraga, F. Reginaldo de. 1987 [ca. 1600]. *Descripción del Perú, Tucumán, Río de la Plata y Chile*. Madrid: Dastin.

Loewen, Jacob. 1967. "Lengua Festivals and Functional Substitutes." *Practical Anthropology* 14, no. 1:15–36.

López, Alejandro M. 2009. "La Virgen, el Árbol y la Serpiente: Cielos e identidades en las comunidades mocovíes del Chaco." PhD diss., Universidad de Buenos Aires.

———. 2017. "Cerrando filas: La mirada menonita sobre los vínculos entre las misiones protestantes en el chaco durante el auge de la 'Nación Católica' (1943–1949)." In *Los evangelios chaqueños: Misiones y estrategias indígenas en el siglo XX*, edited by César Ceriani Cernadas, 41–69. Buenos Aires: Rumbo Sur.

Loukotka, Cestmir. 1968. *Classification of South American Indian Languages*. Los Angeles: UCLA Latin American Center.

Lowrey, Kathleen, 2006. "Bolivia Multiétnico y Pluricultural, Ten Years Later." *Latin American and Caribbean Ethnic Studies* 1, no. 1:63–84.

Ludueña, Gustavo. 2009. "La cultura católica en la imaginación política de las iglesias latinoamericanas." In *Religiones y culturas: Perspectivas latinoamericanas*, edited by Carlos Steil, Eloisa Martín, and Marcelo Camurça, 115–154. Buenos Aires: Biblos.

Lunt, Robert. 2011. *Cien años de la misión anglicana en el Norte Argentino 1911–2011*. Formosa, Argentina: Edición Diócesis de la Iglesia Anglicana en el Norte Argentino.

Maangvayaam'ay'. 2015. Biblioteca de la Memoria Hablada. https://enlhet.org/audio.

Mamani, Walter. 2005. *Estudio sobre impactos socio-ambientales en el territorio ween-hayek y áreas de influencia*. Tarija, Bolivia: Centro de Estudios Regionales para el Desarrollo de Tarija.

Mamonova, Natalia. 2015. "Resistance or Adaptation? Ukrainian Peasants' Responses to Large-scale Land Acquisitions." *Journal of Peasant Studies* 42, no. 3–4:607–634.

Marban, Pedro. 1894 [1701]. *Arte de la Lengua Moxa con su Vocabulario y Catecismo*. Leipzig, Germany: B. G. Teubner.

Martínez, José, and Ely Zulma Villegas. 2005. "Organizaciones indígenas y transnacionales en Bolivia: Las certezas de un futuro predefinido." In *Movimientos indígenas y estado en Bolivia*, edited by Luis Enrique López and Pablo Regalsky, 189–226. La Paz: Plural.

Martínez, P. Diego. 1944 [1601]. *Relación del P. Diego Martínez*. In *Historia general de la Compañía de Jesús en la provincia del Perú, Crónica Anónima de 1600 que Trata del Establecimiento y Misiones de la Compañía de Jesús en los Países de Habla Española en la América Meridional*, vol. 2, edited by F. Mateos, 497–503. Madrid: Consejo Superior de Investigaciones Científicas.

Martínez de Irala, Domingo. 1555. "Carta de Domingo Martínez de Irala al Consejo de Indias, Refiriendo sus Entradas y Descubrimientos por el Río Paraguay hasta el Perú y lo Ocurrido en Aquellas Expediciones y en los Asientos del Río de la Plata." In *Historia y descubrimiento del Río de la Plata y Paraguay*, edited by Mariano Pellizi, 125–133. Buenos Aires: Mayo.

Martínez Sarasola, Carlos. 1992. *Nuestros paisanos los indios: Vida, historia y destino de las comunidades indígenas en la Argentina*. Buenos Aires: Emecé.

Martins Ladeira, Maria Elisa. 2001. "Língua e história: Análise sociolingüística em um grupo terena." PhD diss., Universidade de São Paulo.

Marx, Karl. 1990 [1867]. *Capital*. Vol. 1. London: Penguin Classics.

Mason, John A. 1946. "The Languages of South America." In *Handbook of South American Indians: Bureau of American Ethnology*, edited by Frank Steward, 157–218. Bulletin 143, vol. 2. Washington, DC: Smithsonian Institution.

Matienzo, Juan de. 1566. "Carta del Licenciado Juan de Matienzo, en la que Señala los Lugares donde se Podría Levantar un Puerto en la Mar del Norte para Comunicarse Directamente con España." In *Documentos históricos y geográficos relativos a la conquista colonización rioplatense*, edited by José Torre Revello, 106–113. Buenos Aires: Jacobo Peuser.

Mbembe, Achille. 2003. "Necropolitics." *Public Culture* 15, no. 1:11–40.

McQuown, Norman A. 1955. "The Indigenous Languages of Latin America." *American Anthropologist* 57, no. 3:501–570.

Meador, Melinda, and Maria Julia Balbi. 2019. *Livestock and Products Annual 2019*. GAIN Report. Washington, DC: USDA Foreign Agricultural Services.

Medina, Javier, ed. 2002. *Ñande Reko. La comprensión guaraní de la vida Buena.* La Paz: GTZ.

Meliá, Bartomeu. 1995. *Elogio de la lengua guaraní.* Asunción: Centro de Estudios Paraguayos Antonio Guash.

Merlan, Francesca. 2009. "Indigeneity: Global and Local." *Current Anthropology* 50, no. 3:303–333.

Métraux, Alfred. 1933. "La obra de las misiones inglesas en el Chaco." *Journal de la Société des Américanistes* 25, no. 1:205–209.

———. 1946. "Ethnography of the Chaco." In *Handbook of South American Indians*, edited by Julian Steward, 197–370. Washington, DC: Smithsonian Institution.

Metz, Rosmarie, and Georg Wessling. 2006. *Atlas del Gran Chaco Sudamericano: Educación y capacitación para el desarrollo sostenible del Chaco Sudamericano.* Asunción: GTZ.

Miller, Elmer. 1970. "The Christian Missionary: Agent of Secularization." *Anthropological Quarterly* 43, no. 1:14–22.

———. 1975. "Shamans, Power Symbols, and Change in Argentine Toba Culture." *American Ethnologist* 2, no. 3:477–496.

———. 1979. *Los tobas argentinos: Armonía y disonancia en una sociedad.* Buenos Aires: Siglo XXI.

———. 1995. *Nurturing Doubt: From Mennonite Missionary to Anthropologist in the Argentine Chaco.* Urbana: University of Illinois Press.

———. 1999. *Peoples of the Gran Chaco.* London: Bergin and Garvey.

———. 2002. "Mennonite Chaco Mission, Iglesia Evangélica Unida, and Argentina's Nation-State." *Missiology: An International Review* 30, no. 3:347–360.

Miller, Elmer, and Hilario Wynarczyk. 1988. *Religiosidad y cultura toba. El encuentro de dos cosmos y la problemática de los proyectos de desarrollo.* Buenos Aires: Agencias de Noticias Prensa Ecuménica.

Mingo de la Concepción, Manuel. 1981 [1799]. *Historia de las misiones franciscanas de Tarija entre chiriguanos.* Vol. 2. Tarija, Bolivia: Universidad Boliviana Juan Misael Saracho.

———. 1996 [1791]. *Historia de las misiones franciscanas de tarija entre chiriguanos.* Vol. 1. Tarija, Bolivia: Universidad Juan Misael Saracho.

Mintz, Sidney. 1985. *Sweetness and Power: The Place of Sugar in Modern History.* New York: Penguin.

Mitchell, Timothy. 2002. *Rule of Experts: Egypt, Techno-Politics, Modernity.* Berkeley: University of California Press.

Mölle, Alois. 2008. "Religión, desarrollo y cooperación: Un ensayo teórico y metodológico." *Teoría y Praxis* 13:5–24.

Montagne, Víctor. 1941. "Una maravillosa comarca salteña." *Revista Geográfica Americana* 96:137–148.

Montani, Rodrigo. 2015. "El ingenio como superartefacto. Notas para una etnografía histórica de la cultural material wichí." In *Capitalismo en las selvas*, edited by Lorena Córdoba, Federico Bossert, and Nicolás Richard, 19–44.

Moreton-Robinson, Aileen. 2015. *The White Possessive: Property, Power, and Indigenous Sovereignty.* Minneapolis: University of Minnesota Press.

Morin, Françoise, and Roberto Santana. 2003. "Globalización, transnacionalización y pueblos autóctonos." In *Lo transnacional: Instrumento y desafío para los pueblos indígenas*, edited by Françoise Morin and Roberto Santana, 7–23. Quito: Abya-Yala.

Morínigo, José. 2006. *Puerto Casado: Verbo e imagen de la dignidad*. Asunción: Fondo Nacional de la Cultura y las Artes.

Morrel i Torra, Pere. 2013. "Autonomía guaraní charagua iyambae: Etnografía de una autonomía indígena en construcción." Master's thesis, University of Barcelona.

Muehlmann, Shaylih. 2019. "Clandestine Infrastructures: Illicit Connectivities in the US-Mexico Borderlands." In *Infrastructure, Environment, and Life in the Anthropocene*, edited by Kregg Hetherington, 45–65. Durham, NC: Duke University Press.

Mueller Eckhardt, Ute, and Frank Paul. 2009. "Caminando como misioneros-huéspedes en el Chaco Argentino." In *Misión sin conquista: Acompañamiento de comunidades indígenas autóctonas como práctica misionera alternativa*, edited by Willis Horst, Ute Mueller Eckhardt, and Frank Paul, 65–185. Buenos Aires: Kairós.

Mujía, Ricardo, ed. 1914. *Bolivia-Paraguay: Exposición de los títulos que consagran el derecho territorial de Bolivia, sobre la zona comprendida entre los Ríos Pilcomayo y Paraguay*. La Paz: El Tiempo.

Murton, Galen. 2017. "Border Corridors: Mobility, Containment, and Infrastructures of Development between Nepal and China." PhD diss., University of Colorado Boulder.

Negi, Rohit, and Marc Auerbach. 2009. "The Contemporary Significance of Primitive Accumulation." *Historical Materialism* 14, no. 4:157–166.

Newell, Peter. 2009. "Bio-Hegemony: The Political Economy of Agricultural Biotechnology in Argentina." *Journal of Latin American Studies* 41, no. 1:27–57.

Nielssen, Hilde, Inger Marie Okkenhaug, and Karina Hestad Skeie. 2011. *Protestant Missions and Local Encounters in the Nineteenth and Twentieth Centuries*. Studies in Christian Mission, vol. 40. Leiden, Netherlands: Brill.

Nilsen, Alf G. 2010. *Dispossession and Resistance in India: The River and the Rage*. New York: Taylor and Francis.

———. 2012. "Adivasis in and against the State: Subaltern Politics and State Power in Contemporary India." *Critical Asian Studies* 44, no. 2:251–282.

Nilsen, Alf G., and Laurence Cox. 2013. "What Would a Marxist Theory of Social Movements Look Like?" In *Marxism and Social Movements*, edited by Colin Barker, Laurence Cox, John Krinsky, and Alf Gunvald Nilsen, 63–81. Boston: Brill.

Nino, Bernardino de. 1912. *Etnografía chiriguana*. La Paz: Ismael Argote.

Nordenskiöld, Erland. 1910a. "Exploration ethnographique et archéologique en Bolivie (1908-1909)." *La Géographie: Bulletin de la Société de Géographie* 22, no. 2:97–104.

———. 1910b. *Indianlif i el Gran Chaco (Syd-Amerika)*. Stockholm: Albert Bonners Förlag.

———. 1917. "The Guaraní Invasion of the Inca Empire in the Sixteenth Century: An Historical Indian Migration." *Geographical Review* 4, no. 2:103–121.

———. 1922. *Comparative Ethnographical Studies 5: Deductions Suggested by the Geographical Distribution of Some Post-Columbian Words Used by the Indians of South America*. Gothenburg, Sweden: Elanders Boktryckerei Aktiebolag.

———. 2002 [1912]. *La vida de los indios: El Gran Chaco (Sudamérica)*. Santa Cruz de la Sierra: Apoyo para el Campesino–Indígena del Oriente Boliviano.

OAS (Organization of American States). 2019. *Electoral Integrity Analysis, General Elections in the Plurinational State of Bolivia, October 20, 2019: Preliminary Findings Report to the General Secretariat.* http://www.oas.org/documents/eng/press/Electoral-Integrity-Analysis-Bolivia2019.pdf.

Oberg, Kalervo. 1949. *The Terena and the Caduveo of Southern Mato Grosso, Brazil.* Smithsonian Institution Institute of Social Anthropology Publication No. 9. Washington, DC: Smithsonian Institution.

Occhipinti, Laurie. 2003. "Mujeres como madres, mujeres como agricultoras: Imágenes, discursos y proyectos de desarrollo." *Ecuador Debate* 59:123–126.

———. 2005. *Acting on Faith: Religious Development Organizations in Northwestern Argentina.* New York: Lexington.

———. 2011. "Liberating Development: Religious Transformations of Developmental Discourse." *Anthro-at-Large* 17, no. 1:4–5, 8–11.

O'Faircheallaigh, Ciaran, and Saleem Ali, eds. 2008. *Earth Matters: Indigenous Peoples, Extractive Industries and Corporate Social Responsibility.* Sheffield, England: Greenleaf.

Ong, Aihwa. 1996. "Cultural Citizenship as Subject Making: Immigrants Negotiate Racial and Cultural and Boundaries in the United States." *Current Anthropology* 37, no. 5:737–762.

Ortiz, Edgar. 1986. *Los mataco noctenes de Bolivia.* La Paz: Los Amigos del Libro.

Ott, Willis, and Rebecca Burke de Ott. 1983. *Diccionario ignaciano y castellano con apuntes gramaticales.* Cochabamba: Summer Institute of Linguistics.

Palavecino, Enrique. 1930. "Observaciones etnográficas y lingüísticas de los indios tapiete." *Revista de la Sociedad Amigos de la Arqueología* 4:211–217.

———. 1959/1960. "Algunas notas sobre la transculturación del indio chaqueño." *Runa* 9:379–389.

Palmer, John H. 2005. *La buena voluntad wichí: Una espiritualidad indígena.* Buenos Aires: Asociación para la Promoción de la Cultura y el Desarrollo, Centro de Capacitación Zonal, EPRAZOL, and FUNDAPAZ.

Paraguay, DGEEC (Dirección General de Encuestas, Estadísticas y Censo). 2003. *II censo nacional indígena de población y viviendas 2002: Pueblos indígenas del Paraguay, resultados finales.* Asunción: DGEEC.

———. 2012. *III Censo de comunidades de los pueblos indígenas, resultados finales 2012.* Fernando de la Mora, Paraguay: DGEEC.

Paraguay, MSPBS (Ministerio de Salud Pública y Bienestar Social). 2010. *Política nacional de salud indígena.* Asunción: MSPBS.

———. 2014. *Primera encuesta nacional de factores de riesgo para enfermedades no transmisibles en población indígena.* Asunción: Dirección General de Estadísticas, Encuestas y Censos.

———. 2019. *Proyecto de fortalecimiento del sector público de salud: Marco de planificación para pueblos indígenas.* Asunción: Dirección Nacional de Salud de los Pueblos Indígenas, MSPBS.

Pastore, Carlos. 2008. *La lucha por la tierra en el Paraguay.* 3rd edition. Asunción: Intercontinental.

Perasso, José Antonio. 1987. *Crónicas de cacerías humanas: La tragedia ayoreo.* Colección Sociología. Asunción: El Lector.

Perreault, Tom. 2006. "From the Guerra del Agua to the Guerra del Gas: Resource Governance, Neoliberalism and Popular Protest in Bolivia." *Antipode* 38, no. 1:150–172.

———. 2008. *Natural Gas, Indigenous Mobilization, and the Bolivian State.* Geneva: UN Research Institute for Social Development.

———. 2015. "Mining, Power, and the Limits of Public Consultation in Bolivia." *Journal of Latin American and Caribbean Anthropology* 20, no. 3:433–451.

Perreault, Thomas, and Patricia Martin. 2005. "Geographies of Neoliberalism in Latin America." *Environment and Planning A: Economy and Space* 37, no. 2:191–201.

Petras, James, and Henry Veltmeyer. 2016. *What's Left in Latin America? Regime Change in New Times.* London: Routledge.

Pierce, Joseph, Deborah G. Martin, and James T. Murphy. 2011. "Relational Place-Making: The Networked Politics of Place." *Transactions of the Institute of British Geographers* 36, 1, 54–70.

Pifarré, Francisco, 1989. *Los guaraní-chiriguano.* Vol. 2: *Historia de un pueblo.* La Paz: Centro de Investigación y Promoción del Campesinado.

Polo de Ondegardo, Juan. 1914 [1574]. "Informe Sobre el Origen de los Chiriguanaes y Regiones que han Dominado y Sometido entre el Paraguay y la Cordillera." In *Bolivia-Paraguay: Exposición de los títulos que consagran el derecho territorial de Bolivia, sobre la zona comprendida entre los Ríos Pilcomayo y Paraguay,* edited by Ricardo Mujía, supplement to vol. 2, Época colonial, 82–98. La Paz: El Tiempo.

Portugal, Pedro. 2015. "Revés autonómico indígena pachamamista en Totora Marka." *Pukara* 111:8.

Postero, Nancy, 2007. "Andean Utopias in Morales's Bolivia." *Journal of Latin American and Caribbean Ethnic Studies* 2, no. 1:1–28.

———. 2013. "Bolivia's Challenge to Colonial Neoliberalism." In *Neoliberalism, Interrupted: Social Change and Contested Governance in Contemporary Latin America,* edited by Mark Goodale and Nancy Postero, 25–52. Palo Alto, CA: Stanford University Press.

———. 2017. *The Indigenous State: Race, Politics, and Performance in Plurinational Bolivia.* Oakland: University of California Press.

Postero, Nancy, and Jason Tockman. 2020. "Self-Governance in Bolivia's First Indigenous Autonomy: Charagua." *Latin American Research Review* 55, no. 1:1–15.

Povinelli, Elizabeth. 2002. *The Cunning of Recognition: Indigenous Alterities and the Making of Australian Multiculturalism.* Durham, NC: Duke University Press.

Powell, David. R. 2007. *"Y entonces llegó un inglés": Historia de la Iglesia Anglicana en el Chaco Paraguayo (Volumen conmemorativo de los cien años del templo de Makxawáya).* Asunción: ServiLibro.

Radding, Cynthia. 2005. *Landscapes of Power and Identity: Comparative Histories in the Sonoran Desert and the Forests of Amazonia from Colony to Republic.* Durham, NC: Duke University Press.

Ramos, Alcida Rita. 1992. "The Hyperreal Indian." *Seria Antropologia* 135. Brasilia: Instituto de Ciências Humanas, Departamento de Antropología, Universidade de Brasília.

Ratzlaff, Gerhard. 1999. *La Ruta Transchaco: Proyecto y ejecución*. Asunción: Litocolor SRL.

Reboratti, Carlos. 2010. "Un mar de soja: la nueva agricultura en Argentina y sus consecuencias." *Revista de Geografía Norte Grande*, no. 45:63–76.

Renshaw, John. 2002. *The Indians of the Paraguayan Chaco: Identity and Economy*. Omaha: University of Nebraska Press.

Reyburn, William. 1954. *The Toba Indians of the Argentine Chaco: An Interpretive Report*. Elkhart, IN: Mennonite Board of Missions and Charities.

Ribera, Marco. 2008. *Problemas socio-ambientales de los hidrocarburos en Bolivia*. La Paz: Observatorio Ambiental de Liga de Defensa del Medioambiente.

Ribot, Jesse C., and Nancy L. Peluso. 2003. "A Theory of Access." *Rural Sociology* 68, no. 2:153–181.

Richard, Nicolás. 2008a. "Les Chiens, les hommes et les étrangers furieux: Archéologie des identités indiennes dans le Chaco boréal." PhD diss., École des Hautes Études en Sciences Sociales-CNRS.

———. 2008b. "Los baqueanos de Belaieff: Las mediaciones indígenas en la entrada militar al Chaco." In *Mala guerra*, edited by Nicolás Richard, 291–333.

———, ed. 2008c. *Mala guerra: Los indígenas en la Guerra del Chaco (1932–1935)*. Asunción: CoLibris, Centro de Artes Visuales Museo del Barro, and ServiLibro.

Riester, Juergen, Barbara Schuchard, and Simon Brigitte. 1979. "Los chiriguano." In *Ñande Ñë: Gramática guaraní para castellano hablantes*, edited by Barbara Schuchard, 4–40. Santa Cruz de la Sierra, Bolivia: APCOB.

Rifkin, Mark. 2013. "Settler Common Sense." *Settler Colonial Studies* 3, no. 3–4):322–340.

Rivera Cusicanqui, Silvia. 2010. *Ch'ixinakax utxiwa: Una reflexión sobre prácticas y discursos descolonizadores*. Buenos Aires: Tinta Limón.

Rodgers, Dennis, and Bruce O'Neill. 2012. "Infrastructural Violence: Introduction to the Special Issue." *Ethnography* 13, no. 4:401–412.

Rodrígues de Prado, Francisco. 1839 [1795]. "Historia dos Indios Cavalleiros ou da Naçâo Guaycurú. *Revista do Instituto Histórico e Geográfico do Brazil* 1:21–45.

Rose, Nikolas. 1999. *Powers of Freedom: Reframing Political Thought*. Cambridge, England: Cambridge University Press.

Rose-Redwood, Ruben. 2012. "With Numbers in Place: Security, Territory, and the Production of Calculable Space." *Annals of the American Association of Geographers* 102, no. 2:295–319.

Sahlins, Marshall 1985. *Islands of History*. Chicago: University of Chicago Press.

Saignes, Thierry. 1984. "L'Ethnographie missionaire des sauvages la première description franciscaine des chiriguano (1782)." *Journal de la Société des Américanistes* 70: 21–42.

———. 1990. *Ava y Karai: Ensayos sobre la frontera chiriguano (siglo XVI-XX)*. La Paz: Hisbol.

Sánchez, Zacarías. 1926. "La cuestión de límites con la República de Bolivia." *Boletín del Instituto Geográfico Argentino* 1, no. 2:33–43.

Sánchez Labrador, José. 1910 [1770]. 2 vols. *Paraguay católico con sus principales provincias convertidas á la Santa Fe y vasallaje del Rey de España por la predicación de los misioneros celosos de la Compañía de Jesús en gran parte arruinadas por los mamelucos*

del Brasil y restablecidas por los mismos misioneros, edited by Samuel Alexander La-
fone Quevedo. Buenos Aires: Coni Hermanos.

Sanderson, Alec. 1929. "In Our Doings in the North of the Chaco." *SAMS Magazine* 63,
no. 705 (April): 55.

Sanderson, Jack. 1941. "Report from Mission Campo Flores." *SAMS Magazine* 75, no.
836 (January): 5.

Sanderson, William. 1930. "Work Restarted among the Sanapanas." *SAMS Magazine* 64,
no. 723 (October): 127–128. London: South American Missionary Society.

Santamaría, Daniel J. 1988. "Resistencia anticolonial y movimientos mesiánicos entre
los chiriguanos del siglo XVIII." *Anuario de la Universidad Nacional de Rosario* 13:
169–198.

———. 2001. *Memorias del Jujuy Colonial y del Marquesado de Tojo. Desarrollo integrado
de una secuencia territorial multiétnica, siglos XVI-XVIII*. Seville: Universidad Internacional de Andalucía.

Santamaría, Daniel J., and Marcelo Lagos. 1992. "Historia y etnografía de las tierras bajas
del Norte Argentino: Trabajo realizado y perspectivas." *Anuario del IEHS* 7:75–92.

Sawyer, Suzana. 2004. *Crude Chronicles: Indigenous Politics, Multinational Oil, and Neoliberalism in Ecuador*. Durham, NC: Duke University Press.

Schilling-Vacaflor, Almut, and Jessika Eichler. 2017. "The Shady Side of Consultation and
Compensation: 'Divide-and-Rule' Tactics in Bolivia's Extractive Sector." *Development
and Change* 48, no. 6:1439–1463.

Schmidl, Ulrico. 1881 [1567]. *Historia y descubrimiento del Río de la Plata y Paraguay*.
Buenos Aires: Mayo.

Schmidt, Max. 1903. "Guaná." *Zeitschrift fur Ethnologie* 35:324–336, 560–604.

———. 1938. "Los tapietés." *Revista de la Sociedad Científica del Paraguay* 4, no. 2:36–67.

Schuchard, Barbara. 1979. *Ñande Ñë: Gramática guaraní para castellano hablantes*. Santa
Cruz: APCOB.

———. 1986. "La conquista de la tierra: Relatos guaraníes de Bolivia acerca de experiencias guerreras y pacíficas recientes." *Suplemento Antropológico* 21, no. 2:67–115.

Schwartz, Stuart B., and Frank Salomon. 1999. "New Peoples and New Kinds of People:
Adaptation, Readjustment, and Ethnogenesis in South American Indigenous Societies (Colonial Era)." In *The Cambridge History of the Native Peoples of the Americas*,
edited by Frank Salomon and Stuart B. Schwartz, 3:443–501. Cambridge, England:
Cambridge University Press.

Scott, James C. 1985. *Weapons of the Weak: Everyday Forms of Peasant Resistance*. New
Haven, CT: Yale University Press.

Seelstrang, Arturo. 1977 [1878]. *Informe de la Comisión Exploradora del Chaco*. Buenos
Aires: Eudeba.

Sekhay'-Pva'. 2006–2016. Transcripts of recordings. Apkeltemnaykam' Sekhay'-Pva', Nengvaanemkeskama Nempayvaam Enlhet.

Sieder, Rachel, ed. 2002. *Multiculturalism in Latin America: Indigenous Rights, Diversity,
and Democracy*. New York: Palgrave Macmillan.

Simpson, Audra. 2014. *Mohawk Interruptus: Political Life across the Borders of Settler
States*. Durham, NC: Duke University Press.

Skjerping, Marte. 2011. "Times of Change: Responses to REDD, Deforestation, and Climate Change in Paraguay." Master's thesis, University of Oslo.

Slutzky, Daniel. 2007. *Situaciones problemáticas de tenencia de la tierra en Argentina.* Buenos Aires: Secretaría de Agricultura, Ganadería, Pesca y Alimentos. E-Book (Estudios e Investigaciones, 14). http://redaf.org.ar/wp-content/uploads/2008/08/problematicas-de-tenencia-de-la-tierra.pdf.

Social Capital. 2010. *Linea base social y económica pueblo weenhayek.* Unpublished manuscript. BG Bolivia and Organización de Capitanías Weenayek.

Sousa Santos, Boaventura de. 2010. *Descolonizar el saber, reinventar el poder.* Montevideo: Trilce.

Speed, Shannon. 2017. "Structures of Settler Capitalism in Abya Yala." *American Quarterly* 69, no. 4:783–790.

Spíndola Zago, Octavio. 2016. "Espacio, territorio y territorialidad: Una aproximación teórica a la frontera." *Revista Mexicana de Ciencias Políticas y Sociales* 228:27–56.

Springer, Simon. 2011. "Violence Sits in Places? Cultural Practice, Neoliberal Rationalism, and Virulent Imaginative Geographies." *Political Geography* 30:90–98.

Spronk, Susan, and Jeffery R. Webber. 2007. "Struggles against Accumulation by Dispossession in Bolivia: The Political Economy of Natural Resource Contention." *Latin American Perspectives* 34, no. 2:31–47.

Star, Susan Leigh. 1999. "The Ethnography of Infrastructure." *American Behavioral Scientist* 43, no. 3:377–391.

Stunnenberg, Peter, and Johan Kleinpenning. 1993. "The Role of Extractive Industries in the Process of Colonization: The Case of Quebracho Exploitation in the Gran Chaco." *Tijdschrift Voor Economische en Sociale Geografie* 84, no. 3:220–229.

Suares de Figueroa, Lorenzo. 1965 [ca. 1586]. "Relación de la Ciudad de Santa Cruz de la Sierra, por su Gobernador Don Lorenzo Suárez de Figueroa." In *Relaciones geográficas de Indias-Perú*, edited by Marcos Jiménez de Espada, 1:402–406. Madrid: Atlas.

Surrallés, Alexandre. 2004. "Horizontes de intimidad: Persona, percepción y espacio en los candoshi." In *Tierra adentro: Territorio indígena y percepción del entorno*, edited by Alexandre Surrallés and Pedro García Hierro, 137–162. Copenhagen: International Work Group for Indigenous Affairs.

Susnik, Branislava. 1968. *Chiriguanos I: Dimensiones etnosociales.* Asunción: Museo Etnográfico Andrés Barbero.

———. 1978. *Los aborígenes del Paraguay.* Vol. 1: *Etnología del Chaco Boreal y su periferia, siglos XVI y XVI.* Asunción: Museo Etnográfico Andrés Barbero.

———. 1981. *Los aborígenes del Paraguay.* Vol. 3, part 1: *Etnohistoria de los chaqueños 1650–1910.* Asunción: Museo Etnográfico Andrés Barbero.

———. 2017. *El rol de los indígenas en la formación y en la vivencia del Paraguay.* Asunción: Intercontinental.

Susnik, Branislava, and Miguel Chase Sardi. 1995. *Los indios del Paraguay.* Madrid: MAPFRE.

Tamagno, Liliana. 2001. *Nam Qom Hueta'a Na Doqshi Lma' Los tobas en la casa del hombre blanco: Identidad, memoria y utopía.* La Plata: Al Margen.

———. 2008. "Diversidad/desigualdad en el espacio nacional: Negación-ocultamientoracismo-violencia." In *Nación y diversidad: Territorios identidades y federalismo*, edited by José Nun and Alejandro Grimson, 63–71. Buenos Aires: Edhasa.

Tauli-Corpuz, Victoria. 2015. *Report of the UN Special Rapporteur on the Rights of Indigenous Peoples: Paraguay*. New York: United Nations. http://unsr.vtaulicorpuz.org/.

Taunay, Alfredo Escragnolle. 1868. *Scenas de viagem: Exploração entre os Rios Taquary e Aquidauana no Districto de Miranda*. Rio de Janeiro: Americana.

———. 1875. "Vocabulário da lingua guaná o chané (Provincia de Mato Grosso)." *Revista do Instituto Histórico e Geográfico Brasileiro* 38, no. 2:143–162.

Taussig, Michael. 1980. *The Devil and Commodity. Fetishism in Latin America*. Chapel Hill: University of North Carolina.

———. 1993. *Mimesis and Alterity: A Particular History of the Senses*. New York: Routledge.

Teruel, Ana A. 2005. *Misiones, economía y sociedad: La frontera chaqueña del Noroeste Argentino en el siglo XIX*. Quilmes, Argentina: Universidad Nacional de Quilmes.

Tockman, Jason. 2014. *Instituting Power: Power Relations, Institutional Hybridity, and Indigenous Self-Governance in Bolivia*. PhD diss., University of British Columbia.

Tockman, Jason, and John Cameron. 2014. "Indigenous Autonomy and the Contradictions of Plurinationalism in Bolivia." *Latin American Politics and Society* 56, no. 3:46–69.

Tola, Florencia. 2009. *Les conceptions du corps et de la personne dans un context amérindien*. Paris: L'Harmattan.

———. 2012. *Yo no estoy sólo en mi cuerpo: Cuerpos-personas múltiples entre los tobas del Chaco Argentino*. Buenos Aires: Biblos.

———. 2013. "Introducción: Acortando distancias; el Gran Chaco, la antropología y la antropología del Gran Chaco." In *El Gran Chaco: Ontologías, Poder, Afectividad*, edited by Florencia Tola, Celeste Medrano, and Lorena Cardín, 11–41. Buenos Aires: Rumbo Sur.

Tola, Florencia, and Valentín Suárez. 2016. *El teatro chaqueño de las crueldades: Memorias qom de la violencia y el poder*. Buenos Aires: Rumbo Sur.

Torres Fernández, Patricia. 2007. "Políticas misionales anglicanas en el Chaco Centro-Occidental a principios de siglo XX: Entre comunidades e identidades diversas." *Población y Sociedad* 14:139–176.

Trinchero, Héctor Hugo. 2000. *Los dominios del demonio: Civilización y barbarie en las fronteras de la nación; el Chaco Central*. Buenos Aires: Eudeba.

———. 2007. *Aromas de lo exótico (retornos del objeto): Para una crítica del objeto antropológico y sus métodos de reproducción*. Buenos Aires: SB.

Troeltsch, Ernst. 1951. *El protestantismo y el mundo moderno*. Mexico City: Fondo de Cultura Económica.

Tsing, Anna. 1994. *Friction: An Ethnography of Global Connection*. Princeton, NJ: Princeton University Press.

Tuck, Eve, and K. Wayne Yang. 2012. "Decolonization Is Not a Metaphor." *Decolonization: Indigeneity, Education, and Society* 1, no. 1:1–40.

Tytelman, Carolina. 2016. "Place and Forest Co-Management in Nitassinan/Labrador: St. John's, Newfoundland, and Labrador." PhD diss., Memorial University of Newfoundland.

Última Hora. 2018. "El interés por la soja crece sostenidamente." December 18. https://www.ultimahora.com/el-interes-la-soja-el-chaco-crece-sostenidamente-n2786123.html.

UNHRC (UN Human Rights Council). 2018. *Report of the Special Rapporteur on Contemporary Forms of Slavery, Including Its Causes and Consequences on Her Mission to Paraguay.* New York: UNHRC. https://digitallibrary.un.org/record/1639596?ln=en.

UN Women. 2016. "Strengthening Integrated Services for Indigenous Women Affected by HIV and Violence: Boquerón, Paraguay." Asunción: ONU Mujeres. http://onusidalac.org/1/images/Final-version-April-2017–5095-UN-WOMEN-Violence-and-HIV-EN-LR-web.pdf.

Urban, Greg. 1996. "On the Geographical Origins and Dispersion of Tupian Languages." *Revista de Antropologia* 39, no. 2:61–104.

USAID (US Agency for International Development) and CIRD (Centro de Información y Recursos para el Desarrollo). 2012. *Proyecto de Descentralización de Salud y Participación Comunitaria. Informe Final: Paraguay.* https://www.cird.org.py/institucional/documentos/CIRD_DESCENTRALIZACION%20DE%20SALUD_INFORME%20FINAL.pdf.

Vázquez Recalde, Fabricio. 2011. "Resistencia, Adaptación e Integración en el Chaco Boreal y Central." In *La frontera argentino-paraguaya ante el espejo: Porosidad y paisaje del Gran Chaco y del Oriente de la República del Paraguay,* edited by Eva Morales Raya, Gabriella Dalla-Corte Caballero, Fabricio Vázquez Recalde, and Arturo Landeros Suárez, 99–131. Barcelona: Universitat de Barcelona Publicacions i Edicions.

———. 2013. *Geografía humana del Chaco Paraguayo: Transformaciones territoriales y desarrollo regional.* Asunción: Asociación Paraguaya de Estudios de Población.

Veit, Peter, and Ryan Sarsfield. 2017. *Land Rights, Beef Commodity Chains, and Deforestation Dynamics in the Paraguayan Chaco.* Washington DC: USAID Tenure and Global Climate Change Program.

Villafañe, Benjamín. 1857. *Orán y Bolivia a la margen del Bermejo.* Salta, Argentina: Imprenta del Comercio.

Villagomez Guzmán, Freddy. 2016. "Histórico: Primer gobierno indígena constituido en el país." Centro de Investigación y Promoción del Campesinado. https://cipca.org.bo/analisis-y-opinion/cipcanotas/historico-primer-gobierno-indigena-constituido-en-el-pais.

Villagra, Rodrigo, and Valentina Bonifacio. 2015. "Los maskoy de Puerto Casado y los angaité de Puerto Pinasco: Un recuento de los tiempos del tanino." In *Capitalismo en las selvas,* edited by Lorena Córdoba, Federico Bossert, and Nicolás Richard, 233–270.

Villagra Carron, Rodrigo. 2008. "Nanek añy'a kempohakme o en aquel tiempo de los enojados: Testimonios de los angaité en la Guerra del Chaco." In *Mala guerra,* edited by Nicolás Richard, 67–98.

———. 2010. *The Two Shamans and the Owner of the Cattle: Alterity, Storytelling, and Shamanism amongst the Angaité of the Paraguayan Chaco.* Asunción: Centro de Estudios Antropológicos de la Universidad Católica.

———. 2011. "Del vaingka al choqueo: Sociabilidad y ritual de los angaité a partir de la colonización del Chaco (1880)." *Journal de la Société des Américanistes* 97, no. 2:319–342.

———. 2014. *Meike vakha valayo: Reflexiones etnográficas entorno a los angaité del Chaco*. Asunción: Centro de Estudios Antropológicos de la Universidad Católica.

———. 2018. "Diagnóstico socio-jurídico de tierras y territorios indígenas en Paraguay." *Suplemento Antropológico* 53, no. 1:129–182.

Villar, Diego. 2006. "Repensando el complejo cultural 'chiriguano-chané.'" In *Definiciones étnicas, organización social y estrategias políticas en el Chaco y la Chiquitanía*, edited by Isabelle Combès. 205–224.

Villar, Diego, and Federico Bossert. 2008. "La jefatura entre los chané del Noroeste Argentino." In *Liderazgo, representatividad y control social en el Gran Chaco*, edited by José A. Braunstein and Norma Meichtry, 275–284. Corrientes, Argentina: Eudene, Universidad Nacional del Nordeste.

Viveiros de Castro, Eduardo. 1998. "Cosmological Deixis and Amerindian Perspectivism." *Journal of the Royal Anthropological Institute* 4, no. 3:469–488.

———. 2004. "Perspectival Anthropology and the Method of Controlled Equivocation." *Tipití: Journal of the Society for the Anthropology of Lowland South America* 2, no. 1. http://digitalcommons.trinity.edu/tipiti/vol2/iss1.

Wainwright, Joel. 2008. *Decolonizing Development: Colonial Power and the Maya*. London: Blackwell.

Walkovitz, Judith. 1980. *Prostitution and Victorian Society: Women, Class, and the State*. Cambridge, England: Cambridge University Press.

Warren, Kay B., and Jean E. Jackson. 2002. *Indigenous Movements, Self-Representation, and the State in Latin America*. Austin: University of Texas Press.

Webb, Henry. 1939. "Makthlawaiya." *SAMS Magazine* 73, no. 821 (January): 86–87.

Webber, Michael. 2008. "Primitive Accumulation in Modern China." *Dialectical Anthropology* 32, no. 4:299–320.

Weber, David J. 2005. *Bárbaros: Spaniards and Their Savages in the Age of Enlightenment*. New Haven, CT: Yale University Press.

Whitehead, Neil L. 1992. "Tribes Make States and States Make Tribes: Warfare and the Creation of Colonial Tribes and States in Northeastern South America, 1492–1820." In *War in the Tribal Zone: Expanding States and Indigenous Warfare*, edited by Neil L. Whitehead and Brian Ferguson, 127–150. Santa Fe, NM: School for Advanced Research.

———. 2002. "Arawak Linguistic and Cultural Identity through Time: Contact, Colonialism, Creolization." In *Comparative Arawakan Histories: Rethinking Language Family and Culture Area in Amazonia*, edited by Jonathan Hill and Fernando Santos-Granero, 51–73. Urbana: University of Illinois Press.

Wilde, Guillermo, and Matthias vom Hau. 2010. "'We Have Always Lived Here': Indigenous Movements, Citizenship, and Poverty in Argentina." *Journal of Development Studies* 46, no. 7:1283–1303.

Wolfe, Patrick. 2006. "Settler Colonialism and the Elimination of the Native." *Journal of Genocide Research* 8, no. 4:387–409.

———. 2016. *Traces of History: Elementary Structures of Race*. London: Verso.

Wood, Ellen. M. 2007. "Logics of Power: A Conversation with David Harvey." *Historical Materialism* 14, no. 4:9.

Wright, Pablo. 1983. "Presencia protestante entre aborígenes del Chaco Argentino." *Scripta Ethnologica* 2:73–84.

———. 1998. "El desierto del Chaco: Geografías de la alteridad y el estado." In *Pasado y presente de un mundo postergado: Trece estudios de antropología, arqueología e historia del Chaco y Pedemonte Andino,* edited by Ana A. Teruel and Omar Jerez, 35–56, Jujuy, Argentina: Universidad Nacional de Jujuy.

———. 2002a. "'L'Evangelio': Pentecôtisme indigène dans le Chaco Argentin. *Social Compass* 49, no. 1:43–66.

———. 2002b. "'Ser católico y ser evangelio': Tiempo, historia y existencia en la religión toba." *Antropológicas* 6, no. 13: 61–81.

———. 2003. "Colonización del espacio, la palabra y el cuerpo en el Chaco Argentino." *Horizontes Antropológicos* 9, no. 19:137–152.

———. 2008. *Ser-en-el-sueño: Crónicas de historia y vida toba.* Buenos Aires: Biblos.

Yashar, Deborah. 2005. *Contesting Citizenship in Latin America.* New York: Cambridge University Press.

Ybarra, Megan. 2018. *Green Wars: Conservation and Decolonization in the Maya Forest.* Los Angeles: University of California Press.

Yrigoyen, Raquel. 2009. "De la tutela a los derechos de libre determinación del desarrollo: Participación, consulta y consentimiento: Fundamentos, balance y retos para su implementación." *Amazônica-Revista de Antropologia* 1, no. 2:368–405.

Zapata, Laura. 2013. "Pastoral aborigen y categorías de identificación de poblaciones indígenas en Formosa (1960–1984)." *Uturunku Achachi: Revista de Pueblos y Culturas Originarios* 2:47–62.

Zenteno, Elisa del Carmen. 2008. "Qué rol, qué tarea, que misión tenemos como co-municadores en la comunidad." Red de Comunicación Indígena, *Boletín Mensual* no. 29:4.

Contributors

Denise Humphreys Bebbington (PhD in development policy and management) is research associate professor at Clark University. In her research she has explored the political ecology of natural gas and the implications of the gas economy for both indigenous peoples and regional societies and the dynamics of socioenvironmental conflict and mobilization linked to natural resource extraction and large-scale infrastructure investments in Latin America. She is coauthor with Anthony Bebbington, Abdul-Gafaru Abdulai, Marja Hinfelaar, and Cynthia Sanborn of *Governing Extractive Industries: Politics, Histories, Ideas.*

Mercedes Biocca (PhD in sociology), is associate researcher at the Escuela Interdisciplinaria de Altos Estudios Sociales, Universidad Nacional de San Martín, Argentina. Her research has been published in journals such as *Tipití: Journal of the Society for the Anthropology of Lowland South America* and *Población y Sociedad.* Her research focuses on rural issues associated with extractivism and the relations between indigenous peoples and the state in contexts of dispossession.

Federico Bossert (PhD in anthropology) is a researcher at CONICET (Consejo Nacional de Investigaciones Científicas y Técnicas) and the Instituto de Ciencias Antropológicas, Universidad de Buenos Aires. His research has been published in journals such as *Anthropos, Población y Sociedad,* and *Journal de la Société des Americanistes.* His research focuses on social organization, interethnic relations, ethnohistory, the Andean foothills, and the Chaco region.

Paola Canova (PhD in anthropology) is associate professor in the Anthropology Department and Institute for Latin American Studies, University of Texas at Austin. She is the author of *Frontier Economies: An Intimate*

Ethnography of Ayoreo Women in Paraguay's Chaco. Her research interests include the political ecology of the Chaco, gender and sexuality, indigenous urbanity, and indigenous-state relations.

César Ceriani Cernadas (PhD in anthropology) is a researcher at CONI-CET (Consejo Nacional de Investigaciones Científicas y Técnicas) and a professor at FLACSO (Facultad Latinoamericana de Ciencias Sociales). He is the author of *Nuestros hermanos lamanitas* and *Los evangelios chaque-ños: Misiones y estrategias indigenas en el siglo XX*. His research focuses on religious missions among Chaco indigenous groups and native forms of religious life.

Joel E. Correia (PhD in geography) is assistant professor at the Center for Latin American Studies and faculty member in the Tropical Conserva-tion and Development Program at the Department of Geography and the American Indian and Indigenous Studies Program, University of Florida. His research has been published in *Geoforum, The Journal of Peasant Stud-ies, The Journal of Latin American Geography*, and *Erasmus Law Review*, among others. In his research he investigates the intersections of indig-enous politics, land rights, socioenvironmental (in)justice, and law in the context of extractive development and Latin America, with a particular focus on Paraguay.

Guido Cortez (BA in sociology) is an executive director of the Centro de Estudios Regionales de Tarija, Bolivia. His research focuses on the rela-tions between organizational processes and socioeconomic development in indigenous cultures of the Chaco. His research has been published in journals such as *World Development*, and he is the author of the chapter "Social Change in the Weenhayek People in the Last One Hundred Years" in *Definiciones étnicas, organización social y estrategias políticas en el Chaco y la Chiquitanía*, edited by Isabelle Combès.

Gastón Gordillo (PhD in anthropology) is professor and researcher at the University of British Columbia. He is the author of *Rubble: The Afterlife of Destruction* and *Landscapes of Devils: Tensions of Place and Memory in the Argentine Chaco*. His research focus is the materiality of space, violence, critical theory, and resistance to agribusiness, particularly in the Chaco area.

Bret Gustafson (PhD in anthropology) is professor at Washington University at St. Louis. He is the author of *New Languages of the State: Indigenous Resurgence and the Politics of Knowledge in Bolivia* and coeditor with Nicole Fabricant of *Remapping Bolivia: Resources, Territory and Indigeneity in a Plurinational State*. His research focuses on the anthropology of politics, development, gas development, and indigenous intercultural education.

Silvia Hirsch (PhD in anthropology) is professor and researcher at the Escuela Interdisciplinaria de Altos Estudios Sociales, Universidad Nacional de San Martín, Argentina. She is the author of *El pueblo tapiete de Argentina: Historia y cultura*, editor of *Mujeres indígenas de la Argentina: Cultura, trabajo y poder*, coeditor with Adriana Serrudo of *Educación intercultural bilingüe en la Argentina*, coeditor with Gastón Gordillo of *Movilizaciones indígenas e identidades en disputa en la Argentina: Historias de invisibilización y re-emergencia*, and coeditor with Mariana Lorenzetti of *Salud pública y pueblos indígenas en la Argentina: Encuentros, tensiones e interculturalidad*. Her research focuses on gender, ethnicity, borders, and health and education among indigenous peoples.

Hannes Kalisch (BA in linguistics) is an independent researcher and founder of the Indigenous Working Group Nengvaanemkeskama Nempayvaam Enlhet, in Paraguay. He is the author of *No llores: La historia enlhet de la Guerra del Chaco*, a contributor to *The Paraguay Reader: History, Culture, Politics*, edited by Peter Lambert and Andrew Nickson, and coauthor with Ernesto Unruh of *Wie Schön Ist Deine Stimme*.

Nancy Postero (PhD in anthropology) is professor at the University of California San Diego, codirector of the Human Rights Program at UC San Diego, and codirector of the International Institute at UC San Diego. She is the author of *Now We Are Citizens: Indigenous Politics in Postmulticultural Bolivia* and *The Indigenous State: Race, Politics, and Performance in Plurinational Bolivia*. Her areas of research are race, politics, and political economy among indigenous peoples.

Rodrigo Villagra Carron (PhD in social anthropology) is a lawyer, a researcher of the PRONII (National Incentive Program for Researchers) at CONACYT (National Scientific and Technological Council), Paraguay, and a funder and associate researcher for the NGO Tierraviva, Paraguay. He is a lecturer of indigenous ethnology at the Universidad Federal de Integração Latino-Americana, Foz de Iguaçu, Brazil. He is the author of *The Two Shamans and the Owner of the Cattle: Alterity, Storytelling, and Shamanism among the Angaite of the Paraguayan Chaco* and *Meike makha valayo: No habían Paraguayos; reflexiones etnográficas en torno a los angaité del Chaco*. His research concentrates on indigenous peoples' territoriality, shamanism, interethnic relationships, and applied and legal anthropology.

Index

Page numbers in *italics* refer to illustrations.

Abdo Benítez, Mario, 238
A Buen Tiempo Nacional, 155
Acción Ecológica, 212n17
Accumulation by dispossession, 141–42,
    143–45, 146, 149, 162, 163
Acero, Bolivia, 59, 68
Acharei (Chané man), 47, 49, 52n31
Agribusiness and agriculture: Angaité and,
    121; Chané and, 38, 39, 45; and change
    in Gran Chaco, 1; corn/maize cultiva-
    tion, 108, 154, 216; criollos and, 10; and
    deforestation, 3, 148, 149, 157, 164n7,
    268; Enlhet and, 102, 108; and fencing,
    149, 157; Guaná and, 134; Guaraní and,
    216; Guaraní Ñandeva and, 267; honey
    production, 153; increases in, 22, 148;
    indigenous peoples and, 10, 12, 16, 131, 133,
    141, 145; and infrastructural violence, 184;
    and irrigation, 164n8; Kaskiha and, 134;
    land for, 17–18, 268; mandioca cultivation,
    153; and mechanization, 149; Menno-
    nites and, 102, 108; missionaries and, 87;
    Moonies and, 19; Moqoit and, 142, 156,
    163; nongovernmental organizations and,
    121; organic, 154; peanut cultivation, 108;
    Peronists and, 147–48; and pollution, 149,
    157, 278; Qom and, 141, 142, 148, 149, 154,
    162, 163; Sanapaná and, 134; scholarship
    on, 143–44; sorghum cultivation, 108, 151;
    squash cultivation, 112, 154; sunflower
    cultivation, 151; sweet potato cultivation,
    108, 112, 153; Tapiete and, 257, 263, 265,
    268, 271; and transgenic crops, 142, 148,
    149, 150, 154; vegetable cultivation, 149, 151;
    watermelon cultivation, 112, 154. *See also*
    Cotton production; Soybean production;
    Sugarcane cultivation and processing
Agripino, Pastor, 129
Agroforestry, 87
Aguaragüe gas block, 195, 212n16
Aguaragüe mountain range, 29, 189, 212n16
Aguaray Guazu River, 134
Aguaray ranch, 44
Aguilera, Agustina, 123–24, 126, 127, 128, 137
Aguirre, Juan Francisco, 130
Aikhenvald, Alexandra, 72n8
AIOs (Autonomías Indígenas Originarias
    Campesinas, Indigenous First Peoples Peas-
    ants Autonomies), 219–20
"Ajarise," 67
Alba, Justo, 44
Albó, Xavier, 215, 218
Algarrobal (Irua), Bolivia, 36, 38, 44, *188*
Alternative Program for Conflict Resolution,
    150
Alto Isoso zone, 216
Alvarsson, Jan Ake, 190, 211n4, 213n29
Amazon region, 1, 2, 57, 194, 198
Amazon Watch, 212n17
Amistad Health Clinic, *245*, 248
Ancients (term), 91n8
Andean foothills, 29, 282
Andean Yungas, 29
Andes, 2
Andina company, 195
Angaité (language), 122, 124, 127, 128, 136, 139

Angaité (people): and agriculture, 121, 134–35; assimilation of, 122; and capitalism, 119; and cash transfers, 121; and cattle ranching, 278; and clothing, 129; communities of, *25*, 121, 129; and drinking-water infrastructure, 121; emergence of, as ethnic group, 119, 139; and Enlhet-Enenlhet language family, 93, 119; and environmental impoverishment, 119; and Enxet, 126; evolution of, 131–32, 136, 139; and fishing, 121; and health services, 121; historical documentation on, 129; and housing, 121; and hunting and gathering, 121, 134–35; institutions of, 136; as labor, 120, 121, 122; and land, 119, 120, 121, 129; languages of, 122; leaders of, 136; and Maskoy, 133; and missionaries, 120–21; and nongovernmental organizations, 121; origin of name of, 136; and pensions, 121; and pottery, 134–35; and poverty, 121; religious tensions among, 122; rituals of, 118–19, 122, 124, 127–28, 129, 137, 139; scholarship on, 135–36; and shamans, 118, 136; social customs of, 123, 124; and social impoverishment, 119; subgroups of, 120; terms for, 135–36; and traditional healing practices, 128–29, 140; and wool textiles, 134–35

Angaité-Koalhvok, 139, 140n5

Ángel (Moqoit man), 159

Ángel (Qom man), 153

Anglicans and Anglican Church: Agapito Navarro's family and, 125, 129, 140; arrival of, 80; and cattle ranching, 175, 176; La Herencia program of, 121; and medicine, 83; missions and missionaries of, 86, 175–78, 183, 185n8, 261; and Nivaclé, 134; and resettlement of indigenous peoples, 121; and restitution of indigenous lands, 121

Animals: cattle, 3, 36, 37, 39, 107, 153, 166, 167, 179, 180, 183, 216; cocks, 36; deer, 105; depletion of, 3; eels, 105; fish, 7, 169, 189, 190, 197; goats, 36, 103, 153; Guaraní Ñandeva and, 267; horses, 39, 158; livestock, 6, 10, 15, 149, 160, 169, 216, 268; mules, 158; peccaries, 105; Qom and, 149, 153; sábalo (fish), 211n12; snakes, 36–37. *See also* Cattle ranching

Antaava-Aatkook, Paraguay, *94*, 99, 100, 101, 103, 106

Apa River, 140n3

APG. *See* Asamblea del Pueblo Guaraní (APG, Assembly of the Guaraní People)

Apiaguaki Tumpa (Chiriguano man), 10

Arakuaarenda Cultural Center, 222

Arancibia, María Antonia, 228–29, 230

Arasari (Chané man), 47, 48

Arawak (language): Chané and, 68; changes in, 58; and Chiriguano thesis, 56; and Guaraní language, 67–68, 69; speakers of, 53, 56, 58; suffixes in, 71n5; terms in, 64, 65

Arawak (people): Chiriguano thesis on, 69; communities of, 65, 66, 67; descendants of, 69; diaspora of, 57; and Guaraní and Guaraní speakers, 60, 66, 70; origins of, 57; scholarship on, 67, 72n8; terms for, 70; and weaving, 72n11

Arce, Luis, 210

Argentina: agribusiness and agriculture in, 16, 65, 141, 148, 165n14; and beef exports, 17; and Bolivia, 43, 44, 46, 193; borders of, 6, 46, 267; Catholic Church in, 78, 84, 264; civil unrest and resistance in, 22, 184, 258; and claim to Gran Chaco, 5–6; class in, 261; concept of *desert* in, 5; constitutional reform in, 20–21, 257, 263, 264; deforestation in, 184; development in, 78; European heritage of, 256; foreign companies in, 15; Foster-Seelstrang expedition in, 5; governments of, 74, 78, 84, 147, 257–58, 280; independence of, 3; and industry, 6, 193, 277; infrastructure in, 18, 171; land redistribution in, 147; laws in, 50n1, 147, 263; map of, *4;* missions and missionaries in, 5, 9, 73, 80, 261; national territories and provinces in, 91n9; nongovernmental organizations in, 275; and Paraguay, 6, 169; and reform, 280; violence in, 171; and War of the Triple Alliance, 6, 169. *See also* Argentine Chaco

Argentina Forestry Department, 164n7

Argentina Ministry of Planning and Environment, 150

Argentina Ministry of Social Development (Ministerio de Desarrollo Social), 149, 276n4

Argentina Ministry of the Economy, 164n9

Argentina National Institute for Indigenous Affairs (Instituto Nacional de Asuntos Indígenas), 20, 50n1

Argentine-Bolivian Railway Commission, 7

Argentine Chaco: agribusiness and agriculture in, 15, 16–17, 22; Argentine governments and, 280; borders of, 6; climate in, 3; deforestation in, 184; development in, 74, 76; exploration of, 5; flora in, 3, 277; foreign companies in, 15; Gastón Gordillo in, 277; indigenous peoples in, 7, 8, 9, 10–11, 17, 73, 80, 189, 277; industry in, 5, 6, 15, 16–17, 22; location of, 3; and migration, 6, 7, 80; missions and missionaries in, 5, 6, 7, 8, 9, 73, 74, 80; population of, 7; scarcity in, 11; scholarship on, 26n2; size of, 6; streams in, 3; and transportation, 6, 7; working conditions in, 5, 16

Argentine Episcopal Conference, 91n4

Arias, Miguel, 266

Aringui (Chané man), 66

Aristóbulo (Qom man), 151

Asamblea Constituyente (Constitutional Assembly, Paraguay), 21

Asamblea del Pueblo Guaraní (APG, Assembly of the Guaraní People), 10, 216, 218, 225, 227, 228

Asociación Civil Cacique Taigoyik, 88, 149–50, 164n10

Asociación Comunitaria Colonia Las Tolderías, 156

Asociación de Servicios de Cooperación Indígena Menonita (ASCIM, Association of Indigenous Mennonite Cooperation Services), 267, 276n10

ASOCIANA (Fundación de Acompañamiento Social de la Iglesia Anglicana del Norte Argentino), 87

Assembly of God Church, 8, 270

Association of Aboriginal Communities Lhaka Honhat, 87

Asunción, Paraguay: Agapito Navarro and Navarro family in, 118, 128; health services in, 237, 238, *239*, 251; maps of, *4, 25, 168*; medicine women in, 123; protests in, 125; use of *Chané* in, 58; use of *Chiriguano* in, 71n7

Auerbach, Marc, 144

Autonomía Guaraní Charagua Iyambae, 216–17

Autonomías Indígenas Originarias

Campesinas (AIOCs, Indigenous First Peoples Peasants Autonomies), 219–20

Autonomy: in Bolivia, 18, 22, 215, 216–32, 233, 268, 269, 280; in Paraguay, 13, 21, 119, 242; and race, 221

Auyero, Javier, 238

Ávalos Sánchez, Paraguay, 96

Ayala, Laureano, 125–26, 127–28, 129, 138, 140

Ayentamaklha-Pyespok-Yaata'ay', Paraguay, *94, 99*, 100

Ayoreo (language), 64

Ayoreo (people): communities of, *25*, 247; and cultural adaptation, 20; as foragers, 247; and health services, 239–40, 246, 248–53, 279; and housing, 236; and hygiene, 250; and identity, 20; and migration and mobility, 20, 279; and non-Ayoreo persons, 248; and politics, 20; population of, 247; and religion, 9, 20, 246; scholarship on, 20; sedentarization of, 247; and single parents, 249; and single women's monetization of sexuality, 248–49, 251, 254, 279; and Tapiete, 260; and traditional culture, 246

Ayuda Mutua Hospitalaria, 236

Azara, Félix, 130, 132

Bahía Negra, Paraguay, *4, 6*

Bajo Chaco: Anglicans in, 175–77; cattle ranching in, 167, 169, 173, 174–75, 176, 177, 179–80, 183; climate in, 181, 185n4; deforestation in, 174; fencing in, 174, 177, 179, 180; indigenous peoples in, 167, 174–75, 178, 180, 183, 185n1; and infrastructure, 173, 177; land ownership and rights in, 169, 173, 183; location of, 185n4; Paraguayan government and, 177; pollution in, 181; race in, 173, 183; settler colonialism in, 167, 170, 173, 174, 177, 178, 180; water in, 181–82. *See also* Paraguayan Chaco

Bajo Isoso, Bolivia, 216

Balderas, Reynaldo, 270, 273

Baldus, Herbert, 130

Ballivián, José, 32, 41

Bañado la Estrella, Argentina, 3, *4*

Baptist Church, 8, 151

Barbosa, Pablo Antunha, 140n3

Barrio Obrero Colonia 5, Paraguay, 266–67

Barroso, Maria, 89–90

Bartolina Sisa organization, 228

Basavi (Chané man), 44

Batirayu (Chané man), 64, 66

Bebbington, Denise Humphreys, 187, 280

Berg, Hedvig, 83

Bermejo River: agribusiness along, 148; as border, 3, 6, 29, 133; diversion of, 149; flow of, 2; indigenous peoples along, 131, 147, 189; industry along, 6, 148; maps of, *4, 25;* path of, 281

BG Bolivia. *See* British Gas (BG) Bolivia

Bicentennial Production Financing Program, 150

Biocca, Mercedes: on accumulation by dispossession, 142, 144, 145, 146; on agribusiness, 278; in Chaco Province, Argentina, 142, 147, 151, 152, 155, 159, 164n1; on indigenous demand for government resources, 280; on indigenous dislocation, 278; and indigenous oral histories, 278; on local rationalities, 145, 146; on Moqoit people, 279; on Qom protests, 279; on territoriality, 280

Bioceanic Highway, 179, 184. *See also* Roads

Biraben Castelnuovo, 87

Blaser, Mario, 96

Boggiani, Guido, 5, 130, 132, 134, 135

Bolivia: 2009 constitution of, 22, 214, 217, 219–20, 232; and Argentina, 43, 44, 46, 193; borders of, 6, 46, 58, 267; and Brazil, 193; and Chaco War, 1, 12, 13, 211n7, 262; claims of, on Gran Chaco, 5–6, 66; colonization in, 43; consultation process in, 187–89, 200–207, 208–9, 213n28, 220, 280; elections in, 210, 227–28; exploration in, 5; independence in, 3, 66; left-wing governments in, 240; legislation and decrees in, 196–98, 199–200, 218, 220; maps of, *4, 25;* military of, 190; missions and missionaries in, 5, 8, 9, 66, 262, 270; Mocapoi expedition in, 36, 37; Morales administration in, 18, 22, 192, 199–200, 208, 209, 210, 213n30, 214–15, 220, 225, 232, 234, 268, 280; multicultural policies in, 241; natural resources extraction in, 184, 187, 193, 197, 199–200, 209, 211n7, 214, 225–26, 277, 280; Nordenskiöld in, 67, 69; and ORCAWETA, 209; and Paraguay, 67, 93, 120; political power in, 222; ranching in, 6, 190; and reform, 280; resistance in, 22,

197, 225, 241; and trade, 40; and transportation, 7, 18–19, 235n1; UN High Commission on Human Rights in, 232; and War of the Triple Alliance, 6. *See also* Bolivian Chaco

Bolivia Congress, 220

Bolivia Constituent Assembly, 214, 217, 219, 222

Bolivia Electoral Tribunal, 229

Bolivia Hacienda (Treasury), 230

Bolivia Land Reform Agency, 196

Bolivia Ministry of Autonomies, 220, 221, 229, 230

Bolivia Ministry of Environment and Water, 200

Bolivia Ministry of Health, 229

Bolivia Ministry of Hydrocarbons and Energy, 199, 201, 202–3

Bolivia Ministry of Public Works, 19

Bolivia Ministry of Rural Development, 200

Bolivian Chaco: borders of, 6; capital of, 6; climate in, 3; colonization of, 6; deforestation in, 19; Denise Humphreys Bebbington in, 187; exploration of, 5; flora in, 3; forts in, 6; indigenous peoples in, 7, 9, 189, 259, 261, 266; industry in, 6; location of, 2–3; and migration, 6, 7; missions and missionaries in, 3–5, 6, 7, 8, 9; natural resources extraction in, 18, 187, 280; size of, 6; terrain and topography of, 2, 3, 282; and transportation, 6. *See also* Natural gas extraction

Bolivia Plurinational Constitutional Tribunal, 221

Bolivia State Department, 230

Bolivia Vice Ministry of the Environment, 204, 205

Bossert, Federico, 56, 278, 279, 280–81

BP-Amoco, 195

Braticevic, Sergio, 76

Braunstein, José, 5, 130–31, 135, 164n2, 191

Bravo Company, 129

Brazil: and Bolivia, 193; borders of, 58; cattle ranching in, 198; foreign relations minister of, 140n3; and Gran Chaco, 1, 3, 6; Guana Chané in, 71n4; indigenous peoples in, 57, 60, 61, 89–90, 129, 244; maps of, *4, 25;* multicultural reforms in, 241; and natural gas, 193; nongovernmental organizations in,

89; and Paraguay, 71n4, 169; and War of the Triple Alliance, 6, 169

Brazil-Paraguay Demarcation Commission, 140n3

Brenner, Robert, 144

Briggs, Charles, 250

British Gas (BG) Bolivia: and Bolivian government, 187; and consultation process, 187, 201; Indigenous Development Plan of, 198–99; on indigenous population, 189; and natural gas extraction in Weenhayek territory, 187, 194, 195, 199; and ORCAWETA, 187, 197, 198, 199, 201, 202–6, 211n5, 212n24; Program of Community Relations and Support of, 198; resistance to activities of, 198; and Shell Oil Company/Royal Dutch Shell, 187, 197, 210n3; and Tesoro Petroleum, 187, 198; as UK company, 198; unauthorized activities of, 201

Buckwalter, Albert, 85

Buckwalter, Loida, 85

Buenos Aires, Argentina: and commerce, 29; and communication, 29; Gastón Gordillo in, 277; indigenous peoples in, 38, 49, 52n31, 62; Mocapoi expedition in, 36, 37, 43, 47; as national capital, 6

Bunge corporation, 17

Cabeza de Vaca, Alvar, 58

CAF. See Development Bank of Latin America (CAF, formerly Corporación Andina de Fomento)

Caipependi (Chané village), 30

Caiza Plain, 30, 32, 35, 40, 41

Calchaquíes wars, 133

Camaño y Bazán, Joaquín, 130

Cámara Paraguaya de Exportadores y Comercializadores de Cereales y Oleaginosas (Paraguayan Chamber of Exporters of Cereals), 17

Cameron, John, 220

Camiri, Bolivia, 191

Campanella, Andrés, 33

Campesinos, 186, 189, 200

Campo Alegre, Paraguay, 94, 101

Campo de Alcoba, 44

Campo de Durán ranch, 44

Campo Durán, Argentina: Chané in, 28, 29, 36, 44, 47, 48, 49, 50, 51n8; development of, 49; establishment of, 40; location of, 49; maps of, 4, 25

Campo Flores (Maskoykaha) mission, 120

Campo Jordán, Paraguay, 94, 98, 100

Campo Largo, Paraguay, 93, 94, 97, 101, 107, 117n5

Campo Medina, Argentina, 148

Campo Nuevo, Argentina, 148

Canada, 117n1, 219

Canova, Paola: field work by, 254; and health services for Ayoreo persons, 248, 249, 251, 252; at Paraguay's Ministry of Health conference, 246; on reform in Paraguay, 280; on roads, 279; and Vaela Picanerai, 237–38

Capdevila, Luc, 12, 13

CAPI (Componente de Atención a la Población Indígena, Development Program for the Indigenous Population), 257, 276n4

Capiazuti (Chané settlement), 41

Capiazuti River, 41

Capirenda, Bolivia, 268

Capirendita, Bolivia, 188, 202, 205

Capirendita gas block, 195

Capitalism, 143, 173

Caraparí, Bolivia, 30, 31, 35

Cargill corporation, 17

Caribe (people), 60, 61, 62

Caribe (term), 55, 60

Carío (people), 60, 71n7

Carío (term), 55

Carlos Casado company, 7

Carmelo Peralta, Paraguay, 18–19

Carrasco, Morita, 87, 264

Carvalho, Fernando, 57

Casado, Carlos, 129

Casado (family), 14

Casado company, 14, 19, 133

Castelli, Argentina, 83, 87

Castelnuovo Biraben, Natalia, 76–77

Casuarina (Yaamelket-Aatkok), Paraguay, 94, 103, 106

Catholic Church: and Argentine government, 84, 264; and colonization, 15; criollos and, 12; and development, 77, 78, 80, 86; and education, 88, 242; and evangelism, 80;

Catholic Church—*continued*
and Franciscans, 3–5, 8, 29, 30, 40, 50, 66, 68, 80, 261; and humanitarianism, 86; on integral human development, 92n12; and Jesuits, 5, 58, 63, 130, 133, 134; and missions and missionaries, 8, 73, 76, 90, 211n6, 267, 268; and modernity, 78; organizations of, 76, 87, 88–89, 91n4, 242; presence of, 268; and Protestants, 84; and race, 79; and social and moral change, 78; and status, 84

Catia (Chané man), 44

Cattle ranching: Angaité and, 122, 278; Anglicans and, 175, 176; Brazilians and, 180; British and, 175, 180; and class, 216; and colonization, 40, 42, 49, 180, 183; cooperatives for, 175; and deforestation, 3, 17, 174, 176, 184, 185n6; Enxet and, 167, 170, 178; expansion of, 32, 184, 185n6; as export industry, 175; and fencing, 167, 169, 170, 174, 176, 178, 179, 180; and indigenous autonomy, 222, 228–29; and indigenous migration, 169; and infrastructural violence, 173; in Itiyuro River basin, 49; Koreans and, 180; labor for, 121, 167, 177, 178, 180; land for, 17–18, 21, 41, 120, 167, 169, 170, 174–75, 183, 190, 198, 212n22; Mennonites and, 175, 179, 180; mestizos and, 216; and natural gas extraction, 198; origins of, 3; owners of, 169, 180, 212n22; and pollution, 278; and racism, 173; and stock ponds, 174, 176, 178, 179, 181; as system, 174; and transportation, 166, 176, 178–79, 180

Centeno family, 37

Centro de Estudios Regionales para el Desarrollo de Tarija (CER-DET, Center of Regional Studies for the Development of Tarija), 202, 222

Centro de Investigación y Promoción del Campesinado (CIPCA, Center for Investigation and Promotion of Peasants), 221, 222, 229, 232

Cepeda, Lic., 61, 71n7

Ceriani Cernadas, César, 12, 79, 269, 275, 279

Cerrito, Paraguay, 134

Chaco company, 194, 195, 212n16

Chaco Plain, 29

Chaco Territory/Province, Argentina: accumulation by dispossession in, 142; agribusiness in, 141, 142, 148; as boundary, 15; Catholic Church in, 76, 80, 84; and Córdoba Province, 165n14; cotton production in, 155; creation of, 15; criollos in, 11; deforestation in, 141, 142; departments of, 147; development in, 74; education in, 80; federalization of, 15, 91n9; food scarcity in, 11; government officials in, 150; indigenous peoples and organizations in, 10, 11, 80, 156, 161; industry in, 15; maps of, 4, 25; Mercedes Biocca in, 142, 164n1; missions and missionaries in, 80, 83, 84, 85; mobility in, 164n3; nongovernmental organizations in, 88, 91n2, 156; pollution in, 142; terms for indigenous peoples in, 165n19

Chaco War: Angaité and, 120; causes of, 1, 12, 190, 211n7; Chiriguano migration during, 34; and colonization, 93, 102, 117n1; dates of, 136; Enlhet and, 93, 101, 102, 103, 106, 115, 117n1; impact of, on industry, 14; indigenous peoples and, 12–13, 262; missionaries and, 9; Nivaclé and, 101; participants in, 1, 12; population of Enlhet lands after, 117n1; reterritorialization after, 267; scholarship on, 12, 13, 211n7; Tapiete and, 260, 262; transportation during, 7; Weenhayek and, 190, 197

Chané (language): Chiriguano thesis on, 63; as Guaraní language, 69; Jesuits and, 63; places spoken, 63, 64; scholarship on, 57, 64–65, 69; terms in and derived from, 64–65, 67, 136; variants of, 58

Chané (people): and agriculture, 38, 39–43, 45; artifacts of, 52n30; and Chiriguano, 30, 33, 34, 35, 38, 48, 51n2, 65–66, 67, 69; in Chiriguano thesis, 53, 55, 61, 62, 70; clothing of, 36; communities of, 25, 256, 279; deeds for territory of, 29, 37–38, 39, 40, 41, 43, 44, 47, 48, 49–50, 52n28; diet of, 36, 37; economy of, 38; and enslavement, 35, 53, 55; and fencing, 279; and Guaraní, 53, 55, 56, 68, 281; historical documentation on, 29, 30–33, 39–43, 48, 51n2, 63, 68; as labor, 38, 47, 49; and land, 28–29, 32, 34–35, 37, 39–43, 44–46, 47, 48, 49–50; languages of, 51n11, 53, 54, 56, 57, 59, 64, 68, 69; and livestock, 45; medicines of, 37; and migration, 49, 66, 68; and missions and missionaries, 8, 30, 32, 40, 43, 50, 63; and multiethnicity,

33, 34, 37, 54, 59, 60; and oil firms, 52n30; oral histories of, 33–39, 43, 44, 46, 47–49, 50, 51n10, 52n31; origins of, 68, 69; political leadership of, 33, 43–44, 46–47, 48, 49, 50, 51n9, 52n29; and poverty, 38; scholarship on, 33, 51n4, 64, 65–66; and servitude, 62; settlement patterns of, 30, 32, 49, 50; and settlers/colonists, 38, 39–43, 44–46, 49, 52n27; and Spanish, 68; subgroups of, 57; and Toba, 30, 35–36, 37–38, 51n4, 51n11; and trade, 37–38

Chané (term), 56, 57, 58–59, 62, 68, 69

Chané communities: Acero, 59; Aguaray ranch, 44; Algarrobal, 44; along Andean front, 59, 63, 68; Caipependi, 30; in Caiza Plain, 30; Campo de Alcoba, 44; Campo Durán, 29, 35, 44, 49, 50; Capiazuti, 41; ethnicity in, 34; in foothills, 29, 35, 49, 53, 56, 68; Iquira, 41; isolation of, 32, 34–35; in Isoso region, 54, 68, 69; in Itaki Outlet, 41; Itiyuro Outlet, 42; in Itiyuro River basin, 29, 32, 34, 35, 41–42, 43, 44, 49, 51n10, 54, 69, 72n11; Llanos de Manso, 59; maps of, 31, 32, 45; Mato Grosso, 57; Ñatiurenda, 36; north of Santa Cruz, 59; Pampa Blanca, 42; in Paraguay River region, 54, 59, 65; along Parapetí River, 64, 65, 66, 68; along Pilcomayo River, 30; Piquirenda, 41; Porongo, 59; sales of, to non-Chané persons, 44, 46; Sanandita, 30; Tëtaiguate, 34, 51n10; Tuyunti, 29, 50

Chaparina, Bolivia, 235n1

Charagua Iyambae, Bolivia: 2015 summit meeting in, 229–31, 232; Andean migrants in, 216; as autonomous municipality, 22, 215, 221, 232; and autonomy process, 220–25, 226, 227–32; class in, 216, 221, 229; climate of, 215; conflicts in, 232; deliberative body of, 234; development projects in, 226, 231; Guaraní in, 215–16, 227–28, 233; indigenous values in, 224; leadership of, 216, 218, 224–25, 226, 227, 228, 230, 231, 232, 233, 234–35; location of, 215; maps of, 4, 25; MAS supporters in, 225; Mennonites in, 216; mestizos in, 216, 225, 228–29; municipal revenues in, 234; Nancy Postero in, 217, 221–22, 228, 233; non-Guaraní in, 224, 228; political organization in, 224, 234–35;

population of, 215–16; Quechua in, 228, 231; scholarship on, 217–18; sections of, 216, 219, 226, 228, 229, 230, 231–32; size of, 215

Chiapas, Mexico, 282

Chichimeca (people), 62

Chichimeca (term), 55

Chico (Angaité man), 128

Chile, 282

Chilkara, 37

Chimeo (Chiriguano settlement), 35

Chindika (Chané man), 68

Chiquitano (language), 63, 64

Chiquitano (people), 57

Chiquitos, Bolivia, 3, 63

Chiriguanía, 32, 35, 51n2, 56

Chiriguano (language), 66, 69

Chiriguano (people): alternate terms for, 55; and cannibalism, 34, 55, 61; and Chané, 30, 33, 34, 35, 38, 48, 51n2, 61, 65–66, 67, 69; Chiriguano thesis on, 69, 70; communities of, 35, 63, 64, 65, 67; and enslavement, 35, 55–56; and exchange, 135; as Guaraní group, 10; historical documentation on, 39, 63, 68; languages of, 68; and migration, 34, 35; and missionaries, 30, 33, 39; and Moxeño, 57; oral history of, 33; origins of, 66; and resistance, 10; scholarship on, 33, 71n2; and Spanish, 61; and sugarcane harvests, 34, 35; and Tapiete, 260; territory of, 34, 56; and warfare, 61–62

Chiriguano (term): meanings of, 60, 61–62; modern use of, 56; origins and evolution of, 55, 60, 70, 71n6, 71n7; scholarship on, 71n6; uses of, 55, 60–61

Chiriguano thesis: acceptance of, 53–54, 55, 67; arguments supporting, 58, 63; Bret Gustafson on, 281; changes in, 56; on Chiriguano and Chané peoples, 69; as colonial and national narrative, 55–56, 70, 71n3; foundations of; on Guaraní peoples, 70; on Isoso region Chané, 69; Nordenskiöld and, 67; origins of, 54; tenets of, 53; and term Chiriguano, 55, 59–62

Chomai (Ayoreo man), 237–38

Chorote (language), 86

Chorote (people), 16, 256, 260, 262

Christian Initiative social plan, 87

Chukuri (Chané man), 44–46, 47

Chur, Juan/John Church, 80
Church of God, 84
Cicchetti, Enrique, 83
Ciccone, Florencia, 256
CIDOB. *See* Confederación de Pueblos Indígenas de Bolivia (CIDOB, Confederation of Indigenous Peoples of Bolivia)
CIPCA. *See* Centro de Investigación y Promoción del Campesinado (CIPCA, Center for Investigation and Promotion of Peasants)
Citro, Silvia, 84–85
Class: and accumulation, 143; and cattle ranching, 216; criollos and, 261; Guaraní and, 216, 229; and indigeneity, 215; mestizos and, 216, 222, 229; middle, 215; official report on, 15–16; and sugarcane cultivation and processing, 16, 17
Clastres, Pierre, 223, 282
Clearance (term), 164n6
Cleary, Edward, 271
Clifford, James, 274
Clínica Indígena Filadelfia, 236, 237
Clothing and textiles: Angaité and, 134–35; blankets, 102; cloth, 102; Enlhet and, 102; Enxet and, 134–35; evangelism and, 263; Guaraní and, 231; jackets, 158; missions and missionaries and, 12, 81, 83; Moqoit and, 158; Nivaclé and, 102, 134–35; pants, 102; Paraguayan-style, 129; Protestants and, 81; sandals, 36; shirts, 102, 158; and status, 83; Tapiete and, 269; Toba and, 134–35; wedding dresses, 129; wool, 135
Cochou (Chané man), 33, 34, 35, 38, 48, 51n9
Collective land rights claims. *See* Tierras Comunitarias de Origen (TCOs)
Colonia 15, Argentina, 265
Colonia Cacique Catán (Paraje Las Tolderías), Argentina: accumulation by dispossession in, 147; and agribusiness, 142, 157, 159; colonists' debt in, 159; deforestation in, 160; establishment of, 155, 156; and external support, 160, 161; livestock in, 160; maps of, *25;* Mercedes Biocca in, 159; and migration, 163; neighborhoods of, 156, 160, 161; origin of name of, 165n12; and pollution, 160
Colonia El Pastoril, Argentina, 155
Colonia La Primavera, Argentina, 79

Colorado Party, 243
Columbus, Christopher, 62
Comajuncosa, Antonio, 30–32
Comaroff, Jean, 82
Comaroff, John, 82
Combès, Isabelle: on ancient Zamucos, 135; on Chané, 68, 72n11; on ethnonyms and relationships, 135; on Guaraní, 218; on indigenous peoples and Chaco War, 13; on meaning of *Chiriguano,* 60; on Tapiete, 260; on Weenhayek, 189
Cominges, Juan de, 129
Comisión Zonal de Tierras, 149–50, 164n10
Commission on Autonomies, 219
Componente de Atención a la Población Indígena (CAPI, Development Program for the Indigenous Population), 257, 276n4
Concepción, Paraguay, *4, 166, 168*
Confederación de Pueblos Indígenas de Bolivia (CIDOB, Confederation of Indigenous Peoples of Bolivia): at consultation and participation meeting, 202, 209, 210; and ORCAWETA, 192, 204, 268; and organizing activities, 191; and resistance, 213n30
Consejos locales de salud (local health councils), 245
Cooperativa Pampa del Indio, 148
Coordinadora de Líderes del Bajo Chaco, 125
Cordillera Province, 63
Córdoba (Penek-Saanga), Paraguay, *94, 98, 99,* 100, 101
Córdoba Province, Argentina, 156, 159, 165n14
Corrado, Alejandro, 32, 40, 42–43
Correia, Joel E.: on *cultura indígena,* 185n2; and Enxet-Sur people, 279; field work by, 185n3; on impact of cattle ranching, 180, 278; on indigenous dislocation, 278; on roots of infrastructural violence, 167; on water-borne diseases, 181–82; on water from stock ponds, 185n9; in Yakye Axa, Paraguay, 166–67
Corrientes, Argentina, 91n2
Cortez, Guido, 187, 202, 280
Cortez, Lucas, 190
Corumbá, Brazil, *4,* 66
Costas, Patrón, 52n27
Costas, Ruben, 226, 227, 231

Cotton production: in Argentina, 10, 16, 147, 148, 149, 150, 151, 152, 154, 155, 156, 157–58, 159, 162, 163; cotton cooperatives and, 159; Enlhet and, 102, 108; Guaná and, 134; indigenous people and, 13, 16; Kaskiha and, 134; land for, 147, 148; Mennonites and, 102, 108; Moqoit and, 10, 155, 157–58, 162, 163; origins of, 3; in Paraguay, 102; Qom and, 10, 148, 149, 150, 151, 152, 154, 162; replacement of, with soybeans, 156; Sanapaná and, 134; as transgenic crop, 150, 154; Unión Campesina and, 149, 150, 154; Vilela and, 10

Coutada, Virgilio, 83

Cox, Laurence, 146

Crevaux, Bolivia, *188*, 195, 268

Crévaux, Jules, 5

Criollo (term), 26n1, 91n6, 117n6, 164n5

Criollos (persons): and agriculture, 10; and Chaco War, 106; and class, 261; communities of, 7, 256; and discrimination, 256; and ethnicity, 261; in Gran Chaco, 1; and housing, 81, 263; and indigenous peoples, 10–11, 87, 103, 106, 107, 117n1, 149, 158, 260; languages of, 117n6; and livestock, 10; and migration, 147, 159; and missions, 269; and native territories, 102; origins of, 117n1, 117n6; and poverty, 152, 159; and religion, 12, 79; sales of land by, 156, 159; as settlers, 5, 102; and unemployment, 160

Cruzeño elite, 218

Dario (Qom man), 151

Das Kapital (Marx), 143

Death and the Right Hand (Hertz), 137

Decentralization of Health and Community Participation, 244

Declaration on the Rights of Indigenous Peoples, 20

Decolonization: in Africa, 77; in Asia, 77; Bolivian government and, 214, 225; and dependence, 217; Guaraní and, 215, 217, 224; and indigenous autonomy, 232; and indigenous values, 224; MAS and, 233; and natural resources extraction, 232–33; and racism and discrimination, 217; urban indigenous peoples and, 215; varying practices of, 240

Delgado (litigant), 44, 46

Demócratas (Verdes) political party, 216, 222, 226–27

Department of Alto Paraguay, Paraguay, *4*, 19, *25, 168*, 247

Department of Boquerón, Paraguay: government in, 237; indigenous population of, 247; maps of, *4*, *25, 168;* Paola Canova in, 254; Tapiete in, 262, 266

Department of Chuquisaca, Bolivia, *4*, *25*

Department of Orán, Argentina, 29

Department of Presidente Hayes, Paraguay, *4*, *25*, 140n1, *168*, 176, 185n4

Department of San Martín, Argentina, 29

Department of Santa Cruz, Bolivia: Chaco region of, 215, 229; class in, 216; and gas rents and royalty payments, 225–26; Guaraní in, 216, 225, 226, 230; and indigenous autonomy, 226–27; leadership in, 216, 225, 226, 227; legislature of, 225–26; map of, *4;* mestizos in, 226; and Morales government, 280; political parties in, 216, 226; ranching in, 6; Tapiete in, 262

Department of Tarija, Bolivia, *4*, 6, *25*, 187, *188*, 262

Department of Villa Hayes, Paraguay, 247

"Desde el saber de ellas construimos ciudadanía," 255n4

De Souza, Ilda, 58, 72n8

Development: in Argentina, 22, 49, 74, 76, 78, 258; in Bolivia, 198–99, 226, 231; future research needs of, 90–91; Guaraní and, 218, 223, 233; and humanitarianism, 90; missions and missionaries and, 73, 81, 86, 89–90, 279; and modernity, 77; narrative of, 77; nongovernmental organizations and, 1, 73, 87, 90; and religion, 73, 77, 78–79, 80, 81, 86, 89–90, 279; scholarship on, 77; Tapiete and, 257

Development Bank of Latin America (CAF, formerly Corporación Andina de Fomento), 18

Development Program for the Indigenous Population (CAPI, Componente de Atención a la Población Indígena), 257, 276n4

Diego (religious leader), 79

Dietrich, Wolf, 67, 68, 69

Dirección General de Educación Escolar

Indígena (General Office of Indigenous Schooling and Education), 242

Dirección Nacional de Salud de los Pueblos Indígenas (National Office for the Health of Indigenous Populations), 243

Disciples of Christ, 84

Diseases and health issues: alcoholism, 262, 269; cancer, 250; and Chaco War, 13; cirrhosis, 123; high blood pressure, 236, 237; HIV/AIDS, 249, 251, 252; infant mortality, 83, 87; infections, 250; influenza, 82; kidney stones, 128; malnutrition, 87; maternal mortality, 87; measles, 11; obesity, 247; pesticide-induced, 278; plague, 82; sexually transmitted, 248, 253; smallpox, 11, 82, 103, 106, 107, 115; testing for, 247; tuberculosis, 82, 83, 87, 123, 129, 253; and vaccinations, 83; water-borne illnesses, 179, 181–82, 278. *See also* Health and health care

Don Panos (company), 148, 149, 150, 152–53, 155, 163

D'Orbigny, Alcide, 5

Duarte Frutos, Nicanor, 241

Dulce River, *4*

Eaton family, 125

Ecovia, 271

Ecuador, 240

Education: Catholic Church and, 88, 242; Enxet and, 176–77; Guaraní and, 233; indigenous peoples and, 8, 9, 12, 17, 22, 79, 80, 81, 84, 242; missions and missionaries and, 8, 9, 12, 80, 81, 87, 176–77, 269; and neoliberalism, 22; nongovernmental organizations and, 87, 90, 121; Qom and, 87, 88; Tapiete and, 257, 269, 270, 271, 275; Weenhayek and, 189, 192, 196

El Estribo, Paraguay, 123

El Paso mission station, 176

Embarcación, Salta Province, Argentina, *4, 7*, 79, 82, 83, 262

Emmanuel Mission, 80

ENDEPA (Equipo Nacional de Pastoral Aborigen/National Team of Pastoral Aborigines), 91n4, 164n10

Enenlhet (people), 119

Enenlhet (term), 136

Enimaga (people), 132, 133, 134

Enimaga (term), 132, 133

Enlhet (language): speakers of, 98, 99; terms in, 117n7, 117n8, 117n9, 134, 278

Enlhet (people): adoption of *Enlhet* as name for, 136; and Anglicans, 8; and clothing, 102; and communication, 96, 101–2; communities and settlement patterns of, *25*, 103, 106–7; and concepts of territory and space, 93–95, 100–101, 114–15; contemporary challenges of, 112, 113–14; and criollos and settlers, 103, 106–7, 117n1; diet of, 100, 102, 107, 111; and disease, 103, 106, 107, 115; and Enlhet-Enenlhet language family, 93, 119, 133; and first contact with whites, 101; forebears of, 134; and health care, 107, 108, 110–11; and human-nonhuman interactions, 97–98, 104–5, 107, 110, 113, 115; and identity, 99–100, 101; and intermarriage, 98, 114; as labor, 102–3, 107, 108–9, 112, 113; lands of, 93, *94*, 96, 98, 99, 101, 106–7, 111, 117n1, 278; and livestock, 103; and Mennonites, 9, 102–3, 106–11, 112, 117n1; and mobility, 102–3, 104, 106, 109, 111, 278; and Nivaclé, 98, 99, 101, 102, 103; and Paraguayans, 111, 112; and religion, 9, 107–8, 110–11; resettlement of, 107, 115; and roads, 279; and safety, 111, 112, 113, 114; scholarship on, 117n2; traditions and rituals of, 111, 115–16, 138

Enlhet-Enenlhet language family: cultural variations among, 134–35; evolution of, 132, 136; groups in, 93, 119, 132–33, 139; historical documentation on, 117n2, 132; leaders of, 136; names for, 132; and names for other groups, 132; prefixes in, 120; rituals of, 137–38; scholarship on, 135; shamans among, 136; sociopolitical institutions of, 131; terms in, 135; and Yshir, 133

Ennimá (term), 133

Enslavement: Chané and, 35, 53, 68; Chiriguano and, 35, 55; and colonization, 55; escapees from, 59; Guaná-Chané and, 57–58, 137; Guaraní and, 53, 61, 216; indigenous peoples and, 59, 70; Kadiweu and, 57–58; Mbayá and, 135, 137; Mbaya-Guaykuru and, 57–58; Spanish and, 54, 57, 61, 62, 70

Enxet (language), 122, 134

Enxet (people): and Angaité, 126; and Anglicans, 9, 121, 134, 169, 175, 176–77; and assimilation, 177; and cattle ranching, 167, 169, 170, 178; and Chaco War, 13; and citizenship, 171; communities of, 25, 128, 134, 166, 169; and education, 176–77; and Enlhet-Enenlhet language family, 93, 119, 133; and epidemics, 11; forebears of, 134; and gardening, 169; and health and health services, 166, 179, 181–82; historical documentation on, 130; and human rights violations, 171; and hunting and gathering, 134–35, 169, 180, 181, 185n9; and indigenous culture, 167; and Inter-American Court of Human Rights, 21; and intermarriage, 134; and Joel Correia, 185n2, 185n3; as labor, 121, 167, 169, 170, 177, 179, 184; and land, 21–22, 121, 167, 169, 170–71, 178, 179, 184; and livestock, 169; and Maká, 134; and Maskoy, 133; and Maskoy language family, 185n1; and mobility, 169, 179, 180; names of, for other groups, 132; naming of, 136, 185n1; and Nivaclé, 134; oral histories of, 13; and pottery, 134–35; and poverty, 121; and racism, 173; and religion, 11, 167, 185n2; resettlement of, 121; and resistance, 11, 168, 170–71, 182; rituals of, 138; and safety, 171; scholarship on, 185n1; and settler colonialism, 167–68, 169, 177; and shamen, 125; standard of living of, 167; and state services, 167, 170, 171; and Toba Qom, 134; and traditional healing practices, 123, 128–29; traditional practices of, 185n2; and transportation, 166, 167, 181; and unemployment, 167; and water, 171, 181; and wool textiles, 134–35
Enxet-Sur (people), 185n1, 279
Equipo Nacional de Misiones (National Missionary Team), 267
Escobar, Arturo, 240
Escondido, Bolivia, 195
Espinillo, Argentina, 80
Ethnos 360 (New Tribes Mission), 9, 185n8, 246
Eurnekian, Eduardo, 149, 153
Evangelical Baptist Church, 151
Evangelical Church of the Río de la Plata, 84
Evangelical Methodist Church of Argentina, 84

Evangelical Mission Assembly of God, 79, 83
Evangelical Superior Institute of Theological Studies (ISEDET), 88
Evangelism: and Catholicism, 80; and clothing, 263; criollos and, 12; indigenous peoples and, 12, 73, 74, 79, 80, 81, 257, 258, 259; and literacy, 263; and modernization, 263; scholarship on, 276n6; tenets of, 263
Exploraciones (Cominges), 129

Fabricant, Nicole, 213n30
Family Federation for World Peace and Unification (Korean Holy Spirit Association for the Unification of World Christianity, "Moonies"), 19, 20
Farmer, Paul, 172
Federación de Pueblos y Organizaciones Indígenas Chaco del Paraguay (Federation of Indigenous Peoples and Organizations of the Paraguay Chaco), 267–68
Federación Pilagá, 88
Fernández (colonist), 158
Fernández, Rubén, 127
Fernando (Moqoit man), 158, 159
Fernheim Colony, 9, 117n1, 247, 255n1
Ferreyra, Tomás, 272–73
Filadelfia, Paraguay: Ayoreo in, 236, 240; Christian community in, 249; communities near, 267; as economic hub, 9; Enlhet in, 102; health care in, 236–37, 240, 245, 248, 249, 252; maps of, 4, 25, 94, 168; Mennonites in, 102, 117n1, 236; neighborhoods of, 236; Paola Canova in, 254
Flecha, Asencio, 130
Flores, Damacio, 140n5
Flores, Tranquilino, 134
Foods and beverages: aitipí, 36; alcohol, 128, 138, 269; atikui, 36; beef, 37, 173, 175, 179; bread, 107; bush meat, 111; carob meat, 102; chicken and vegetable stew, 204; consumption of, during rituals, 138; dairy products, 173, 179; fish, 100, 102, 149, 189, 190, 211n11, 263; fruits, 189, 190; honey, 166, 189, 190, 263; mate, 83, 124, 185n9; meat, 158, 190; sorghum flour, 107
Formosa (city), Argentina, 4, 25, 80, 117n6

Formosa Territory/Province, Argentina: agribusiness in, 148; Anglicans in, 83; Catholic Church in, 76, 80, 89; César Ceriani Cernadas in, 79; diseases in, 82; establishment of, 15; federalization of, 91n9; Gastón Gordillo in, 277–78; maps of, *4, 25*; nongovernmental organizations in, 88, 89, 91n2; as part of central Chaco, 3; and Protestantism, 84; railroads in, 7; resistance in, 10
Fortín Falcón (Kenma'lha, Fort Falcón), Paraguay, *94,* 98
Fortín Infante Rivarola/Pikasu, Paraguay, 267
Fortín Nanawa, Paraguay, *94*
Fortín Saavedra (Fort Saavedra), Paraguay, *94,* 100
Foster-Seelstrang expedition, 5
Foundation of Social Accompaniment of the Anglican Church of Northern Argentina, 87
Franciscans: in Argentina, 261; and Chané, 40, 50, 68; and Guaraní, 66; and missions, 3–5, 8, 29, 30; withdrawal of, 8. *See also* Catholic Church
Free Swedish Mission in Bolivia (Misión Sueca Libre en Bolivia), 190, 192, 196, 197, 211n10, 271
Friends of the Earth, 212n17
Fundación de Acompañamiento Social de la Iglesia Anglicana del Norte Argentino (ASOCIANA), 87
Fundación para el Desarrollo en Justicia y Paz (FUNDAPAZ, Foundation for Development in Justice and Peace), 76, 87, 91n3
Furlong, Guillermo, 130

Galarza, Nicanor, 41, 42
Galtung, Johan, 172
Galvão, Rufino Enéas Gustavo, 140n3
García Linera, Álvaro, 210
GASYRG, 194
General Necochea Agricultural Colony, Chaco Province, Argentina, 155
General San Martín, Chaco Province, Argentina, 147, 149
German Catholic Church, 77
Giannecchini (missionary), 33, 39
Giordano, Mariana, 74
Glassman, Jim, 144
Glauser, Pascual, 125

Gobernación de Boquerón, 237. *See also* Department of Boquerón, Paraguay
Gobierno Autónomo Guaraní Charagua Iyambae, 234. *See also* Charagua Iyambae, Bolivia
Gómez, Mariana, 76
Gómez, René, 217, 218, 233
González, Amancio, 133
González, Eligio, 128–29
González, Hebe, 256
González, Josué Emanuel, 128
González, Lorena, 123, 128–29, 137, 140
González, Osvaldo, 128, 129
Gordillo, Gastón, 171, 173, 277, 282
Gorgotoqui (language), 63
Gran Chaco: agribusiness in, 1, 3, 277, 281; animals in, 281; biodiversity in, 1, 3; borders of, 7; capitalist expansion in, 13; and Chaco War, 1; characteristics of, 281–82; and climate change, 282; climate in, 3, 5, 281; competing factions in, 1, 2; countries in, 6; deforestation in, 3, 17, 26n2, 282; disputes over, 5; earth ethnologies of, 130; economy in, 19; exploration in, 3, 5, 29, 32, 129, 130; fencing in, 277; flora in, 2, 277, 281; frontiers in, 2, 282; historical documentation on, 3, 5, 130; indigenous peoples in, 1, 5, 9–10, 11, 29, 36, 182, 190, 260, 275, 277, 278; industry in, 1, 3, 5, 18, 19, 193, 211n7, 277; infrastructure in, 18–19; location of, 1, 281; map of, *4;* mestizos in, 190; and migration, 7; missions and missionaries in, 5, 8, 129, 130; nights in, 281–82; nongovernmental organizations in, 1, 77; population of, 1; ranching in, 6, 277; regions of, 2–3; rivers in, 2, 281; sale of lands in, 6; scholarship on, 2, 5, 26n2, 281; settlement in, 5, 6; size of, 1; soil in, 281; soldiers in, 190; sunlight in, 281; terrain in, 281; topography of, 5; transportation in, 6, 18, 277; water resources in, 3. *See also* Argentine Chaco; Bolivian Chaco; Paraguayan Chaco
Gran Chaco Province, Bolivia, 6, 29, 40, *188*
Grigotá (Chané man), 59
Gringos, 91n6
Grubb, W. Barbrooke, 8, 130, 135, 138, 175–76, 177
Guaná (language), 57, 69
Guaná (people), 93, 119, 131, 133, 134, 136

Guana Chané: as Arawak population, 56–57; communities of, 57, 58, 59, 70, 71n4, 137; and enslavement, 135, 137; and Guaraní speakers, 66; and hierarchy, 137; historical documentation on, 59; and Jesuits, 58; languages of, 57, 58; and Mbaya, 135; and mobility and migration, 58, 71n4; reputation of, 58; terms used by, 135

Guaraní (language): Angaité and, 122; and Arawak language, 67–68, 69; Chané and, 53, 54, 58; and Chiriguano thesis, 53, 56, 63, 281; introduction of, 13; meetings in, 222; places spoken, 63, 69; prevalence of, 53; required use of, 229; scholarship on, 65, 68–69; speakers of, 54, 55, 56, 59, 61, 64, 66, 117n6, 124, 127, 281; Tapiete and, 260; terms and phrases in, 39, 64, 65, 67, 122, 136, 189, 217, 224, 227, 233; use of *i* in, 51n7; use of {#}-*tá* suffix in, 59; variants of, 69

Guaraní (people): and activism, 215–16, 280; and agriculture, 216; and Arawak, 60, 67, 70; and autonomy, 215, 216–19, 220–21, 222–31, 232, 233; and Bolivian government, 215, 217, 225, 227–28; and cannibalism, 53, 55, 60; and Chaco War, 12–13; and Chané, 53, 56, 68, 281; and Chiriguano thesis, 53, 54, 55, 56, 62, 69, 70, 281; communities of, 7, *25*, 54, 55, 58, 59, 67, 69, 71n2, 71n5, 119, 189, 256, 267; conflict among, 218, 222–23, 233; and consensual decision making, 191; and culture, 20, 233; and development, 218, 223, 233; and diplomacy, 234; and education, 233; and enslavement, 53, 55, 61, 216; and identity, 12–13, 20; and Inca Empire, 67, 71n6; and intermarriage, 268, 274; and labor, 65, 216; leaders of, 217, 223; and livestock, 216; and migration, 13, 20, 48, 49, 54, 65; and missions and missionaries, 82, 211n6, 267; and Moxeño, 57; and multiterritoriality, 266, 273–74; and nongovernmental organizations, 10; and oil companies, 52n30, 218, 223, 233; oral histories of, 48; organizations of, 269; origins of, 281; political organization of, 274; and politics, 218, 222, 225, 226–28, 233–34; and religion, 20; and resistance, 225; scholarship on, 20, 67, 69, 71n2, 217–18; settlement patterns of, 216; and Silvia Hirsch, 256; and Spanish, 54, 55,

56, 58–59, 60–61; subgroups of, 216, 218; and Tapiete, 260, 268, 274; terms for, 60–61, 281; territories of, 59, 218, 223

Guaraní (term), 54, 55, 64

Guaraní Ñandeva: and access to water, 267, 268; and agriculture, 267; communities of, 25, 267; and employment, 267; leaders of, 267; and livestock, 267; origins of, 267; in Paraguay, 266, 268, 274, 276n9; population of, 276n9; Silvia Hirsch and, 273. *See also* Tapiete (people)

Guaraní Occidentales, 267

Guaraní region, 63–64

Guarumbaque (Chané man), 41–42, 44–45, 46, 47, 52n28, 52n31

Guaykurú (language group), 131, 132

Guaykurú (people), 5, 131

Guirapembi, Bolivia, 64

Gupta, Akhil, 172

Gustafson, Bret, 57, 281

Guyra Paraguay, 17

Haako'-Pya'yeem (Mennonite), 107–8, 110

Haesbaert, Rogério, 259, 265–66

Hallin, Daniel, 250

Harder Horst, René, 275

Hardy, Charles, 15

Hardy, Richard, 15

Harvey, David, 141, 142, 143, 144

Harvey, Penelope, 167, 182

Hayes, Rutherford B., 6

Health and health care: Ayoreo and, 236–37, 239–40, 246, 248–54, 279; and contraception, 249; and decentralization, 244–45; facilities for, 236–37, 245; funding and supplies for, 237–38, 245; and hygiene, 8, 250, 270, 279; ignorance about, 249; indigenous peoples and, 238–39, 243–44, 247; medications and supplies for, 237, 238, 251; Mennonites and, 236–37; missions and, 9, 80, 81–83, 84, 269; and pollution, 278; Qom and, 80; and racism and discrimination, 249, 251, 253, 254; Tapiete and, 275; and traditional healing practices, 107, 110–11, 123, 128, 153, 246; training in cross-cultural approaches to, 252; and transportation, 237, 247, 250; women and, 236–38, 239–41, 246, 247, 248–49, 253, 254

Hertz, Robert, 137
Hetherington, Kregg, 172
Hinu Parava, 33, 34, 51n9
Hirsch, Silvia: and Guaraní, 256; and Guaraní Ñandeva, 273; on indigenous dislocation, 278; and Tapiete, 256, 257, 263, 264, 270, 272, 273, 279, 281
hooks, bell, 178
Horst, Willis, 85
Hospital Filadelfia, 236
Hospital Materno-Infantil Villa Choferes del Chaco, 237, 250
Huenuán, Catalina, 51n8
Humahuaca route, 29
Humanitarianism, 73, 75, 81–82, 83, 86, 90
Hydrocarbon extraction. See Natural gas extraction; Natural resources extraction

Ibibobo, Bolivia, 4, 188, 195
I Encuentro Trinacional Tapiete, 271
Ijoya (Ayoreo woman), 250–51
Ikua, Argentina, 37
Imaca (term), 133
Inca Empire, 67, 71n6
INCUPO. See Instituto de Cultura Popular (INCUPO, Institute of Popular Culture)
Indalecio (Wichí person), 83
INDI. See Instituto Nacional del Indígena (INDI, National Institute for Indigenous Affairs)
Indiana, USA, 85
Indigenista, 76, 91n1
Indigenist Association of Paraguay, 267
Indigenous Communication Network, 88–89
Indigenous Development Plan, 198–99, 206, 209
Indigenous peoples: Aguaze, 61; Angaité-Koalhvok, 139, 140n5; Apipón, 131; Arauaca, 62; Auca, 62; Ava, 216, 218; Aymara, 225, 234; Caniba, 62; Caribe, 60, 61, 62; Darío, 60, 71n7; Chaco, 130, 131; Chamacoco, 5; Chaná, 135; Chanameshma, 120; Charrua, 62; Chichimeca, 62; Chiquitos, 135; Chorote, 9, 16, 256, 260, 262; Chulupi, 256; Echoaladi, 57; Enenlhet, 119; Enimaga, 132, 133, 134; equestrian, 131, 134; Guaná, 93, 119, 131, 133, 134, 136; Guarayu, 57, 60; Guatate, 61; Guatiao, 62; Guaycuro, 61; Guaykurú,

5, 131; Guisnay, 189; Ignaciano, 57; Isoseño, 69, 216, 218; Isoso Guaraní, 72n11; Itatine, 57; Kadiweu, 57, 58; Kaskiha, 132, 134; Kinikinau, 57, 66, 72n8; Koeteve, 120; Konhongnava, 120; Koonaava'atsam, 120; Koonalhma, 120; Kovalhok, 120; Layana, 57; Lengua, 130, 132, 133; Lengua-Maskoy, 132; Lule, 131; Machicui, 132; Maká, 13, 98, 134; Malvala, 131; Manjui, 9; Mapuche, 282; Maskoy/Maskoi, 119, 131, 133, 136, 175; Mataguayo, 30, 131; Mbayá, 129, 130, 135, 137; Mbaya-Caduveo, 131; Mbaya-Guaykuru, 57, 58; Mocoví, 74, 81, 131, 165n12; Mohawk, 219; Moxeño, 57, 59, 66; Parapetiguasu, 216; Payaguá, 130, 132; Pilagá, 9, 13, 25, 74, 80, 81, 82, 133; Qomle'ec (Toba), 278; Quechua, 64, 225; Sújen/Sujin/Seugen, 132; Tapuy, 64; Terena, 54, 57, 66; Toba-Enenlhet, 93; Toba-Maskoy, 132; Toba Qom, 134; Toothli, 132; Trinitario, 57; Tsané, 57; Tsirakua, 64; Tupi, 61; Vejoz, 189; Vilela, 10, 131; Wichí-Guisnay, 13; Xaané, 57; Xâne, 57; Yanaygua, 64; Yshir, 133, 137; Yshir-Chamacoco, 135; Zamuco, 131, 135, 260. See also Angaité (people); Angaité-Koalhvok; Arawak (people); Ayoreo (people); Chané (people); Chané communities; Chiriguano (people); Enlhet (people); Enxet (people); Guana Chané; Guaraní (people); Guaraní Ñandeva; Moqoit (people); Nivaclé (people); Qom (people); Sanapaná people; Tapiete (people); Toba (people); Weenhayek people; Wichí (people)
Indigenous Peoples Health Division, 123
Indigenous Peoples Institute, 257
Indigenous women: and activism, 20, 76, 87; and health services, 236–38, 239–41, 246, 247, 248–49, 253, 254; marginalization of, 19; as medicine women, 123; official reports on, 255n4; violence against, 55, 249, 255n4, 270
Industry: and Chaco War, 14; logging, 1, 3, 5, 6, 41, 49, 177, 185n7; lumber, 10, 13, 15, 120; palm oil production, 174, 182; ranching, 1; rubber production, 65; tannin production, 3, 7, 13, 14, 15, 16, 120, 122, 129, 133, 175, 177, 185n7; timber milling, 5, 6, 7, 263. See also Agribusiness and agriculture; Cotton production; Natural gas extraction; Natural

resources extraction; Sugarcane cultivation and processing

Infrastructural violence: and capitalism, 173; and cattle ranching, 172–73, 178; and colonialism, 173; and deforestation, 184; and drinking water, 167, 171, 173, 178, 179, 182, 279; Enxet and, 168, 182; and fences, 172–73, 178, 179, 279; and gender, 181; and human rights violations, 171; and indigenous land rights, 167, 171, 173, 178, 183; in Indonesia, 172; and labor, 167, 171, 178, 183; and race and racism, 173, 183; and roads, 171, 173, 178–79, 279; scholarship on, 167–68, 171, 172, 173–74; and settler colonialism, 173, 174; and state services, 171; and violence, 167, 171–72. *See also* Settler colonialism

Ingenio La Esperanza, Argentina, 261

Inimicá/Imaca. *See* Enimaga (people)

Instituto de Cultura Popular (INCUPO, Institute of Popular Culture), 76, 88, 91n2, 91n3, 164n10

Instituto de Previsión Social, 255n1

Instituto Nacional del Desarrollo Rural y de la Tierra (National Institute for Land and Rural Development), 19

Instituto Nacional del Indígena (INDI, National Institute for Indigenous Affairs), 237, 238, *239*, 241–42

Instituto Superior Evangélico de Estudios Teológicos (ISEDET), 88

Intendencia del Ejército, 238

Inter-American Court of Human Rights (IACHR), 21, 125, 170, 171, 180, 181–82

Inter-American Development Bank, 18, 194, 241–42, 276n4

Inter-American Foundation, 156

Interfluvio Turco-Bermejito, 87

International Labor Organization Convention on Indigenous and Tribal Peoples (ILO 169), 20

International Product Corporation (IPC), 120, 121

Iopeité (settlement), 38

Iquira (settlement), 41

Irala, Domingo Martínez de, 58, 71n5

Irua (Algarrobal), Bolivia, 36, 38, 44, *188*

Isiporenda, Bolivia, 64

Isla Chané island, 58

Isoso region: Chané in, 64, 67, 68; and Chiriguano thesis, 54; development in, 231; Guaraní in, 67, 231; Guaraní speakers in, 68–69; indigenous peoples in, 34, 52n21; location of, 64, 260; Nordenskiöld and, 64, 67, 68–69; and Salinas salt flats, 71n5; Tapiete in, 260; weaving in, 72n11

Itaki Outlet, 32, 41

Itatine (people), 57

Itatines (place), 61, 71n7

Itau, Bolivia, 30, 35, 198

Itau mission, 30

Itika region, 38, 51n11

Itiyuro (settlement), 41, 44

Itiyuro region: altitude of, 29; cattle ranching in, 49; Chané in, 29, 41, 44, 46, 49, 52n27, 54, 64, 69, 72n11; colonization in, 38, 40, 42, 49; development in, 49; ecosystem in, 29; Guaraní language in, 69; historical documentation on, 30; industry in, 34, 35, 49; location of, 29, 68; mapping of, 42; map of, *31*; missionaries in, 43; non-indigenous peoples in, 29–30, 32, 34; Nordenskiöld in, 72n11; railroad in, 49; transfer of, from Bolivia to Argentina, 43

Itiyuro River: as boundary, 37, 41; indigenous peoples along, 32, 35; industry along, 29; mapping of, 29, 30; settlements along, 40, 51n12

Itiyuro River basin: Chané in, 279, 280–81; location of, 69

Iyambae, Enrique, 52n21

Jakatimbae Gorge, 32

Japan International Cooperation Aid, 245

Jerusai (Chané woman), 38, 47

Jesuits, 5, 58, 63, 130, 133, 134. *See also* Catholic Church

Johnsen, Bergen, 82, 83, 90

Jolis, Giuseppe, 59, 68

Jonsson, Olof, 262

Jorge (teacher), 229, 230

José (Moqoit man), 155, 159, 160

Juan Max Boettner Hospital, 123

Jujuy Province, Argentina, 7, 16, 80, 82, 211n6

Junta vecinal (neighborhood association), 216, 228, 230

Kaamiri (Chané man), 36
Kaipependi region, 64, 68
Kalisch, Hannes, 132, 135, 278, 279
Kam'aatkok-Ketsek (Enlhet woman), 105–6
Kapi (Chané man), 36
Kapura (Toba man), 36, 37
Karanday Puku community, 138
Karova Guazu, Paraguay, 123, 124, 125, 126, 127
Kaymaap-Tes (Enlhet man), 101
Keane, Webb, 77
Kenma'lha (Fortín Falcón), Paraguay, *94, 98*
Kidd, Stephen William, 11, 169, 177
Kilómetro 1, Bolivia, *188,* 195
Kilómetro 6, Argentina, 262
Kinikinau (language), 57, 64, 65
Kinikinau (people), 57, 66, 72n8. *See also*
    Chané (people)
Kirchner, Cristina, 258, 280
Kirchner, Néstor, 258, 280
Klassen, Pamela, 82
Korean Holy Spirit Association for the
    Unification of World Christianity (Family
    Federation for World Peace and Unification,
    "Moonies"), 19, 20
Koronsai (Chané man), 38
Kuruyuki, Bolivia, 10

La Curvita, Argentina, 262, 265
La Forestal Land, Timber, and Railways Com-
    pany, 15, 16
Laguna Blanca, Argentina, 80
Laguna Negra, Paraguay, 267–68, 271
Laguna Rey mission, 120
La Herencia (program), 121, 123
La Leona, Paraguay, 122, 125, 126
Land of the Enlhet, 93. *See also* Enlhet (people)
La Patria, Paraguay, 121, 122, 123, 124, 125,
    126–28
La Paz, Bolivia, 6, 42, 47, 52n21, 52n31, 230
Lapegna, Pablo, 146
Larkin, Brian, 173, 174
Las Lomitas, Argentina, *4, 7*
Las Palmas sugar refinery, 15, 16, 147
Lavazza, Hugo, 269, 275
La Vertiente, Bolivia, *188,* 195
Leake, Andrew, 180
Lebowitz, Michael, 145
Ledesma, Jujuy Province, Argentina, 211n6

Ledesma sugar plantation, 47
Legislation and decrees: in Argentina, 20, 50n1,
    147, 164n9, 257, 263, 264, 268; in Bolivia, 22,
    196, 197, 199–200, 218, 220, 268; in Paraguay,
    15, 19, 21, 147, 236, 241, 242, 244, 245, 268
Lengua (people), 130, 132, 133
Lengua (term), 132, 140n4
Lengua-Maskoy (people), 132
Lengua-Maskoy (term), 133
Leone, Miguel, 76
Levien, Michael, 144
Lha'akme-Yaamelket (Campo Jordán), Para-
    guay, *94,* 100
Lhaapangkalvok (Filadelfia), Paraguay. *See*
    Filadelfia, Paraguay
Lhamalhtengyava' (Paratodo), Paraguay, *94,*
    103
Li, Tania M., 152, 172, 173, 174, 182
Lida, Miranda, 78
Lilly (teacher), 229
Lima, Upper Peru, 58, 61
Lizárraga, F. Reginaldo de, 58, 62
Llanos de Manso region, 59
Local rationalities, 142, 145–47, 162, 163. *See*
    also Accumulation by dispossession
Loewen, Jacob, 137
Loida (Ayoreo woman), 250
Loma Plata, Paraguay, 9, *94,* 102, 117n1
Loma Pytá, Paraguay, *94,* 99
López, Aurelio, 86
López, Mártires, 141, 154, 163
López, Salustiano, 86
López, Serafín, 125
Los Monos, Bolivia, 195
Los Suris, Bolivia, *188,* 195
Loukotka, Cestmir, 72n11
Lowrey, Kathleen, 72n11
Lugo, Fernando, 243
Luis (Qom man), 148, 151–52, 154

Maalhek (Tinfunke), Paraguay, *94,* 99, 100
Maangvayaam'ay' (Enlhet man): on agricul-
    ture, 112; birth of, 96, 98; changes during life
    of, 113; on conversion to Christianity, 107–8,
    112; on Enlhet land title, 112; on Enlhet mo-
    bility, 108; on Enlhet resettlement, 98, 107,
    109; on Enlhet territory and settlements,
    97, 100, 101; on Enlhet youth, 112; family

of, 98–99, 101, 102–3, 110–11; on human-nonhuman interactions, 97–98, 104–5, 116; identity of, 99; on languages, 98–99, 103; and Mennonites, 98, 102, 107–9, 112, 116; movement and resettlement by, 102–3; and Nivaclé, 100, 101, 102; photo of, 97; on space, 98, 106; and traditional healing practices, 107, 110–11

Maapekmentek, Paraguay, 94, 109

Machicui (people), 132

Machicui, Machikúy (term), 132

Magariños, Manuel Rodríguez, 32, 40, 41, 43

Maká (language), 133

Maká (people), 13, 98, 134

Makok'jey, Paraguay, 100

Makxawáya (Mission Station), 176

Mala guerra (Richard), 12

Malvinas/Falklands War, 86

Mamani, Rosa, 228, 231

Mandasai (Chané woman), 35–38, 39, 43, 50, 51n8

Mansilla (Criollo), 159

Marban, Pedro, 64–65

March for Land & Territory, 197

Marcos (pastor), 79

Margarita gas block, Bolivia, 198

Mariana (Moqoit woman), 160

Mariana (Qom woman), 147, 165n13

Mariano (Qom man), 154, 155

Mariscal Estigarribia, Paraguay, 4, 25, 94, 99

Martínez, Diego, 63

Martínez, Horacio, 262, 269

Martínez, Pedro, 84, 148

Marx, Karl, 143

Marxism, 144, 145

MAS. See Movimiento al Socialismo (MAS)

Maskoy/Maskoi (people), 119, 131, 133, 136, 175

Maskoy/Maskoi (term), 132, 133

Maskoykaha (Campo Flores) mission, 120

Maskoy language family, 185n1

Mason, John A., 58

Masse, Bialet, 15

Mataco-Mataguayo language group, 131, 132, 133, 260

Matacos noctenes, 189, 190, 211n4. See also Weenhayek people

Mato Grosso do Sul, Brazil: indigenous languages in, 58, 63, 64, 72n8; indigenous peoples in, 54, 57, 63, 72n8, 129; location of, 54

Mbaya (langauge), 136

Mbayá (people), 129, 130, 135, 137

Mbaya-Caduveo, 131

Mbaya-Guaykuru, 57, 58

Meike makha valayo (Villagra Carron), 127

Meliá, Bartomeu, 217

Mendoza, Pedro José Nolasco, 155

Menno Colony, 9, 107, 117n1, 247

Mennonite Fraternal Workers, 85, 86

Mennonites: and agriculture, 108; and Angaité, 122; arrival of, 93, 117n1, 175; and Ayoreo, 9, 240, 248–49, 253, 279; and Casado family, 14; in Charagua, 216; and colonization, 7; and cooperation with indigenous peoples, 108; cooperatives of, 185n6; and dairy operations, 179; and deforestation, 185n6; and Enlhet, 9, 98, 102–3, 106–11, 112, 116, 117n1; and family of Agapito Navarro, 128; in Gran Chaco, 1; and health care, 236–37, 249, 253, 255n1; and industry, 18; and labor, 102–3, 108–9; language of, 117n1; and missions, 8, 185n8; and Nivaclé, 9; and nongovernmental organizations, 276n10; origins of, 6, 9, 117n1, 247; and Paraguayan government, 6; and politics, 216; and publications in native languages, 85; and ranching, 18, 179, 180; settlements and colonies of, 14, 102, 247, 279; and Tapiete, 271; and transportation, 7

Merlan, Francesca, 242

Mesa Interinstitutional de Salud (Inter-Institutional Health Committee), 243

Mestizos: and cattle ranching, 216; and class, 216, 222; communities of, 14, 130; and indigenous autonomy, 221–22, 225, 228; as political leaders, 226; and racism, 222; as settlers, 190

Methodism, 83

Métraux, Alfred, 5, 33, 71n2, 83, 130

Mexico, 5, 55

Miguel (Qom man), 79–80

Miller, Elmer, 5

Mingo de la Concepción, Manuel, 68

Misereor organization, 77

Misión (term), 261

Misión Escalante, 94

Misión Evangélica Bautista, 148
Misión Los Tapietes, 258, 261, 263, 265, 266, 271, 273
Misión Sueca Libre en Bolivia. *See* Free Swedish Mission in Bolivia (Misión Sueca Libre en Bolivia)
Mission (concept), 261
Mission Guaraní, 55
Missionization: and agriculture, 87; Catholics and, 76; changes in philosophies of, 85, 86–87, 88, 90; and civilizing activities and ethos, 82, 83, 90; and cooperative activities, 87, 89–90; and development, 89–90, 279; and diet, 80; and education, 80, 87; entities involved in, 77–78; goals of, 75; and health, 82–83, 87; and humanitarianism, 90; and hygiene, 80, 279; ideological framework of, 75; and indigenous citizenship, 79; and indigenous displacement, 279; and indigenous resistance, 11; Protestants and, 90; and race, 82; scholarship on, 75, 76; and social engineering, 90; and social good, 77–78; and territorial issues, 87
Mission of Santa Cruz, 63
Missions and missionaries: and agriculture, 151; alliances among, 81; Anglican, 43, 80, 83, 86, 87, 98, 120–21, 130, 134, 169, 175–78, 183, 185n8; Argentine, 85; and assimilation, 177; British, 80, 81, 82, 86; Catholic, 8, 73, 90, 267; Catholic, Franciscan, 3–5, 29, 30, 40, 66, 80, 211n6; Catholic, Jesuit, 5, 63, 129, 130, 133, 134, 211n6; and cattle ranching, 175; and Chaco War, 9; Chané and, 30, 32, 40, 63; Chiriguano and, 30, 33, 39; and citizenship, 81; and civilizing activities and ethos, 8, 12, 81; criollos and, 269; and culture, 8, 79, 124, 269; and development, 73, 81, 86; and education, 8, 9, 12, 80, 81, 176–77, 269, 270; Enlhet and, 97, 101; Enxet and, 169, 175; and ethnography, 81; European, 85; Evangelical Baptist, 151; evolution of, 79; German, 86; goals of, 80; Guaraní, 55; Guaraní and, 211n6; and health and health services, 8, 9, 80, 81, 82, 83, 86, 87, 269; and hygiene, 8, 83, 270; and indigenous communities, 7, 9, 269; indigenous perceptions of, 269; and indigenous rights, 79; and labor, 81, 175–78; and land, 8, 177, 180; and languages, 81; and

legal support for indigenous communities, 86; Maskoy and, 175; and material culture, 81; Mennonite, 85–86; models for, 81; Nivaclé and, 101; and nongovernmental organizations, 87; North American, 81, 82; Norwegian, 9, 79, 82, 83, 90; Pentecostal, 86, 190; Protestant, 8, 73, 79, 80, 81, 90; purposes of, 269; Qom and, 151; and race, 82; and religious conversion, 8; and religious leaders, 80; as safe havens, 8, 269; Sanapaná and, 175; Scandinavian, 81, 86; scholarship on, 8, 82, 269; and science, 82; and social work, 79, 86; as sources of support, 151, 152; Swedish, 9, 79, 83, 190, 192, 262, 270; training of pastors by, 9; Weenhayek and, 211n6; Wichí and, 211n6
Mission Station (Makxawáya), 176
Mocapoi (Chané man): and Chukuri, 47; death of, 47, 48; and Erland Nordenskiöld, 35, 38, 43, 46; expedition of, 33, 35–38, 39, 40, 43, 47, 48–49, 50, 51n11, 52n31; family of, 46, 47, 51n9; and Guarumbaque, 47; as leader, 35, 43, 44, 46, 47, 51n9
Mocoví (language), 85
Mocoví (people), 74, 81, 131, 165n12
Mocoví, Antonio, 155–56
Modernity, 77, 78–79, 263
Molina (Chané man), 47
Montelindo River, *4, 94*, 134
Moonies, 19, 20
Moqoit (people): and agribusiness and agriculture, 142, 156, 157–58, 162, 163; and assimilation, 157, 161; and child rearing, 161; and clothing, 158; communities of, *25*, 142, 155; diet of, 158; and displacement and dispossession, 10, 146; and external support, 156, 158–59, 162, 163, 165n14; and family, 157–58; and hunting and gathering, 156, 157, 158; as labor, 156, 157, 158, 159, 160, 162, 163; lands of, 155, 156, 157, 163; languages of, 161, 165n16; leaders of, 155; and livestock, 160; and mobility and migration, 155, 157, 163; and poverty and prosperity, 157, 158; and resistance, 10, 11, 159–60, 161–62, 163, 279; and settlers, 155–56, 158–59; and unemployment, 157, 160; work culture of, 161
Morales, Evo: on Chaco War, 211n7; on economic liberation, 232; election of, 199, 214,

228; and environment, 225; exile of, 210; and highway through TIPNIS, 235n1; and indigenous development projects, 231; and indigenous language, 268; and indigenous leaders, 196; as indigenous person, 214, 228; and indigenous rights, 18, 22, 214–15, 220, 225, 234, 268, 280; mestizos on, 229; and natural resources extraction, 18, 225, 232–33; opposition to, 210, 213n30, 225, 226, 235n1; and ORCAWETA, 192; presidency of, 18, 22, 192, 199–200, 208, 209, 210, 213n30, 214–15, 220, 225, 232, 234, 268, 280; scholarship on, 214–15; supporters of, 216

Moreno, Juan, 38, 51n12

Morin, Françoise, 273

Mormons, 8

Morrel i Torra, Pere, 217, 218, 223, 224

Mount Tëtaiguate, 34, 51n10

Movimiento al Socialismo (MAS): and 2015 Charagua summit, 231; and APG, 227, 228; and Bartolina Sisa, 228; Guaraní and, 225, 226, 227–28, 231; and indigenous autonomy, 222, 225, 226, 227, 232; as indigenous party, 226; and indigenous peoples, 200, 207, 208, 209, 210, 213n30, 215; and indigenous rights, 225; leadership of, 210; and natural resources extraction, 199–200, 209, 210, 213n30, 215; and nongovernmental organizations, 209; opposition to, 225; as party of Evo Morales, 192, 199, 208, 209, 210, 213n30, 215; platform of, 225, 233; supporters of, 216

Moxeño (language), 57, 64

Moxeño (people), 57, 59, 66. *See also* Chané (people)

Moxos, Bolivia, 63

Muehlmann, Shaylih, 173

Mueller-Eckhardt, Ute, 86

Mujía, Ricardo, 67

Multiculturalism, 238–40

Multiterritoriality: Gran Chaco residents and, 2; Guaraní and, 266, 273–74; as indigenous heritage, 7; scholarship on, 273; Tapiete and, 257, 258–59, 262, 265, 266, 271, 273, 275, 276

Municipal Hospital, 83

Naineck, Argentina, 79

Nam Cum Mission, 85

Nanaava'a (Fortín Nanawa), Paraguay, *94,* 98

Nanawa mission, 134

Ñandereta Mbajape Tenta Tappii (Tapiete Trinational Organization), 271

Napalpí (Reducción Aborigen Napalpí), Argentina, 27n8

Napalpí rebellion, 10–11

Narciso (Moqoit person), 156, 159

Nataahap, Paraguay, *94,* 99

Na'tee-Ptelhla-Maaset (Fortín Saavedra), Paraguay, *94,* 100

National Aboriginal Pastoral Team (ENDEPA), 76

National AIDS Program, 252

National Cancer Hospital, 251

National Health System for Indigenous Peoples, 244

National Institute of Indigenous Affairs, 149

National Insurance Agency, 257

National Register of Non-Catholic Religious Associations, 84, 85

Ñatiurenda (Chané settlement), 36

Natochí (shaman), 11

Natural gas extraction: companies involved in, 189, 193, 194, 195, 197, 198–206, 211n7; conflicts related to, 187; and consultation, 187–89, 197, 199–206; customers for, 193; expansion of, 187, 198; Guaraní and, 218; legislation and decrees related to, 196, 199–200; steps in, 193–94, 199; Weenhayek and, 187–89, 193–96, 199–204, 207–8, 210, 211n5, 280

Natural resources extraction: in Argentina, 21, 22; in Bolivia, 18, 187, 199–200, 209, 210, 211n7, 213n30, 214, 215, 225–26, 232–33, 277, 280; and decolonization, 232–33; hydrocarbon, 21, 22; impact of, 1; mineral, 21; resistance to, 21; revenues from, 22; scholarship on, 18; tannin, 7; and transportation, 19; wood, 3

Navarro, Agapito: burial site of, 124; death and death ritual of, 118, 119, 122, 123, 124–28, 129, 130, 136, 137, 138–40; family of, 123–24, 126, 127, 128–29, 137, 140; illnesses of, 123; and Rodrigo Villagra Carron, 123, 126; as shaman, 127; as village leader, 124, 127

Navarro, Carolina, 129

Navarro, Félix, 124–25, 126

Navarro, Gregorio, 124, 125, 126–27, 128, 140

Navarro, María, 123, 124, 126, 128

Navarro, Remigio, 123, 124, 126, 129, 137

Navarro, Victor, 125

Navarro, Wilfredo, 126

Negi, Rohit, 144

Negro, Simeón, 93, 113, 116

Ñemboati Guasu deliberative body, 234

Nempeena-Amyep (Waldrode), Paraguay, 94, 107

Neoliberalism: and access to resources, 22; and accumulation by dispossession, 141; and agribusiness, 145, 148, 153, 159, 162; and education, 22; and environment, 22; and health services, 22, 250; and indigenous rights, 233, 240, 241, 246; international financial institutions and, 241–42; and multiculturalism, 239, 240, 241, 244, 246; nongovernmental organizations and, 244; overturning of and opposition to, 215, 239, 240; period of, 148, 280; and privatization, 241; and race, 246; scholarship on, 142, 143, 144; subalterns in, 146, 159, 162, 240, 244

Neuland (Neu-Halbstadt, Peetempok, urban center), 4, 9, 94, 109, 117n1

Neuland (Neu-Halbstadt) Colony, 9, 103, 106, 110, 117n1, 247

New Imperialism, The (Harvey), 143

New Tribes Mission (Ethnos 360), 9, 185n8, 246

Nilsen, Alf G., 146

Ñimaqa (term), 133

Nino, Bernardino de, 66, 67

Nivaclé (language), 98, 99

Nivaclé (people): and agriculture, 134–35; and Chaco War, 13; and clothing and textiles, 102, 134–35; communities of, 99, 100, 101, 134, 267; and Enlhet, 97, 98–99, 100–101, 102, 103; and Enxet, 134; forebears of, 132, 134; and hunting, 134–35; languages of, 98, 99; and Mataco-Mataguayo language group, 132; and missions and missionaries, 9, 134, 267; and Pierre Clastres, 282; and pottery, 134–35; subgroups of, 98–99; and Tapiete, 260; territory of, 117n1

Nongovernmental organizations (NGOs): and 2015 Charagua summit, 230; activities of, 78; and agriculture, 87, 88, 90, 121; and agroecology, 91n2; and agroforestry, 87;

Anglican, 87; and autonomy, 220; and cash transfers, 121; Catholic, 87, 88–89, 91n4, 242; and civil rights, 88; and community, 89, 91n2; and cooperative action, 77, 87, 88; and cultural diversity, 90; and culture, 89, 90; and decentralization, 244; and development, 1, 73, 87; and drinking-water infrastructure, 121; and ecology and environment, 1, 88, 90, 91n2; and education, 87, 90, 121; and ethnic categories, 76; and fair trade, 88; faith-based, 76, 90; and family, 89; and food security, 88; and gender issues, 90; and health services, 87, 90, 121, 244–45; and housing, 121; and human development, 90; and human rights, 90; impact of, 89; indigenist, 21; and indigenous lands, 21, 87, 88, 89, 90, 121; and indigenous languages, 89, 122; and indigenous rights, 19, 88, 89, 91n2, 241; and individual responsibility, 77; and knowledge appropriation, 76; and labor, 76; and MAS, 209; Mennonites and, 276n10; and multicultural reforms, 241; as negotiators, 212n13; Norwegian, 89; and Paraguayan constitution, 241; and pensions, 121; and political ideals, 76; political power of, 155; and religion, 89–90; scholarship on, 76–77, 87, 89–90; and social categories, 76; and social programs, 87; during Stroessner regime, 241; Tapiete and, 257, 264, 275; and transnational corporations, 194; and women's rights, 76

Nonhuman societies, 104–5

Nora (Qom woman), 154

Nordenskiöld, Erland: on Arawak, 67; and Bolivian government, 67; and Chané, 32, 33, 34, 43, 44, 48, 51n9, 64, 65–66, 67; and Chiriguano, 64, 67; as ethnographer, 130; on Guaraní and Inca Empire, 67; and Guaraní speakers, 68–69; on Isoso Chané, 72n11; on Itiyuro Chané, 72n11; linguistic data of, 69–70; and Mocapoi, 35, 38, 43; modern Chané interest in scholarship of, 39; on Portuguese and Incas, 67; scholarship by, 5; on sugar production sites, 16; and Tapietes, 261; third Bolivian expedition by, 63–64

Norway, 77

Nueva Jerusalem, Paraguay, 128

Ñuflo de Chávez, 59

Nukkachi, Paraguay, 100
Núñez Cabeza de Vaca, Alvar, 58

Oblates of Mary Immaculate, 267
Occhipinti, Laurie, 76
Oilwatch Rainforest Action Network, 212n17
Olsson, Rudolph Jalmar, 262, 270
O'Neill, Bruce, 171
Orán region, 35, 40
Orbigny, Alcide D', 5
Organización de Capitanías Weenhayek de Tarija (ORCAWETA, Organization of Weenhayek Captaincies of Tarija): activities of, 192; and Bolivian government, 192; and British Gas, 197, 198, 199, 201, 202–6, 211n5, 212n24; conflicts with, 206; consolidation of, 192; creation of, 191, 197, 268; government recognition of, 197; Guido Cortez and, 187; and internal conflict, 191–92; issues addressed by, 191, 196; leaders of, 190, 204, 208, 209–10, 211n8; and sales of Weenhayek lands, 208; and Shell Oil, 212n24; structure of, 191; and Swedish missionaries, 192; Tapiete and, 212n14, 268–69; and Transierra, 197; Weenhayek and, 191, 192, 196, 208, 211n5, 268–69
Organización Guaraní Ñandeva, 267
Overseas Private Investment Corporation, 194
Oviedo, Ramón, 125

Pablo (Moqoit man), 157–58
Paeklha'pe' (Loma Plata), Paraguay, 94, 102
Página 12, 150
Paisano (term), 165n19
Palavecino, Enrique, 130, 261
Palmar Grande, Bolivia, 188, 195
Palo Marcado project, 188, 195, 197, 199, 201, 204
Pampa Blanca, Argentina, 42
Pampa Chica, Argentina, 148
Pampa del Cielo, Argentina, 155
Pampa del Indio, Argentina: accumulation by dispossession in, 147, 149; agribusiness and agriculture in, 142, 147, 148, 151, 153; capital of, 150; countryside conflict in, 149, 164n9; criollos in, 147; deforestation in, 149; dispossession in, 162–63; economy of,

148; and external support, 160; location of, 4, 147; Mercedes Biocca in, 147, 151, 152; and migration, 147; nongovernmental organizations in, 149–50, 153–55; pollution in, 149, 150; protests and resistance in, 11, 150, 161; water access in, 149, 150
Pampas, 3
Pampeana region, Argentina, 165n14
Pando, José Manuel, 42
Pantanal region, 58
Paragua (Chané leader), 32, 33, 40, 41, 43, 44
Paraguay: agribusiness and agriculture in, 19, 268; and Argentina, 6, 169; and beef exports, 17; and Bolivia, 67, 93, 120, 169; borders of, 6, 267; and Brazil, 71n4, 169; Catholic Church in, 15; and cattle ranching, 166, 175; and Chaco War, 1, 12, 13, 262; Chané delegation to, 37; claims of, on Bolivian Chaco, 67; and colonization, 15; deforestation in, 184, 268; democracy in, 247; departments in, 140n1; Duarte Frutos administration in, 241; education in, 242; and Enxet, 172, 182; ethnic classification in, 122; exploration of, 5; foreign companies in, 14; Guaraní in, 55, 58, 67; health care in, 236–37, 238–39, 243–44, 253, 254, 255n1; human rights violations by, 172; hydrocarbon reserves in, 211n7; independence in, 3; indigenous peoples in, 118, 122, 124, 131, 169, 170–71, 241, 242–43; and Inter-American Court of Human Rights, 21–22; Irala in, 71n5; laws in, 236, 241, 244, 268; Lugo administration in, 243; maps of, 4, 25, 94, 168; Mennonites in, 276n10; missions and missionaries in, 9, 55, 175–78; Mocapoi expedition in, 36, 37; natural resources extraction in, 18, 277; and Pilcomayo River canal, 211n12; population of, 247; privatization in, 241; reform in, 21, 238–41, 242, 244, 246, 247, 251, 253, 280; resistance in, 184; sale of state lands by, 14; and settler colonialism, 177, 184; Spanish in, 54, 59, 61; state agencies in, 255n3; Stroessner regime in, 21, 117n10, 119, 121, 239, 241, 268, 280; Tapiete in, 257, 258, 259, 260, 262, 271; Tapiete trinational meeting in, 271; and transportation, 18–19, 184, 237, 247; and Uruguay, 169; and War of the Triple Alliance, 6, 169

Paraguayan Chaco: agribusiness and agriculture in, 17–18, 19, 21; Angaité in, 9; aqueduct in, 18; Ayoreo in, 9; borders of, 6; Chamacoco in, 5; climate in, 3, 174; colonization in, 93, 119, 177; decentralization in, 247; deforestation in, 17, 19, 184, 185n6; departments in, 247; economy in, 9, 248; Enlhet-Enenlhet linguistic family in, 119; Enlhet in, 9; exploration of, 5; fencing in, 183–84; foreign companies in, 6, 14; Guaycurú in, 5; health services in, 236–37, 239–40, 245, 247, 248–49, 251–52, 255n1; historical documentation on, 130; indigenous peoples in, 11, 14, 57, 119, 180, 237, 255n4, 279; industry in, 14, 18, 177, 185n7; Joel Correia in, 185n3; labor in, 248; lands in, 6, 14–15, 19, 21, 119–20, 180, 183–84, 279; location of, 3; Manjui in, 9; map of, 168; Max Schmidt in, 262; Mennonites in, 6, 9, 18, 175, 185n6; missions and missionaries in, 8, 9, 11, 175, 177; Moonies in, 19; Nivaclé in, 9, 282; nonindigenous communities in, 15; Paraguayan state and, 119, 169, 183; population of, 247, 255n1; racism in, 279; ranching in, 6, 17–18, 19, 21, 174, 175, 179, 180, 183, 185n6, 279; settlement patterns in, 15; size of, 6; Tapiete in, 261, 266, 274; terrain and topography of, 3, 282; transportation in, 18, 120, 179, 183, 184
Paraguayan Chaco Indian Association, 176
Paraguayan Chamber of Exporters of Cereals (Cámara Paraguaya de Exportadores y Comercializadores de Cereales y Oleaginosas), 17
Paraguayan Institute for Indigenous Affairs, 125
Paraguayans, 102, 111, 112, 120, 127
Paraguay Instituto Nacional del Indígena (INDI), 21
Paraguay Ministry of Defense, 21, 241
Paraguay Ministry of Education, 242
Paraguay Ministry of Health, 123
Paraguay Ministry of Linguistic Policies, 122
Paraguay Ministry of Public Health, 243, 245, 246, 247, 254
Paraguay Ministry of War and Marines, 247
Paraguay River: aqueduct from, 18; as border, 118, 176, 177; indigenous communities along, 7, 54, 70, 120, 129, 137; industry along, 6, 7, 14, 175; maps of, 4, 25; non-indigenous communities along, 7; tributaries of, 134
Paraguay River region: Arawak in, 66; Chané in, 54, 59, 63, 65; Chiriguano in, 66; Guana Chané in, 57, 58, 71n4
Paraguay Secretaría de la Mujer, 255n4
Paraiso, Paraguay, 122, 126, 128
Paraje Las Tolderías (Colonia Cacique Catán), Argentina: accumulation by dispossession in, 147; and agribusiness, 142, 157, 159; as alternate name for Colonia Cacique Catán, 165n12; colonists in, 159; deforestation in, 160; establishment of, 155, 156; and external support, 160, 161; livestock in, 160; map of, 25; Mercedes Biocca in, 159; neighborhoods of, 156, 160, 161; and pollution, 160
Paraná River, 4, 15, 25, 118
Parapetí River, 64, 65, 68, 260
Parapetí River region, 69
Paratodo, Paraguay, 94, 103
Paul, Frank, 86
Payaguá people, 130, 132
Pedersen, Cyril, 83
Pedersen, Per, 83
Pedro (Moqoit man), 158, 165n16
Pedro P. Peña, Paraguay, 267
Peetempok (Neuland, Neu-Halbstadt, urban center), 4, 9, 94, 109, 110, 117n1. See also Neuland (Neu-Halbstadt) Colony
Penek-Saanga (Córdoba), Paraguay, 94, 99, 100, 101
Pentecostals, 84, 85, 122, 167, 185n8, 211n6
Perón, Juan, 78, 84, 147, 148, 280
Person (concept), 74
Peru, 29, 59, 61
Petroandina, 195
Petrobras, 195
Picanerai, Vaela, 236, 237, 238, 252
Pifarré, Francisco, 234
Pikasu/Fortín Infante Rivarola, Paraguay, 267
Pilagá (language), 85
Pilagá (people): agency of, 80; and Chaco War, 13; communities of, 25; and Maká, 133; and missionaries and missionization, 74, 80, 82; and religion, 81
Pilcomayo River: as boundary, 3, 6, 29, 133, 176, 260, 266; canal from, 211n12; during Chaco War, 190; Chané term for, 51n11;

evangelism along, 262; fishing in, 263; flow of, 2; indigenous peoples along, 13, 30, 35, 134, 189, 190, 261, 262, 265, 274, 278; maps of, *4, 25, 31, 94, 188;* military sites along, 6, 40; natural gas pipelines under, 195, 201; ranching along, 6; settlement along, 40; wetlands of, 281

Pilcomayo River region, 131, 132

Pink Tide, 240

Pipa (Chané man), 36

Piquirenda (settlement), 41

Plants: algarrobo (carob) trees, 3; fruit trees, 3; grasses, 174; indigenous peoples and, 3; industrial uses of, 3; pacará, 37; quebracho (Schinopsis) trees, 3, 15, 19; scrub brush, 166; and traditional healing practices, 128; tusca trees, 37

Platanillo, Paraguay, *94,* 99

Plurinational Constitutional Tribunal, 224

Plurinational Institute of Culture and Language, 268

Pocitos, Argentina, 7, 37

Política Nacional de Salud Indígena (National Policy on Indigenous Health), 243

Polo de Ondegardo, Juan, 61

Porongo, Bolivia, *4,* 59, 68

Porto Murtinho, Brazil, *4,* 18

Portuguese (language), 71n7

Portuguese (people), 67, 70

Postero, Nancy: field work by, 217, 221–22, 228, 230, 233–34; on Guaraní activism, 280; scholarship by, 213n30, 214–15, 235, 240

Pottery, 131, 133, 134

Pozo Brillante (Tengkat), Paraguay, *94,* 98, 99

Pozo Colorado, Paraguay, *4,* 166, *168*

Pozo Hondo, Argentina, 18

Primitive accumulation, 143, 144. *See also* Accumulation by dispossession

Program of Community Relations and Support, 198

Property ownership, undivided joint, 44, 52n23

Protestants and Protestantism: Argentine regulation of, 84; denominations of, 8; and development, 77, 78–79; and ethnography, 81; and indigenous agency, 80; and indigenous citizenship, 81; and languages, 81; and literacy, 85; and material culture, 81; and medicine, 81; and missions, 8; and modernity, 78–79; and progress, 81; scholarship on, 78

Provincial Institute of Indigenous Peoples (Instituto Provincial de los Pueblos Indígenas de Salta), 264

Provincial Institute of the Aborigen (Instituto Provincial de la Aborigen), 264

Provincial Water Administration, 150

Proyecto Ñandeva Guaraní, 267

Puente Kaigue, Paraguay, 122, 128

Puerto Casado, Paraguay, *4,* 14, 19, 20, 136

Puerto Pinasco, Paraguay, 120

Puesto de Salud Amistad, 237

Punta Riel, Paraguay, 7

Qad'aqtaxanaxanec (Our Messenger), 85

Qom (language), 85, 275

Qom (people): agency of, 80, 279; and agribusiness and agriculture, 16, 148, 149, 151, 152–53, 154, 162; César Ceriani Cernadas and, 79; and civil rights, 88; on colonization, 165n13; communities of, *25,* 142, 147, 148, 155, 256, 262; and criollos, 149; and cultural adaptation, 20; and cultural rights, 11, 16; and debt, 148; and diet, 11; and displacement and dispossession, 10, 141, 146, 147, 152–53, 162–63; and Don Panos company, 149, 150, 152–53, 155; and education, 87, 88; and external support, 151–52, 154, 162; and health, 80, 82; and hunting and gathering, 147, 149, 150; and identity, 20; as labor, 147, 148, 149, 164n6; lands of, 147, 148, 149, 164n4; lawsuit by, 149; leaders of, 141, 147, 165n13; and livestock, 149, 153; and Mercedes Biocca, 151, 155; and missionaries and missionization, 75, 80, 82, 86, 87–88; and mobility and migration, 20, 82, 147, 148, 149; and Peronist government, 84–85, 147; political culture of, 161; and politics, 20; population of, 147; and poverty and prosperity, 151, 155; publications of, 85; and religion, 20, 74, 79, 80, 81, 84, 85, 88, 151, 262; and resistance, 10, 11, 141, 149–50, 161, 162, 163, 279; scholarship on, 20; social organization of, 147, 164n2; on stigma of indigenous peoples, 152; and Tapiete, 260; and territorial rights, 87, 88; and traditional medicines, 153; and unemployment, 148,

Qom (people)—*continued*
150; wages for, 16; and water access, 149, 150; and women's empowerment, 87; working conditions of, 16
Qomle'ec (Toba) people, 278
Quechua (language), 71n6, 216
Quechua (people), 64, 225

Ramal Salto-Jujeño region, Argentina, 17
Ranching, 1, 6, 19, 45, 99. *See also* Cattle ranching
Reconquista Santa Fe Province, Argentina, 91n2
Red de Comunicación Indígena (RCI), 88–89
Red Tape (Gupta), 172
Reducción Aborigen Napalpí, Argentina, 27n8
Resistance: and accumulation by dispossession, 143, 145; and agribusiness, 145; against British Gas (BG) Bolivia, 198; and capitalism, 143; Chiriguano and, 10; CIDOB and, 213n30; and dislocation, 10; Enxet and, 11, 168, 170–71, 182; and factory closures, 144; Guaraní and, 225; and labor abuses, 10–11; and land issues, 10–11, 21–22, 144, 145; and local rationalities, 146; and missionization, 11; and mobility, 10; Moqoit and, 10, 11, 159–60, 161–62, 163, 279; and multicultural policies, 241; and natural resources extraction, 21; and privatization, 144; and proposed highway through TIPNIS, 197; Qom and, 10, 11, 141, 142, 149–50, 161, 162, 163, 279; and self-determination, 219, 279, 282; and settler colonialism, 184, 197; Vilela and, 10
Resistencia, Chaco Province, Argentina, 4, 25, 88, 150, 188
Revolutionary Communist Party, 164n10
Reyburn, William, 85
Riacho Mosquito, Paraguay, 119, 136
Richard, Nicolás, 12, 135
Riester, Juergen, 67
Río de la Plata, 55, 61
Río Montelindo. *See* Montelindo River
Río Pilcomayo. *See* Pilcomayo River
Rio Verde, Paraguay, 123
Rivera Cusicanqui, Silvia, 234
Rivero, Pablo, 203, 204
Roads: bioceanic highway, 18, 179, 184; condition of, 247; construction of, 6; financing

for, 18; indigenous calls for, 182, 231; and infrastructural violence, 279; missions and, 176, 177, 179; and modernization, 179; at Napalpí, 10; and natural resources extraction, 179, 198, 280; and protest, 279; ranching and, 177, 178–79; and reshaping of Gran Chaco, 277; Ruta 5, 166, 170, 176, 179, 180, 182, 184; and safety, 279; taxes for maintenance of, 10; through TIPNIS, 225, 235n1; Trans-Chaco Highway, 168, 179, 237, 247
Roboré, Bolivia, 4, 18
Rodgers, Dennis, 171
Rodolfo (Moqoit man), 157
Rodríguez de Francia, José Gaspar, 119
Roque Sáenz Peña, Argentina, 85
Rosa (Moqoit woman), 161
Rosarina company, 120
Rosario, Santa Fe Province, Argentina, 83
Royal Dutch Shell, 197, 210n3, 211n7. *See also* British Gas (BG) Bolivia; Natural gas extraction; Shell Oil Company
Ruiz, Eulogia, 127
Russia, 6, 9, 117n1, 247

Saanga-Kloom, Paraguay, 94, 105
Saignes, Thierry, 60, 71n2, 71n3
Saipurú, Bolivia, 68
Salado River, 4, 131, 133
Salazar ranch, 125
Salinas mission, 30
Salinas Province, Bolivia, 29, 40
Salinas salt flats, 71n5
Salta Province, Argentina: Catholic Church in, 80; departments in, 29; disease in, 82; Guaraní in, 7, 256; indigenous peoples in, 264; maps of, 4, 25; missions in, 29, 83; Mocapoi expedition in, 36; as part of central Chaco, 3; railroads in, 7; social projects in, 80; sugarcane cultivation and processing in, 16; Tapiete in, 256, 261, 274
Samuwate, Bolivia, 268, 270, 273
Sanabria (indigenous man), 80
Sanandita (Chané village), 30
San Antonio, Villa Montes, Bolivia, 188, 195, 211n6
Sanapaná people: and Anglicans, 121, 175; and cotton, 134; and Enlhet-Enenlhet language family, 93, 119; as labor, 121; and land rights,

121, 125; and Maskoy people, 133; and pottery, 134; and poverty, 121; resettlement of,
121; retention of *Sanapaná* as name for, 136;
villages of, 125

Sánchez Labrador, José, 58, 129

San Fernandez, Paraguay, 127

San Martín, José de, 49

Santa Cruz de la Sierra, Bolivia: governor of,
60; indigenous peoples in, 58, 71n5; map of,
4; markets in, 191; railroad in, 7; ranching
in, 6; Spanish in, 58, 61, 71n5

Santa Cruz Province, Argentina, 57, 59

Santa Fe Province, Argentina: as boundary,
15; map of, *4*; medical missionaries in, 83;
Moqoit in, 155, 157; nongovernmental organizations in, 91n2, 91n3

Santana, Roberto, 273

Santa Teresita, Paraguay, 267

Santiago, Argentina, 160

Santiago del Estero Province, Argentina, *4*,
91n2, 157, 165n17

Sapiranda, Moises, 196, 201, 202, 203, 204

Saul (Weenhayek man), 202

Sawhoyamaxa, Paraguay: access to drinking
water in, 171, 181; as Enxet community, 166;
health in, 181–82; human rights abuses in,
172, 173; and infrastructural violence, 172,
173; Joel E. Correia in, 167, 180, 181–82; and
land, 170–71, 173, 181, 182; location of, *168,
169*–70; marginalization of residents of,
178; Maskoy language family in, 185n1; and
mobility, 180–81; origins of, 183; population
of, 185n1; and Ruta 5, 166, 167, 169–70, 179,
180; and state services, 173; and transportation, 167

Schmidl, Ulrico, 57, 58, 71n5, 130

Schmidt, Max, 262

Schuchard, Barbara, 67

Scott, James, 159

Sebastián (Qom man), 152

Seco River mission, 32

Seelstrang, Arturo, 5

Sekhay'-Pva' (Enlhet man), 105, 111

Settler colonialism: and capitalism, 184; and
cattle ranching, 173, 175, 177, 180, 183, 184;
definition of, 167; and deforestation, 184;
Enxet and, 167–68, 169, 177; expansion of,
184; and fencing, 167, 172–73, 174, 177, 179,

180; and indigenous assimilation, 177; and
indigenous labor, 167, 171, 175, 177, 178, 180;
and indigenous lands, 170, 171, 172, 173,
175, 177, 178, 179, 180; and infrastructural
violence, 167, 172–73, 174, 183; Paraguayan
government and, 177; and race and racism,
173, 180; and religion, 177, 180; and roads,
167, 177; scholarship on, 173, 175, 177, 178;
and stock ponds, 167, 174

Shell Oil Company, 194, 195, 197, 210n3,
212n24. *See also* British Gas (BG) Bolivia;
Natural gas extraction; Royal Dutch Shell

Simon, Brigitte, 67

Simpson, Audra, 219

6 de Marzo, Paraguay, 122, 124, 126, 128, 129

So'khalheem (Nivaclé man), 101

Solano, Belarmino: and 2014 Bolivian national
elections, 228; and 2015 Charagua summit,
230, 231, 232; and indigenous autonomy,
227, 231, 232, 233; as mayor of Charagua,
224, 227, 230, 231, 232; on political organization in Charagua, 224

Sombrero Piri, Paraguay, 125

Sousa Santos, Boaventura de, 95–96

South American Missionary Society (SAMS),
8–9, 176

Soybean production: and access to resources,
142; and deforestation, 17, 142, 157; expansion of, 159, 162; extent of, 141; and globalized capitalism, 277; government assistance
for, 154; indigenous participation in, 145;
irrigation for, 164n8; land for, 21, 141, 156;
margins of, 184; and mobility, 157; Moqoit
and, 156, 162; and pollution, 142, 157, 278;
Qom and, 141, 154, 162; resistance to, 145;
taxes on, 164n9; transgenic varieties for,
17, 142

Spain, 3, 5

Spanish (language): Moqoit and, 161, 165n16;
publications in, 85; speakers of, 117n6, 124,
127, 164n1, 222, 237; Tapiete and, 258; terms
in, 65, 122, 132, 140n4, 165n17, 165n18, 189

Spanish (persons): and Arawak speakers, 58;
and Chané, 68; and Chiriguano, 61; and
colonization, 119; and El Dorado, 57; and
enslavement, 54, 57, 61, 62, 70; and exploration, 5; and Guaraní, 59; and Inca Empire,
67; and indigenous languages, 65; and

Spanish (persons)—*continued*
intermarriage, 61; and labor, 57; and land, 57, 59; rebellions against, 61; scholarship on, 67; and Wichí, 211n6
Speed, Shannon, 175, 177, 178
Springer, Simon, 172
Spronk, Susan, 146
Standard Oil, 49, 211n7. *See also* Natural gas extraction; Natural resources extraction
Star, Susan, 172
"State of the Working Classes in Argentina, The" (Masse), 15–16
Steigenga, Timothy, 271
"Strengthening Integrated Services for Indigenous Women Affected by HIV and Violence: Boquerón Paraguay," 255n4
Stroessner, Alfredo, 117n10, 119, 121, 239, 241, 280
Suares de Figueroa, Lorenzo, 60–61
Sucre, Bolivia, 221
Sugarcane cultivation and processing: and class, 16, 17; companies engaged in, 15, 147; and deforestation, 17; and disease, 82; economic importance of, 147; impact of, on indigenous peoples, 13–14, 17, 261; indigenous labor for, 15, 16, 17, 35, 47, 147, 261, 263; and indigenous migration, 7; land for, 15; locations of, 15, 17, 34, 35, 47; oral histories of, 263; origins of, 16; and pollution, 17; scholarship on, 16, 17; settlements arising from, 17; and transportation, 15; and water resources, 17
Survival International, 212n17
Susnik, Branislava: on Chimeo/Itau/Caraparí split, 35; and Grand Chaco ethnohistory, 5; on groups in Pilcomayo River region, 134; on late 18th-century Toba offensive, 51n4; on link between Chanameshma and Angaité, 135–36; on peoples in Chaco interior, 135; scholarship on work of, 130; use of *Chanameshma* by, 120
Sweden, 77. *See also* Free Swedish Mission in Bolivia (Misión Sueca Libre en Bolivia)
Swedish Evangelical Mission, 211n6
Swedish Free Mission. *See* Free Swedish Mission in Bolivia (Misión Sueca Libre en Bolivia)

Taigoyik (Qom man), 147, 148, 165n13
Taikoriki (Toba man), 36
Taokoriki (Toba man), 51n11
Tapanaik (Qom man), 11
Taparindu (Chané man), 47, 50
Tapiete (language), 257, 258, 268, 269, 271, 274
Tapiete (people): and 1994 Argentine Constitutional Convention, 264; and activism, 263, 264; and agribusiness and agriculture, 16, 257, 263, 265, 268, 271; and alcoholism, 262, 269, 270; and assimilation, 269–70, 275; assistance for, 275; and autonomy, 269; and Ayoreo, 260; and carnival, 271; and Chaco War, 13, 262; and Chorote, 260; and class, 261; and clothing, 269; communities of, 25, 64, 191, 256, 257, 258, 259, 261, 265, 266–67, 268, 271, 274; and community resources, 275; and criollos, 260, 273; and cultural adaptation, 20; and cultural rights, 16, 257, 268, 271, 274, 275; and development, 257; and discrimination, 275; and displacement, 269, 270; economic situation of, 258; and education, 257, 269, 270, 271, 275; and exchange networks, 262; and family size and composition, 258, 263, 265; and fishing, 263, 265; and government assistance, 263; and Guaraní, 268, 274; and Guaraní/Chiriguano, 260; and health care, 275; historical documentation on, 276n7; and housing, 257; and hunger, 262, 270; and hunting and gathering, 263, 265, 268; and hygiene, 270; and identity, 20, 257, 273, 274, 275, 276, 279; and intermarriage, 257, 260, 261, 262, 263, 266, 268, 274; and kinship, 271, 273, 274, 275, 276; as labor, 260, 261; and land, 22, 257, 258, 260, 263, 265, 268, 274, 275; languages spoken by, 257, 258, 260, 262, 266, 268, 269, 274, 275; leaders of, 264; marginalization of, 273; and migration and mobility, 13, 20, 258, 259, 261, 262, 266, 281; and multiterritoriality, 257, 258–59, 262, 265, 266, 271, 273, 274, 275, 276, 281; and Nivaclé, 260; and nongovernmental organizations, 191, 212n14, 268–69, 275; oral histories of, 258, 269; origins of, 260; and political organization, 274; and politics, 20, 273, 274; population of, 260, 268; and

poverty, 262, 270; and Provincial Institute of Indigenous Peoples, 264; and Qom, 260; and race and ethnicity, 261; relationship of, with governments, 275–76; and religion, 20, 257, 258, 259, 260, 262–63, 266, 269–71, 272–73, 274, 276, 279, 281; resources for, 271; in rural areas, 258, 265, 266, 274; scholarship on, 20, 256–57, 260, 271; and Silvia Hirsch, 256, 257, 279, 281; and standard of living, 265, 271; and TCO, 22; terms for, 260, 266; and traditional celebrations, 270; and transportation, 265; trinational meetings of, 271–72, 274; in urban areas, 258, 265, 275; and violence, 262, 269, 270; and wages, 16; and Weenhayek, 268, 274; and Wichí, 260; working conditions of, 16

Tapiete Institute of Culture and Language, 268

Tapiete IV, Argentina, 265

Tapiete Trinational Organization (Ñandereta Mbajape Tenta Tappii), 257, 264, 271–73

Tarija, Bolivia, 4, 6, 35, 191

Tartagal, Salta Province, Argentina: Chané in, 47, 256; Chorote in, 256; Chulupi in, 256; communities near, 262, 265; criollos in, 256, 261, 263; Guaraní in, 256; housing projects in, 263; leadership of, 263; location of, 256; maps of, 4, 25; and migration, 266; Misión Los Tapietes in, 261; Qom in, 256; ranching in, 6; religion in, 263, 270; Silvia Hirsch in, 256; Tapiete in, 256, 261, 262, 263, 265, 266; Tapiete trinational meeting in, 271, 272; urbanization of, 261; Wichí in, 256; women in, 270

TCO Weenhayek. See Tierras Comunitarias de Origen (TCOs): Weenhayek and

Tengkat (Pozo Brillante), Paraguay, 94, 98, 99

Tenjoke', Paraguay, 100

Terena (language), 57, 64, 65

Terena (people), 54, 57, 66. See also Chané (people)

Territorio Indígena y Parque Nacional Isiboro Sécure (TIPNIS, Isiboro Sécure Indigenous Territory and National Park), 213n30, 225, 235n1

Tesoro Bolivia Petroleum Company, 195, 197, 198

Tëtaiguate (Chané settlement), 34

Teuco River, 4, 25

Thouar, Alfred, 5

Tierras Comunitarias de Origen (TCOs): Bolivian constitution and, 22; establishment of, 268; obstacles to, 198; sales of lands covered by, 208; Tapiete and, 22; Weenhayek and, 188, 196, 197, 199, 201, 202, 204–5, 206, 212n16

Tierraviva, 121, 123, 125, 128

Timboy, Bolivia, 188, 194, 195

Tinfunke, Paraguay, 94, 98, 99, 100

TIPNIS. See Territorio Indígena y Parque Nacional Isiboro Sécure (TIPNIS, Isiboro Sécure Indigenous Territory and National Park)

Toba (Chané term), 51n11

Toba (language), 134

Toba (people): and agriculture, 134–35; and Chané, 30, 35–36, 37, 38, 51n4, 51n11; forebears of, 134; and Guaikurú language group, 132; as Guaykurú people, 131, 132; and hunting, 134–35; and Maká, 133; and Maskoy, 133; oral histories of, 278; political leaders of, 51n11; and pottery, 134–35; and religion, 85; scholarship on, 51n4; terms used by, 132; and wool textiles, 134–35

Toba-Enenlhet people, 93

Toba-Maskoy people, 132

Toba Qom people, 134

Tockman, Jason, 220, 235

Tomaklha'-Apetek-Setaaha' (Loma Pytá), Paraguay, 94, 99

Totora Marka, Bolivia, 221

Transierra, 194, 195, 197

Transnationalism. See Multiterritoriality

Transportation: of beef and dairy commodities, 173, 179, 180; buses, 231; of capital, 180; and economic growth, 279; fluvial, 6; impact of, 6–7; indigenous peoples and, 178, 181; of laborers, 180; and natural resources extraction, 19; ports, 15; and railroads, 3, 6, 7, 15, 16, 18–19, 49, 120; trucks, 166–67; walking, 36, 37, 111, 167, 237. See also Roads

Transredes, 194, 195

Trees. See Plants

Troeltsch, Ernst, 78

Tucumán, Argentina, 133

Tucumán Ethnological Institute, 33
Tucumán Province, Argentina, 80
Tumbakiki (Toba man), 36
Tuntey, Bolivia, *188*, 211n10
Tupí-Guaraní language family, 260
Tupi people, 61
Tuyunti, Argentina, 29, 37, 47, 50, 51n8

Uacapi (Chané man), 47
UN Declaration of the Rights of Indigenous
    Peoples, 214
UN General Assembly, 20
UN High Commission on Human Rights, 232
Unión Campesina, 149–50, 153, 163, 164n10
Unitec Agro S.A., 148, 149, 150, 164n7
United Bible Societies, 85
United Evangelical Church, 74, 79, 85
United Missions Board (Junta Unida de Misio-
    nes), 83–84, 87–88
United States, 2, 5, 6, 15, 219
"Unknown people in an unknown land,
    An . . ." (Grubb), 130
Unruh, Ernesto, 135
UN Women, 251
Upper Per
Uruguay, 169
Urundey, Paraguay, 128
US Aid for International Development (US-
    AID), 244, 245

Vaca, Abilio, 219, 227–28
Van Nivel, Enrique, 32
Vázquez, Cristian, 76
Vega, Juan, 265
Velásquez, Dionisio, 63
Venezuela, 240
Verde River, 6
Verdes (Demócratas) political party, 216, 222,
    225, 226–27
Villa Bermejito, Argentina, 87
Villagra Carron, Rodrigo: and Agapito Na-
    varro, 123, 126; and Angaité, 278; and death
    ritual of Agapito Navarro, 125–28, 140;
    ethnographic and ethnohistorical materials
    collected by, 119; family of, 123, 128; and
    family of Agapito Navarro, 123–24, 125–29;
    and grave of Agapito Navarro, 124, 137; on

shamanic visions, 278; and Yooksa'a ritual,
    138
Villa Montes, Bolivia: as border, 189; maps of,
    4, 25, 188; military base in, 203; missions
    in, 190, 211n6; and Morales government,
    280; and Palo Marcado project, 197, 201–2;
    protests in, 210; Tapiete in, 268; Toba in, 36;
    Weenhayek in, 190, 196, 201–2
Villar, Diego, 68, 69, 72n11
Voces originarias (Aboriginal Voices), 88
Vom Hau, Matthias, 264
Vuaruyi (Chané woman), 51n9

Waldensian Church of the Río de la Plata, 84
War of the Triple Alliance, 6, 14, 71n4, 119, 169
Water and Maintenance Provincial Company
    Service, 150
Webber, Jeffery, 146
Webber, Michael, 144
Weber, Max, 78
Weenhayek people: and begging, 190; and Bo-
    livian government, 196–98, 200–201, 204–5,
    207; and Bolivian military, 190; and Chaco
    War, 190, 197; and class, 280; communities
    of, *25*, 189, 190, 202, 211n5; conflicts among,
    200, 201–4, 206, 208, 210, 211n5, 280; culture
    of, 189, 201; and diet, 189, 190, 211n11; and
    discrimination, 190; and education, 189,
    192, 196; ethnic group of, 189; and external
    employment, 189; and fishing, 190–91, 197,
    211n11; and food crises, 191; and hunting and
    gathering, 189, 190, 191; income of, 191; and
    intermarriage, 274; as labor, 190, 211n9; and
    land, *188*, 190, 191, 193, 194, 196–99, 200, 201,
    204–5, 207, 208, 210, 212n20, 280; leaders
    of, 189, 202, 203–4, 205, 206, 207, 210, 211n5;
    and migration and mobility, 190, 197, 211n9;
    and missions and missionaries, 196, 197,
    211n6, 213n29; and natural gas extraction,
    187–89, 193–96, 199–204, 207–8, 210, 211n5,
    280; and ORCAWETA, 191, 192–93, 196,
    208, 209, 211n5, 268; and religion, 211n6;
    resettlement of, 190; scholarship on, 189;
    socio-political organization of, 191, 197,
    211n5; and Spanish, 190; standard of living
    of, 191; subgroups of, 189; and Tapiete, 268,
    274; terms for, 189, 211n4

Wichí (language), 85, 86, 211n6

Wichí (people): agency of, 80; communities of, *25,* 155, 256, 262; and cultural rights, 16; ethnic group of, 189; and evangelism, 81, 262; lands of, 32; and migration, 82; and missions and missionaries, 75, 80, 82; and Spanish, 211n6; and sugarcane cultivation and processing, 16; and Tapiete, 260; and wages, 16; working conditions of, 16

Wichí-Guisnay people, 13

Wiky'i (term), 191

Wilde, Guillermo, 264

Wolfe, Patrick, 173

Women. *See* Indigenous women

Wood, Ellen, 144

World Bank, 194, 241

World War I, 15

World War II, 77

Wright, Pablo, 74

Xakmok Kásek, Paraguay, 120, 125

Yaamelket-Aatkok (Casuarina), Paraguay, *94,* 103, 106

Yaasek-Yaamelket, Paraguay, *94,* 100

Yacimientos Petrolíferos Fiscales (YPF), 49, 52n30, 203, 204

Yacimientos Petrolíferos Fiscales de Bolivia (YPFB): and consultation process, 200, 201, 202, 203, 204, 205, 206, 213n27; in Wee-hayek territory, 193, 195

Yacuiba, Bolivia: assignment of, to Bolivia, 6; leaders of, 42; maps of, *4, 188;* and Palo Marcado natural gas project, 201–2; and railroads, 7; representative of, 44; Ween-hayek in, 201–2

Ya'kal'a (Platanillo), Paraguay, *94,* 99

Yakatimbae, Argentina, 37

Yakye Axa, Paraguay: access to drinking water in, 171, 181–82; cattle ranching in, 176; and dispossession, 173; as Enxet community, 167; health in, 181–82; human rights abuses in, 172, 173; and infrastructural violence, 173; Joel E. Correia in, 166, 180, 181–82; and land, 170–71, 181, 182; location of, *168,* 169–70; marginalization of residents of, 178; Maskoy language family in, 185n1; and migration and mobility, 180–81, 185n1; origins of, 183; Paraguayan state and, 182; photo of, *170;* population of, 185n1; and roads, 166, 167, 169–70, 179, 180, 182; and state services, 173; and violence, 172

Yarigua, Ruth, 226, 233

Yave Sage mission, 120

Ya'yeem-Peehe, Paraguay, *94,* 109–10

Yerba Buena, 37

YPFB. *See* Yacimientos Petrolíferos Fiscales de Bolivia (YPFB)

Yrigoyen, Hypólito, 147, 155, 164n4

Yunchan, Bolivia, *188,* 195

Zapallar, Argentina, 11

Zapata, Laura, 76

Zapatista collectives, 282

Zenteno, Elisa del Carmen, 88–89